New York City For Dummies,®
3rd Edition

W9-AUB-955

Manhattan Subways

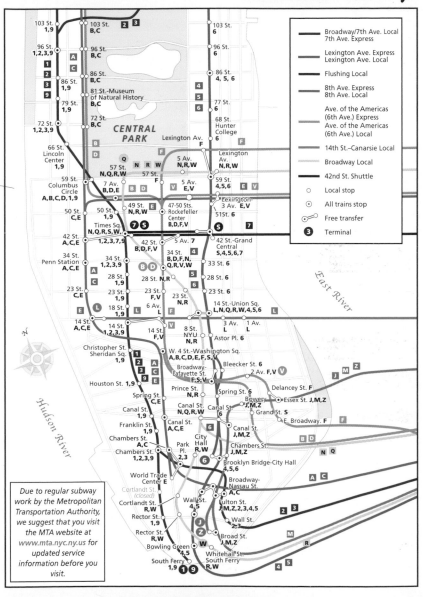

Legend:

- ━━━ Broadway/7th Ave. Local 7th Ave. Express
- ━━━ Lexington Ave. Express Lexington Ave. Local
- ━━━ Flushing Local
- ━━━ 8th Ave. Express 8th Ave. Local
- ━━━ Ave. of the Americas (6th Ave.) Express Ave. of the Americas (6th Ave.) Local
- ━━━ 14th St.–Canarsie Local
- ━━━ Broadway Local
- ━━━ 42nd St. Shuttle
- ○ Local stop
- ⊙ All trains stop
- ⌒ Free transfer
- ❸ Terminal

CENTRAL PARK

East River

Hudson River

Subway Stops for New York's Top Attractions

Attraction	Subway Stop

MUSEUMS

American Museum of Natural History..... **B** **C** to 81st St.

The Cloisters... **A** to 190th St.

Ellis Island.. **4** **5** to Bowling Green or **N** **R** to Whitehall St.

Guggenheim Museum.............................. **4** **5** **6** to 86th St.

Intrepid Sea-Air-Space Museum.............. **A** **C** **E** to 42nd St.-Port Authority

Metropolitan Museum of Art.................. **4** **5** **6** to 86th St.

Museum of Modern Art.......................... **E** **V** to Fifth Ave

★ ★

PARKS

Central Park... **1** **9** **A** **C** **B** **D** to 59th St.-Columbus Circle

★ ★

HISTORIC BUILDINGS AND ARCHITECTURE

Brooklyn Bridge....................................... **4** **5** **6** to Brooklyn Bridge-City Hall

Chrysler Building..................................... **4** **5** **6** **7** **S** to Grand Central-42nd St.

Empire State Building.............................. **B** **D** **F** **V** **N** **R** **Q** **W** to 34th St.-Herald Sq.

Grand Central Terminal........................... **4** **5** **6** **7** **S** to Grand Central-42nd St.

Rockefeller Center................................... **B** **D** **F** **V** to 47-50th Sts.-Rockefeller Center

Staten Island Ferry.................................. **1** **9** to South Ferry (first 5 cars)

Statue of Liberty...................................... **4** **5** to Bowling Green, **N** **R** to Whitehall St.

United Nations.. **4** **5** **6** **7** **S** to Grand Central-42nd St.

Yankee Stadium.. **4** **B** **D** to 161st St-River Ave-Yankee Stadium

★ ★

NEIGHBORHOODS

Chinatown.. **6** **J** **M** **Z** **N** **R** **W** to Canal St.

Greenwich Village.................................... **A** **C** **E** **B** **D** **F** **V** to West 4th St.

Times Square.. **1** **2** **3** **7** **N** **R** **W** **S** to 42nd St-Times Square

Wall Street... **4** **5** to Wall St. or **N** **R** to Rector St.

★ ★

CHURCHES

Cathedral of St. John the Divine.............. **1** to Cathedral Parkway (110th St.)

St. Patrick's Cathedral.............................. **B** **D** **F** **V** to 47-50th Sts.-Rockefeller Center or **E** **V** to Fifth Avenue/53rd St.

Copyright © 2005 Wiley Publishing, Inc. All rights reserved.
Item 6945-7.
For more information about Wiley Publishing, call 1-800-762-2974.

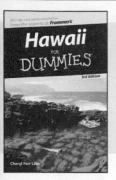

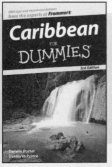

New York City

FOR

DUMMIES®

3RD EDITION

by Brian Silverman

WILEY

Wiley Publishing, Inc.

New York City For Dummies, 3rd Edition
Published by
Wiley Publishing, Inc.
111 River St.
Hoboken, NJ 07030-5774
www.wiley.com

Copyright © 2005 by Wiley Publishing, Inc., Indianapolis, Indiana

Published simultaneously in Canada

No part of this publication may be reproduced, stored in a retrieval system, or transmitted in any form or by any means, electronic, mechanical, photocopying, recording, scanning, or otherwise, except as permitted under Sections 107 or 108 of the 1976 United States Copyright Act, without either the prior written permission of the Publisher, or authorization through payment of the appropriate per-copy fee to the Copyright Clearance Center, 222 Rosewood Drive, Danvers, MA 01923, 978-750-8400, fax 978-646-8600. Requests to the Publisher for permission should be addressed to the Legal Department, Wiley Publishing, Inc., 10475 Crosspoint Blvd., Indianapolis, IN 46256, 317-572-3447, fax 317-572-4355, e-mail: brandreview@wiley.com

Trademarks: Wiley, the Wiley Publishing logo, For Dummies, the Dummies Man logo, A Reference for the Rest of Us!, The Dummies Way, Dummies Daily, The Fun and Easy Way, Dummies.com and related trade dress are trademarks or registered trademarks of John Wiley & Sons, Inc., and/or its affiliates in the United States and other countries, and may not be used without written permission. Frommer's is a trademark or registered trademark of Arthur Frommer. Used under license. All other trademarks are the property of their respective owners. Wiley Publishing, Inc., is not associated with any product or vendor mentioned in this book.

For general information on our other products and services or to obtain technical support, please contact our Customer Care Department within the U.S. at 800-762-2974, outside the U.S. at 317-572-3993, or fax 317-572-4002.

Wiley also publishes its books in a variety of electronic formats. Some content that appears in print may not be available in electronic books.

Library of Congress Control Number: 2004114076

ISBN: 0-7645-6945-7

Manufactured in the United States of America

10 9 8 7 6 5 4 3 2 1

3B/RY/RQ/QU/IN

WILEY

About the Author

Brian Silverman has written about travel, food, sports, and music for publications such as *Saveur, Caribbean Travel & Life, Islands, American Way, The New Yorker*, and *The New York Times*. He is the author of several books, including *Going, Going, Gone: The History, Lore and Mystique of the Home Run* and co-editor of *The Twentieth Century Treasury of Sports*. Brian lives in New York, New York with his wife and children.

Author's Acknowledgments

I feel I should thank Charles Salzberg for recognizing my true literary talent and recommending me as a potential author of a *For Dummies* book.

Publisher's Acknowledgments

We're proud of this book; please send us your comments through our Dummies online registration form located at www.dummies.com/register/.

Some of the people who helped bring this book to market include the following:

Editorial

Developmental Editor:
Kathleen Warnock

Project Editor:
Sherri Cullison-Pfouts

Copy Editor: Elizabeth Rea

Cartographer: Roberta Stockwell

Editorial Managers:
Michelle Hacker,
Christine Meloy Beck

Editorial Assistant:
Melissa S. Bennett

Senior Photo Editor: Richard Fox

Cover Photos:

Front Cover Photo:
© Mitchell Funk/Getty Images

Back Cover Photo:
© Mitchell Funk/Getty Images

Cartoons: Rich Tennant,
www.the5thwave.com

Composition

Project Coordinator: Kristie Rees

Layout and Graphics:
Lauren Goddard, Michael Kruzil,
Lynsey Osborn,
Melanee Prendergast,
Heather Ryan, Julie Trippetti

Proofreaders: Carl William Pierce,
Charles Spencer, Brian H. Walls,
TECHBOOKS Production
Services

Indexer: TECHBOOKS Production
Services

Publishing and Editorial for Consumer Dummies

Diane Graves Steele, Vice President and Publisher, Consumer Dummies

Joyce Pepple, Acquisitions Director, Consumer Dummies

Kristin A. Cocks, Product Development Director, Consumer Dummies

Michael Spring, Vice President and Publisher, Travel

Brice Gosnell, Associate Publisher, Travel

Kelly Regan, Editorial Director, Travel

Publishing for Technology Dummies

Andy Cummings, Vice President and Publisher, Dummies
Technology/General User

Composition Services

Gerry Fahey, Vice President of Production Services

Debbie Stailey, Director of Composition Services

Contents at a Glance

Maps at a Glance

Table of Contents

Introduction

*T*he diversity, depth, resilience, and spirit of New York have been chronicled so much in the news and in films and books that it's almost a cliché. But in New York's case, the cliché is not only accurate, but it's also one we New Yorkers take pride in. And New Yorkers usually disdain clichés. We like things to be new, fresh — exciting. In a way, New Yorkers have short attention spans; a restaurant, show, club, or store may be the hottest thing to hit the city for a couple of months, and then another opens or is discovered, and that once-hot place quickly becomes passé.

But not everything has to be new and hot for New Yorkers. We don't always appreciate change because it means we may have lost something we had come to love. New Yorkers respect the old standards — places and things that never change. Those are essential ingredients that make up New York. What would we do without that reassuring sight of the Lady in the harbor? Or the gleaming spire of the Empire State Building? Or the perfect pizza? Or a Sunday in Central Park? Or the rumbling of the trains beneath the earth? Or the sounds of jazz from a Village club? So even though New York is ever-changing, its core remains the same. And we wouldn't have it any other way.

In the pages that follow, I do my best to guide you to what's hot and new, without leaving out the old standards. I tell you where to find the best New York has to offer. I steer you to places both on and off the beaten path. But really, what I hope to accomplish in this book is to present New York as simply as possible so that you can decide what path you want to be on during your visit.

About This Book

Maybe this is your first trip to New York, or maybe you're a repeat visitor; in either case, I assume that you want to find out what you need to know plus a little bit more. But I don't want to overload you with information, which is very easy to do when you're talking about New York.

This book is both a guidebook *and* a reference book. You can read it cover to cover, or you can jump in anywhere to find the information you want about a specific task, such as finding a hotel or working out your budget. Whether you're sitting in your living room trying to make a reservation or standing on the corner of 42nd Street and Fifth Avenue wondering where to eat, *New York City For Dummies,* 3rd Edition, is set up so that you can get the facts, analysis, and recommendations you want, quickly.

Dummies Post-it® Flags

As you're reading this book, you'll find information that you'll want to reference as you plan or enjoy your trip — whether it be a new hotel, a must-see attraction or a must-try walking tour. Mark these pages with the handy Post-it® Flags included in this book to help make your trip planning easier!

Please be advised that travel information is subject to change at any time — this is especially true of prices. I therefore suggest that you write or call ahead to confirm prices and details when making your travel plans. The author, editors, and publisher cannot be held responsible for readers' experiences while traveling. Your safety is important to us, however, so I encourage you to stay alert and be aware of your surroundings. Keep a close eye on cameras, purses, and wallets, all favorite targets of thieves and pickpockets.

Conventions Used in This Book

In this book, I've included lists of hotels, restaurants, and attractions. As I describe each, I often include abbreviations for commonly accepted credit cards. Take a look at the following list for an explanation of each:

> AE: American Express
>
> DC: Diners Club
>
> DISC: Discover
>
> MC: MasterCard
>
> V: Visa

I've divided the hotels into two categories: my personal favorites and those that don't quite make my preferred list but still get my hearty seal of approval. Don't be shy about considering these "runner-up" hotels if you're unable to get a room at one of my favorites or if your preferences differ from mine — the amenities offered by the runners-up and the services that each provides make all these accommodations good choices to consider as you determine where to rest your head at night.

I also include some general pricing information to help you as you decide where to unpack your bags or dine on the local cuisine. I've used a system of dollar signs to show a range of costs for one night in a hotel (the price refers to a double-occupancy room) or a meal at a restaurant (included in the cost of each meal is soup or salad, an entrée, dessert, and a non-alcoholic drink). Check out the following table to decipher the dollar signs:

Cost	Hotel	Restaurant
$	$85–$150	Less than $25
$$	$150–$250	$25–$35
$$$	$250–$350	$35–$45
$$$$	$350–$450	$45–$60
$$$$$	$450 and up	$60 and up

For those hotels, restaurants, and attractions that are plotted on a map, a page reference is provided in the listing information. If a hotel, restaurant or attraction is outside the city limits or in an out-of- the-way area, it may not be mapped.

Foolish Assumptions

As I wrote this book, I made some assumptions about you and what your needs may be as a traveler. Here's what I assumed about you:

✔ You're an experienced traveler who hasn't had much time to explore New York and wants expert advice when you finally do get a chance to enjoy that particular locale.

✔ You're an inexperienced traveler looking for guidance when determining whether to take a trip to New York and how to plan for it.

✔ You're not looking for a book that provides all the information available about New York or that lists every hotel, restaurant, or attraction available to you. Instead, you're looking for a book that focuses on the places that will give you the best or most unique experience in New York.

If you fit any of these criteria, then *New York City For Dummies* gives you the information you're looking for!

How This Book Is Organized

This book is divided into six parts covering the major aspects of your trip. Each part is further broken down into specific components so that you can go right to the subtopic you want (you don't have to read all about nightlife if you're just looking for a jazz club, for example). Following are brief summaries of the parts.

Part 1: Introducing New York City

In this part, I give you my opinion on the very best of New York when it comes to hotels, attractions, events, and restaurants. This part also includes some basic information on culture, history, architecture, and food, along with the differences the seasons make in determining when you may want to come to New York and a yearly calendar of events.

Part 2: Planning Your Trip to New York City

This part covers the nitty-gritty of trip planning: how to manage your money and plan your budget for your New York visit; how to get to New York; whether you should join an escorted tour or choose a package tour; what to do if you have special needs; and other minute details.

Part 3: Settling into New York City

This part is all about getting around, from the moment your plane lands or you step off the train or bus. I cover ground transportation into the city, the public transit system, and sights to see on foot. This part also includes information about the many New York neighborhoods and what makes them distinct. From there, I explain New York lodging and how to find the best room rate, and then I give you my favorite hotels along with a number of very good runners-up. Finally, this part includes a chapter on eating in New York. Here I give you an overview of the food scene in New York, along with snacking options like pizza, bagels, dessert, and cheap eats.

Part 4: Exploring New York City

This part describes what to see and do, from touring famous buildings to attending a TV show taping. This part also includes a chapter on shopping the local stores. Here, I point out the best shopping neighborhoods and the city's best stores. To help you fit in all that you want to see without getting worn out, I also provide some sample itineraries to help you organize your time in the city.

Part 5: Living It Up after Dark: New York City Nightlife

This part covers New York's major arts attractions, from Broadway shows to clubs, and gives you an idea of what each activity costs and how to get discount tickets. I also include a chapter on nightclubs, places to have a drink, and other more or less civilized forms of relaxation.

Part 6: The Part of Tens

The Part of Tens gives you a few of my top tens of New York. You can take them seriously. Or you can take them for what they are — fun. Either way, I think you will enjoy them.

In back of this book I've included an appendix — your Quick Concierge — containing lots of handy information you may need when traveling in New York, like phone numbers and addresses for emergency personnel or area hospitals and pharmacies, lists of local newspapers and magazines, protocol for sending mail or finding taxis, and more. Check out this appendix when searching for answers to lots of questions that may come up as you travel. You can find Quick Concierge easily because it's printed on yellow paper.

Icons Used in This Book

Keep your eyes peeled for icons, which appear in the margins throughout the book. These little pictures serve as a kind of shorthand or code to alert you to special information. Here's the decryption key:

 Keep an eye out for the Bargain Alert icon as you seek out money-saving tips and/or great deals.

 The Best of the Best icon highlights the best New York has to offer in all categories — hotels, restaurants, attractions, activities, shopping, and nightlife.

 Watch for the Heads Up icon to identify annoying or potentially dangerous situations, such as tourist traps, unsafe neighborhoods, budgetary rip-offs, and other things to beware of.

 Find out useful advice on things to do and ways to schedule your time when you see the Tip icon.

 Look to the Kid Friendly icon for attractions, hotels, restaurants, and activities that are particularly hospitable to children or people traveling with kids.

 Secret little finds or useful resources that are worth the extra bit of effort to get to or find are highlighted by the Worth the Search icon.

Where to Go from Here

Sure, New York can seem overwhelming, but it doesn't have to be. It can seem budget-busting, but it doesn't have to be. In New York, you can find something for everyone — and that's what makes it so special. This book, and all it offers, should help assuage any fears or apprehensions you may have as it guides you to a fun and stress-free trip to the Big Apple.

Part I

Introducing New York City

I love visiting New York. When we're landing at LaGuardia, the look on the fans' faces in the upper deck of Shea Stadium is priceless!

In this part . . .

1 give you a taste of the best of New York City, with a spotlight on the top restaurants, hotels, attractions, sights, and sounds that make up this unique city. I do my best to guide you to what's hot and new, as well as the old standards. I tell you where to find the best New York has to offer, and I steer you to places both on and off the beaten track.

In this part, I also give you a brief history of New York City, as well as overviews of the architecture and cuisine, and I finish up with a list of books and films you may enjoy as you get ready to hit the town.

Chapter 1

Discovering the Best of New York City

In This Chapter

▶ Celebrating the most festive parades and seasons

▶ Finding rooms in the best hotels, both grand and budget

▶ Enjoying meals at the most delicious restaurants and street eats

▶ Visiting Lady Liberty and other top attractions

▶ Giving the credit card a workout at the top shops

▶ Choosing the spots with the best nightlife

*W*elcome to New York City! No matter when you visit, there's sure to be something of interest going on. In this chapter, I list my choices for the best events, hotels, restaurants, attractions, shopping, culture, and nightlife.

Whether you're looking for a world-class hotel, exotic cuisine to enjoy, or the view from the Empire State building, I have no doubt you'll soon compile your own "Best of" list . . . but here's a good place to start!

Best Events

Best Parade: West Indian-American Day Carnival and Parade. Held on Eastern Parkway in Brooklyn, this is the biggest parade in New York. The music (calypso, soca, reggae, and Latin), the amazing costumes, and the incredible Caribbean food make this an unforgettable experience. If you're lucky enough to be in town on Labor Day, don't miss it. See Chapter 3.

Best Street Festival: Ninth Avenue International Food Festival. Held for one weekend (usually in the middle of May), this festival is the perfect illustration of the ethnic diversity in the city. You can taste foods from local restaurants and sample cuisines from Afghani to Peruvian. See Chapter 3.

Downtown Orientation

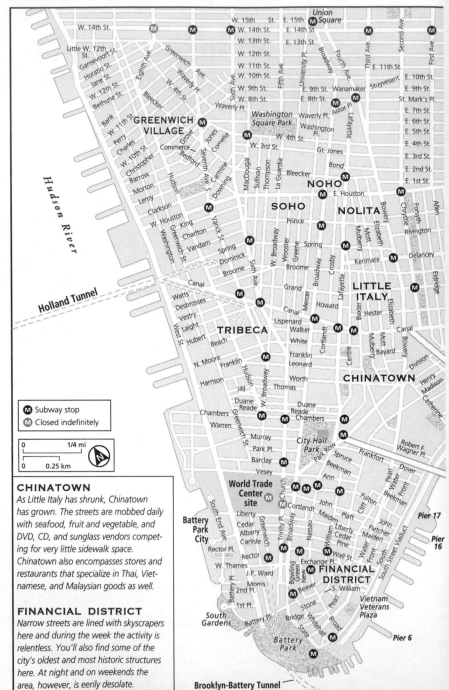

CHINATOWN

As Little Italy has shrunk, Chinatown has grown. The streets are mobbed daily with seafood, fruit and vegetable, and DVD, CD, and sunglass vendors competing for very little sidewalk space. Chinatown also encompasses stores and restaurants that specialize in Thai, Vietnamese, and Malaysian goods as well.

FINANCIAL DISTRICT

Narrow streets are lined with skyscrapers here and during the week the activity is relentless. You'll also find some of the city's oldest and most historic structures here. At night and on weekends the area, however, is eerily desolate.

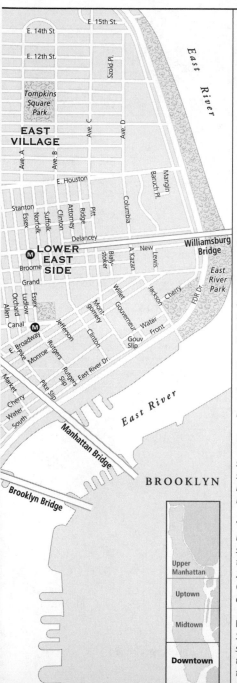

GREENWICH VILLAGE

The once-famous Bohemian enclave where off-beat became the Beats is still the city's best people-watching neighborhood. You won't find any high-rises here, just quaint, narrow streets and beautifully preserved brownstones and townhouses.

NOHO

I'm not sure why this very tiny stretch of furniture stores, boutiques, and a few restaurants has been designated a neighborhood, but it has. Maybe the powers that decide these things wanted a companion to SoHo so they came up with NoHo (North of Houston Street).

EAST VILLAGE

The East Village now is home to some of the city's most interesting restaurants and despite its counter-culture reputation, real estate prices are very "establishment."

NOLITA

Here's another neighborhood that has a cute acronym (North of Little Italy). This is really old Little Italy in architecture, but there is nothing old about the very hip boutiques and cafes that are sprinkled throughout the relatively small enclave.

SOHO

What once was an artist's destination has become a very affluent and very trendy tourist destination. You'll find just about all the top designer names in retail here housed in historic cast-iron buildings.

LOWER EAST SIDE

This is where so many immigrants, especially Jewish, settled as their first home in America. And there is still some of that old world feel to the neighborhood but it is fading fast as it becomes the city's newest hot spot for restaurants, bars, and clubs.

TRIBECA

In the 1980s TriBeCa (Triangle Below Canal), with its sprawling lofts and hip restaurants, became one of the most desirable places to live. After September 11, 2001 and its close proximity to the World Trade Center, the area lost a bit of its luster, but that was only temporary. TriBeCa is thriving once again.

LITTLE ITALY

Sadly, this once unique and charming neighborhood, squeezed by the expansion of Chinatown, has shrunk to a mere block or two. And what's left, with very few exceptions, is nothing like what it once was. You can't even get a good plate of pasta here anymore.

Midtown Orientation

MIDTOWN EAST
The heart of corporate Manhattan, Midtown East is also where you'll find such landmarks as Grand Central Station, the Empire State Building, St. Patrick's Cathedral, the Chrysler Building, and the United Nations.

MIDTOWN WEST
This bustling sprawl of an area includes many of the city's best hotels, the Art Deco masterpiece, Rockefeller Center, and a neighborhood called Hell's Kitchen where you'll find some of the city's most ethnically diverse restaurants.

TIMES SQUARE/ THEATER DISTRICT
In the truly American tradition, everything here is big and gaudy and, as a result, the streets here are constantly crammed with people who have come to gawk at the big and the gaudy — meaning the neon wonderland of Times Square.

MURRAY HILL
This is a quiet, mostly residential neighborhood. On its southern fringe is the Indo-Pakistani enclave known as Curry Hill.

GRAMMERCY PARK
The heart of this neighborhood is the postcard-perfect little park that's so exclusive you need a key to get into it. You don't need a special key to live in the quaint and very beautiful brownstones that surround the park, but you do need money. Many of the buildings here date back to the 1800s, giving the area a real 19th century feel.

FLATIRON AND UNION SQUARE
Cheaper rents attracted many publishing and media businesses and, as a result, the neighborhood is now bursting with restaurants and clubs. Along with Union Square, and the wildly popular greenmarket, the Flatiron Building embodies the spirit of this vibrant neighborhood.

CHELSEA
With galleries everywhere, Chelsea is now one of the city's arts centers. There is an almost small town feel to this neighborhood, which has also become the center for the city's gay population.

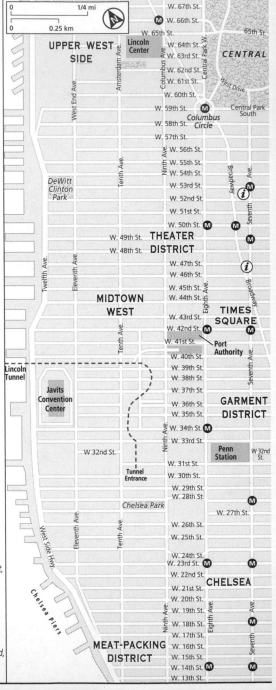

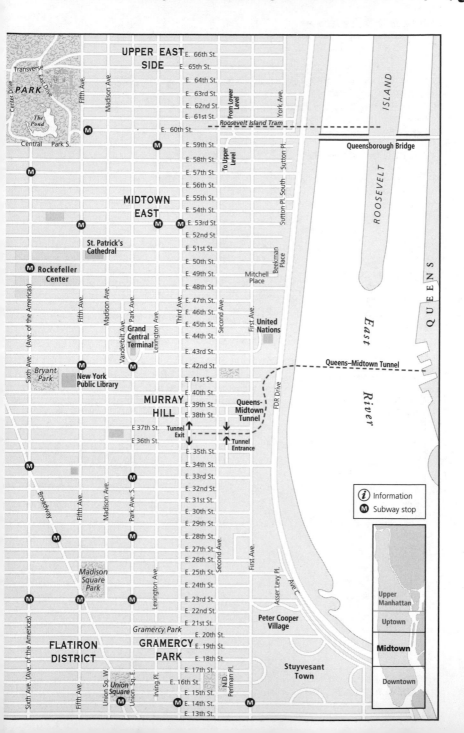

Uptown Orientation

CENTRAL PARK

This 843-acre nature retreat in the heart of Manhattan is one of the great parks of the world. Even if nature is not your thing, from the Central Park Zoo to the Carousel, from playgrounds to skating rinks, there is something for everyone in Central Park.

UPPER WEST SIDE

This mostly residential neighborhood also features landmarks like Lincoln Center, the Museum of Natural History, and the Cathedral of St. John the Divine and is enviable because it is surrounded by two great parks, Central Park and Riverside Park.

UPPER EAST SIDE

Long the address of the rich and famous, the Upper East Side is also the home to the Metropolitan Museum of Art, the Guggenheim, and other fantastic museums along "Museum Mile." You'll also find a thick concentration of restaurants and bars, and, of course, some great and very expensive shopping along tony Madison Avenue.

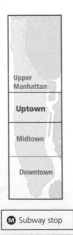

Upper Manhattan

Uptown

Midtown

Downtown

Ⓜ Subway stop

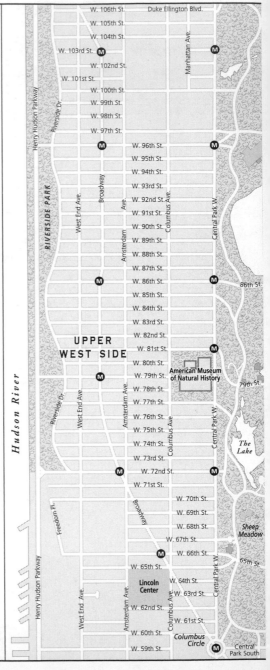

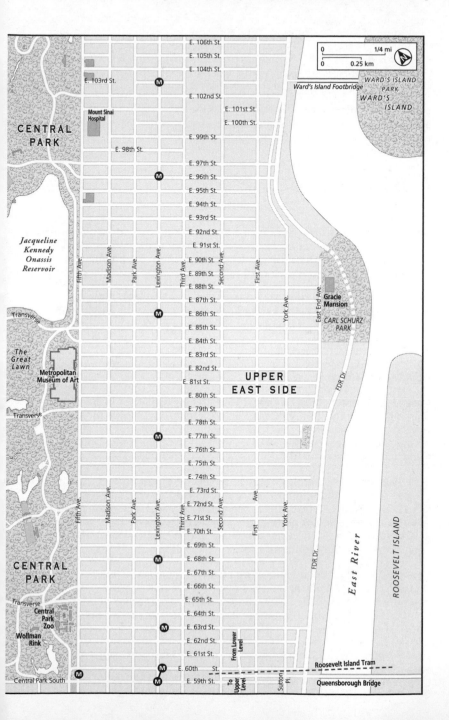

Best Time of Year to Come to New York: Summer. Most people prefer the temperate days of fall to visit New York, and that's when the city is most crowded; but my personal favorite season is summer, when the streets are empty, restaurants and shows are easier to get into, and countless free outdoor cultural events abound.

Best Day to Come to New York: New Year's Day. You've skipped the insanity of New Year's Eve and arisen fresh and sober. Get out on the town early; you have the city practically to yourself.

Best Hotels

For more information on all the hotels listed, refer to Chapter 9.

Best Hotel: Ritz-Carlton New York Central Park. The combination of a great location (just across from Central Park); large, well-outfitted rooms; typically excellent Ritz-Carlton service; and the magnificent restaurant **Atelier** (see Chapter 10) make this Ritz the city's all-out best.

Best Hotel for Classic New York Elegance: The Waldorf=Astoria. This hotel is a glorious throwback to old New York glamour — and it's often surprisingly affordable, considering the top-quality accommodations.

Best for Classic Old World Elegance: Hotel Plaza Athénée. That European feel pervades the hotel from the old-world design to the first-rate concierge service.

Best Trendy Hotel: Tribeca Grand Hotel. Trendy may not be for everyone, but trendy the Tribeca Grand is. With its atrium lobby and the bustling Church Lounge, the hotel is a gathering spot for film, fashion, and music industry people and a magnet for the trendy locals in the equally hip neighborhood.

Best Times Square Hotel: Westin New York at Times Square. If you choose to spend more money to be around the crowds, noise, and illumination of Times Square, this is the place for you. Located on Eighth Avenue, the hotel is not quite in the middle of Times Square, but the 45-story tower gives you views of the neon one block away. *And* the rooms are thankfully soundproofed.

Best Moderately Priced Hotel: The Lucerne. This is my favorite hotel on the Upper West Side and one of my favorites in New York. The homey, neighborhood feel of the hotel combined with exceptional service and nice-sized, well-equipped rooms make this a very attractive mid-priced option.

Best Budget Hotel: Chelsea Lodge. If you don't mind sharing a toilet with other guests, this charming hotel offers impeccable comforts — including an actual sink and shower — at a budget price.

Best for Families: The Doubletree Guest Suites Times Square. This place boasts an entire floor of childproof suites, complete with living rooms for spreading out, kitchenettes for preparing light meals, and a Kids Club (for ages 3–12), which features a playroom, an arts-and-crafts center, and computer and video games.

Best Romantic Hotel: Sofitel New York. How can an almost 400-room hotel be romantic? Maybe it's because the hotel is French-owned and staying here feels like you've escaped for a naughty tryst in Paris.

Best Hotel Restaurant: Atelier. With so many excellent restaurants in hotels, it's hard to believe that hotel food was once mocked. At Atelier, in the Ritz-Carlton, Central Park, Chef Gabriel Kreuther, former chef de cuisine at Jean-Georges (another incredible hotel restaurant), performs culinary magic.

Best Hotel Bar: Bemelmans Bar in the Carlyle Hotel. Named after book illustrator Ludwig Bemelmans, who created the *Madeline* books and painted the mural in the bar, this romantic, charming bar features white-gloved service and wondrous cocktails conceived by master mixologist Audrey Saunders.

Best Hotel for Museum Going: The Stanhope Park Hyatt New York. Across the street from the Metropolitan Museum of Art and within walking distance from the Guggenheim, Whitney, Cooper Hewitt, and Frick Museums, you can't find a better base than this elegant hotel for taking in the museums.

Best Restaurants

For more information on the restaurants listed, head to Chapter 10.

Best Restaurant: Eleven Madison Park. Higher praise has consistently gone to chef/restaurateur Danny Meyer's other restaurants, including the much-praised Gramercy Park Tavern, and as a result this gem often gets overlooked, which is a shame. It's a magnificent restaurant on every level. The Art Deco room is spectacular, the service almost otherworldly — and the food is truly memorable.

Best Special Occasion Restaurant: Chanterelle. If you want to impress that special loved one, you won't ever go wrong if you choose Chanterelle. The food is consistently superb, the room lovely and intimate, and the service impeccable.

Best for Romance: Café des Artistes. If the murals of the naked wood nymphs don't get you in the mood, the old school French cooking coupled with traditional, white-gloved service certainly will.

Best Chinese: New York Noodletown. With all the culinary wonders that Chinatown has to offer, this is a tough choice. Noodletown's my current favorite, where the soups are always fresh and comforting and anything that's salt-baked is guaranteed to be sublime.

Best French: Daniel. For faultless French cooking, nobody does it better than Chef Daniel Boulud, especially here at his signature restaurant.

Best Italian: 'Cesca. It's difficult to find a restaurant that presents dishes totally original to New York, but 'Cesca, with its truly farmhouse rustic cuisine does just that — and very successfully.

Best Mexican: Pampano. Another new arrival in New York, and I, for one, am grateful for it. Seafood is what they do best here and that includes the amazing ceviches and the lobster tacos.

Best Seafood: rm. The things Rick Moonen, the chef of this three-star restaurant, can do with denizens of the deep is truly amazing.

Best Steak: Peter Luger Steak House. Don't expect great service. Don't expect an intimate atmosphere. But do expect the finest steak in New York — and that's saying something.

Best Jewish Deli: Katz's Delicatessen. This deli's the choice among those who know their kreplach, knishes, and pastrami. No cutesy sandwiches named for celebrities here — just top-notch Jewish classics.

Best Burger: Burger Joint. Who woulda thunk that a fancy hotel like **Le Parker Meridien** would be the home to a place called Burger Joint that serves great burgers at great prices?

Best Pizza: Patsy's Pizzeria. This great East Harlem pizzeria has been cranking out coal-oven pizza since 1932. It was the favorite of Frank Sinatra, who used to have Patsy's pizzas packed and shipped to him in Vegas.

Best Breakfast: Good Enough to Eat. They've been lining up on Amsterdam Avenue on weekend mornings for over 20 years to get a taste of chef/owner Carrie Levin's bountiful home-cooked breakfasts.

Best Dessert: Fiamma Osteria. Many impressive pastry chefs work around the city, but few of them can top the remarkable Elizabeth Katz. Her creations make you want to skip the entrees and head straight for dessert.

Best Ice Cream: Brooklyn Ice Cream Factory. A treat from the Ice Cream Factory is the perfect reward after a brisk walk across the Brooklyn Bridge. Rich homemade ice cream with a view of the Manhattan skyline — that's a tough combination to beat.

Best Bagel: Absolute Bagels. These aren't huge, like some bagels you can find these days, but they're always hot and baked to perfection.

Best Hot Dog: Gray's Papaya. The hot dogs are so good here that it's tough to eat just one. But even though they're delicious, stop at two if you know what's best for you.

Best Times Square Restaurant: Virgil's Real BBQ. Times Square is a restaurant wasteland with bad theme restaurants or overpriced national chains. Virgil's, in a sense, is a barbecue-theme restaurant, but they do an excellent job of smoking meats.

Best for the Kids: Bubby's. With great pancakes, macaroni and cheese, peanut butter, spaghetti, and other comfort foods that kids love on the menu, Bubby's will please even the pickiest eater.

Best Neighborhood for Food: Hell's Kitchen. The area around this neighborhood, especially on Ninth Avenue, has so many different eating possibilities that you could spend your entire vacation — breakfast, lunch, and dinner — trying them all.

Best Attractions

For more information on the attractions below, please refer to Chapter 11.

Best Attraction: Statue of Liberty. If you have time to do only one thing on your visit to New York, sail to the Statue of Liberty. No other monument embodies the nation's, and the world's, notion of political freedom and economic potential more than Lady Liberty. She's also the ultimate symbol of New York; the personification of the city's vast diversity and tolerance. While visitors were denied access to the Statue's interior after the September 11, 2001 terrorist attack on the World Trade Center, 2004 saw a welcomed easing of security restrictions. Visitors are now allowed to explore the Statue of Liberty museum, peer into the intricate inner structure through a glass ceiling near the base of the statue, and enjoy the 360-degree views from the observation deck on top of the 16-story pedestal.

Best Skyscraper: Empire State Building. Like the Statue of Liberty, the Empire State Building, once again the tallest building in New York, is one of the city's definitive icons. The view from the 86th-floor observatory is unforgettable.

Best-Looking Building: Chrysler Building. This award goes to the chrome-topped, gargoyle-laden Art Deco masterpiece, the Chrysler Building.

Best Historic Building: Grand Central Terminal. Even if you don't have to catch a train, make sure you visit this beaux-arts gem that was built in 1913 and beautifully restored in the 1990s to recapture its initial brilliance.

Best Museum: American Museum of Natural History. You could spend your entire visit to New York at this 4-square-block museum; there's that much to see. From the famed Dinosaur Hall to the adjoining Rose Center for Earth and Space, the Museum of Natural History houses the world's greatest natural science collection.

Best Art Museum: Metropolitan Museum of Art. It's not only the best art museum in New York, but the best in North America as well. The number of masterworks housed here is mind-boggling.

Best Museum for Older Children: Intrepid Sea-Air-Space Museum. This humongous retired aircraft carrier offers almost as many thrills as a theme park.

Best Museum for Younger Children: Children's Museum of Manhattan. This museum is strictly hands-on and designed for ages 2–12. Beyond the normal exhibits, something special is always happening here.

Best Park: Central Park. Though New York has many wonderful parks, Central Park has no real competition here. It's one of the world's greatest urban refuges, serving as a center of calm and tranquility amongst the noise and bustle of Manhattan.

Best Location in Central Park for a Picnic: The Pool. At 100th Street, the Pool is like being in another world. It's relatively quiet and undiscovered, and with weeping willows, ducks, geese, egrets, and a hawk or two, this watering hole is an oasis of tranquility.

Best Place to Take the Kids: Central Park. Again, head to Central Park. With a lovely carousel, a zoo, two ice-skating rinks, and numerous playgrounds and ball fields, Central Park is a children's wonderland.

Best Street: Broadway. Fifth Avenue has the reputation, but it has lost some luster in the past few years with the proliferation of chain and theme stores, so my pick is Broadway. As it stretches from one end of Manhattan to the other, no street captures the city's diversity better than Broadway.

Best Neighborhood to Stroll: Greenwich Village. Though I'm partial to the Upper West Side, I have to give the nod here to Greenwich Village. With its historic streets, hidden cafes, cozy restaurants, and eccentric characters, Greenwich Village is a constant, but pleasant, barrage on the senses.

Best Bridge: Brooklyn Bridge. New York is a city of bridges connecting the various islands to the mainland and beyond. But none equals the splendor and originality of the Brooklyn Bridge. Walking across it is a must.

Best Free Attraction: Staten Island Ferry. With views of the Statue of Liberty, Ellis Island, lower Manhattan, the Verrazano Narrows Bridge, and the rest of New York Harbor — and the chance to mingle with commuters — you can't beat the price of this ride.

Best Shopping

For more information on the stores listed, skip to Chapter 12.

Best Store: Saks Fifth Avenue. Not as overwhelming as other department stores, Saks is consistently good. And don't miss those window displays at Christmas.

Best Clothes Store: Barney's. This store is the pinnacle with prices to match.

Best Bookstore: Coliseum Books. This book-lover's paradise is a mini-superstore (if there is such a thing) with the heart of an independent.

Best Music Store: Tower Records. A huge selection and frequent sales make this my personal favorite.

Best Shopping Zone: SoHo, NoHo, and NoLita. All three neighborhoods are within easy walking distance of one another and feature the newest, trendiest boutiques.

Best Culture and Nightlife

For more information on the listings below, jump to Chapters 15 and 16.

Best Performance Space: Carnegie Hall. You can find few greater performance spaces in the world than this one. Visually and acoustically brilliant, Carnegie Hall regularly attracts an amazing array of talent.

Best Free Cultural Event: Shakespeare in the Park. Imagine Shakespeare performed by stars, under the stars, in Central Park. No wonder it has become a New York institution.

Best Children's Theater: Paper Bag Players. For children ages 4–9, this group performs in the winter only and offers tales told in imaginative and original ways.

Best Jazz Club: Village Vanguard. The acoustics and sight lines aren't great, but you can't do better for finding consistent, good-quality jazz.

Best Rock Club: Mercury Lounge. This venue is intimate, but not obscure. The Merc is the best for hard-edged rock and roll.

Best Comedy Club: Gotham Comedy Club. Comfortable and sophisticated, this is where the best come to hone their acts.

Best Pub: Ear Inn. Located in an old hanger-on in chic SoHo, I hope it continues to survive amongst the lush lounges that surround it.

Best Dive Bar: Subway Inn. Sure, I know you came to New York to go to a dive bar. Enter the Subway Inn, and it's as if you stepped into a 1940s moody film noir — minus the cigarette smoke, of course.

Best Bar With a View: Rise Bar, in the Ritz-Carlton Battery Park Hotel. With views of Lady Liberty, New York Harbor, and incredible sunsets, this bar is worth seeking out even if you're not staying at the hotel.

Chapter 2

Digging Deeper into New York City

● ●

In This Chapter

▶ Exploring the history of New York City

▶ Appreciating Manhattan's architecture

▶ Tasting the local cuisine

▶ Absorbing New York City through films and books

● ●

*N*ew York is not an obscure destination. Even people in the most remote parts of the globe know about the Empire State Building and the Statue of Liberty. But no matter how much you know (or don't know) about New York, it may help you to get a little background on the city before you arrive. Here's a quick overview — historical timelines, architectural highlights, culinary tidbits, a recommended reading and films list — that may help you discover a part of what makes New York unique.

Hunting Down a Little History

The area that became New York City was the home to many Native Americans before Giovanni da Verrazano arrived in 1524. Even though Verrazano didn't stay, a bridge was named after him. And it wasn't until 1609, when Henry Hudson, while searching for the Northwest Passage, claimed it for the Dutch East India Company, that New York was recognized as a potential, profitable settlement in the New World.

Hudson (the river that separates Manhattan from the mainland is named after him) said of New York, "It is as beautiful a land as one can hope to tread upon." The treading didn't really start until years later, but by 1625, Dutch settlers established a fur trade with the locals and called their colony New Amsterdam. A year later, Peter Minuit of the Dutch West India Company made that famous deal for the island. He bought New Amsterdam from the Lenape Tribe for what has widely been reported as $24.

New Amsterdam became a British colony in the 1670s, and during the Revolutionary War it was occupied by British troops. England controlled New York until 1783 when it withdrew from the city two full years after the end of the American Revolution. Two years after *that*, New York was named the first capital of the United States. The first Congress was held at Federal Hall on Wall Street in 1789, and George Washington was inaugurated president. But New York's tenure as the capital didn't last long. A year later, the government headed south to the newly created District of Columbia.

By 1825, New York City's population swelled to 250,000 and rose again to a half-million by mid-century. The city was a hotbed of Union recruitment during the Civil War; in the 1863 draft riots, Irish immigrants violently protested the draft and lynched 11 African Americans.

With industry booming, the late 19th century was termed the "Gilded Age." New York City was an example of this label in action; millionaires built mansions on Fifth Avenue, while rows of tenements teeming with families (made up of the cheap, mostly immigrant laborers who were employed by the industrial barons) filled the city's districts. In 1880, the city's population boomed to 1.1 million.

New York City timeline: 1524-1792

1524 Giovanni da Verrazano sails into New York Harbor.

1609 Henry Hudson sails up the Hudson River.

1621 The Dutch West India Company begins trading from New York City.

1626 The Dutch pay 60 Guilders ($24) to the Lenape Tribe for the island of New Amsterdam.

1664 The Dutch surrender New Amsterdam to the British and the island is renamed after the brother of King Charles II, The Duke of York.

1765 The Sons of Liberty burn the British Governor in effigy.

1776 Independence from England is declared.

1789 The first Congress is held at Federal Hall on Wall Street, and George Washington is inaugurated.

1792 The first stock exchange is established on Wall Street.

New York City timeline: 1820-1929

1820 New York City is the nation's largest city with a population of 124,000.

1863 The draft riots rage throughout New York; 125 people die including 11 African Americans who are lynched by mobs of Irish immigrants.

1883 The Brooklyn Bridge opens.

1886 The Statue of Liberty is completed.

1892 Ellis Island opens and begins processing over a million immigrants yearly.

1904 The first subway departs from City Hall.

1920 Babe Ruth joins the New York Yankees.

1929 The stock market crashes.

More European immigrants poured into the city between 1900 and 1930, arriving at Ellis Island and then fanning out into neighborhoods like the Lower East Side, Greenwich Village, Little Italy, and Harlem. With the city population in 1930 at 7 million and a Depression raging, New York turned to a feisty mayor named Fiorello La Guardia to help turn things around. With the help of civic planner Robert Moses, who masterminded a huge public works program, the city was remade. Moses did some things well, but his highway, bridge, tunnel, and housing projects ran through (and sometimes destroyed) many vibrant neighborhoods.

While most of the country prospered after World War II, New York, with those Moses-built highways and a newly forming car culture, endured an exodus to the suburbs. By 1958, the Dodgers had left Brooklyn and the Giants had left the Polo Grounds in Upper Manhattan. This economic slide climaxed in the late 1970s with the city's declaration of bankruptcy.

As Wall Street rallied during the Reagan years of the 1980s, New York's fortunes also improved. In the 1990s, with Rudolph Giuliani — whom they haven't named anything after yet — as the mayor, the city rode a wave of prosperity that left it safer, cleaner, and more populated. The flip side of this boom was that Manhattan became more homogenized. Witness the Disney-fication of Times Square — the ultimate symbol of New York's homogenization — and the growing gap between the rich and poor.

Everything changed on September 11, 2001, when terrorists took down the Twin Towers of the World Trade Center. But New York's grit and verve showed itself once more, as the city immediately began to rebound emotionally and financially from that terrible tragedy. As this book goes to press, plans are progressing to break ground on the new Freedom Tower to be built on the World Trade Center site.

New York City timeline: 1931-2004

1931 The Empire State Building opens and is the tallest building in the world.

1939 The New York World's Fair opens in Flushing Meadows, Queens.

1947 The Brooklyn Dodgers sign Jackie Robinson, the first African American to play in the Major Leagues.

1957 Elvis Presley performs live in New York on The Ed Sullivan Show.

1969 The Gay Rights movement begins with the Stonewall Rebellion in Greenwich Village.

1990 David Dinkins is elected as the first African-American mayor of New York City.

2000 The New York Yankees beat the New York Mets in the first Subway Series in 44 years. New York's population exceeds 8 million.

2001 Terrorists use hijacked planes to crash into the Twin Towers of the World Trade Center, which brings both towers down and kills more than 3,000 people.

2003 Smoking is banned in all restaurants and bars.

2004 Ground breaks on the Freedom Tower to be built on the site of the World Trade Center.

Looking at Local Architecture

I admit it: I'm no architectural scholar. I'm easy. I see a building, and if it looks old and sturdy and has ornate design, I'm impressed. New York has many of these buildings, along with a slew of tall, sleek, modern buildings. The architectural styles in New York are as diverse as the population. Table 2-1 lists some of New York's more prominent styles, dates, and structures that represent those styles.

Table 2-1   New York Examples of Architectural Styles

Architectural Style	Building
Georgian (1700–1776)	St. Paul's Chapel (1766)
Greek Revival (1820–1860)	Federal Hall National Memorial (1842)
Gothic Revival (1830–1860)	Trinity Church (1846)
Early Skyscraper (1880–1920)	Flatiron Building (1902), Woolworth Building (1913)

Architectural Style	Building
Beaux Arts (1890–1920)	U.S. Customs House (1907), Grand Central Station (1913), New York Public Library (1911)
Art Deco (1925–1940)	Chrysler Building (1930), Empire State Building (1931), Rockefeller Center (1940)
Art Moderne (1930–1945)	Radio City Music Hall (1932)
Postmodern (1975–1990)	Sony Building (1984)

Lauding the Local Cuisine

I dare you to define the local cuisine of New York: Is it a hot dog with mustard? Pastrami on rye? A bagel and a schmear? A "slice" (of pizza, of course)? It's all of them and more. The cuisine of New York is the cuisine of the world. A little bit of everything goes into the melting pot, and the mix is constantly changing. A few years ago, you couldn't get good Mexican food. Now, with the influx of thousands of Mexican immigrants, good, authentic Mexican restaurants abound.

But what defines New York cuisine is not just different ethnic foods, but the different trends, styles, and types of restaurants. Food is important in New York. And it's also big business. This is a city where a hamburger can sell from $3 to $30, or an omelet with mounds of caviar can sell for $1,000. It's also the city where you can find a restaurant where the only item on the menu is peanut butter. Or another restaurant that only sells variations of rice pudding. Everyone can find something to eat in New York. For a list of some of New York's best restaurants in every category, see Chapter 10.

Recommending Books and Movies

New York City has inspired writers for hundreds of years, and filmmakers since the invention of the form. You might gain another level of understanding of the city by reading or watching some of the following novels, non-fiction works, or films.

New York City on paper

For the definitive history of New York City from its birth to the end of the 19th century, you won't find a better read than the Pulitzer Prize-winning *Gotham: A History of New York City to 1898,* by Edwin G. Burrows and Mike Wallace (Oxford University Press, 1998). Another recommended historical look at the growth of New York City — this one told in a breezy narrative tone — is *Epic of New York City: A Narrative History*, by Edward Robb Ellis (Kodansha, 1990).

One of master biographer Robert A. Caro's early works, *The Power Broker: Robert Moses and the Fall of New York* (Vintage, 1975), focuses on how the vision of master builder Robert Moses transformed New York to what it became in the second half of the 20th century.

In *Great Bridge: The Epic Story of the Building of the Brooklyn Bridge* (Simon & Schuster, 1983), David McCullough devotes his estimable talents to the story of the building of the Brooklyn Bridge.

The companion volume to a PBS Series (see *New York: A Documentary Film* later in this chapter), *New York: An Illustrated History,* by Ric Burns, Lisa Ades, and James Sanders (Knopf, 2003) uses lavish photographs and illustrations to show the growth of New York City.

The great essayist E.B. White's classic, *Here is New York* (Little Bookroom, 1999), is as relevant today as it was in 1948 when it was written. Another timeless masterpiece is Miroslav Sasek's illustrated children's book from 1960, *This is New York* (Universe Books, 2003). Both books are available in recent reprints.

New York City on film

Few places are as cinematic as New York City. Filmmakers sometimes think of the city as a character itself. The list of movies in which New York plays a crucial role is too long to cover in depth, but some of these top New York City movies are worth renting before you visit.

Possibly the best New York City promotional film is the musical *On The Town,* with Gene Kelly and Frank Sinatra. This film is about three sailors who spend their 24-hour leave exploring Gotham. Shot on location, all the landmarks, circa 1949, are captured in Technicolor.

Woody Allen is known as a New York filmmaker and proudly shoots all his films in the city. One of his best and a good, but maybe a bit dated, look at neurotic New York is 1977's *Annie Hall*.

Following in Woody Allen's footsteps are director Rob Reiner and writer Nora Ephron, the team who made *When Harry Met Sally* in 1989. It's a gorgeous cinematic tribute to New York. By the way, the famous "I'll have what she's having" scene was filmed in Katz's Delicatessen (see Chapter 10 for more on this famous deli).

"I love this dirty town," says Burt Lancaster in the gritty, crackling *Sweet Smell of Success*. In this beautifully photographed black-and-white movie from 1957, Lancaster plays malicious gossip columnist J.J. Hunsecker, and Tony Curtis is perfectly despicable as the groveling publicist, Sidney Falco.

Another filmmaker identified with New York is Martin Scorsese. He has made many films in which New York plays a central role, including *Mean Streets* (1973), *The Age of Innocence* (1993), and 2002's *Gangs of New*

York, which was actually filmed in Italy. But the one film where New York is a character, and not a very flattering one, is *Taxi Driver*. The Academy Award–nominated 1976 movie about an alienated and psychotic taxi driver is tough and bloody, but if you want to see images of pre-cleanup Times Square, check this film out.

The best history of New York on video is the Ric Burns documentary, *New York: A Documentary Film* (1999). The seven-disc, 14-hour DVD (also available on VHS) with a poignant, post-9/11 epilogue is a must-see for anyone interested in the evolution of this great city.

Chapter 3

Deciding When to Go

. . . .

In This Chapter

▶ Choosing the best time to visit New York City

▶ Keeping your cool (or dressing warmly!)

▶ Flipping through the calendar of events

. . . .

*B*ecause New York offers such a wide variety of attractions and sights, people visit the city year-round, regardless of the weather. In addition to giving you the lowdown on New York life during each season, this chapter includes a calendar of events if you'd like to plan your visit around a particular activity.

Revealing the Secrets of the Seasons

Summer or winter, rain or shine, great stuff is always going on in New York City, so I can't really tell you a "best" time to go. I can, however, give you some of the pros and cons, season by season.

Winter: With the exception of the first few weeks in December, winter is a great time to come to New York if you're searching for bargains. Hotel rates are at their lowest, tickets to top shows are attainable, and reservations at the best restaurants are very manageable. But if your idea of a vacation doesn't involve walking around bundled in layers of protective clothing to insulate you from the biting cold (in a city where the skyscrapers function as wind tunnels), then don't come during a New York winter.

Spring: This is the wettest time of year, but in between the showers, the flowers in the park bloom and the temperatures are more pedestrian-friendly. As a result, the tourists make their way back to the city and hotel rates begin to rise, especially in late spring.

Summer: The city is sticky, streets begin to radiate a pungent stench, and tempers can be testy. Why then, do I love the summer in New York so much? Because I've got so many free outdoor events, like concerts and plays, to choose from. Restaurants are less crowded, museums and other attractions are more manageable, I can picnic in Central Park, and I can walk around in shorts, sandals, and a T-shirt.

Fall: With mild temperatures and dry days, fall is New York's best weather season. But it's also the busiest time of year in the city. Everyone is back to school or work; street fairs continue through the early fall; and reservations at restaurants and hotels are tougher to snag. You'll also be hard-pressed to find bargains during this period.

To get an idea of the kind of temperatures and weather you may experience during a particular month in New York, take a look at Table 3-1.

Table 3-1 Average Temperature and Rainfall in New York City

	Jan	Feb	Mar	Apr	May	Jun	Jul	Aug	Sept	Oct	Nov	Dec
Daily temp.(°F)	38	40	48	61	71	80	85	84	77	67	54	42
(°C)	3	4.5	9	16	21.5	26.5	29.5	29	25	19.5	12	5.5
Days of rain	11	10	11	11	11	10	11	10	8	8	9	10

Marking Your Calendar: Year-round New York

Regardless of when you plan to visit New York, you can find events that draw people to the Big Apple by the millions. This section lists the highlights, month by month.

January

New York National Boat Show, Jacob K. Javits Convention Center. Expect to find a leviathan fleet of boats and marine products from the world's top manufacturers. Call ☎ **212-984-7000,** or visit www. boatshows.com or www.javitscenter.com. First or second week in January.

 Winter Restaurant Week. Participating fine-dining restaurants offer two- or three-course fixed-price lunches for a price that corresponds to the year ($20.03 in 2003, $20.04 in 2004, and so on). For a list of restaurants and exact dates, go to www.restaurantweek.com. Second week in January.

February

Chinese New Year, Chinatown. The famous dragon parade and fireworks highlight this two-week celebration. Call ☎ **212-484-1222** for information. Late January/early February.

Westminster Kennel Club Dog Show, Madison Square Garden. More than 2,500 dogs and their owners compete for the top prize in mid-February. Call ☎ **212-465-6741** for information.

March

 Ringling Brothers and Barnum & Bailey Circus, Madison Square Garden. Don't miss the parade from Twelfth Avenue and 34th Street to the Garden the morning before the show opens. Call ☎ 212-465-6741 for information. March through April.

St. Patrick's Day Parade, Fifth Avenue between 44th and 86th streets. Make sure to wear green to this parade of 150,000 marchers showing their love of all things Irish. Call ☎ 212-484-1222 for information. March 17.

April

Greater New York International Auto Show, Javits Convention Center. This car show, featuring classics, futuristic models, and everything in between, is the largest in the United States. Call ☎ 800-282-3336 or 212-216-2000 for information. First week in April.

The Easter Parade, Fifth Avenue from 49th to 57th streets. Silly hats abound; the *New York Times* recently featured a picture of a ferret attending the parade in an Easter bonnet. Call ☎ 212-484-1222 for information. Easter Sunday.

May

Fleet Week, Intrepid Sea-Air-Space Museum. A plethora of ships and thousands of crew members visit New York during Fleet Week; activities include flyovers, ship tours, 21-gun salutes, and more. Call ☎ 212-245-0072 for information or check www.fleetweek.navy.mil. Last week in May.

Ninth Avenue International Food Festival, 37th to 57th streets. Food, entertainment, and music come together to make this 20-block fair a must-see. Call ☎ 212-581-7029 for information. Third weekend in May.

June

Hudson River Festival, parks and public spaces of Battery Park City. Free concerts along the river. Call ☎ 212-945-0505 for information. June through August.

The Puerto Rican Day Parade and **Lesbian and Gay Pride Week and March,** Fifth Avenue. Both parades are in June. The Puerto Rican Day Parade is the third week of June while the Lesbian and Gay Pride March is the last week in June.

Museum Mile Festival, Fifth Avenue from 82nd to 104th streets. Free admission to the nine museums of the famous mile-long stretch of Fifth Avenue plus live music and street performers make this a mile of fun. Call ☎ 212-606-2296 for information. June 11.

Restaurant Week. Participating restaurants around the city offer two- or three-course lunches for $20.04 in 2004 (it'll cost one cent more in 2005!). (See the entry for "Winter Restaurant Week" under January events.) Third week in June.

SummerStage, Central Park at 72nd Street. Free afternoon concerts feature a wide range of contemporary groups and often some big-name performers. Call ☎ 212-360-2777 for information. The concerts run through August.

July

Fourth of July fireworks. Get to as high a vantage point as you can to watch any of the several fireworks shows that light up the skyline. Usually, the fireworks are set off from barges in the East River. Call ☎ 212-695-4400 for information. July 4.

Midsummer Night's Swing, Lincoln Center Fountain. Dance under the summer skies to a live band. Call ☎ 212-546-2656 for information. Throughout July.

Mostly Mozart, Avery Fisher Hall, and **Lincoln Center Festival,** Lincoln Center. The former is an important appointment for classical music fans, while enthusiasts of dance, opera, ballet, and theater enjoy the latter. Call ☎ 212-875-5030 (Avery Fisher Hall) and ☎ 212-546-2656 (Lincoln Center) for information. July and August.

 Shakespeare in the Park, Central Park. The Public Theater stages a free play by the Bard each summer at the Delacorte Theater in Central Park. Shows often feature top stars. Call ☎ 212-861-2777 or 212-539-8750, or visit www.publictheater.org for information. Throughout July and August.

August

Harlem Week, Harlem and other public areas around the city, including City Hall, Gracie Mansion, Columbia University, and the Schomburg Center. This week-long celebration features theater, symposia, art, sport, and the famous Harlem Jazz and Music Festival. Call ☎ 212-283-3315 or visit www.harlemdiscover.com/harlemweek for information. August.

Lincoln Center Out-of-Doors, Damrosch Park, Lincoln Center. Treat yourself to free concerts and dance performances. Call ☎ 212-546-2656 for information. August.

U.S. Open Tennis Championships, Flushing Meadows, Queens. The world's best tennis players gather for the final Grand Slam tournament of the year. Call ☎ 718-760-6200 or visit www.usopen.org for information. The two weeks before and after Labor Day.

September

West Indian-American Day Carnival and Parade. This annual Brooklyn event is New York's largest and best street celebration. Come for the extravagant costumes, pulsating rhythms (soca, calypso, reggae), bright colors, folklore, food (jerk chicken, oxtail soup, Caribbean soul food), and two million hip-shaking revelers. The route can change from year to year, but it usually runs along Eastern Parkway from Utica Avenue to Grand Army Plaza (at the gateway to Prospect Park). Call ☎ 212-484-1222 or 718-625-1515 for information. Labor Day.

New York Film Festival, sponsored by the Film Society of Lincoln Center. This two-week festival has seen many important premieres over the years. Get your tickets in advance. Call ☎ 212-875-5610 for information. September through October.

October

Greenwich Village Halloween Parade, West Village/Chelsea. Not your average group of trick-or-treaters, this parade — the nation's largest public Halloween parade — features outrageous costumes and people (soon to be outnumbered by boring floats advertising radio stations and the like). Call ☎ 212-484-1222 for information. October 31.

Next Wave Festival, Brooklyn Academy of Music. Enjoy experimental dance, theater, and music. Call ☎ 718-636-4100 for information. October through December.

November

Big Apple Circus, Lincoln Center. You don't have to be a kid to enjoy this fabulous spectacle. Call ☎ 212-268-2500 for information. November through January.

Macy's Thanksgiving Day Parade, Central Park West/Broadway. Some people think that watching the balloon inflation the night before is even more fun than the parade itself. Call ☎ 212-494-5432 or 212-494-4495 for information. Thanksgiving Day (late November).

New York City Marathon, ends in Central Park. Join this race, which runs through all five boroughs, or stand at the sidelines to cheer on the thousands of competitors. Call ☎ 212-860-4455 for the exact route and more information. First Sunday in November.

December

Rockefeller Center Christmas Tree Lighting, Rockefeller Center. Prepare to join thousands of others to watch the lighting of the huge tree, which remains on display through the New Year. Call ☎ 212-632-3975 or 212-632-4000 for information. Early December.

New Year's Eve, Times Square. Okay, if freezing your buns off amongst thousands of intoxicated people from everywhere but New York is what you've wanted to do all your life, than this is the place for you. You won't find many New Yorkers there. But arrive early or you'll get a better view of the ball dropping from your hotel room television set. Call ☎ 212-768-1560 or 212-354-0003 (the hotline) for information. December 31.

Part II
Planning Your Trip to New York City

In this part . . .

1 suggest ways to get the most value out of your travel budget and prepare you for how much things cost in New York City. I also discuss your options for getting to New York City, whether you're flying, driving, or taking the train.

I also discuss planning resources that can be a big help for families, seniors, travelers with disabilities, and gay and lesbian travelers coming to the city.

Finally, I discuss the important details, from renting a car to travel insurance, staying in touch with home, and following the latest information on airline security.

Chapter 4

Managing Your Money

In This Chapter

▶ Deciding how to spend your money
▶ Cutting the costs, but not the fun
▶ Getting, carrying, and keeping your funds

*N*ew York has a way of devouring your cash. With almost as many ATMs (and their accompanying fees) as there are things to spend money on, the Big Apple can be a big budget-buster. But as long as you set realistic goals for your spending and plan ahead, you don't have to worry about mortgaging the house to finance your trip. In this chapter, I share ways you can get the best value for your dollars without going broke.

Planning Your Budget

New York has a reputation as one of the most expensive cities to live in, not only in the United States, but in the world. So dismiss any notions that you can get off on the very cheap here. But that reputation is also exaggerated; you can spend a week in the Big Apple for somewhat less than a king's ransom. In fact, you can make your trip to New York wallet-friendly in lots of ways. You just have to know what you're doing and do a bit of groundwork.

Hotel

The biggest challenge in terms of saving money in New York is finding an affordable place to stay. As I discuss in Chapter 9, a decent hotel room in New York can run at least $150 per night, including a hotel tax of 15.25 percent. This expense is the biggest drain on your budget unless you want to share a bathroom or explore a youth hostel — and you don't want to do that, do you? So definitely look for bargains, but do be realistic. A hotel room is going to cost you some dough.

Transportation

First off, pack comfortable walking shoes — walking is the preferred mode of transportation in New York. Next, invest in a MetroCard (the major form of admittance to New York's public transportation). One ride on the subway costs $2 (although you can purchase an "unlimited" MetroCard . . . more about that later in this chapter), and if you transfer to a bus, the transfer is free. The New York subway system is a marvel. At times it is overcrowded (try to avoid riding on it at rush hour), and in the summer, the stations can be extremely toasty (even though all the trains are air-conditioned), but no other means of transportation can get you to your destination within the city cheaper and faster. See Chapter 8 for more information about getting around New York.

Buses, which accept both MetroCards and exact change, are also an inexpensive alternative to the subway and a nice way to see the city. But with many stops and the regular heavy traffic in Manhattan, they can be extremely slow.

Yellow cabs are the city's other great resource. They're usually plentiful — they say approximately 19,000 cabs are on the streets at any given time — and you can usually get a cab without too much hassle (except on rainy days and at the pre-theater hour). Cabs offer relatively affordable rides, particularly if you're in a group of up to three people. They're also the most convenient way to get to parts of town where the subway doesn't go. You pay $2.50 as soon as the cabbie turns on the meter, plus 40¢ per ⅕ mile or 30¢ per minute when stuck in traffic. There's also a 50¢ night-time surcharge and a $1 surcharge Mon–Fri, from 4–8 p.m.

As signs all over Manhattan say: "Don't Even THINK About Parking Here." If you're considering renting a car in New York or using your own car for transportation around town, think again. (Find more discussion on parking and driving in Chapter 7.)

Food

You can get every conceivable kind of food in New York at just about any price. We all know about those three- and four-star restaurants that may cost more than two nights at a New York hotel, but not as well-known are those hidden gems (and there are plenty) that cost you less than $20 for an excellent meal. If you want to save even more, you can always get pizza, bagels, hot dogs, falafel, and other (surprisingly) good street food throughout New York to satisfy your hunger pangs. Chapter 10 offers tips on selecting food that fits both your appetite and your budget.

Sights

Entrance fees vary from attraction to attraction. If you're planning on visiting a lot of them, consider buying a CityPass, which gets you reduced admission to six of the city's top attractions for $45 (a savings of more than 50 percent of what you would pay for separate admissions). See Chapter 11 for more information about places and things to see in the city.

Some attractions request a suggested contribution for admission, which means that you can pay whatever you want. But be reasonable — if you offer up a couple of dollars to get a family of six into the Metropolitan

Museum, you're likely to get a sneer with your tickets. Some museums also offer a free admission night, which, for obvious reasons, is usually the busiest night of the week. See the individual museum listings in Chapter 11 for details.

Shopping

When it comes to shopping, only you know how much you want to spend. You can find bargains in New York on electronics, CDs, and because of the many options, clothes as well. But unless you happen upon a sample sale or another sale, top designer duds are going to cost you. (Of course, you can buy designer knockoffs on the street, but the quality is somewhat less than the real thing, to say the least.)

Nightlife

Again, how much you spend on nightlife entertainment depends on what you're interested in doing. At the top end are Broadway shows, which average $75 and up for the best orchestra seats, and supper clubs where you can see a cabaret act for around $60, not including drinks. If you just want to people-watch at a wine bar or pub around happy hour, you'll be hard-pressed to spend more than $20.

Typical day-to-day purchases

Table 4-1 gives you an idea of what you can expect to pay for typical purchases in New York.

Table 4-1   What Things Cost in New York City

Item	Price
Subway or city bus ride	$2
Bottle of water	$1
Slice of pizza	$2–$3.50
Hot dog from a street vendor	$1–$3
Coffee (standard cuppa joe at a diner, not Starbucks-style)	60¢–$1
New York Yankees baseball cap from street vendor	$5–$10
Ticket to top of the Empire State Building	$10
Cover charge at a Village jazz club (excluding 1- or 2-drink minimum)	$15–$30
Boat ride around Manhattan on the Circle Line, adult	$25
Ride on the Staten Island Ferry	Free

(continued)

Table 4-1 *(continued)*

Item	Price
Admission to the Guggenheim Museum, adult	$15
Hotel bar martini	$10–$15
Three-course prix fixe at Chanterelle	$95

Taxes

Regular sales tax is 8.65 percent — not a small amount, especially if you buy expensive stuff. Remember that advertised prices, from restaurants to hotels to most shops, almost always exclude sales tax. The prices in this book also do not include sales tax.

Keep an eye out for "tax free" weeks on clothing and shoes, which are usually declared a couple times a year.

Hotel taxes run 15.25 percent. If you think this seems ridiculous, be glad that you didn't plan your trip a few years ago, when the hotel tax was 19.25 percent! (Occasionally, things in New York do get cheaper.) A room charge of $2 per night is also added to your bill. Remember to ask whether the price quoted to you includes these additional amounts, both for travel packages and hotel rooms; they can make quite a difference.

Tips

Bottom line: Expect to tip for every service you get in New York. Use the following guidelines when tipping:

- ✔ **Waiters:** Simply double the tax on your bill and round up to the nearest dollar (which is a tip of about 17 percent). Often, restaurants add the tip (15 to 20 percent) to the bill automatically for parties of six or more.

- ✔ **Bartenders:** If you're just drinking at a bar, 10 to 15 percent takes care of it.

- ✔ **Taxi drivers:** No matter how bumpy the ride, tip 15 percent.

- ✔ **Everybody else:** Bellhops get $1 or $2 per bag, maids get $1 per day, coat-check people get $1 per garment, and automobile valets get $1.

Cutting Costs, But Not the Fun

You can cut costs in plenty of ways — some little and some big. Note the Bargain Alert icons scattered throughout this book, which offer hints on ways to trim the fat from your budget. While you're planning a trip, keep a few things in mind:

✔ **Travel at off-peak times.** Although New York doesn't have a real off-season, the prices at some hotels during nonpeak times are half of what they are during the peak travel seasons. See Chapter 3 for a discussion of the New York travel seasons.

✔ **Check out a package tour.** A package deal may get you your airfare and hotel, as well as other aspects of your trip, for a good price. See the section on package tours in Chapter 5 for suggestions of specific companies to call.

✔ **Always ask for discount rates.** You won't get them if you don't ask for them. Don't forget to mention your membership in any clubs that may earn you a discount.

✔ **Ask if your kids can stay in your room with you.** You may have to pay a few extra dollars to have them stay with you, but it sure beats paying for a second room.

✔ **Reserve a room with a refrigerator and coffeemaker.** You don't have to slave over a hot stove to cut a few costs; several motels have minifridges and coffeemakers. Buying supplies for breakfast saves you money — and probably calories.

✔ **Try expensive restaurants at lunch instead of dinner.** Lunch tabs are usually a fraction of what dinner costs at most restaurants, and the menu often offers many of the same specialties, only sometimes in smaller portions. Many of New York's best restaurants participate in Restaurant Week in January and June — $20 and some change nets you a two- or three-course lunch — and some extend this fixed-price bargain throughout the summer or even year-round.

✔ **Don't use the hotel phone.** Some hotels in the moderate-to-expensive range now offer free local calls from rooms, but don't count on it. Instead, if you have one, bring your cell phone and use it. See Chapter 7 for more info.

✔ **Stay away from the minibar.** I know it's tempting, but if you want a snack, pick one up at the closest deli. Open that minibar and crack open that can of peanuts . . . and then a beer, and before long you've spent $20 on a snack.

✔ **Use the buses and subways.** Taxis get expensive quickly, especially in gridlock traffic. See Chapter 8 for hints on navigating the public transit system.

✔ **Buy a daily or weekly MetroCard pass.** See Chapter 8 for more info about the MetroCard and its budget-saving powers.

✔ **Walk a lot.** A good pair of walking shoes can save lots of money in taxis and other local transportation. As a bonus, you get to know your surroundings more intimately because you explore at a slower pace.

✔ **Seek out small local restaurants.** Often not only is the food less expensive, but it's also better than some of what you get at the big name tourist traps. Turn to Chapter 10 for suggestions.

✔ **Visit museums that have a "suggested donation," or go on the nights that are free.** See Chapter 11 to find out which days and nights are free at my favorite museums.

✔ **Buy your Broadway and Off-Broadway tickets at TKTS.** You can get same-day performances for some of Broadway's best shows by standing in line at the TKTS booth in Times Square or downtown at the South Street Seaport. See Chapter 14 for more info.

✔ **Buy your drinks at happy hour.** Many bars throughout the city have happy hours, usually between the hours of 4–8 p.m. or thereabouts, when you can save considerably on the price of a drink.

✔ **Go to jazz clubs early in the week, when many do not have cover charges.** See Chapter 15 for more info.

Handling Money

New York is one of the safest cities in the country, but that doesn't mean you should go around carrying wads of cash (although you should always make sure you have at least $20 in taxi fare on hand). Below are the best ways to access money in New York.

You're the best judge of how much cash you feel comfortable carrying or what alternative form of currency is your favorite. That's not going to change much on your vacation. True, you're probably going to be moving around more and incurring more expenses than you generally do (unless you happen to eat out every meal when you're at home), and you may let your mind slip into vacation gear and not be as vigilant about your safety as when you're in work mode. But, those factors aside, the only type of payment that isn't quite as easy to use when you're away from home is your personal checkbook; remember, some places don't accept out-of-town checks.

Using ATMs and carrying cash

The easiest and best way to get cash away from home is from an ATM (automated teller machine). The **Cirrus** (☎ 800-424-7787; www.mastercard.com) and **PLUS** (☎ 800-843-7587; www.visa.com) networks span the globe; look at the back of your bank card to see which network you're on; then call or check online for ATM locations at your destination. Be sure you know your personal identification number (PIN) before you leave home. Also keep in mind that many banks impose a fee (from $1–$2) every time your card is used at a different bank's ATM. On top of this fee, the bank from which you withdraw cash may charge its own fee. To compare banks' ATM fees within the U.S., visit www.bankrate.com. For international withdrawal fees, contact your bank. If your own bank doesn't have branches in New York, call to find out if it's affiliated with a bank in the city. Doing so may save you the extra $1.50 or more charge for using a nonaffiliated ATM. Many banks limit the amount of money per day that you can withdraw from an ATM; before you depart, be sure you know your bank's daily withdrawal limit.

ATM machines are everywhere in New York, including in banks, super-markets, and delis. You can get cash at any hour of the day or night, but you pay a higher surcharge at the non-bank affiliated ATMs. Some clubs (where there's no reentry after you leave) have up to a $5 surcharge, so make sure you have enough cash on you when you go in. Most ATMs are linked to a national network like Cirrus or Plus, and it's more than likely your home bank is a member of one of those networks.

Some credit cards let you get cash advances at ATMs. However, inter-est rates for cash advances are often significantly higher than rates for credit card purchases. More importantly, you start paying interest on the advance the moment you receive the cash.

Charging ahead with credit cards

Credit cards are a safe way to carry money. They also provide a conven-ient record of all your expenses, and they generally offer relatively good exchange rates. You can also withdraw cash advances from your credit cards at banks or ATMs, provided you know your PIN. If you've forgotten yours, or didn't even know you had one, call the number on the back of your credit card and ask the bank to send it to you. It usually takes 5 to 7 business days to get this information, although some banks pro-vide the number over the phone if you tell them your mother's maiden name or some other personal information to verify your identity.

Some credit card companies recommend that you notify them of any impending trip abroad so that they don't become suspicious when your card is used numerous times in a foreign destination and consequently block your charges. Even if you don't call your credit card company in advance, you can always call the card's toll-free emergency number if a charge is refused — a good reason to carry the phone number with you. But perhaps the most important lesson here is to carry more than one card with you on your trip; a card may not work for any number of rea-sons, so having a backup is the smart way to go.

Toting traveler's checks

These days, traveler's checks are less necessary because most cities have 24-hour ATMs that allow you to withdraw small amounts of cash as needed. However, keep in mind that you're likely going to be charged an ATM withdrawal fee if the bank is not your own; so, if you're with-drawing money every day, you may be better off with traveler's checks — provided that you don't mind showing identification every time you want to cash one.

You can get traveler's checks at almost any bank. **American Express** offers denominations of $20, $50, $100, $500, and (for cardholders only) $1,000. You pay a service charge ranging from 1 to 4 percent. You can also get American Express traveler's checks over the phone by calling ☎ 800-221-7282; Amex gold and platinum cardholders who use this number are exempt from the 1 percent fee.

Visa offers traveler's checks at Citibank locations nationwide, as well as at several other banks. The service charge ranges between 1.5 and 2 percent; checks come in denominations of $20, $50, $100, $500, and $1,000. Call ☎ 800-732-1322 for information. AAA members can obtain Visa checks without a fee at most AAA offices or by calling ☎ 866-339-3378. **MasterCard** also offers traveler's checks. Call ☎ 800-223-9920 for a location near you.

If you choose to carry traveler's checks, be sure to keep a record of their serial numbers separate from your checks in the event that they're stolen or lost. You get a refund faster if you know the numbers.

Dealing with a lost or stolen wallet

Be sure to contact all your credit card companies the minute you discover your wallet has been lost or stolen, and file a report at the nearest police precinct. Your credit card company or insurer may require a police report number or record of the loss. Most credit card companies have an emergency toll-free number to call if your card is lost or stolen; they may be able to wire you a cash advance immediately or deliver an emergency credit card in a day or two. Call the following emergency numbers in the United States:

✔ **American Express** ☎ 800-221-7282 (for cardholders and traveler's check holders)

✔ **MasterCard** ☎ 800-307-7309 or 636-722-7111

✔ **Visa** ☎ 800-847-2911 or 410-581-9994

For other credit cards, call the toll-free number directory at ☎ 800-555-1212.

If you need emergency cash over the weekend when all banks and American Express offices are closed, you can have money wired to you via **Western Union** (☎ 800-325-6000; www.westernunion.com).

Identity theft or fraud are potential complications of losing your wallet, especially if you've lost your driver's license along with your cash and credit cards. Notify the major credit-reporting bureaus immediately; placing a fraud alert on your records may protect you against liability for criminal activity. The three major U.S. credit-reporting agencies are **Equifax** (☎ 800-766-0008; www.equifax.com), **Experian** (☎ 888-397-3742; www.experian.com), and **TransUnion** (☎ 800-680-7289; www.transunion.com). Finally, if you've lost all forms of photo ID, call your airline and explain the situation; they may allow you to board the plane if you have a copy of your passport or birth certificate and a copy of the police report you filed.

Chapter 5

Getting to New York City

● ●

In This Chapter

▶ Taking a plane, train, or automobile
▶ Choosing between a package or escorted tour
▶ Finding the best package or tour for your needs

● ●

*Y*ou can get to New York in a variety of ways, depending on where you're starting from. Choosing the best mode of transit for your needs and preference depends on distance, convenience, and cost. Are you willing to arrange your own transportation? Or would you prefer to have someone else make all the arrangements (such as a travel agent or tour company)? When you arrive, do you want to explore the city by yourself? Or do you want the company of a group? In this chapter, I give you the pros and cons of each option.

Choosing the Airport

Three major airports serve New York City: **LaGuardia, JFK,** and **Newark Liberty.** The city is easily accessible from all three (see Chapter 8 for details on transportation between airport and city), although choosing to arrive at one or another may affect the price of your ticket. If you're looking for the best price, be flexible and accept a flight to any of these three airports. However, if saving money isn't your first priority, you may want to consider these differences:

  ✔ **LaGuardia Airport,** in northern Queens, is the closest airport to Manhattan (therefore, the cab rides from the city are cheaper and get you to and from the airport faster). It's also the smallest of the three. Although the number of flights allowed to arrive here has increased in recent years, the choices are more limited than at the other two airports. This is primarily a domestic, not an international, airport. Also, the increased number of flights has led to an increase in delays.

> ✔ **John F. Kennedy International Airport,** in southern Queens, is the official international airport for New York. Its international status makes it the largest and busiest airport in the metro area in terms of the volume of arrivals and departures (although Newark may have overtaken it). Also, of the three major airports, it's the farthest from the city center.

> ✔ **Newark International Airport** is in New Jersey but is somewhat closer to Manhattan than JFK, especially if your accommodations are on the West Side or downtown.

Two other airports in outlying areas service New York City: Westchester Airport in White Plains, New York (25 miles north of the city), and MacArthur Airport in Islip, Long Island (50 miles east of the city). MacArthur is the closest airport that budget carrier Southwest Airlines services. However, the inconvenience and high cost of getting into the city from these out-of-the-way airports far outweigh the money you save by using them.

Flying to New York

If you're in the Northeast or mid-Atlantic, flying may be only one of your options for reaching New York City (see the sections below on arriving by car, train, and bus). If, however, you're coming from further away, then flying is probably your best bet. You have a lot of options when it comes to airlines, number of flights, and price range (from no-frills to first-class).

Finding out which airlines fly there

Almost every major domestic carrier serves at least one of the New York–area airports; most serve two or all three. The major ones include:

> ✔ **America West** (☎ 800-327-7810; www.americawest.com)

> ✔ **American** (☎ 817-967-2000; www.aa.com)

> ✔ **Continental** (☎ 800-525-3273; www.continental.com)

> ✔ **Delta** (☎ 800-221-1212; www.delta.com)

> ✔ **Northwest** (☎ 800-225-2525; www.nwa.com)

> ✔ **US Airways** (☎ 800-428-4322; www.usairways.com)

> ✔ **United** (☎ 800-864-8331; www.united.com)

In addition to the domestic airlines, many international carriers serve JFK and Newark airports. Among the ones who offer the most frequent service are:

> ✔ **British Airways** (☎ 0845-77-333-77; www.british-airways.com)

> ✔ **Virgin Atlantic** (☎ 0870-380-2007; www.virgin-atlantic.com)

✔ **Air Canada** (☎ 888-247-2262; www.aircanada.ca)

✔ **Aer Lingus** (☎ 0818-365000; www.aerlingus.ie)

✔ **Qantas** (☎ 13-13-13; www.qantas.com.au)

✔ **Air New Zealand** (☎ 0800-737-000; www.airnewzealand.co.nz)

The "no-frills" airlines like **JetBlue** (☎ 800-JETBLUE; www.jetblue. com); **Airtran** (☎ 800-AIRTRAN; www.airtran.com); **ATA** (☎ 800-I-Fly-ATA; www.ata.com); and **Independence Air** (☎ 1-800-FLY-FLYi; www.flyi.com) frequently offer rock-bottom rates to New York City from destinations across the country. If you like flying Southwest, the nearest that budget carrier comes to New York City is MacArthur Airport on Long Island, about 50 miles east of New York City.

Getting the best deal on your airfare

Competition among the major U.S. airlines is unlike that of any other industry. Every airline offers virtually the same product (basically, a coach seat is a coach seat is a . . .), yet prices can vary by hundreds of dollars.

Business travelers who need the flexibility to buy their tickets at the last minute and change their itineraries at a moment's notice — and who want to get home before the weekend — pay (or at least their companies pay) the premium rate, known as the *full fare.* But if you can book your ticket far in advance, stay over Saturday night, and are willing to travel midweek (Tuesday, Wednesday, or Thursday), you can qualify for the least expensive price — usually a fraction of the full fare. On most flights, even the shortest hops within the United States, the full fare is close to $1,000 or more, but a 7- or 14-day advance purchase ticket may cost less than half of that amount. Obviously, planning ahead pays.

The airlines also periodically hold sales, in which they lower the prices on their most popular routes. These sale fares have advance purchase requirements and date-of-travel restrictions, but you can't beat the prices. As you plan your vacation, keep your eyes open for these sales, which tend to take place in seasons of low travel volume — January through March here in New York. You almost never see a sale around the peak summer vacation months of July and August, or around Thanksgiving or Christmas, when many people fly, regardless of the fare they have to pay.

Consolidators, also known as *bucket shops,* are great sources for international tickets, although they usually can't beat the Internet on fares within North America. Start by looking in Sunday newspaper travel sections; U.S. travelers should focus on the *New York Times, Los Angeles Times,* and *Miami Herald.*

Bucket shop tickets are usually nonrefundable or rigged with stiff cancellation penalties, often as high as 50 to 75 percent of the ticket price, and some put you on charter airlines with questionable safety records.

Several reliable consolidators are worldwide and available on the Net. **STA Travel** (☎ 800-781-4040; www.statravel.com), the world's leader in student travel, offers good fares for travelers of all ages. **Flights.com** (☎ 312-332-0090; www.flights.com) started in Europe and has excellent fares worldwide. **FlyCheap** (☎ 800-FLY-CHEAP or 800-359-2432; www.flycheap.com) is owned by package-holiday megalith MyTravel and so has especially good access to fares for sunny destinations. **Air Tickets Direct** (☎ 800-778-3447; www.airticketsdirect.com) is based in Montreal and leverages the currently weak Canadian dollar for low fares.

Booking your flight online

The "big three" online travel agencies, **Expedia** (www.expedia.com), **Travelocity** (www.travelocity.com), and **Orbitz** (www.orbitz.com) sell most of the air tickets bought on the Internet. (Canadian travelers should try www.expedia.ca and www.travelocity.ca; U.K. residents can go to www.expedia.co.uk and www.opodo.co.uk.) Each has different business deals with the airlines and may offer different fares on the same flights, so shopping around is wise. Expedia and Travelocity also send you an e-mail notification when a cheap fare becomes available to your favorite destination. Of the smaller travel agency Web sites, **SideStep** (www.sidestep.com) receives good reviews from users. It's a browser add-on that purports to "search 140 sites at once," but in reality it only beats competitors' fares as often as other sites do.

Great **last-minute deals** are available through free weekly e-mail services provided by the airlines. Most of these deals are announced on Tuesday or Wednesday and must be purchased online. Most are only valid for travel that weekend, but some fares (such as Southwest's) can be booked weeks or months in advance. Sign up for weekly e-mail alerts at airline Web sites or check mega-sites that compile comprehensive lists of last-minute specials, such as **Smarter Living** (www.smarterliving.com). For last-minute trips, www.site59.com in the U.S. and www.lastminute.com in Europe often have better deals than the major-label sites.

If you're willing to give up some control over your flight details, use an *opaque fare service,* like **Priceline** (www.priceline.com) or **Hotwire** (www.hotwire.com). Both offer rock-bottom prices in exchange for travel on a "mystery airline" at a mysterious time of day, often with a mysterious change of planes en route. The airlines are all major, well-known carriers — and the possibility of being sent from Philadelphia to Chicago via Tampa is remote. But your chances of getting a 6 a.m. or 11 p.m. flight are pretty high. Hotwire tells you flight prices before you buy; Priceline usually has better deals than Hotwire, but you have to play their "name your price" game. *Note:* In 2004, Priceline added non-opaque service to its roster. You now have the option to pick exact flights, times, and airlines from a list of offers — or opt to bid on opaque fares as before.

 You can sign up for the email bargain newsletters for all the major airlines at one time by logging on to **Smarter Living** (www.smarter living.com), or you can go to each individual airline's Web site. Airline sites also offer schedules, flight booking, and information on late-breaking bargains.

Driving to New York City

If you're visiting New York from the Northeast or mid-Atlantic, certainly consider driving your car; but just as certainly, park it after you get here.

 Some long-term outdoor lots charge less than $35 a day for parking. You can find these lots along the West Side Highway and in the 50s west of Eighth Avenue. Also ask if your hotel has an arrangement with a nearby parking lot for a discount on their daily rate. Most do, but you may not have in-and-out privileges.

You also can park near a commuter train station in New York, New Jersey, or Connecticut and take the commuter rail into the city. You still have to find parking near the station, but it's somewhat cheaper than parking in Manhattan. For information about PATH train stations in New Jersey, contact the Port Authority of New York & New Jersey (☎ **800-234-PATH** or 800-234-7284; www.panynj.gov). The Metropolitan Transportation Authority (MTA) New York City Transit (www.mta.info) operates not only the city's subways and buses but also the Long Island Rail Road (☎ **718-217-LIRR** or 718-217-5477), which serves Long Island (no kidding!), and the Metro-North Railroad (☎ **212-532-4900**), which serves upstate New York and Connecticut.

 In all cases, plan your arrival to avoid rush hours. Traffic jams in New York can be dreadful at the points of connection between the island of Manhattan and the surrounding metropolitan area (where all the airports are located). At rush hour, tunnels and bridges completely clog up. And don't think that you can get around the traffic by "reverse commuting" — coming into the city when everybody is leaving — because it doesn't work that way. Even if most of the traffic is outbound at around 5 p.m., a significant number of people commute back to Manhattan and the number of inbound lanes is actually reduced to help the traffic that's leaving get out more quickly.

Try to arrive well outside the peak hours of 8–10 a.m. and 4:30–7 p.m. The weekend rush is the worst. In summer, outbound traffic starts as early as 2 p.m. on Fridays, and inbound traffic on Sunday evenings is absolutely nightmarish.

Arriving by Other Means

If you don't want to fly or drive, many modes of land-based transportation service New York City.

By train

New York is well served by **Amtrak** (☎ **800-USA-RAIL** or 800-872-7245; www.amtrak.com). The most convenient route to New York City is the Northeast Corridor line, which runs between Washington, D.C. and Boston. If you're coming from anywhere on this line, taking the train is a lot smarter than taking a plane. The ride is likely to be shorter: You don't have to commute in traffic to and from the airport; you don't need to be there two hours in advance to check in and pass through security, and there's no waiting on the other end to collect your luggage. The train is also more comfortable — no dry airplane air, more freedom to stroll along the aisle, more room to work or sleep, and so on. Be sure to book in advance.

The train isn't necessarily cheaper, though. Prices on Amtrak remain high, but it offers specials and package tours that are worth looking into. Call ☎ **800-872-7245** for information about special rates, or check the Web site.

Amtrak trains arrive at Penn Station on the West Side, a hub for land transportation in the heart of the city. The average round-trip fare to New York on regular trains is around $126 from Boston (a 4½-hour journey); $168 and up from Chicago (a 16- to 18-hour trip, usually overnight); and $142 from Washington, D.C. (about 3½ hours). Note that these are coach fares, which means (except for Chicago) that seats are unreserved and not guaranteed (that is, if all the seats are full, you have to stand). You can reserve a seat in the pricier business-class and first-class wagons if you don't want to risk standing.

Amtrak has instituted new security measures: To buy a ticket, you must show a photo ID, such as a driver's license or passport.

Amtrak's recently introduced **Acela** (www.acela.com) express train cuts down on travel time, although you pay for that perk. For example, the New York–Boston run costs about $220 round-trip. Travel on Acela between Washington, D.C., and New York takes about 2 hours and 45 minutes; between Boston and New York about 3 hours.

By Bus

The bus can be a viable option for getting to New York City if you're coming from as far north as Boston, as far south as Washington, D.C., and as far west as the middle of Pennsylvania. Offering express bus service from several northeastern and mid-Atlantic cities, **Peter Pan Bus Lines** (☎ **800-237-8747**; www.peterpanbus.com) features wide-bodied coaches equipped with video cassette players (which show movies during the trip), climate control, and plenty of overhead storage compartments. Buses arrive at the Port Authority Bus Terminal at 42nd Street and Eighth Avenue, connecting directly to subways, city buses, and taxis.

For other regional bus companies (there are more than 20) that offer runs to New York City, check with the Port Authority (☎ 212-564-8484; www.panynj.gov/tbt/pabframe.HTM).

 The bus is probably the cheapest way to reach New York from most cities in the Northeast (with discount fares available for seniors, students, and children). Travel time from Washington D.C. to New York City is between three and four hours, from Philadelphia usually less than two hours.

 If you decide to ride the bus to New York City, make sure of two things:

✔ Book your trip on an express bus, or you'll spend a few more hours getting there.

✔ Try to get on a Peter Pan bus. Greyhound/Trailways runs on the same line and books through the same Web site, but their buses aren't nearly as comfortable as Peter Pan buses, and you may end up in the middle of, say, the Maine to Miami run. (The code on the Web site is PPP for Peter Pan, GLI for Greyhound/Trailways).

Joining an Escorted Tour

You may be one of the many people who love escorted tours. The tour company takes care of all the details and tells you what to expect at each leg of your journey. You know your costs upfront, and you don't get many surprises. Escorted tours can take you to the maximum number of sights in the minimum amount of time with the least amount of hassle.

 If you decide to go with an escorted tour, I strongly recommend purchasing travel insurance, especially if the tour operator asks to you pay upfront. But don't buy insurance from the tour operator! If the tour operator doesn't fulfill its obligation to provide you with the vacation you paid for, don't think that they'll fulfill their insurance obligations either. Get travel insurance through an independent agency. (I tell you more about the ins and outs of travel insurance in Chapter 7.)

When choosing an escorted tour, along with finding out whether you have to put down a deposit and when final payment is due, ask a few simple questions before you buy:

✔ **What is the cancellation policy?** Can they cancel the trip if they don't get enough people? How late can you cancel if you're unable to go? Do you get a refund if you cancel? If they cancel?

✔ **How jam-packed is the schedule?** Does the tour schedule try to fit 25 hours into a 24-hour day, or does it give you ample time to relax by the pool or shop? If getting up at 7 a.m. every day and not returning to your hotel until 6 or 7 p.m. sounds like a grind, certain escorted tours may not be for you.

✔ **How large is the group?** The smaller the group, the less time you spend waiting for people to get on and off your bus or public transportation. Tour operators may be evasive about this, because they may not know the exact size of the group until everybody has made reservations, but they should be able to give you a rough estimate. Also, get an idea of the general age range of the group; whether the tour's geared to seniors, students, families, or some other demographic may affect your decision to sign up.

✔ **Is there a minimum group size?** Some tours have a minimum group size and may cancel the tour if they don't book enough people. If a quota exists, find out what it is and how close the operator is to reaching it. Again, tour operators may be evasive in their answers, but the information may help you select a tour that's sure to happen.

✔ **What exactly is included?** Don't assume anything. You may have to pay to get yourself to and from the airport. A box lunch may be included in an excursion, but drinks may be extra. How much flexibility do you have? Can you opt out of certain activities, or does the bus leave once a day with no exceptions? Are all your meals planned in advance? Can you choose your entree at dinner?

Depending on your recreational passions, I recommend one of the following tour companies:

✔ **Globus** (☎ 866-755-8581; www.globusandcosmos.com) sometimes runs first-class independent tours of New York (often as part of a larger, multi-city itinerary). A "host" is available to answer questions but doesn't take you around the city, except on a designated day. The package includes everything — hotel, local transportation, and even tips. Check the Web site for the most up-to-date tour offerings.

✔ **Maupintour** (☎ 800-255-4266 or 913-843-1211; www.maupintour.com) specializes in lavish "grand tours." These escorted tours often feature Broadway shows and an excursion to the Hudson Valley. The cost of a tour may run about $2,000 per person depending on the options you select, plus airfare.

Choosing A Package Tour

For lots of destinations, package tours can be a smart way to go. In many cases, a package tour that includes airfare, hotel, and transportation to and from the airport costs less than the hotel alone on a tour you book yourself. That's because packages are sold in bulk to tour operators, who resell them to the public.

Package tours can vary a good bit in terms of what's provided. Some offer a better class of hotels than others; others provide the same hotels for lower prices. Some book flights on scheduled airlines; others sell charters. In some packages, your choice of accommodations and travel days may be limited. Some let you choose between escorted vacations and independent vacations; others allow you to add on just a few excursions or escorted day trips (also at discounted prices) without booking an entirely escorted tour.

To find package tours, check out the travel section of your local Sunday newspaper or the ads in the back of national travel magazines such as *Travel & Leisure, National Geographic Traveler,* and *Condé Nast Traveler.* **Liberty Travel** (call ☎ **888-271-1584** to find the store nearest you; www.libertytravel.com) is one of the biggest packagers in the Northeast and usually boasts a full-page ad in Sunday papers.

Other good sources of package deals are the airlines themselves. Most major airlines offer air/land packages, including **American Airlines Vacations** (☎ 800-321-2121; www.aavacations.com), **Delta Vacations** (☎ 800-221-6666; www.deltavacations.com), **Continental Airlines Vacations** (☎ 800-301-3800; www.covacations.com), and **United Vacations** (☎ 888-854-3899; www.unitedvacations.com). Several big **online travel agencies** — Expedia, Travelocity, Orbitz, Site59, and Lastminute.com — also do a brisk business in packages. If you're unsure about the pedigree of a smaller packager, check with the Better Business Bureau in the city where the company is based, or go online at www.bbb.org. If a packager won't tell you where it's based, don't purchase anything from them.

In addition to the resources just mentioned, you can also check out these options.

- ✔ **New York City Vacation Packages** offers a wide variety of packages year-round, some of them at unbeatable prices. Call ☎ **888-692-8701,** check www.nycvp.com, or send an e-mail to info@nycvp.com.

- ✔ **NYC & Company,** the city's Convention and Visitors Bureau, offers special packages, usually during the slower first months of the year. Call ☎ **800-NYC-GUIDE** or 800-NYC-VISIT, or check www.nycvisit.com for information about these packages. At press time, NYC & Company was offering the NYC Freedom Package starting at $157 per person for a one-night stay, including hotel, a Broadway show, and one dinner gift certificate.

- ✔ The Web site www.vacationpackager.com can link you up with many different operators — about 150 in all! — and help you design your own package.

Chapter 6

Catering to Special Travel Needs or Interests

- -

- -

*N*ew York may seem intimidating, but if you can get over your initial awe, you may find that things are easier for people with special needs here than in other cities. New York offers so many things to see and do that anybody can find something suitable, and specialized services are available for just about everything and everyone.

Traveling with the Brood: Advice for Families

Forget Disney World — New York is the true kid capital of the United States. And don't believe the hype about it being unsafe. As long as parents — and children — come prepared, you can have a safe, enjoyable, enriching experience that the kids will long remember.

If you have trouble getting your kids out of the house in the morning, dragging them thousands of miles away may seem like an insurmountable challenge. But family travel can be immensely rewarding, giving you new ways of seeing the world through smaller pairs of eyes.

Familyhostel (☎ 800-733-9753; www.learn.unh.edu/familyhostel) takes the whole family, including kids ages 8–15, on moderately priced domestic and international learning vacations. Lectures, field trips, and sightseeing are guided by a team of academics.

You can find good family-oriented vacation advice on the Internet at sites, such as the **Family Travel Forum** (www.familytravelforum.com), a comprehensive site that offers customized trip planning; **Family Travel Network** (www.familytravelnetwork.com), an award-winning site that offers travel features, deals, and tips; **Traveling Internationally with Your Kids** (www.travelwithyourkids.com), a comprehensive site that offers customized trip planning; and **Family Travel Files** (www.thefamilytravelfiles.com), which offers an online magazine and a directory of off-the-beaten-path tours and tour operators for families.

Parents should research all the places the family plans to visit; see Chapter 8 for descriptions of New York's neighborhoods. Parents and children should go over safety issues before leaving (see the Quick Concierge appendix); be sure to create a plan so that children know what to do if they get lost.

Finding a family-friendly hotel

Finding a hotel that caters to children may be your biggest concern when traveling to New York. But you're in luck — some New York hotels market special services just for families, including play areas and programs. Be sure to ask about these services when you call for a reservation.

If watching your wallet is a concern, look for a hotel that lets children stay in your room for free. You may also want to consider getting a room with a kitchenette; eating some meals in your room (or preparing and taking food with you) can help defray food costs. In Chapter 9, look for the Kid Friendly icons next to hotels that offer family-friendly options.

Getting around

If you and your children don't want to tangle with public transportation from the airport or around the city, you can always take taxis. But if your children are patient enough, you can get almost anywhere on the bus or subway. Make sure to review the safety tips I give in Chapter 8 and in the Quick Concierge appendix before hitting the road. (By the way, children under 3 feet, 8 inches tall ride New York's subways for free.)

Finding baby-sitting services

Many hotels have baby-sitting services or can provide lists of reliable sitters. If your hotel can't make a recommendation, try the **Baby Sitters Guild** (☎ 212-682-0227) or the **Frances Stewart Agency** (☎ 212-439-9222). These sitters are licensed, insured, and bonded and take your children on an outing.

Touring the town

To help you plan outings with your children, look for the Kid Friendly icons throughout this book, which point out places of particular interest to children. You'll find this icon next to such sights as the Empire State

Building, the Bronx Zoo, Central Park Zoo, the Statue of Liberty, the Museum of Natural History, and Central Park. For more information about planning activities for children, pick up a copy of Frommer's *New York City with Kids* (Wiley).

Time Out New York, a magazine that comes out every Wednesday, is an excellent source for finding out about child-friendly activities and events. Look for the "Kids" listings near the back of the magazine. They also recently launched a new magazine, *Time Out New York Kids,* which helps to steer you in the right direction for fun with your kids.

For teenagers, some neighborhoods may be more interesting than others. Downtown neighborhoods (such as Chelsea, the East and West Villages, SoHo, NoHo, and NoLiTa) have younger crowds, lots of alternative music stores, coffee shops, and funky clothing stores. (For more detailed descriptions of these neighborhoods, see Chapter 8.) Fans of MTV's *Total Request Live* may want to check out the show's Times Square studios.

Making Age Work for You: Advice for Seniors

Mention the fact that you're a senior citizen when you make your travel reservations. Although all the major U.S. airlines except America West have cancelled their senior discount and coupon book programs, many hotels still offer discounts for seniors. In most cities, New York included, people over the age of 60 qualify for reduced admission to theaters, museums, and other attractions, as well as discounted fares on public transportation.

Members of **AARP** (formerly known as the American Association of Retired Persons), 601 E St. NW, Washington, D.C. 20049 (☎ **888-687-2277** or 202-434-2277; www.aarp.org), get discounts on hotels, airfares, and car rentals. AARP offers members a wide range of benefits, including *AARP: The Magazine* and a monthly newsletter. Anyone over 50 years of age can join.

Many reliable agencies and organizations cater to the 50-plus market. **Elderhostel** (☎ **877-426-8056;** www.elderhostel.org) arranges travel-study programs for those aged 55 and over (and a spouse or companion of any age) in the United States and in more than 80 countries around the world. Most courses last five to seven days in the United States (2–4 weeks abroad), and many include airfare, accommodations in university dormitories or modest inns, meals, and tuition. Some courses recently offered in New York City are "Five Days, Five Boroughs," "Secret Places, Secret Views of New York City," and "Autumn in New York."

Recommended publications offering travel resources and discounts for seniors include: the quarterly magazine ***Travel 50 & Beyond*** (www.travel50andbeyond.com); ***Travel Unlimited: Uncommon Adventures***

for the Mature Traveler (Avalon); *101 Tips for Mature Travelers,*
available from Grand Circle Travel (☎ 800-221-2610 or 617-350-7500;
www.gct.com); *The 50+ Traveler's Guidebook* (St. Martin's Press);
and *Unbelievably Good Deals and Great Adventures That You
Absolutely Can't Get Unless You're Over 50* (McGraw-Hill), by
Joann Rattner Heilman.

 Seniors get a 50 percent discount on bus and subway fares in New York
(see the following section for more info). Be sure to carry identification
with proof of age.

Accessing New York City: Advice for Travelers with Disabilities

Most disabilities shouldn't stop anyone from traveling, because more
options and resources exist than ever before. In general, New York is
progressive in its efforts to make the city accessible for the disabled.
Equal access is now mandated by law, but implementation has been
gradual and is not complete. The city makes progress every day,
though; you may want to check on the latest changes.

Travel agencies and organizations

Many travel agencies offer customized tours and itineraries for travelers
with disabilities.

- ✔ **Flying Wheels Travel** (☎ 507-451-5005; www.flyingwheels
  travel.com) offers escorted tours and cruises that emphasize
  sports and private tours in minivans with lifts.

- ✔ **Access-Able Travel Source** (☎ 303-232-2979; www.access-able.
  com) offers extensive access information and advice for traveling
  around the world with disabilities.

- ✔ **Accessible Journeys** (☎ 800-846-4537 or 610-521-0339; www.
  disabilitytravel.com) offers travel planning and information
  for mature travelers, slow walkers, wheelchair travelers, and their
  families and friends.

- ✔ **Big Apple Greeter** (☎ 212-669-2896, TTY 212-669-8273; www.
  bigapplegreeter.org) offers tours for travelers with disabilities
  free of charge. As with its other tours (see Chapter 18), advance
  reservations are necessary.

- ✔ **FEDCAP Rehabilitation Services,** 211 W. 14th St., New York, NY
  10011 (☎ 212-727-4200) can provide you with information about
  membership and summer tours.

Organizations that offer assistance to travelers with disabilities include:

- ✔ **MossRehab ResourceNet** (www.mossresourcenet.org): Provides a library of accessible travel resources online.

- ✔ **American Foundation for the Blind (AFB)** (☎ 800-232-5463; www.afb.org): A referral resource for the blind or visually impaired that includes information on traveling with Seeing Eye dogs.

- ✔ **Hospital Audiences, Inc.,** 220 W. 42nd St., 13th Floor, New York, NY 10036 (hotline ☎ 888-424-4685, local 212-575-7676, TTY 212-575-7673; www.hospitalaudiences.org): Some of HAI's programs include "Describe," which allows theatergoers who are blind or visually impaired enjoy theater with audio-describers giving a summary of the action onstage. The hotline provides accessibility information to performance and art venues and about programs that are signed for the hearing impaired. You also can order *Access for All*, the accessibility guidebook on city cultural institutions, for $5.

- ✔ **The New York Society for the Deaf,** 817 Broadway, 7th Floor, New York, NY 10003 (☎ TTY 212-777-3900; www.nysd.org): Provides travel tips for the hearing impaired.

- ✔ **Society for Accessible Travel & Hospitality,** 347 Fifth Ave., Suite 610, New York, NY 10016 (☎ 212-447-7284; www.sath.org): Offers a wealth of travel resources for people with all types of disabilities and recommends access guides, travel agents, tour operators, companion services, and more. Annual membership costs $45 for adults and $30 for seniors and students.

For more information specifically targeted to travelers with disabilities, the community Web site **iCan** (www.icanonline.net/channels/travel/index.cfm) has destination guides and several regular columns on accessible travel. Also check out the quarterly magazine *Emerging Horizons* ($14.95 per year, $19.95 outside the U.S.; www.emerginghorizons.com); **Twin Peaks Press** (☎ 360-694-2462), offering travel-related books for travelers with special needs; and *Open World Magazine,* published by SATH (subscription: $13 per year, $21 outside the U.S.).

Hotels

Some older, smaller, and budget hotels have not been updated to current access regulations. However, other hotels, including chains such as Hilton, offer features that accommodate wheelchairs, like roll-in showers, lower sinks, and extra space for maneuverability. Simply ask for one of these accessible rooms when you make your reservation.

Transportation

Taxis are required by law to take persons with disabilities, wheelchairs, and guide dogs. For getting into the city from one of the airports, the **Gray Line Shuttle** (☎ 800-451-0455 or 212-315-3006) has minibuses with lifts. The vans go only to Midtown hotels, and you must make a reservation to get a ride.

All buses in Manhattan and 95 percent of New York City buses are equipped with wheelchair lifts and special areas where the bus seats fold up to make extra room. The buses also "kneel," lowering their front ends so that the first step is more accessible. Wheelchair passengers don't have to request these bus services in advance; just show up at the bus stop. The driver can help put a wheelchair on the ramp and secure the chair inside the bus.

Subway access for travelers with disabilities is still limited, but the MTA New York City Transit keeps working at increasing accessibility. You can certainly experience the thrill of a New York subway ride by boarding and getting off at the accessible stations, but the bus is a much more flexible option. The following are wheelchair-accessible stations and lines in Manhattan:

- ✓ Brooklyn Bridge/City Hall (4/5/6)
- ✓ 14th Street/Union Square (4/5/6/N/Q/R/W)
- ✓ 34th Street/Herald Square (B/D/F/Q/N/R/V/W)
- ✓ 42nd Street/Port Authority Bus Terminal (A/C/E)
- ✓ Grand Central/42nd Street (4/5/6)
- ✓ 50th Street (southbound only, C/E)
- ✓ 51st Street (6)
- ✓ Lexington/63rd Street (F)
- ✓ 66th Street/Lincoln Center (1/2)
- ✓ 125th Street (4/5/6)
- ✓ 175th Street (A)
- ✓ Roosevelt Island (F)

Accessible stations are marked with an icon on the free subway map distributed in the subway. You also can get a free brochure, *Accessible Transfer Points,* from MTA Customer Assistance, 370 Jay St., Room 702, Brooklyn, NY 11201 (☎ **718-330-3322;** TTY 718-596-8273). Braille subway maps are available from **The Lighthouse, Inc.,** 111 E. 59th St., New York, NY 10022 (☎ **800-334-5497** or 212-821-9200), which also produces concerts and exhibitions by the vision impaired.

Seniors and persons with disabilities get a 50 percent discount with the MTA. Getting a discount MetroCard takes a little planning, however. You need to get an application by writing to Customer Assistance Division, MTA, 370 Jay St., 7th Floor, Brooklyn, NY 11201. Or you can download the application from the MTA Web site (www.mta.info) or call ☎ **718-243-4999.**

Following the Rainbow: Advice for Gay and Lesbian Travelers

New York ranks with San Francisco as one of the most gay-friendly cities in the United States. Greenwich Village and Chelsea have large gay populations, and the West Village and Chelsea areas offer abundant nightlife.

Many agencies offer tours and travel itineraries specifically for gay and lesbian travelers.

- **Above and Beyond Tours** (☎ 800-397-2681; www.abovebeyond tours.com) is the exclusive gay and lesbian tour operator for United Airlines.

- **Now, Voyager** (☎ 800-255-6951; www.nowvoyager.com) is a well-known San Francisco–based gay-owned and -operated travel service.

- **International Gay & Lesbian Travel Association** (IGLTA) (☎ 800-448-8550 or 954-776-2626; www.iglta.org) provides information about gay-friendly hoteliers, tour operators, and airline representatives. It offers monthly newsletters and a membership directory that's updated once a year. Annual membership is $200, plus a $100 fee for new members.

The following are a few of the major gay organizations in New York City:

- **The Lesbian, Gay, Bisexual & Transgender Community Center,** 208 W. 13th St. between Seventh and Eighth avenues (☎ 212-620-7310; www.gaycenter.org) is a fabulous source of information, and also offers literally hundreds of events and activities each month, from readings, films, and dances to advice and medical referrals. Call or visit the Center's excellent Web site to get information about the programs it sponsors. The Center also offers a list of gay-friendly accommodations and a calendar of local cultural events.

- **The Organization of Lesbian and Gay Architects and Designers** (☎ 212-475-7652) offers a free map of lesbian and gay historical landmarks.

- **Gay Men's Health Crisis (GMHC),** 119 W. 24th St. (☎ 212-807-6655; www.gmhc.org) has an AIDS hotline, serves anyone with HIV, and offers a wide variety of programs.

For the most up-to-date information about events and entertainment, try any of the city's gay-friendly publications. The weekly *Time Out New York* (www.timeoutny.com) includes a comprehensive gay and lesbian section. *HX Magazine* (www.hx.com), a free publication available in restaurants, clubs, and bars, lists events around town. *Gay City News* (www.gaycitynews.com) appears every other Thursday, and

The New York Blade News (www.nyblade.com), a weekly newspaper, is published on Thursdays. *GoNYC Magazine* is free glossy monthly that focuses on articles and listings of interest to the lesbian community (www.gonycmagazine.com).

The following travel guides are available at most travel bookstores and gay and lesbian bookstores.

> ✔ *Out and About* (☎ **800-929-2268** or 415-644-8044; www.outand about.com) offers guidebooks and a newsletter ($20/yr; 10 issues) packed with solid information on the global gay and lesbian scene.

> ✔ *Spartacus International Gay Guide* (Bruno Gmünder Verlag; www.spartacusworld.com/gayguide) and *Odysseus* are both good, annual English-language guidebooks focused on gay men.

> ✔ The *Damron* guides (www.damron.com) include annual books for gay men and lesbians.

> ✔ *Gay Travel A to Z: The World of Gay & Lesbian Travel Options at Your Fingertips* by Marianne Ferrari (Ferrari International; Box 35575, Phoenix, AZ 85069) is a very good gay and lesbian guidebook series.

New York City also has two GLBT bookshops: the oldest gay bookstore in the country (founded in 1967) — the **Oscar Wilde Bookshop** at 15 Christopher Street (☎ **212-255-8097**; www.oscarwildebooks.com) and **Creative Visions Books & Video** at 548 Hudson St. (☎ **800-434-7126** or 212-645-7573; www.creativevisionsbooks.com).

Chapter 7

Taking Care of the Remaining Details

*O*h, how I hate those little details — the ones I always forget. But if I had paid more attention to those details, I could have avoided all the last-minute hassles I've experienced on trips. Go over the points in this chapter so that you don't make the same mistakes I always do when traveling.

Renting a Car: Not in New York!

One of the first questions that comes to mind when organizing a trip is: "Do I need to rent a car?" In New York, the answer is clear: No! You just don't need one; New York is a great walking city, and you can take fast and cheap public transportation almost anywhere. Need I mention that gas is seriously expensive; parking can be a nightmare; and driving the city streets is — more often than not — a high-speed, high-stakes game of dodge 'em that's *not* for the weak of heart? (Not to mention that you probably don't want to spend valuable time and $185 *cash* at the car pound should your car get towed!)

Playing It Safe: Travel and Medical Insurance

Three kinds of travel insurance are available to you: trip-cancellation insurance, medical insurance, and lost luggage insurance. The cost of travel insurance varies depending on the cost and length of your trip, your age and health, and the type of trip you're taking, but expect to pay 5–8 percent of your total vacation cost. Here's my advice on all three insurance options:

- ✔ **Trip-cancellation insurance** helps you get your money back if you have to back out of a trip, if you have to go home early, or if your travel supplier goes bankrupt. Permissible reasons for cancellation can range from sickness to natural disasters to the State Department declaring your destination unsafe for travel. (Insurers usually won't cover vague fears, though, as many travelers discovered when they tried to cancel their trips in October 2001 because they were wary of flying.)

    Travel Guard International (www.travelguard.com) can supply you with a list of companies that they consider to be high-risk (that is, with a reputation of not providing what they promise, or not refunding your money satisfactorily in case of a cancellation), as well as companies whose product they won't insure. Protect yourself further by paying for the insurance with a credit card — by law, consumers can get their money back on goods and services not received if they report the loss within 60 days after the charge is listed on their credit card statement.

    Many tour operators, particularly those offering trips to remote or high-risk areas, include trip-cancellation insurance in the cost of the trip or can arrange insurance policies through a partnering provider. This option is a convenient and often cost-effective way for you to obtain insurance, but make sure the tour company is a reputable one. Some experts suggest you avoid buying insurance from the tour or cruise company you're traveling with, saying it's better to buy from a third party insurer than to put all your money in one place.

- ✔ **Medical insurance** coverage doesn't make sense for most people travelling domestically. Most existing health policies cover you if you get sick away from home — but check before you go, particularly if you're insured by an HMO.

- ✔ **Lost luggage insurance** is not necessary for most travelers. On domestic flights, checked baggage is covered up to $2,500 per ticketed passenger. On international flights (including U.S. portions of international trips), baggage coverage is limited to approximately $9.07 per pound, up to approximately $635 per checked bag.

    If you plan to check items more valuable than the standard liability, see if your valuables are covered by your homeowner's policy, get baggage insurance as part of your comprehensive travel-insurance package, or buy Travel Guard's "BagTrak" insurance (which you can purchase through a Travel Guard affiliated insurance agent). Don't buy overpriced insurance at the airport from your airline. Be sure to take any valuables or irreplaceable items on the plane in your carry-on luggage, because many valuables (including books, money, and electronics) aren't covered by airline policies.

If your luggage is lost, immediately file a lost-luggage claim at the airport, detailing the luggage contents. For most airlines, you must report delayed, damaged, or lost baggage within four hours of arrival. After your luggage is found, airlines are required to deliver it directly to your house or destination free of charge.

For more information on luggage insurance, contact one of the following recommended insurers:

- ✔ **Access America** (☎ 866-807-3982; www.accessamerica.com)
- ✔ **Travel Guard International** (☎ 800-826-4919; www.travel guard.com)
- ✔ **Travel Insured International** (☎ 800-243-3174; www.travel insured.com)
- ✔ **Travelex Insurance Services** (☎ 888-457-4602; www.travel ex-insurance.com)

Staying Healthy When You Travel

Getting sick ruins your vacation, so I *strongly* advise against it (of course, last time I checked, the bugs weren't listening to me any more than they probably listen to you). New York won't make you sick more than any other city, and the water is safe to drink. Beyond that, take this basic advice for keeping your health in tiptop shape.

For domestic trips, most reliable healthcare plans provide coverage if you get sick away from home.

Before leaving on your trip, talk to your doctor if you have a serious and/or chronic illness; she may make some recommendations for keeping yourself healthy and comfortable while you travel. For conditions such as epilepsy, diabetes, or heart problems, register with **MedicAlert** (☎ **888-633-4298;** www.medicalert.org) and wear your identification tag, which alerts doctors to your condition and gives them access to your records through MedicAlert's 24-hour hotline. The United States **Centers for Disease Control and Prevention** (☎ **800-311-3435;** www. cdc.gov) provides up-to-date information on health hazards by region and offers tips on food safety.

Staying Connected by Cellphone or E-mail

Staying in touch with the folks at home (or with each other) is much easier these days thanks to the rapidly expanding cellphone networks and various plans that give you plenty of unlimited minutes. Access to the Internet from your phone or at hotel or public terminals (or from your own laptop, via wi-fi, or via a handy modem cord and plug) also makes communicating while traveling much less complicated.

Using a cellphone across the U.S.

Just because your cellphone works at home doesn't mean it works elsewhere in the country (thanks to our nation's fragmented cellphone system). But it's a good bet that your phone works in major cities. To be sure, take a look at your wireless company's coverage map (usually available on the Web site) before heading out. If you need to stay in touch at a destination where you know your phone won't work, rent a phone that you're sure will have service from **InTouch USA** (☎ **800-872-7626;** www.intouchusa.com) or a rental car company, but beware that you pay $1 a minute or more for airtime.

If you're not from the U.S., you may be appalled at the poor reach of our **GSM (Global System for Mobiles) wireless network,** which is used by much of the rest of the world. Your phone probably works in most major U.S. cities, but you may not be able to send SMS (text messages) home — something Americans tend not to do anyway, for various cultural and technological reasons. Assume nothing when it comes to using your cellphone in another city — call your wireless provider and get the full scoop. In a worst-case scenario, you can always rent a phone; InTouch USA delivers to hotels.

Accessing the Internet away from home

Travelers have any number of ways to check their e-mail and access the Internet on the road. Of course, using your own laptop — or even a phone, PDA (personal digital assistant), or electronic organizer with a modem — gives you the most flexibility. But even if you don't have a computer, you can still access your e-mail and even your office computer from cybercafes.

Taking advantage of cybercafes

Although no definitive directory for cybercafes exists — these are independent businesses, after all — two places to start looking are www.cybercaptive.com and www.cybercafe.com.

Some of the places where you can check your e-mail in New York include:

- ✔ The **Times Square Visitors Center:** 1560 Broadway, between 46th and 47th streets (☎ 212-768-1560; open daily 8 a.m.–8 p.m.)

- ✔ **easyInternetcafé:** 235 W. 42nd St., between Seventh and Eighth avenues (☎ 212-398-0775; www.easyeverything.com; open 24 hours)

- ✔ **CyberCafe:** in Times Square at 250 W. 49th St., between Broadway and Eighth Avenue (☎ 212-333-4109; www.cyber-cafe.com), and in SoHo at 273 Lafayette St., at Prince Street (☎ 212-334-5140)

> ✔ **Kinko's:** numerous locations, including 100 Wall St., at Water Street
> (☎ 212-269-0024); near City Hall at 105 Duane St., between Broadway
> and Church Street (☎ 212-406-1220); 245 Seventh Ave., at 24th St.
> (☎ 212-929-2679); 60 W. 40th St., between Fifth and Sixth avenues
> (☎ 212-921-1060); 221 W. 72nd St., at Broadway (☎ 212-362-5288)

Finding other ways to surf the Web

Aside from formal cybercafes, most **youth hostels** have at least one
computer you can use to access the Internet. And most **public libraries**
offer Internet access free or for a small fee. Avoid **hotel business centers**
unless you're willing to pay exorbitant rates. (More hotels are offering
free Internet access in their business centers, but it's not something
they all do.)

Most major airports now have **Internet kiosks** scattered throughout
their gates. These kiosks, which you may also see in shopping malls,
hotel lobbies, and tourist information offices, give you basic Internet
access for a per-minute fee that's usually higher than cybercafe prices.
The kiosks' clunkiness and high prices mean they should be avoided
whenever possible.

To retrieve your e-mail, ask your **Internet Service Provider (ISP)** if it has
a Web-based interface tied to your existing e-mail account. (Translation:
You can access your e-mail from any computer just by visiting your ISP's
Web page and signing in with your account info.) If your ISP doesn't have
such an interface, you can use a free service from **mail2web** (www.mail2
web.com) to view and reply to your home e-mail. For more flexibility, you
may want to open a free, Web-based e-mail account with **Yahoo! Mail**
(mail.yahoo.com). (Microsoft's Hotmail is another popular option, but
Hotmail has severe spam problems.) Your home ISP may be able to for-
ward your e-mail to the Web-based account automatically.

If you need to access files on your office computer, look into a service
called **GoToMyPC** (www.gotomypc.com). This service provides a Web-
based interface for you to access and manipulate a distant PC from
anywhere — even a cybercafe — provided your "target" PC is on and
has an always-on connection to the Internet (such as with digital cable).
The service offers top-quality security, but if you're worried about hack-
ers, use your own laptop rather than a cybercafe computer to access the
GoToMyPC system.

If you're bringing your own computer with you as you travel, the buzz-
word in computer access is **wi-fi** (wireless fidelity). More and more
hotels, cafes, and retailers are signing on as wi-fi "hotspots," allowing
you to get a high-speed connection without cable wires, networking
hardware, or a phone line. You can get a wi-fi connection one of several
ways. Many laptops sold in the last year have built-in wi-fi capability (an
802.11b wireless, Ethernet connection). Mac owners have their own networking technology called Apple AirPort. For those travelers with older

computers, an 802.11b/**wi-fi card** can be purchased for around $50 and plugs into your laptop. You sign up for wireless access service much as you do cellphone service, through a plan offered by one of several commercial companies that have made wireless service available in airports, hotel lobbies, and coffee shops, primarily in the U.S. (followed by the U.K. and Japan). **T-Mobile HotSpot** (www.t-mobile.com/hotspot) serves up wireless connections at more than 1,000 Starbucks coffee shops nationwide. **Boingo Wireless** (www.boingo.com) and **Wayport** (www.wayport.com) have set up networks in airports and high-class hotel lobbies. **iPass** (www.ipass.com) providers also give you access to a few hundred wireless hotel lobby setups. Best of all, you don't need to be staying at the Four Seasons to use the hotel's network; just set yourself up on a nice couch in the lobby. The wireless companies' pricing policies can be Byzantine, with a variety of monthly, per-connection, and per-minute plans, but in general you pay around $30 a month for limited access — and as more and more companies jump on the wireless bandwagon, prices are likely to get even more competitive.

Certain places also provide **free wireless networks** in cities around the world. To locate these free hotspots, go to www.personaltelco.net/index.cgi/WirelessCommunities.

If wi-fi is not available at your destination, most business-class hotels throughout the world offer dataports for laptop modems, and a many hotels in the U.S. offer free high-speed Internet access using an Ethernet network cable. You can bring your own cables, but most hotels rent them for around $10. **Call your hotel in advance** to find out about your options.

In addition, major Internet Service Providers (ISPs) have **local access numbers** around the world, allowing you to go online by simply placing a local call. Check your ISP's Web site or call its toll-free number and ask how you can use your current account away from home, and how much it costs. If you're traveling outside the reach of your ISP, the **iPass** network has dial-up numbers in most of the world's countries. You have to sign up with an iPass provider, who then tells you how to set up your computer for your destination(s). For a list of iPass providers, go to www.ipass.com and click on "Individual Purchase." One solid provider is **i2roam** (☎ **866-811-6209** or 920-235-0475; www.i2roam.com).

Keeping Up with Airline Security Measures

With the federalization of airport security, procedures at U.S. airports are more stable and consistent than ever. Generally, you won't be delayed if you arrive at the airport **one hour** before a domestic flight; if you show up late, tell an airline employee so that you can (hopefully) be whisked away to the front of the line.

Don't leave home without a **current, government-issued photo ID,** such as a driver's license or passport. Keep your ID at the ready to show at check-in, at the security checkpoint, and sometimes even at the gate. (Children under 18 don't need government-issued photo IDs for domestic flights, but they do for international flights to most countries.)

In 2003, the Transportation Security Administration (TSA) phased out **gate check-in** at all U.S. airports. And **e-tickets** have made paper tickets nearly obsolete. With an e-ticket, you can beat the ticket-counter lines by using airport **electronic kiosks** or even **online check-in** options from your home computer. Online check-in involves logging on to your airline's Web site, accessing your reservation, and printing out your boarding pass — and the airline may even offer you bonus miles to do so! If you're using a kiosk at the airport, bring the credit card you used to book the ticket or your frequent-flier card (you may not be able to print out your boarding pass without the credit card used for purchase, and you want to make sure your frequent-flier miles are credited properly). Print out your boarding pass from the kiosk and simply proceed to the security checkpoint with your pass and photo ID. If you're checking bags or looking to snag an exit-row seat, you can do so using most airline kiosks. Even the smaller airlines are employing the kiosk system, but always call your airline to make sure these alternatives are available. **Curbside check-in** is also a good way to avoid lines, although a few airlines still ban curbside check-in, so call before you go.

Security checkpoint lines are getting shorter than they were in 2002, but some doozies remain. If you have trouble standing for long periods of time, tell an airline employee; the airline can provide a wheelchair to make your wait more comfortable. Speed up security by **not wearing metal objects** like big belt buckles. If you've got metallic body parts, a note from your doctor can prevent a long chat with the security screeners. Keep in mind that only **ticketed passengers** are allowed past security, except for folks escorting disabled passengers or children.

Federal rules dictate **what you can carry on** a plane and **what you can't.** The general rule is that sharp things are out, nail clippers are okay, and food and beverages must be passed through the X-ray machine — but screeners can't make you drink from your coffee cup. Bring food in your carry-on rather than checking it, as explosive-detection machines used on checked luggage have been known to mistake food (especially chocolate, for some reason) for bombs. Travelers in the U.S. are allowed one carry-on bag, plus a "personal item," such as a purse, briefcase, or laptop bag. Carry-on hoarders can stuff all sorts of things into a laptop bag; as long as it has a laptop in it, it's still considered a personal item. The TSA has issued a list of restricted items; check its Web site (`www.tsa.gov/public/index.jsp`) for details.

Airport screeners may decide that your checked luggage needs to be searched by hand. You can now purchase luggage locks that allow screeners to open and re-lock a checked bag if hand-searching is necessary.

Look for Travel Sentry certified locks at luggage or travel shops and Brookstone stores (you can buy them online at www.brookstone. com). These locks, approved by the TSA, can be opened by luggage inspectors with a special code or key. For more information on the locks, visit www.travelsentry.org. If you use something other than TSA-approved locks, your lock may be cut off your suitcase if a TSA agent needs to hand-search your luggage.

Part III
Settling Into New York City

The 5th Wave   By Rich Tennant

Of all the boutique hotels in New York City, you had to pick one called "The D'Lapa Dated".

In this part . . .

1 help you get oriented in New York City with logistical information (getting around and where to find information on the city once you're here) and the lowdown on where to stay and where to eat.

Chapter 8

Arriving and Getting Oriented

*W*hether you're landing at one of the three major area airports, alighting from Amtrak, or taking the family car to New York City, this chapter helps you get to where you're going.

Getting from the Airport to Your Hotel

The New York airports, like airports in most cities, are located away from the center of things — LaGuardia and Kennedy are in the borough of Queens, and Newark Airport is across the Hudson River in New Jersey. From any of these airports, taking a taxi is the easiest and most hassle-free option, but it's also the most expensive. Another possibility is to use a car service or van service (see the following sections for information). At the cheaper end, you can take a bus or a train.

 If you take a cab, make sure that a uniformed, official taxi dispatcher hails your cab. Always stand in the official taxi line and take a licensed New Jersey taxi or New York City yellow cab. If someone approaches you offering a cab ride, just keep walking toward the cab line; illegal drivers, who may take you on an unwelcome ride, abound at all three main airports. Remember that taxis are required by law to take no more than four people, and you should always tip 15 percent of the fare, regardless of whether the driver helps you with your bags.

From JFK

John F. Kennedy International (JFK) is New York's largest airport. Its several terminals are located along a great loop. Each terminal has a taxi stand, bus stops, and car service pickup points. After collecting your luggage, follow the "Ground Transportation" signs or the signs for the closest exit to the transportation of your choice.

A cab from JFK to Manhattan takes about 45 minutes, depending on the traffic (which can be fierce), and costs a flat rate of $45 plus tolls and tip. The toll is $4 each for the Queens Midtown Tunnel and the Triborough Bridge; the Queensborough Bridge is free, as are the Williamsburg and Manhattan bridges, but they can get very crowded. Still, if your destination is downtown and the Williamsburg and Manhattan bridges are free of construction, they should be your best bets to get into the city quickly. Your cab driver should know the fastest way into town considering the traffic situation. If you arrive at night (between 8 p.m. and 6 a.m.), you have to pay a 50¢ night surcharge and a $1 surcharge Monday through Friday from 4–6 p.m.

A private car service (a "limo" in New York-ese) is another option. In fact, a ride in a private car can cost a little less than a cab ride. Also, the driver meets you just outside the baggage claim area, so you don't have to wait in line for a cab. Following are some of the car companies that service JFK; call ahead for a reservation.

- ✔ **Allstate:** ☎ **800-453-4099** or 212-741-7440
- ✔ **American Ground Transportation:** ☎ **800-NYC-LIMO** or 800-692-5466
- ✔ **Sabra:** ☎ **212-777-7171**

Another possibility is to take a shared transportation service (a "minivan" in New York lingo). Follow the "Ground Transportation" signs upon your arrival and sign up at one of the desks. Options include:

- ✔ **Gray Line Air Shuttle** (☎ **800-451-0455** or 212-315-3006; www.graylinenewyork.com) has vans that depart every 20 minutes and serve major hotels between 23rd and 63rd streets in Manhattan. The fare is $19 to the airport and $14 from the airport; children under 6 ride free. If you buy a round-trip Gray Line ticket at the airport when you arrive, you get the $14 fare both ways (for a total of $28) and save $5. Call 24 hours in advance for pickup; hourly pickup is available from hotels.

- ✔ **New York Airport Service** (☎ **800-872-4577,** 718-875-8200, or 212-875-8200; www.nyairportservice.com) offers regular bus service to and from Manhattan. The buses stop outside each terminal at JFK; follow the directions to ground transportation and wait by the sign. When boarding the bus at the airport, purchase your ticket on the bus or from the dispatcher at the sign. Buses leave every 20 minutes. The bus makes three stops in Manhattan: across

New York Metropolitan Area

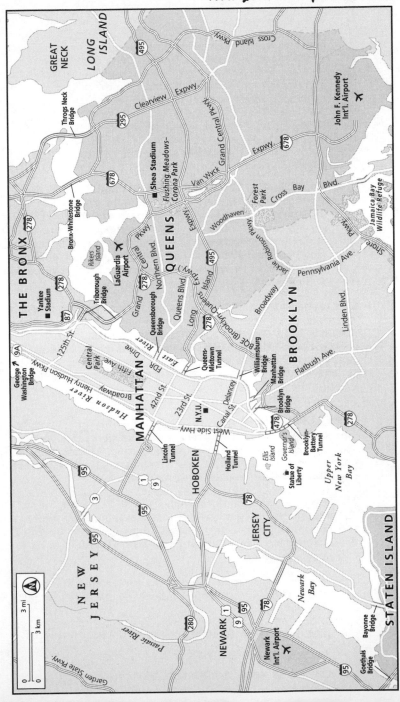

from Grand Central Terminal (the southeast corner of 42nd Street and Park Avenue), the Port Authority Bus Terminal (42nd Street and Eighth Avenue), and Penn Station (1 Penn Plaza between 31st and 33rd streets, just off Seventh Avenue). The price is $13 one-way or $23 round-trip; children under 12 ride free, but watch out for the limit of one free child per full fare adult. You can take advantage of a $1 discount for tickets purchased on the Web site; discounted rates are available for students and seniors, but only if tickets are purchased from the ticket counters in Manhattan. Add $2 for the Midtown Hotel Shuttle, which serves hotels between 33rd and 57th streets. When you leave New York, you can take the bus service from any of these three stops, but you need to call 24 hours in advance to reserve a hotel pickup.

✔ **Super-Shuttle** (☎ **800-BLUE-VAN** or 212-BLUE-VAN; www.super shuttle.com) has vans on call 24 hours a day to all destinations in Manhattan. The price is $13 to or from the airport if you're staying at a hotel; if you're staying at a residential address, the price is $15 from the airport and $22 to the airport for the first passenger in your party and $9 for each additional passenger; children under 3 ride free. You can reserve in advance for your pickup to head back to the airport.

Last *and* least is public transportation. Going from JFK to Manhattan by public transportation is *really* cheap but *really* time-consuming. This option is best reserved for those traveling light and with more time than money. For $5, **AirTrain JFK**, which opened late in 2003 takes you to Jamaica Station where you can connect with the A, E, J, and Z; the E, J, Z to Jamaica Station; or the Howard Beach/JFK Airport Station where you can take the A train into Manhattan.

From LaGuardia

Smaller than JFK, LaGuardia receives fewer flights than its two New York–area counterparts — but, paradoxically, it experiences more flight delays, according to the FAA. Just step outside the terminal at the baggage-claim level for ground transportation.

The fare for a taxi ride from LaGuardia to Midtown runs about $20 to $30 plus tolls and tip. The toll is $4 each for the Queens Midtown Tunnel and Triborough Bridge; the Queensborough Bridge is free, as are the Williamsburg and Manhattan bridges. Allow 30 minutes or more for this trip, depending on traffic.

A private car service is also an option (see "From JFK," earlier in this chapter). Call ahead to one of these reliable car companies for a reservation:

✔ **Allstate:** ☎ **800-453-4099** or 212-333-3333

✔ **Tel-Aviv:** ☎ **800-222-9888** or 212-777-7777

✔ **Carmel:** ☎ **800-922-7635** or 212-666-6666

New York Airport Service (☎ **800-872-4577**, 718-706-9658, or 718-875-8200; www.nyairportservice.com) also serves LaGuardia. It offers the same service to and from LaGuardia as for JFK (see the preceding section). Buses leave every 20 minutes, and the cost is $10 one-way or $17 round-trip (children under 12 free, $1 Internet discount, discounted rates for students and seniors available only from the service's ticket counters in Manhattan). Add $2 for the Midtown Hotel Shuttle service.

Shared transportation services are a good option from LaGuardia as well. Follow the "Ground Transportation" signs upon your arrival and sign up at one of the desks.

Super-Shuttle (☎ **800-BLUE-VAN** or 212-BLUE-VAN; www.supershuttle.com) has vans on call 24 hours a day to all destinations in Manhattan. The price is $13 to and from the airport if you're going to a hotel; if you're staying at a private residence, the price is $15 from the airport and $22 to the airport for the first passenger in your party and $9 for each additional passenger. Children under 3 ride free. You can reserve in advance for pickup to go back to the airport.

 As for public transportation, the **M60 bus** gets you from the airport to a choice of subway stops: first the Astoria Boulevard stop in Queens on the N/W line, then into Manhattan at one of the subway stops on 125th Street (4/5/6, 2/3, or A/B/C/D subway lines), and finally to the Cathedral Parkway/110th Street stop and the 116th Street/Columbia University stop on the 1 subway line. Another possibility: The **Q48** and **Q33** buses bring you to a stop of the 7 train in Queens, which eventually takes you to Times Square. Curbside bus signs and stops are clearly marked. If you're using the bus-and-subway system's MetroCard, you're allowed free transfers to approved connecting buses and subways within two hours of initial card use. In both cases, you face a complicated, two-hour odyssey that you shouldn't attempt unless you're really looking to save money.

From Newark

Although it's in New Jersey, Newark is closer to Manhattan than JFK, especially if your final destination is downtown or the West Side of Manhattan. The Air Train to Newark airport has been a revelation, connecting Newark's three terminals with the long-term parking lots and with the Rail Link (the railroad station of Newark Airport). From there, you can catch a train directly into New York Penn Station ($11.15). See the end of this section for details.

The airport taxi dispatcher sets the price of a cab — about $34 to $45 — from Newark to Manhattan based on your destination, to which you add toll and tip. You pay a $6 inbound-only toll (toward Manhattan) for either the Holland Tunnel or the Lincoln Tunnel, and you should tip 15 percent. You will most likely take a New Jersey cab on the way in and a New York cab on the way back to the airport. The trip takes about 40 minutes each way.

You can take a private bus as well. **Olympia Airport Express** (☎ 212-964-6233; www.olympiabus.com) offers regular service between Newark and destinations in Manhattan for $12 each way or $24 round-trip (children under 30 inches tall ride free, seniors and travelers with disabilities pay $5 — but only if you buy your ticket at the ticket counters). Buses run every 20 minutes, and the ride takes 30 minutes or longer, depending on traffic. From the Grand Central Station stop (at 120 E. 41st St. between Park and Lexington avenues), you can transfer to Olympia Trails' **Midtown Shuttle**, which takes you to any destination between 30th and 65th streets for an additional $5 (you can purchase the ticket at the airport). Other stops in Manhattan are Penn Station (at the northwest corner of 34th Street and Eighth Avenue) and the Port Authority Bus Terminal (gates 316 and 317 at the Airport Bus Center, on 42nd Street between Eighth and Ninth avenues).

In the airport, follow the "Ground Transportation" signs and stop at the Olympia Airport Express counter, or go directly to the bus stop outside that corresponds to your destination; you can buy your ticket at the counter or from the driver. If you're traveling from Manhattan, you can find a dispatcher on duty at the bus stop at 34th Street and 8th Avenue and a counter in the Airport Bus Center; at the 41st Street stop, you can buy your ticket from the Western Union office or from the driver.

Another possibility is to take a mini-van. Follow the signs for ground transportation upon your arrival and sign up at one of the desks.

  ✔ **Super-Shuttle** (☎ 800-BLUE-VAN or 212-BLUE-VAN; www.super shuttle.com) has vans on call 24 hours a day to all destinations in Manhattan. The price is $13 to or from the airport if you're going to a hotel; if you're staying at a private residence, the price is $15 from the airport and $22 to the airport for the first passenger in your party and $9 for any additional passengers; children under 3 ride free. You can reserve in advance for pickup to go back to the airport.

  ✔ **Newark Airport Express** (☎ 877-8-NEWARK or 877-863-9275; www.graylinenewyork.com) has vans every 20 minutes serving hotels between 23rd and 63rd streets. The fare is $14 to and $19 from Newark Airport; children under 6 ride free; round-trip is $28.

You also can take public transportation:

  ✔ To get to the **AirTrain** (☎ 800-772-2222 or 973-762-5100; www.air trainnewark.com) from your terminal, take the airport monorail (monorail stations are located in each terminal) to the Rail Link station served by Amtrak and New Jersey Transit, where you can catch a direct train to New York Penn Station (a 20-minute ride). Trains run every 20 minutes on weekdays and every half-hour on weekends; service is less frequent in the evening after 9 p.m. A one-way trip on New Jersey Transit is $11.15 for adults and $9.05 for children and seniors. Purchase tickets from the automated vending machines in the station; if you purchase a ticket from the conductor on the train, add $5 to the price.

✔ An even cheaper option is to catch a **New Jersey Transit train** to Newark Penn Station (a five-minute ride; $6.80 adults and $5.80 children and seniors), where you can hop a **PATH train** to Manhattan. The PATH train works quite well and costs only $1.50. From Newark, the train makes four stops in New Jersey and five stops in Manhattan, which are Christopher Street (in Greenwich Village on Hudson Street), 9th Street, 14th Street, 23rd Street, and 33rd Street, all along Sixth Avenue. Allow about 40 minutes for the trip between Newark Penn Station and 33rd Street.

Note that the PATH train to Manhattan is *very* crowded with commuters during morning rush hour and from Manhattan during the evening rush hour. If you're toting luggage, paying the extra $3 to take the train from the airport directly to New York Penn Station is far easier.

From MacArthur Airport (Long Island)

Although I don't recommend flying into MacArthur Airport in Islip, Long Island, 50 miles east of Manhattan, the budget airline Southwest flies there. So if you get a rock-bottom fare on Southwest, you may decide it's worth it to fly into MacArthur. Be aware that taxi service into the city is not available from there, but you can reserve a private car (a limo, as we say in New York), which costs about $100 for a 1½-hour trip. Call **Colonial Transportation** (☎ **800-464-6900** or 631-589-3500; www.colonialtransportation.com) for reservations.

Another option is to take the shuttle, also run by Colonial Transportation (a white van marked "Express Service") from outside the terminal to the Ronkonkoma train station. From there you can take the Long Island Rail Road (☎ **718-217-5477**) into New York Penn Station. A shuttle comes every 20 minutes and costs $5; the train ride costs about $10, depending on the time of day. The trip takes about 1 hour and 45 minutes.

Finally, you can use the **Hampton Jitney** (☎ **800-936-0440** or 631-283-4600; www.hamptonjitney.com). Take a local cab to the Jitney's bus stop in Ronkonkoma for about $15, and then catch the bus (a 1½-hour ride) into Manhattan for $25.

Arriving by Train

As I mention in Chapter 5, Amtrak offers regular service to New York from many other cities in the United States. Amtrak trains arrive at Penn Station (between Seventh and Eighth avenues and 31st and 33rd streets), a large, noisy space with fast-food outlets galore and cramped waiting areas.

From the station, you can take a cab to wherever you're headed; signs guide you to the taxi stand on Penn Plaza Drive, a passageway situated between Penn Station (close to Eighth Avenue) and the Long Island Rail Road Terminal (LIRR, close to Seventh Avenue).

Another option is public transportation; the station is well connected with the 1/2/3/A/C/E trains and several buses. However, this isn't the best alternative, especially if you're unfamiliar with the city and you have a lot of luggage. Elevators are virtually unheard of in New York's subway stations, so count on lugging your bags up and down multiple flights of stairs.

Arriving by Car

I don't recommend having a car in New York for the reasons I outline in Chapter 7. If you decide to arrive by car, you'll immediately understand why I tried to dissuade you.

You know you're approaching New York when the traffic and signs multiply beyond all expectations. Open your eyes and sharpen your senses; if you're unfamiliar with the tangle of highways, thoroughfares, and parkways, then getting into Manhattan can be a nerve-racking experience. Remember that you won't find signs for Manhattan; signs give the names of specific tunnels, bridges, and streets instead.

If you arrive from the west or south, the **New Jersey Turnpike** is your jumping-off point to Manhattan. Take exit 14C for the **Holland Tunnel** (which lets you out around Canal Street in Manhattan), exit 16E for the **Lincoln Tunnel** (which deposits you in far-west Midtown at 42nd Street), or exit 18, the turnpike's end, for the **George Washington Bridge** (which lets you out at 181st Street, far uptown). The inbound-only toll (toward Manhattan) is $6; you pay no outbound toll (you're free to leave, so to speak).

From the north, take the **Deegan Expressway** (I-87); from the northeast, take the **New England Thruway** (I-95) to the Bruckner Expressway. To get to the east side of Manhattan, follow the signs to the Triborough Bridge ($4 toll in both directions), but then be careful to follow the signs to **FDR Drive** and avoid going on to Queens — unless that's your destination. FDR Drive runs along the East River all the way to the southern tip of Manhattan and has exits at different points. If you want to get to the west side of Manhattan, exit I-87 at the Sawmill River Parkway and follow it to the Henry Hudson Parkway, pass the Henry Hudson Bridge (a $2 toll), and you can find yourself on the **West Side Highway**, which runs along the Hudson on the west side of the island to its southern tip and has exits at different streets.

 When approaching a toll plaza, stay in the lanes marked "Cash" and *not* "EZ-Pass," (unless, of course, you *have* an EZ-Pass). EZ-Pass is a toll payment system where a scanner identifies your car by an electronic tag mounted on your windshield and deducts the toll from a prepaid account. No attendants man the EZ-Pass booths, so you can't pay cash in those lanes.

 If you're coming from the Northeast, many of the contiguous states have an EZ-Pass program, and your tag from the other states also works in New York City.

The **Cross Bronx Expressway** runs east-west and connects to the George Washington Bridge; you can use it to get to whichever side of the island you want, but its traffic jams are infamous (especially on days when the Yankees play at home).

After you're on the West Side Highway or FDR Drive, take the exit closest to your destination — all exits have street names — and calm down: You've made it to New York!

Figuring Out the Neighborhoods

Getting to know New York and all its neighborhoods is easy (see the "Manhattan Neighborhoods" map). Most of the city's famous sights are on the island of Manhattan, bounded by the Hudson River to the west and the East River — guess where? — to the east. With the exception of a few of the downtown streets, the main avenues run north-south and the streets run east-west.

Downtown

"Downtown" is both a place and a state of mind; physically, everything below 14th Street is considered downtown. Chelsea, the Flatiron District, and Gramercy Park are not, strictly speaking, downtown, but I've included them in this section because they're in that nebulous zone that's neither Downtown nor Midtown.

Lower Manhattan and the Financial District

Lower Manhattan is where the city was born and as a result, the area is home to some of the most important historic landmarks, including Trinity Church, South Street Seaport, and the Brooklyn Bridge.

Much of the area is considered the **Financial District** but may be even more famous now as **Ground Zero.** Until September 11, 2001, the Financial District was anchored by the **World Trade Center,** with the World Financial Center complex and Battery Park City to the west, and **Wall Street** running crosstown a little south and to the east. Now, a gaping hole sits where the Twin Towers and five other buildings stood.

Ground Zero has been cleaned, and a beautiful, though temporary, PATH station has reopened. Designs for what will eventually be constructed on the site have finally been approved, but it will be years before those

Manhattan Neighborhoods

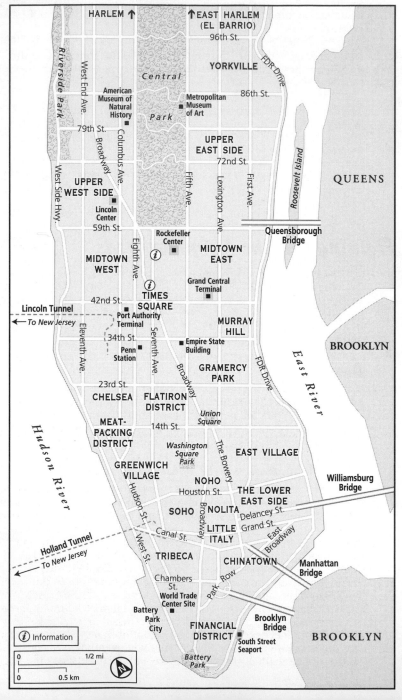

HARLEM ↑   ↑EAST HARLEM
            (EL BARRIO)
            96th St.

Central

YORKVILLE

West End Ave.

American Museum of Natural History

Metropolitan Museum of Art

86th St.

79th St.

Park

UPPER EAST SIDE
72nd St.

Riverside Park

Columbus Ave.

Broadway

UPPER WEST SIDE

Fifth Ave.

Lexington Ave.

First Ave.

Roosevelt Island

QUEENS

West Side Hwy.

Lincoln Center
59th St.

Rockefeller Center

(i)

Queensborough Bridge

Eighth Ave.

MIDTOWN WEST

(i)
TIMES SQUARE

MIDTOWN EAST

Grand Central Terminal

42nd St.

Lincoln Tunnel
← To New Jersey

Port Authority Terminal

MURRAY HILL

BROOKLYN

Eleventh Ave.

34th St.
Penn Station

Seventh Ave.

Empire State Building

23rd St.

Broadway

GRAMERCY PARK

East River

FDR Drive

CHELSEA   FLATIRON DISTRICT

MEAT-PACKING DISTRICT

14th St.

Union Square

Hudson River

GREENWICH VILLAGE

Washington Square Park

The Bowery

EAST VILLAGE

NOHO
Houston St.

Williamsburg Bridge

SOHO NOLITA

THE LOWER EAST SIDE

Hudson St.

Broadway

LITTLE ITALY

Delancey St.

Grand St.

Holland Tunnel
To New Jersey

Canal St.

West St.

TRIBECA

CHINATOWN

East Broadway

Manhattan Bridge

Chambers St.

Park Row

World Trade Center Site

Battery Park City

FINANCIAL DISTRICT

Brooklyn Bridge

South Street Seaport

BROOKLYN

(i) Information

Battery Park

0   1/2 mi

0   0.5 km

designs are fully realized. For more information about visiting the World Trade Center site, see Chapter 11.

City Hall remains the northern border of the district, abutting Chambers Street. Most of the streets of this neighborhood are narrow concrete canyons, with Broadway serving as the main uptown-downtown artery. Just about all the major subway lines congregate here before they either end or head to Brooklyn.

Since September 11, 2001, the rebuilding process has been long and difficult for downtown New York, the area hardest hit economically by the terrorist attacks. But Lower Manhattan has so much to offer, and the local community has united to revitalize and promote the area. Check out these Web sites for useful information on new developments and exciting events that you can find downtown. Both www. lowermanhattan.info and www.downtownny.com, the Web site for the Alliance for Downtown New York, Inc., are updated daily.

TriBeCa, Chinatown, Little Italy, and the Lower East Side

TriBeCa, the acronym for the **Tri**angle **Be**low **Ca**nal (Street), is one of the city's hippest residential neighborhoods. It's an area of residential lofts inhabited by artists and celebrities, as well as the home of some of the most fashionable and chic restaurants in town. Hip doesn't translate into big crowds, though; the neighborhood, especially at night, is very quiet. Canal Street runs straight across the island, going through the heart of **Chinatown,** which lies to the east of TriBeCa. Chinatown is a sprawling neighborhood that bursts with shops selling Asian wares, cheap souvenirs, bootleg DVDs and CDs, and counterfeit watches, bags, and sunglasses (more about these offerings in Chapter 12). The streets are lined with Asian restaurants of every variety, and the sometimes very ripe aroma of fish from the countless fish stalls fills the air.

North of Chinatown and centered around Mott and Mulberry streets is **Little Italy.** The neighborhood, squeezed by the northern encroachment of Chinatown, has sadly been reduced to not much more than a tourist trap, with just a few remaining cafes, stores, and mediocre restaurants. To the east and north of Little Italy is the **Lower East Side,** a historic area that was a Jewish ghetto in the 19th century. The neighborhood is now a bubbling mix of hipster-trendy (alternative music clubs, adventurous new restaurants) and old-world remnants from its historic past. The farther east you go, the sketchier the neighborhood can get.

Orchard Street is where you can find great bargain hunting in many old-world fabric and clothing stores that thrive between club-clothes boutiques and trendy lounges. Keep in mind that the old-world shops close early on Friday afternoon and remain closed all day on Saturday (the Jewish Sabbath). The exponentially expanding trendy set can be found in the blocks between Allen and Clinton streets south of Houston and north of Delancey, with more new shops, bars, and restaurants popping up in the blocks to the east every day. The **Lower East Side**

Business Improvement District operates a neighborhood visitor center at 261 Broome St., between Orchard and Allen streets (☎ 866-224-0206 or 212-226-9010), that's open daily from 10 a.m. to 4 p.m. (sometimes later). Stop in for an Orchard Street Bargain District shopping guide (which they can also send you in advance), plus other information on this historic yet freshly hip 'hood. You can also find shopping, dining, and nightlife directories online at www.lowereastsideny.com.

Greenwich Village, the East Village, SoHo, and NoHo

SoHo (which stands for **so**uth of **Ho**uston Street — pronounced "*HOW*-ston," not "*HYOO*-ston") is famous for its cast-iron architecture and, in the past 25 years, its thriving art scene. The art scene, however, is not as thriving is it was just a decade ago, with just a few galleries remaining; artists can no longer afford the astronomical rents. Still, SoHo's cachet has been established and you can find numerous chic boutiques and some interesting restaurants here as well. The eastern part of SoHo, rebaptized **NoLiTa** (**no**rth of **Li**ttle **Ita**ly), is where young, innovative fashion and accessory designers have opened small shops. The neighborhood has merged north into **NoHo** (**no**rth of **Ho**uston), a small, fashionable area just east of Broadway and north of Houston Street. You can find some of the city's most trend-setting restaurants here.

Greenwich Village, also called simply "the Village," is a center of art, dining, shopping, music, and gay life. The neighborhood is roughly bordered by Houston Street to the south and 14th Street to the north. Known for its architecture, the Village has the shortest street in the city (Weehawken, just one block long) and the narrowest house (on Bedford Street, where poet Edna St. Vincent Millay once lived). It's an area that never sleeps, yet it still manages to give off a sense of quiet and beauty. Within the Village itself is the **West Village,** west of Seventh Avenue, which is the historic center of New York's gay community and is centered around Sheridan Square and Christopher Street. It has a residential feel, with beautiful tree-lined streets and comfortable neighborhood cafes. East of Broadway, the Village becomes the **East Village,** a center for alternative music and dance clubs, which draws a younger, edgier crowd. More raw and less polished, and despite rising rents, the East Village still clings proudly to its seediness. Despite that forced seediness, some excellent restaurants and a growing number of boutiques can be found in the East Village. The area between the East Village and West Village (that is, between Broadway and Seventh Avenues) is simply referred to as the Village. In the middle sits Washington Square Park, landmarked by the park's famous arch.

Chelsea, the Flatiron District, and Gramercy Park

Chelsea, which extends from 14th Street to 26th Street and from the Hudson River to Fifth Avenue, is now the city's largest gay community. The neighborhood lays claim to lots of art galleries and many cutting-edge cafes and restaurants. East of Chelsea is the **Gramercy Park** area — a quiet, elegant, moneyed neighborhood known for its jewel of a park and handsome architecture. In between are **Union Square** and the **Flatiron District,** a lively hub of New York life that was home to New York's dot-com companies in the late 1990s, before the virtual economy went bust. This area, bordered by the historic Flatiron Building to the north (at Broadway and Fifth at 23rd Street) and Union Square to the south, is where members of the fashion industry — models, advertising people, photographers, and so on — meet and eat.

Midtown

Midtown is roughly defined by 26th Street to the south and 59th Street to the north. This is concrete canyon territory, where skyscrapers block out most of the sun and sky. During the day, Midtown is a hectic center of commerce, seething with people on their way to or from work, while at night, the restaurant scene is lively and generally very expensive. This is the city's biggest hotel neighborhood, with choices running the gamut from cheap to chic.

Within Midtown to the southeast lies **Murray Hill,** just east of Fifth Avenue and below 42nd Street. It's a mixture of business and residential property, where a 40-story slab may rub up against a five-story apartment building. The Murray Hill area is safe and quiet — for New York. The Empire State Building is the major sightseeing stop here. Above 42nd Street is **Midtown East,** which is more commercial and includes a number of famous shops that line 59th Street between Fifth and Lexington. The main attractions in this area are the United Nations, Grand Central Terminal, St. Patrick's Cathedral, Rockefeller Center, and the stunning Chrysler Building. The stretch of **Fifth Avenue** from Saks at 49th Street extending to the Plaza Hotel at 59th is home to the city's most high profile haute shopping, including Tiffany & Co. and Bergdorf Goodman. Here you can find the city's finest collection of grand hotels, mostly along Lexington Avenue and near the park at the top of Fifth.

To the southwest lies the **Fashion** or **Garment District** (roughly between 26th and 42nd streets west of Fifth Avenue), with its array of fabric shops and wholesale fashion stores. At the heart of it, at the intersection of 34th Street, Broadway, and Sixth Avenue (also called the Avenue of the Americas), is **Herald Square,** a bustling (some would say choked-with-crowds) shopping area. Herald Square is the home of Macy's, and with ongoing development, more national chain stores are appearing all the time. Other than that, it's a pretty grim commercial area that lacks any real charisma.

Farther north, on the west side, is **Times Square,** a once legendary — some would say colorful — place full of peep shows and sex shops until a business partnership completed an ambitious (and completely transforming) improvement campaign. Times Square is now a family-oriented area with renovated theaters and the famous neon, which is bigger, brighter, and louder than ever (including the largest TV screen in the world, the Sony Jumbotron). Crowds are sometimes impenetrable, so be prepared for a major jostling. Just up Broadway is the **Theater District.** The area churns with activity, and the scale is grand, so it's not the kind of place to step out for a casual stroll under the trees (there aren't any, anyway). Famed Restaurant Row is close by on 46th Street. A number of hotels are centered around Times Square, so if you don't mind the crowds, generally higher prices, and want to be as close as possible to the pulse of the city, this is where you want to be.

Just west of the Theater District is **Hell's Kitchen,** probably the most picturesquely named neighborhood in New York City. Once a rough-and-tumble immigrant community and the home turf of Irish gangs, Hell's Kitchen has seen some gentrification. In an amusing example of New York's constant effort to reinvent itself, real-estate developers have pushed to rename the area "Clinton Hill" or "Theater District West," but thankfully, the natives have resisted those monikers. Ninth Avenue has blossomed into one of the city's finest dining avenues; just stroll along and choose from a world of great, inexpensive dining options, from American diner to Mediterranean to traditional Thai.

Uptown

Most of the northern part of the island of Manhattan is comprised of three major neighborhoods, each with their own distinct characters.

The Upper West Side

Located to the west of Central Park, the **Upper West Side** is bordered by Columbus Circle, the new Time Warner Center and Lincoln Center to the south, and Columbia University and the Cathedral of St. John the Divine to the north. The area is home to some beautiful, historic residential buildings, such as The Dakota, where John Lennon lived and died, and The Ansonia, once the home of Babe Ruth. Other streets are lined with brownstones, townhouses, and apartment buildings. In the past decade, the area has grown tremendously with a proliferation of superstores, movie theaters, and some very good new restaurants. Also in this neighborhood, you find the American Museum of Natural History. Though it's a bit away from the action of midtown and downtown, the Upper West Side is a good option for reasonable hotels.

The Upper East Side

To the east of Central Park and stretching to the East River, the **Upper East Side**'s main draw is Museum Mile, a stretch of Fifth Avenue that includes the Metropolitan Museum of Art, the Guggenheim, the Museum of the City of New York, the International Center of Photography, the Frick Museum, and the Jewish Museum, all within a walkable stretch. Madison Avenue from 60th Street well into the 80s is the monied crowd's main shopping strip. The neighborhood has an upper-crust, old-money feel and, west of Lexington Avenue, is generally pretty quiet after sundown. East of Lexington along Third, Second, and First avenues, you encounter a number of lively restaurants and clubs.

Harlem

Harlem stretches from about 96th Street east of Fifth Avenue and 110th Street west of Fifth to 155th Street. **Spanish Harlem** (El Barrio) runs between East 100th and East 125th streets. Harlem real estate has shot up the past few years; restaurants, new apartments, and clubs are beginning to line the streets, and historic brownstones are constantly being restored. Exploring the area is becoming safer and safer, and that's a very good thing considering there's so much to see here, such as the Morris-Jumel Mansion, the Schomburg Center, the Studio Museum, and the Apollo Theatre. Above Harlem, you'll find **Washington Heights** and Fort Tryon Park, home to the Cloisters annex of the Metropolitan Museum of Art.

Finding Information after You Arrive

The following places can help you get your bearings after you arrive in New York:

✓ **NYC & Company** (the former Convention & Visitors Bureau) has a **Visitor Information Center** (810 Seventh Avenue between 52nd and 53rd streets; ☎ 212-484-1200; www.nycvisit.com; open Mon–Fri 8:30 a.m.–6 p.m., Sat–Sun 9 a.m.–5 p.m.) where you can find useful printed material, pick up coupons for theaters and attractions, and buy tickets for New York's top sights, as well as the CityPass (see Chapter 11). Together with American Express and CitySearch.com, NYC & Co. has developed electronic kiosks at various locations in the city, called Ticket axis (see the second-to-last item in this list). Using the touch-screen, you can get directions and get information about attractions and events.

✓ The **Grand Central Partnership** (Grand Central Terminal, East 42nd Street and Vanderbilt Avenue; open Mon–Fri 8:30 a.m.–6:30 p.m., Sat–Sun 9 a.m.–6 p.m.) offers an information window inside Grand Central Terminal and a cart outside.

✓ The **Manhattan Mall** (Sixth Avenue and 32nd Street; open Mon–Sat 10 a.m.–8 p.m., Sun 11 a.m.–6 p.m.; ☎ 212-465-0500) offers traveler information on the first floor.

✓ The **34th Street Partnership** (Penn Station, Seventh Avenue between 31st and 33rd streets; open Mon–Fri 8:30 a.m. to 5:30 p.m., Sat–Sun 9 a.m.–6 p.m.; ☎ 212-868-0521) has a window inside Penn Station and an information cart at the Empire State Building at Fifth Avenue and 32nd Street. You find carts at Greeley Square (32nd Street at Broadway and Sixth Avenue) in the summer and at Madison Square Garden (above Penn Station at Seventh Avenue and 32nd Street) in above-freezing weather. The carts open a little later and close a little earlier than the indoor window.

 ✔ **Ticket axis kiosks** are electronic touch-screen kiosks offering information and tickets at the touch of a finger. The number of locations is increasing, but at press time, kiosks can be found at the Visitor Information Center (see first bullet in this list), New York Skyride (on the second floor of the Empire State Building), Intrepid Sea-Air-Space Museum, Circle Line Tours, Museum of the City of New York, New York Hall of Science (in Queens), New York Botanical Gardens (in the Bronx), Museum of American Financial History (26 Broadway at Wall Street), and Brooklyn Museum of Art (Brooklyn).

 ✔ The **Times Square Visitors Center,** 1560 Broadway, between 46th and 47th streets (where Broadway meets Seventh Ave.), across from the TKTS booth on the east side of the street (☎ **212-768-1560;** www.timessquarebid.org), is the city's top info stop. This pleasant and attractive center features a helpful info desk offering loads of citywide information. There's also a tour desk selling tickets for Gray Line bus tours and Circle Line boat tours; a Metropolitan Transportation Authority (MTA) desk staffed to sell MetroCard fare cards, provide public transit maps, and answer all your questions about the transit system; a Broadway Ticket Center providing show information and selling full-price show tickets; ATMs and currency exchange machines; and computer terminals with free Internet access courtesy of Yahoo!. It's open daily from 8 a.m. to 8 p.m.

Getting Around New York

You may not be used to riding a subway, taking a bus, hailing a taxi, or, yes, walking to where you want to go, but that's what New Yorkers do (few own cars, and those who do use them only on weekends to get out of the city). You'll find yourself doing the same. The guidelines and tips in this section will have you navigating the island of Manhattan like a native in no time. Remember that taxis, subways, and most buses run 24 hours a day.

Traveling by subway

Besides walking, riding the subway is my preferred mode of transportation. And some 3.5 million people seem to agree with me each day, because they ride it too. The subway is quick, inexpensive, relatively safe, and pretty efficient, as well as being a genuine New York experience.

The subway runs 24 hours a day, 7 days a week. The rush-hour crushes are roughly from 8–9:30 a.m. and from 5–6:30 p.m. on weekdays; the trains are relatively uncrowded the rest of the time.

The subway fare is $2 (half price for seniors and those with disabilities), and children under 44 inches tall ride free (up to three per adult).

Finding the entrance and getting on board

You can easily locate a subway entrance along the sidewalk by looking for a set of stairs that heads underground. Most stops also have signs above them that list the lines that run through those stations.

Some subway entrances close at night. Each stairway has a globe on top of it that's supposed to tell you whether the entrance is open (green for open, red for closed), but the globes aren't always accurate; look down the stairs to find out whether the entrance is open (a big clue is if there's a locked gate at the bottom of the staircase!).

The famous New York City subway token was phased out in 2003 and now the only way to gain entry to the subway is with the **MetroCard,** a magnetically encoded card that debits the fare when swiped through the turnstile (or the fare box on any city bus). After you're in the system, you can transfer freely to any subway line that you can reach without exiting your station. MetroCards also allow you **free transfers** between the bus and subway within a two-hour period.

MetroCards can be purchased from each station's staffed token booth (which is what they're still called, even though the token itself has been phased out), where you can only pay with cash. At the ATM-style vending machines now located in just about every subway station, you can pay with cash, credit cards, and debit. See the section "Understanding the MetroCard," later in this chapter, for details.

The Cheat Sheet at the front of this book shows you the pertinent subway stops, and all the maps in this book also show subway stops. You can usually find a subway map inside each subway car, on the platform, and on the wall in the subway station. You also can get a detailed subway map from the token booth inside each station.

Getting where you want to go

If you need directions in the subway, trying to get information from the token-booth attendant can be frustrating. The acoustics are horrible, the people behind you are impatient, and it's difficult to make yourself heard (and even harder to understand the resulting directions). Instead, pick out a friendly or knowledgeable face; you'd be surprised how willing we New Yorkers are to help out.

The orientation of the subway system is mainly north-south (or uptown-downtown); you can find only a few points at which the lines go straight east-west. To travel up and down the west side (and also to the Bronx and Brooklyn), take the 1, 2, 3, or 9 line; the A, C, E, or F line; or the B or D line.

The N, R, Q, and W lines first cut diagonally across town from east to west and then snake under Seventh Avenue before shooting out to Queens.

The crosstown S line, the Shuttle, runs back and forth between Times Square and Grand Central Terminal. The 7 line also goes from Times Square to Grand Central Station (with a stop at Fifth Avenue). Farther downtown, across 14th Street, the L line works its own crosstown magic.

Lines have assigned colors on subway maps and trains — red for the 1, 2, 3, 9 line; green for the 4, 5, 6 trains; and so on — but nobody ever refers to them by color. Always refer to them by number or letter when asking questions. Within Manhattan, the distinction between different numbered trains that share the same line is usually that some are express and others are local.

Express trains often skip about three stops for each one that they make; express stops are indicated on subway maps with a white (rather than solid) circle. Local stops usually come about 9 blocks apart.

Directions are almost always indicated using "Uptown" (northbound) and "Downtown" (southbound), so be sure to know what direction you want to head in. The outsides of some subway entrances are marked UPTOWN ONLY or DOWNTOWN ONLY; read carefully, because it's easy to head in the wrong direction. After you're on the platform, check the signs overhead to make sure that the train you're waiting for is traveling in the right direction. If you do make a mistake and get on the wrong train, it's a good idea to wait for an express station, like 14th Street or 42nd Street, so you can get off and change for the other direction without paying again.

Staying safe

To keep yourself safe in the subway, heed this advice:

✔ At night, use the off-hours waiting areas, which are usually close to the exits to the street. They're clearly marked with signs overhead.

✔ Don't tempt thieves by displaying money or valuables on the subway.

✔ Don't try to stop a subway door that's closing. You can end up with a bruised hand or arm — or something more serious. Just wait for the next train.

✔ Always stand a few feet back from the tracks on the subway platform.

✔ Avoid subways late at night, and splurge on a cab after about 10 or 11 p.m. — it's money well spent to avoid a long wait on a deserted platform. Or take the bus.

Traveling by bus

The New York City bus system reaches far and wide, traveling to just about all points of the city on a north-south *and* an east-west grid. You even get a tour of the city as you ride! Remember that because traffic can be horrific during the day, buses are much slower going than the subway.

To check out the bus routes, grab one of the free city bus maps available right by the front door of every bus and also in the booths at subway stations. If you want to scan the routes before you get to town, you can access full bus maps via the Internet at www.mta.info.

Bus stops are located every couple of blocks along each route. The stop is either a small, glass-walled shelter or a simple sign on a post (blue with a bus icon) stating the bus numbers. Each bus has a sign above the windshield that flashes its route and end destination. Schedules for buses are posted at most bus stops and are relatively reliable. The buses run every 5 to 20 minutes or so, depending on the time of day.

 Some buses are labeled "Limited" and make only a few major stops along the line; they're particularly useful when you want to go a long distance. Buses making express stops only have an orange "Limited" sign placed on the dashboard to the right of the driver. Limited bus stops also display the orange sign.

Like the subway fare, **bus fare** is $2 — half price for seniors and riders with disabilities, free for children under 44 inches (up to three per adult). The fare is payable with a **MetroCard** or **exact change.** Bus drivers don't make change, and fare boxes don't accept dollar bills or pennies. You can't purchase MetroCards on the bus, so you have to have them before you board.

If you pay with a MetroCard, you can transfer to another bus or to the subway for free within two hours. If you pay cash, you must request a **free transfer** slip that allows you to change to an intersecting bus route only (legal transfer points are listed on the transfer paper) within one hour of issue. Transfer slips cannot be used to enter the subway.

All buses in Manhattan, and 95 percent of New York City buses in the other boroughs, are equipped with wheelchair lifts and special areas where the seats in the back fold up to make room for securing wheelchairs on board. The buses also "kneel," scrunching down when they stop so that the first step is not quite so high up.

 The Alliance for Downtown New York's **Downtown Connection** offers a free bus service that provides access to important Downtown destinations including Battery Park City, the World Financial Center, and South Street Seaport. The service, which operates from 10 a.m. to 8 p.m. seven days a week, brings Lower Manhattan residents, workers, and visitors closer to Downtown businesses, events, shopping, and attractions.

The Downtown Connection's five-mile route runs in two directions: from Chambers Street on the West Side to Beekman Street on the East Side. The service makes stops at dozens of locations and is able to transport about 30 passengers per bus (20 seats and 10 standees). Six buses run on weekdays and four buses on the weekend.

The climate-controlled buses are ADA-wheelchair accessible and run on ultra-low sulfur fuel. Each vehicle is also equipped with diesel-particulate filters and electronically controlled fuel-injected engines. For more information on the Downtown Connection, call the Downtown Alliance at ☎ 212-566-6700, or visit www.downtownny.com.

Understanding the MetroCard

The MetroCard fare card is a high-tech system that encodes a certain number of rides on a magnetic strip on the back of a thin plastic card. MetroCards are accepted on both buses and subways and have a lot of advantages over tokens: They don't weigh a ton, you can slip the card in your wallet or pocket, you can buy and recharge it in an automatic vending machine, you get a free ride for every $10 you spend, and last but not least, you get one free transfer between bus and subway (or vice versa) for each ride as long as you make the transfer within two hours of your initial boarding.

Two types of MetroCards are available for purchase:

✔ **Pay-Per-Ride** is the regular card I just described, which can be used for up to four people by swiping up to four times (bring the whole family). You can put any amount from $4 (two rides) to $80 on your card. Every time you put $10 or $20 on your Pay-Per-Ride MetroCard, it's automatically credited with an additional 20 percent — that's one free ride for every $10 you spend, or six trips for the price of five. You can refill your card at any subway station at any time until its expiration date, which is usually about a year from the date of purchase.

✔ **Unlimited-Ride** can't be used for more than one person at a time or more frequently than 18-minute intervals. These cards are available in four values: the **Daily Fun Pass,** which allows you a day's worth of unlimited subway and bus rides for $7; the **7-Day MetroCard,** for $21; and the **30-Day MetroCard,** for $70. Seven- and 30-day Unlimited-Ride MetroCards can be purchased at any subway station or MetroCard merchant.

Fun Passes can't be purchased at token booths — you can only buy them at a MetroCard vending machine, from a MetroCard merchant, or at the MTA information desk at the Times Square Visitors Center.

Unlimited-Ride MetroCards go into effect *the first time you use them* — so if you buy a card on Monday and don't use it until Wednesday, Wednesday is when the clock starts ticking. A Fun Pass is good from the first time you use it until 3 a.m. the next day, while 7- and 30-day MetroCards run out at midnight on the last day. These unlimited MetroCards can't be refilled; throw them out once they've been used up and buy a new one.

In addition to being sold in the subway, MetroCards are sold at many hotels and in thousands of shops all over town (if a shop offers the card, it has a sign in its window saying so).

The MetroCard has one corner snipped off and a small hole on one side. To use your MetroCard in the subway, swipe the card horizontally through the reader in the same direction you're traveling, with the cut-off corner on top and at the back (and between your fingers) and the little hole leading the way. To use your MetroCard on the bus, insert the card downward into the machine with the snipped-off corner up and to the left, the little hole on the bottom and the side with the magnetic strip facing you. The machine eats the card momentarily and then spits it back out and beeps — also displaying, for your information, how much money is left on your card.

 Seniors and persons with disabilities get a 50 percent discount with the MTA New York City Transit. You can apply for the discount by writing to Customer Assistance Division, MTA, 370 Jay St., 7th Floor, Brooklyn, NY 11201. Or you can download the application from the MTA Web site (www.mta.info), or call ☎ **718-243-4999.** You can recharge your discounted MetroCard at the vending machines and ticket booths in subway stations.

Traveling by taxi

Sometimes I actually have to shell out the big bucks to take a cab. Like when I'm late, it's not rush hour, and I need to be somewhere fast. Or when I'm not near public transportation, if I'm with a group of three or four, or if it's just too late at night and I want to be home safe and fast, then a taxi is my best option.

Taking a cab costs you $2.50 for the initial charge, plus 40¢ per ⅕ mile or 40¢ per 120 seconds waiting charge, plus a 50¢ night surcharge (from 8 p.m.–6 a.m.). The average fare in Manhattan is $6.25.

 When you're waiting on the street for an available taxi, look at the **medallion light** on the top of oncoming cabs. If the light is out, the taxi is in use. When the center part (the number) is lit, the taxi is available — this is when you raise your hand to flag the cab. If all the lights are on, the driver is off duty. A taxi can't take more than four people, so expect to split up if your group is larger. If it's raining and it's rush hour and everyone is looking for a cab, either be prepared to battle it out amongst the seasoned New York cab riders, or do what I do and head for the nearest subway station.

Follow these suggestions to make your ride as smooth as possible:

> ✔ When announcing your destination to the driver, speak clearly. Remember that English is probably not your driver's first language.

✔ Try to know the cross-street of your destination ("Third Avenue and 41st Street"). Many drivers don't know the city as well as you may expect, and if you give a specific street address (like "1500 Broadway"), the driver may not immediately know the exact location, and his confusion may end up costing you more money.

✔ If your driver is driving too fast for you, ask him nicely to slow down. You have the right to a safe (as well as a smoke-free and noise-free) trip.

✔ Have your money ready (you can track the charge on the meter; remember to add the 50¢ night surcharge). You want to disembark rapidly to avoid traffic jams.

✔ Have small bills with you when boarding a cab; drivers generally don't accept bills larger than $20.

✔ Tip 15 percent.

✔ Ask for a receipt: It has the taxi registration number on it, which is a useful detail if you forget something in the car.

✔ Check that you have all your belongings before leaving. Taxi drivers are usually very honest, but the same is not necessarily true of the customers who use the cab immediately after you.

✔ Disembark from the curbside door to avoid the stream of traffic that is dodging around your stopped vehicle on the other side.

✔ Wear a seat belt — accidents can happen.

✔ Remember your taxi's medallion number (which is listed on your printed receipt). If you leave anything behind in the cab or if you want to register a complaint, call the Taxi and Limousine Commission Consumer Hotline (☎ **212-NYC-TAXI** or 212-692-8294) and reference the medallion number to help identify your driver.

Seeing New York on Foot

Walking is one of the preferred modes of transportation in New York — at least it's one of mine. Walking not only lets you ponder the wonder that is New York, it's also good exercise. And best of all: It's free.

When walking in New York, however, don't do as we New Yorkers do. We zigzag across the streets, rush against the lights, dodge taxis and buses, and tempt fate on an almost daily basis. So be smart and exercise some caution when walking. Always be careful when crossing the street, even when you have the light; drivers sometimes get distracted. And cross only at crosswalks. Keep your eyes open for distracted walkers who sometimes resemble NFL blockers. And if your head is up gawking at some amazing edifice, do it while you're immobile. Otherwise you may find yourself flattened by one of those blockers.

Walk as if you're driving, staying to the right. Unfortunately, most bicyclists seem to think that the traffic laws don't apply to them; they often blithely fly through red lights and dash the wrong way on one-way streets, so be on your guard.

As I mentioned, walking is sometimes faster than taking the bus and sometimes even taking a taxi. Traffic can move through Midtown at a snail's pace — especially during rush hours — and pedestrians typically outdistance cars and buses by blocks.

If you plan to do a lot of walking, be sure to bring comfortable shoes! You'll not only be on your feet seeing the city all day, but you'll probably be on your feet indoors, too — you can rack up a lot of mileage inside the Metropolitan Museum of Art, for example.

Chapter 9

Checking In at New York's Best Hotels

. . . .

In This Chapter

▶ Choosing the right hotel for you
▶ Finding the best room rate
▶ Arriving without a reservation
▶ Deciding among New York's best hotels
▶ Choosing a backup if your favorite isn't available

. . . .

*W*ith more than 230 hotels and 63,000 hotel rooms, the sleeping options in New York are staggering. Do you want to spend most of your travel budget on a luxurious hotel? Do you want to stay close to the flickering neon lights of Times Square? Do you want a room with a view of Central Park? Do you want a room vastly bigger than your linen closet back home? These are just some of the questions you need to ask yourself before you book a room.

Getting to Know Your Options

In some cities and regions, chain hotels might be the most prevalent option, but that's not the case in New York City. In this section, I briefly discuss nationally known chains with hotels in New York as well as one-of-a-kind hostelries you can find only in New York. A few bed and breakfasts are worth investigating if you like that kind of place to stay, and I cover them, too. If you're staying awhile (more than a few days), I also give you leads on short-term apartment rentals and why you might want to consider that option.

Independent hotels

Most of the hotels I list in this chapter fall in the class of independent hotels (versus hotel chains) because I feel that such hotels give you more of a taste of the city. Don't be misled, though; in New York, inde-pendent hotels include everything from huge business hotels run by large corporations — or by the master builder, Donald Trump — to small boutique hotels that are family-owned and run the gamut from very expensive to inexpensive.

Chain hotels

Just a few of the hotels I list in this chapter are major national chains. Far from the kind of cookie-cutter sameness you may find elsewhere, the chains I choose, usually moderate to inexpensive in price, hold up well in comparison to similarly located independent hotels. (See the Quick Concierge appendix for the toll-free numbers and Web sites of New York's major chain hotels.)

Bed & Breakfasts and inns

New York is not the Berkshires, where there are B&Bs galore. Still, the city has some very nice B&Bs and inns (usually in historic brownstones in residential neighborhoods) that offer quaint alternatives to the typically big, cold behemoth of a hotel the city is more famous for. If you'd like to check out some B&B options, try these associations and reservation agencies:

- ✔ **A Hospitality Company,** 247 W. 35th St., 4th Floor, New York, NY 10001 (☎ 800-987-1235 or 212-813-2244; www.hospitalityco.com)

- ✔ **At Home In New York Inc.,** P.O. Box 407, New York, NY 10185 (☎ 212-956-3125; Fax: 212-247-3294; www.athomeny.com)

- ✔ **City Lights Bed & Breakfast,** 308 E. 79th St., New York, NY 10021 (☎ 212-737-7049; Fax: 860-533-1738; www.citylightsbandb.com)

- ✔ **Manhattan Lodgings,** 70 E. 10th St., Suite 18C, New York, NY 10003 (☎ 212-677-7616; Fax: 212-253-9295; www.manhattanlodgings.com)

- ✔ **New York Bed and Breakfast Reservation Center,** 331 W. 57th St., Suite 221, New York, NY 10019 (☎ 212-977-3512; E-mail: smartsleep@aol.com)

Short-term apartment rentals

If you want to look into renting a furnished apartment or subletting someone's place as an alternative to staying in a hotel, try the following companies:

- ✔ **Manhattan Getaways** (☎ 212-956-2010; Fax: 212-265-3561; www.manhattangetaways.com)

- ✔ **New York Habitat** (☎ 212-255-8018; Fax: 212-627-1416; www.nyhabitat.com)

- ✔ **NYC Residence** (☎ 212-226-2700; Fax: 212-226-7555; www.nycresidence.com)

Finding the Best Room at the Best Rate

In all but the smallest accommodations, the rate you pay for a room depends on many factors — chief among them being how you make your reservation. A travel agent may be able to negotiate a better price with certain hotels than you can get by yourself. (That's because the hotel often gives the agent a discount in exchange for steering his or her business toward that hotel.)

The **rack rate** is the maximum rate a hotel charges for a room. It's the rate you get if you walk in off the street and ask for a room for the night. You sometimes see these rates printed on the fire/emergency exit diagrams posted on the back of your door.

Hotels are happy to charge you the rack rate, but you can almost always do better. The best way to avoid paying the rack rate is surprisingly simple: Just ask for a cheaper or discounted rate. You may be pleasantly surprised.

Room rates (even rack rates) change with the season, as occupancy rates rise and fall. But even within a given season, room prices are subject to change without notice, so the rates quoted in this book may be different from the actual rate you receive when you make your reservation.

 As you proceed with the selection process, don't forget that the basic rate a hotel charges you isn't what you end up paying. The hotel tax in New York City is 13.25 percent, and don't forget the room charge of $2 per night. When you reserve a room, make sure to find out whether the price you're being quoted includes taxes.

You don't have to just take the room and rate that a hotel offers you. With a little know-how, you can get the room you want at a price you can afford.

Below are some tried-and-true tips to help you locate the best room for the best available price.

Trying out a travel agent

Hotels sometimes have discount rates that they offer only to travel agents; business is business, and a travel agent represents more business and more dollars than little old you. A good side of this equation is that, when the city is full, no rooms are available, and you're pulling your hair out, your travel agent may have the juice to get you a room even when you've been told, "Sorry, we're full up."

Taking the do-it-yourself approach

The following tips can help you save money on your room if you decide to reserve a room without using a travel agent:

✔ **Ask for the best rate.** Sometimes the easiest approach is a straightforward one. A hotel typically won't extend its discount room rates unless you ask for them.

✔ **Mention your memberships.** When you reserve a room, mention your membership in AAA, AARP, frequent-flyer programs, and any other corporate rewards programs you belong to. These memberships may shave a few dollars off your room rate.

✔ **Call all available numbers.** Most hotels have both a local number and an 800 central reservation number. Sometimes these numbers have different rate information. Call both numbers and compare the rates that each one gives you.

Choosing your season carefully

Room rates can vary dramatically — by hundreds of dollars in some cases — depending on what time of year you visit. Winter (January through March) is best for bargains, with summer (especially July and August) coming in at second. Fall is the busiest and most expensive season after Christmas, but November tends to be quiet and rather affordable, as long as you're not booking a parade-route hotel on Thanksgiving weekend. All bets are off at Christmastime — expect to pay top-dollar for everything. See Chapter 3 for more information on the best time to visit the city.

Going uptown or downtown

A New York subway can whisk you anywhere you want to go in minutes, so you don't have to stay in Midtown, where the most expensive hotels are.

 You get the best value for your money by staying *outside* the Theater District, in the residential neighborhoods where real New Yorkers live, like Greenwich Village, Chelsea, Murray Hill, or the Upper West Side.

Visiting over a weekend

If your trip includes a weekend, you may be able to save big. Business hotels tend to empty out on weekends, and rooms that go for $300 or more Monday through Thursday can drop dramatically, as low as $150 or less, after the execs have headed home. These deals are especially prevalent in the Financial District, but they're often available in tourist-friendly Midtown, too. Look in the Travel section of the Sunday *New York Times* for some of the best weekend deals, which are also often advertised on a hotel's Web site. Or just ask when you call.

Buying a money-saving package deal

A travel package that gets your plane tickets and your hotel stay for one price just may be the best bargain of all. In some cases, you get airfare, accommodations, transportation to and from the airport, plus extras like a sightseeing tour or discount coupons to shows or restaurants. All this may be less than the hotel alone would have cost had you booked it yourself. See Chapter 5 for more information.

Investigating reservation services

These outfits usually work as consolidators, buying up or reserving rooms in bulk, and then dealing them out to customers at a profit. You can get 10 to 50 percent off; but remember, these discounts apply to rack rates — inflated prices that people rarely end up paying. You may get a decent rate, but always call the hotel directly to see if you can do better. See Chapter 5 for more information.

Surfing the Web for hotel deals

Shopping online for hotels is generally done one of two ways: by booking through the hotel's own Web site or through an independent booking agency (or a fare-service agency like Priceline). These Internet hotel agencies have multiplied in mind-boggling numbers of late, competing for the business of millions of consumers surfing for accommodations around the world. This competitiveness can be a boon to consumers who have the patience and time to shop and compare the online sites for good deals — but shop you must, for prices can vary considerably from site to site. And keep in mind that hotels at the top of a site's listing may be there for no other reason than that they paid money to get the placement.

Of the "big three" sites, **Expedia** offers a long list of special deals and "virtual tours" or photos of available rooms so you can see what you're paying for (a feature that helps counter the claims that the best rooms are often held back from bargain-booking Web sites). **Travelocity** posts unvarnished customer reviews and ranks its properties according to the AAA rating system. Also reliable are **Hotels.com** and **Quikbook.com.** An excellent free program, **TravelAxe** (www.travelaxe.net), can help you search multiple hotel sites at once — even ones you may never have heard of — and conveniently lists the total price of the room, including the taxes and service charges. Another booking site, **Travelweb** (www.travelweb.com), is partly owned by the hotels it represents (including the Hilton, Hyatt, and Starwood chains) and is plugged directly into the hotels' reservations systems — unlike independent online agencies, which have to fax or e-mail reservation requests to the hotel, a good portion of which get misplaced in the shuffle. More than once, travelers have arrived at the hotel, only to be told that they have no reservation. To be fair, many of the major sites are undergoing improvements in service and ease of use, and Expedia will soon be able to plug directly into the reservations systems of many hotel chains — none of which can be bad news for consumers. In the meantime, it's a good idea to **get a confirmation number** and **make a printout** of any online booking transaction.

In the opaque Web site category, **Priceline** and **Hotwire** are even better for hotels than for airfares; at both sites, you're allowed to pick the neighborhood and quality level of your hotel before offering up your

money. Priceline's hotel product is much better at getting five-star lodging for three-star prices than at finding anything at the bottom of the
scale. I've had excellent results booking rooms on Priceline for out-of-
town guests, getting particularly good rates ($50 a night in a suite hotel!)
in late December/January, as well as a $90 a night rate in a good hotel
on a summer weekend in July.

Priceline's booking process allows you to select which neighborhood
you want to stay in; start with downtown and the Upper East and West
Sides with your lowest bids.

On the down side, many hotels stick Priceline guests in their least
desirable rooms. Be sure to go to the BiddingforTravel Web site (www.
biddingfortravel.com) before bidding on Priceline; it features a fairly
up-to-date list of hotels that Priceline uses in major cities. For both
Priceline and Hotwire, you pay upfront, and the fee is nonrefundable.
Note: Some hotels do not provide loyalty program credits or points or
other frequent-stay amenities when you book a room through opaque
online services.

In addition, you can read descriptions of some hotels online through
NYC & Company, the New York City Convention & Visitors Bureau
(☎ 212-484-1222; www.nycvisit.com). Some of the descriptions offer
links to individual hotel Web sites, allowing you to book your room
online. **Hotelguide.com** (www.hotelguide.com) is another source of
information about New York hotels. **Citysearch** (newyork.citysearch.
com) and **TripAdvisor** (www.tripadvisor.com) have hotel guides as
well.

Consider joining the **Playbill Online Theater Club** (www.playbill
club.com), a free service that offers some excellent members-only
rates at select city hotels in addition to discounts on theater tickets.

Finding the Top-notch Room

After you make your reservation, asking one or two more pointed questions can go a long way toward making sure you get the best room in
the house. Always ask for a corner room; they're usually larger, quieter,
and have more windows and light than standard rooms, and they don't
always cost more. Also ask if the hotel is renovating; if it is, request a
room away from the renovation work. Inquire, too, about the location
of the restaurants, bars, and discos in the hotel — all sources of annoying noise.

Street noise in New York can be deafening, but many hotels have double-
paned or soundproofed windows. If you're a light sleeper, ask whether
the room you've booked is facing the street or off the street. And if you
aren't happy with your room when you arrive, talk to the front desk. If
they have another room, they should be happy to accommodate you,
within reason.

Arriving without a Reservation (Not Recommended)

Your lodging options may be limited if you arrive without a reservation. However, making a few phone calls can get you a room most of the time.

As with airline travel, services that call themselves consolidators or wholesalers purchase lots of rooms at a big discount and then pass some of the savings on to you. The hotel stays full, the consolidator makes money, and you may save a lot (or only a little) in the bargain. Money aside, consolidator and reservation services often can get you a room when you can't find one anywhere else. The service usually makes you pay for your stay upfront and in full; however, you've gotta pay sometime, and this way, the figure may be more like what you had in mind.

If you arrive in New York without a reservation and have trouble booking directly with the hotels, then try the following bureaus:

- **Quikbook** (☎ 800-789-9887; www.quikbook.com): Covers 50 hotels; discounts can reach 60 percent

- **Turbotrip.com** (☎ 800-473-7829; www.turbotrip.com): Provides comprehensive lodging and travel information for destinations throughout the United States and worldwide

- **Hotel Discounts** (☎ 800-715-7666; www.hoteldiscounts.com): Is another good source for last minute reservations

New York City's Best Hotels

New York City can be an expensive place, and the number one cause of this expense is the cost of your hotel room. You won't get the same kind of space that you can expect in other places, so I've broken down what sort of space and amenities you can expect at each price level.

Getting what you pay for: Picking a price range

Each hotel listing is prefaced with a number of dollar signs ranging from one ($) to five ($$$$$), corresponding to price. Here's a glance at what you can expect in terms of room size and standard amenities in each of these price categories:

- **$ ($85–$150):** These hotels are true bargains, but services are sparse. Your room will probably be small, you might have to share a bathroom, and don't expect room service, fitness equipment, movie or cable channels, or bellhops.

✔ **$$ ($150–$250):** Expect these rooms to be a little larger and of better quality and comfort than those in the first category. You may have access to a fitness center and business facilities, and the hotel may throw in a complimentary continental breakfast.

✔ **$$$ ($250–$350):** Typically, you get room service, a phone with a dataport, probably a refrigerator and perhaps some kind of minimal cooking facility, cable TV and/or VCR, free access to a health club, complimentary breakfast or beverages (and possibly afternoon wine and cheese), and an on-site restaurant.

✔ **$$$$ ($350–$450):** On top of the amenities listed for the preceding category, you can expect plenty of space, fine furnishings, a variety of dining and drinking options in the hotel, and excellent service. Because these hotels often cater to businesspeople, they sometimes offer special amenities like complimentary car service to the Financial District.

✔ **$$$$$ ($450 and up):** In this range, you get more than a place to stay: You get an experience. These hotels have style, elegance, and a reputation for impeccable service.

Affinia Dumont
$$$ Midtown East

Located a bit away from the center of midtown, but still within easy walking distance of Herald Square shopping, the Empire State Building, Madison Square Garden, and Grand Central Station, this may be New York's only fitness suite hotel. When you book a room, you can request a "Fit Kit" that will be prepared, with no extra charge, to be used if you only have time to work out in your room. The hotel also has a complete fitness spa with the most advanced weights, cardio equipment, and massage and skin treatments. But even if you don't want to break a sweat during your stay, the hotel features amenities that make it a very attractive option, including a full kitchen, at least one 27-inch television, a large desk with an ergonomic chair, the "Affinia Bed" with a custom-designed mattress, four-selection "pillow menu," and a minibar stocked with unusual options, such as health elixirs.

See map p. 108. 150 E. 34th St. (between 2nd and 3rd avenues, three blocks east of the Empire State Building). ☎ *212-481-7600 or 212-320-8019. Fax: 212-889-8856. www.affinia.com. Subway 6 to 33rd Street. Valet parking: $27. Rack rates: $340–$625 suites. AE, DC, MC, V.*

The Benjamin
$$$$ Midtown East

From the Jazz Age design of the exterior and lobby, you would never know that the Benjamin is a relatively new hotel. But after you check into your spacious room and notice the numerous high-tech amenities, such as Bose Wave radios, Internet browsers for the televisions, high-speed Internet access, and an ergonomic chair at an executive desk with moveable workstation, you know you are definitely in the 21st century. Many of the amenities are geared toward business travelers, but why should they be the only ones to experience all this comfort and luxury? All rooms are airy, but the deluxe studio and one-bedroom suites are extra large. The hotel even offers a few one-bedroom suites with terraces. How many hotels can boast a "sleep concierge" who consults with you and recommends the right choice from a "pillow menu" of 11 choices? Lexington Avenue can get very busy most weeknights and mornings, so if you're a light sleeper, book a room off Lexington. Bathrooms feature Frette robes, under-the-counter TV speakers, a shower caddy, and shower water pressure that's headstrong enough to make you think you've just experienced a deep-tissue massage.

See map p. 108. 125 E. 50th St. (at Lexington Avenue). Close to Rockefeller Center, St. Patrick's Cathedral, and Saks Fifth Avenue. ☎ *888-4-BENJAMIN or 212-320-8002, or 212-715-2500. Fax: 212-715-2525.* www.thebenjamin.com. *Subway: 6 to 51st Street; E, F to Lexington Avenue. Parking: $35. Rack Rates: $420–$530 studios and suites. AE, DC, DISC, MC, V.*

Broadway Inn
$$ **Midtown West**

With its easygoing vibe, this Theater District hotel is a real charmer. The rooms are basic but comfy, outfitted in an appealing neo-Deco style with firm beds, good-quality linens and textiles, and nice bathrooms (about half have showers only). The whole place is impeccably kept. If more than two of you are traveling or you're looking to stay a while, the suites — with pullout sofa, microwave, minifridge, and lots of closet space — are a great deal. The location can be noisy, but double-paned windows keep the rooms surprisingly peaceful; still, ask for a back-facing one if you're extra sensitive to noise. The service is great here; you're given a hotline number upon check-in to call if you need any assistance, and a nice, simple, and free breakfast is included in the room rate. The location is perfect for theatergoers, but take note, this four-story building doesn't have an elevator.

See map p. 108. 264 W. 46th St. (at Eighth Avenue). Located on Restaurant Row and steps from many Broadway theaters. ☎ *800-826-6300 or 212-997-9200. Fax 212-768-2807.* www.broadwayinn.com. *Subway: A, C, E to 42nd Street. Parking: $20, 3 blocks away. Rack rates: $135–$225 double. Rates include continental breakfast. AE, DC, DISC, MC, V.*

Casablanca Hotel
$$ **Midtown West**

Despite its hokey Hollywood-Morocco theme, the Casablanca is an excellent value and a very good Theater District hotel choice. You get a free breakfast, and coffee, tea, and cookies are served all day with wine and cheese available most evenings. Free passes to a nearby health club also contribute to the value you get here. The rooms aren't huge, but they're perfectly comfortable with platform beds, ceiling "Casablanca" fans, two-line phones, bathrobes, and double-paned windows for quiet. The

Downtown Hotels

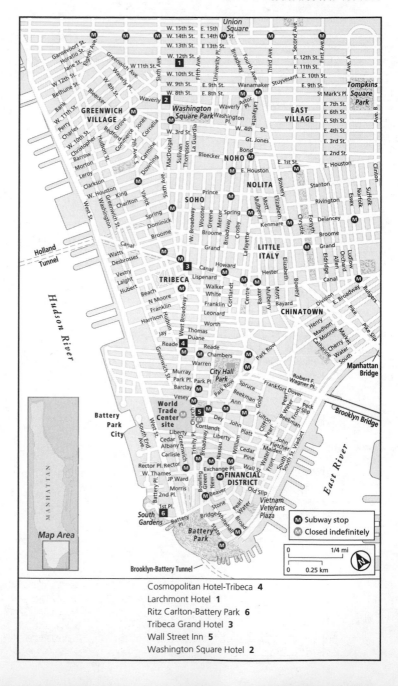

Cosmopolitan Hotel-Tribeca **4**
Larchmont Hotel **1**
Ritz Carlton-Battery Park **6**
Tribeca Grand Hotel **3**
Wall Street Inn **5**
Washington Square Hotel **2**

Midtown Hotels

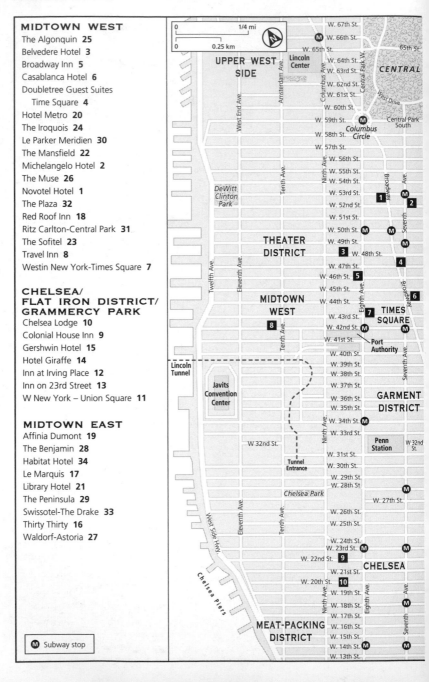

MIDTOWN WEST

The Algonquin **25**
Belvedere Hotel **3**
Broadway Inn **5**
Casablanca Hotel **6**
Doubletree Guest Suites
   Time Square **4**
Hotel Metro **20**
The Iroquois **24**
Le Parker Meridien **30**
The Mansfield **22**
Michelangelo Hotel **2**
The Muse **26**
Novotel Hotel **1**
The Plaza **32**
Red Roof Inn **18**
Ritz Carlton-Central Park **31**
The Sofitel **23**
Travel Inn **8**
Westin New York-Times Square **7**

**CHELSEA/
FLAT IRON DISTRICT/
GRAMMERCY PARK**

Chelsea Lodge **10**
Colonial House Inn **9**
Gershwin Hotel **15**
Hotel Giraffe **14**
Inn at Irving Place **12**
Inn on 23rd Street **13**
W New York – Union Square **11**

MIDTOWN EAST

Affinia Dumont **19**
The Benjamin **28**
Habitat Hotel **34**
Le Marquis **17**
Library Hotel **21**
The Peninsula **29**
Swissotel-The Drake **33**
Thirty Thirty **16**
Waldorf-Astoria **27**

Ⓜ Subway stop

0   1/4 mi
0   0.25 km

UPPER WEST SIDE

Lincoln Center

CENTRAL

Columbus Circle

Central Park South

DeWitt Clinton Park

THEATER DISTRICT

MIDTOWN WEST

TIMES SQUARE

Port Authority

Lincoln Tunnel

Javits Convention Center

GARMENT DISTRICT

Penn Station

Tunnel Entrance

Chelsea Park

CHELSEA

MEAT-PACKING DISTRICT

West End Ave.
Amsterdam Ave.
Columbus Ave.
Central Park W.
West Drive
Ninth Ave.
Tenth Ave.
Twelfth Ave.
Eleventh Ave.
Eighth Ave.
Seventh Ave.
Broadway
West Side Hwy.
Chelsea Piers

W. 67th St.
W. 66th St.
W. 65th St.
65th St.
W. 64th St.
W. 63rd St.
W. 62nd St.
W. 61st St.
W. 60th St.
W. 59th St.
W. 58th St.
W. 57th St.
W. 56th St.
W. 55th St.
W. 54th St.
W. 53rd St.
W. 52nd St.
W. 51st St.
W. 50th St.
W. 49th St.
W. 48th St.
W. 47th St.
W. 46th St.
W. 45th St.
W. 44th St.
W. 43rd St.
W. 42nd St.
W. 41st St.
W. 40th St.
W. 39th St.
W. 38th St.
W. 37th St.
W. 36th St.
W. 35th St.
W. 34th St.
W. 33rd St.
W 32nd St.
W. 31st St.
W. 30th St.
W. 29th St.
W. 28th St.
W. 27th St.
W. 26th St.
W. 25th St.
W. 24th St.
W. 23rd St.
W. 22nd St.
W. 21st St.
W. 20th St.
W. 19th St.
W. 18th St.
W. 17th St.
W. 16th St.
W. 15th St.
W. 14th St.
W. 13th St.
W 32nd St.

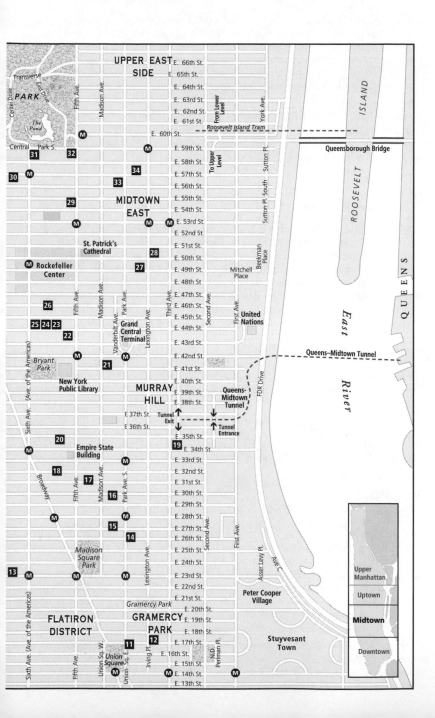

bathrooms are spacious and come with oversized showers. Everybody at the Casablanca Hotel goes to **Rick's Café**, where you can sit by the fire sipping a cappuccino from a serve-yourself machine. A tiled second-floor courtyard is also ideal for summer lounging, and the rooftop deck is a perfect vantage point for watching the New Year's ball drop. Needless to say, if you're planning on spending New Year's here, expect to pay a premium and reserve *well* in advance!

See map p. 108. 147 W. 43rd St. (just east of Broadway). In the heart of Times Square.
☎ *888-922-7225 or 212-869-1212.. Fax: 212-391-7585.* www.casablancahotel.
com. *Subway: N, R, 1, 2, 3, 9 to 42nd Street/Times Square. Parking: $25 next door.*
Rack rates: $169–$265 double. Rates include continental breakfast. AE, DC, MC, V.

The Carlyle
$$$$$ Upper East Side

This Upper East Side legend is a magnet for visiting dignitaries. They come for the impeccable service as well as the elegant ambiance. Rooms range from singles to seven-room suites, some with terraces and full dining rooms. All have marble bathrooms with whirlpool tubs and all the amenities you'd expect from a hotel of this caliber — and price. The lobby was renovated recently; the marble floors and columns, the original clock, and the Piranesi prints and murals were all restored and new features have been added, such as Baccarat light fixtures, a new reception desk, and an expanded concierge space. **Café Carlyle**, the supper club where living legend Bobby Short still holds court, still attracts top names in cabaret. **Bemelmans Bar** (named after children's book illustrator Ludwig Bemelmans, who created the Madeline books and painted the mural here) is one of my top spots for cocktails, and the hotel's restaurant, **Dumonet**, is a star in its own right.

See map p. 111. 35 E. 76th St. (at Madison Avenue). (One block north of the Whitney Museum.) ☎ *800-227-5737 or 212-744-1600. Fax: 212-717-4682..* www.thecarlyle.
com. *Subway: 6 to 77th Street and then walk 1 block west on 76th Street to Madison Avenue. Parking: $50. Rack rates: $495–$750 double. Pets accepted. AE, DC, MC, V.*

Chelsea Lodge
$ Chelsea

This small hotel housed in a Chelsea brownstone is not only a charmer, but it's also a great value for those on a tight budget. Though the rooms are small, everything is in top notch condition. Rooms on the first floor have high ceilings and give the appearance of being bigger. Beds are full-size and each room has its own sink and in-room shower stall; toilets are shared. I really like the location in the heart of trendy, yet residential Chelsea, and coupled with the stylishness of the rooms, you'd be hard-pressed to do better for the money. Best for couples rather than shares.

See map p. 108. 318 W. 20th St. (between Eighth and Ninth avenues). ☎ *800-373-1116 or 212-243-4499. Fax: 212-243-7852..* www.chelsealodge.com. *Subway: 1, 9 to 18th Street; C, E to 23rd Street. Parking: about $20 nearby. Rack rate: $105 double. AE, DC, DISC, MC, V.*

Uptown Hotels

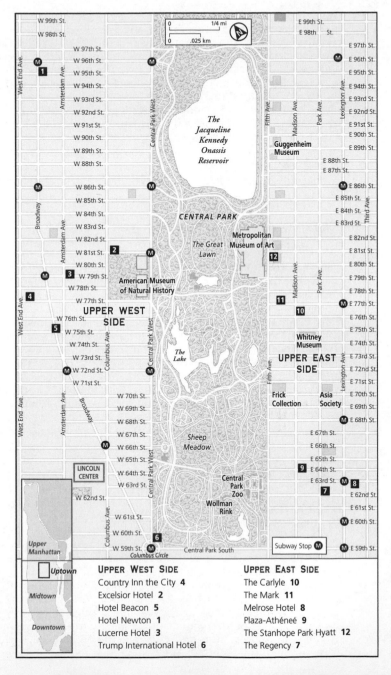

Uptown		
Midtown		
Downtown		

UPPER WEST SIDE
Country Inn the City **4**
Excelsior Hotel **2**
Hotel Beacon **5**
Hotel Newton **1**
Lucerne Hotel **3**
Trump International Hotel **6**

UPPER EAST SIDE
The Carlyle **10**
The Mark **11**
Melrose Hotel **8**
Plaza-Athénéé **9**
The Stanhope Park Hyatt **12**
The Regency **7**

Cosmopolitan Hotel–Tribeca
$ TriBeCa

If you're looking for a budget hotel and you don't want to share a bathroom, go downtown to this perfectly decent TriBeCa choice. The modern IKEA-ish furniture includes a work desk and an armoire (a few rooms have a dresser and hanging rack instead); for a few extra bucks, you can have a love seat, too. Beds are comfy, and sheets and towels are of good quality. Rooms are small but make the most of the limited space, and the whole place is pristine. The TriBeCa location is safe, superhip, and subway-convenient. Don't expect much in the way of services here, but this is still a perfectly acceptable choice for the money.

See map p. 107. 95 W. Broadway (at Chambers Street). ☎ *888-895-9400 or 212-566-1900. Fax: 212-566-6909.* www.cosmohotel.com. *Subway: 1, 2, 3, 9 to Chambers Street. Parking: $20, 1 block away. Rack rates: $119–$149 double. AE, DC, MC, V.*

Doubletree Guest Suites Times Square
$$$ Midtown West

This all-suite hotel in the center of cacophonous Times Square is comparable in price to many hotels that only feature standard rooms. Each spacious suite has a separate bedroom, a dining/work area, and a living room with a pullout sofa, a wet bar with microwave and coffeemaker, two TVs with Sony PlayStation, and multiple dual-line phones. For business travelers, conference suites are large enough for small meetings and feature good workstations. This is a great option for families, with a floor of childproof family-size suites and special amenities for kids. The Kids Club, designed by Philadelphia's Please Touch Museum for children ages 3 to 12, features a playroom, an arts-and-crafts center, and computer and video games. Cribs and strollers are available, and there's even a room-service menu just for kids.

See map p. 108. 1568 Broadway (at 47th Street and Seventh Avenue). ☎ *800-222-TREE or 212-719-1600. Fax: 212-921-5212.* www.doubletree.com. *Subway: N, R to 49th Street. Parking: $35. Rack rates: $199–$750 suite. Children under 12 stay free in parent's suite. AE, DC, DISC, MC, V.*

Excelsior Hotel
$$ Upper West Side

If the Lucerne (see listing later in this chapter) is booked and you still want to stay on the Upper West Side, the Excelsior is a perfectly acceptable mid-priced alternative. The location, across from the Museum of Natural History and just steps from Central Park, is hard to beat, and the hotel has a fresh, comfortable feel to it. The guest rooms boast high-quality furnishings, commodious closets, two-line phones, thick terry bathrobes, a work desk, free bottled water, and full-length dressing mirrors for those of you who appreciate them. The recently remodeled bathrooms are attractive and well-outfitted. The two-bedded rooms are large enough to accommodate budget-minded families (a few even have two queens), and suites feature pullout sofas. Because the hotel's in a low-rise residential area, all rooms receive generous light. The second floor boasts a clubby lounge with a working fireplace, gorgeous leather seating, writing desks, and a large flat-screen TV with VCR and DVD player.

See map p. 111. 45 W. 81st St. (between Columbus Avenue and Central Park West). ☎ *800-368-4575 or 212-362-9200. Fax: 212-721-2994.* www.excelsiorhotelny. com. *Subway: B, C to 81st Street/Museum of Natural History. Parking: $27 nearby. Rack rates: $180–$225 double. Children 12 and under stay free in parent's room. AE, DC, DISC, MC, V.*

Gershwin Hotel
$ Flatiron District

Look for the glowing protruding horns and you know you've found the Gershwin. And those unusual horns tell you pretty much what the Gershwin is all about: It's an artsy, funky, fun, yet budget-conscious hotel. Each floor, hallway, and room is decorated with original art by different artists. The standard rooms are clean and bright, with Picasso-style wall murals and Phillippe Starck-ish takes on motel furnishings. Superior rooms are best, as they're newly renovated and well worth the extra $10; all have either a queen bed, two twins, or two doubles, plus a newish private bathroom with cute, colorful tile. The lobby was recently revovated, and a new hip bar, **Gallery at the Gershwin,** was added. The hotel is more service-oriented than you usually see at this price level, and the staff is very professional.

See map p. 108. 7 E. 27th St. (between Fifth and Madison avenues). ☎ *212-545-8000. Fax: 212-684-5546.* www.gershwinhotel.com. *Subway: N, R, 6 to 28th Street. Parking: $25, 3 blocks away. Rack rates: $99–$189 double. AE, MC, V.*

Habitat Hotel
$ Midtown East

If you're short on funds but big on style, the Habitat is calling your name. The rooms are designed in a natural palette accented with black-and-white photos. The quality is very good for a hotel of this price range, from the firm mattresses to the plush towels to the pedestal sinks in every room. The bathrooms are immaculate; choose between shared (one for every three to four rooms), private, or a semiprivate "minisuite" (two rooms sharing an adjacent bathroom — great for friends traveling together). Most of the double rooms have twin beds; only a few queens are available, but hey, who says twin beds can't be romantic? You can always improvise. The location is central to transportation. This hotel's a rare budget choice in this corporate neighborhood.

See map p. 108. 130 E. 57th St. (at Lexington Avenue). ☎ *800-497-6028 or 212-753-8841. Fax: 212-838-4767.* www.habitatny.com. *Subway: 4, 5, 6 to 59th Street; E, F to Lexington Avenue. Parking: $25. Rack rates: $75–$115 double with shared bathroom; $125–$185 double with private bathroom. Rates include continental breakfast. AE, DC, DISC, MC, V.*

Hotel Giraffe
$$$$ Flatiron District

Built just five years ago in the fashionable Madison Park area, this hotel has a cozy, intimate, lived-in feel to it. Guest rooms evoke an urban European character with high ceilings, velveteen upholstered chairs, and original black-and-white photographs from the '20s and '30s. All the rooms are good-sized with high ceilings, and deluxe rooms and suites feature French doors that lead to small balconies with large windows and remote-controlled blackout shades. Bathrooms are spacious with plenty of marble counter space and glass-paneled doors. But the services are what really separate this hotel from so many others. In the hotel's elegant lobby, you can find a continental breakfast, and coffee, cookies, and tea are available there all afternoon. Wine, cheese, and piano music are offered each evening. The lovely rooftop garden is also the perfect place for a glass of wine in the evening or morning coffee during warm weather.

See map p. 108. 365 Park Ave. South (at 26th Street). ☎ *877-296-0009 or 212-685-7700. Fax: 212-685-7701.* www.hotelgiraffe.com. *Subway: 6 to 28th Street. Parking: $24. Rack rates: $325–$425 double. Rates include continental breakfast and evening wine and cheese accompanied by piano music. AE, DC, MC, V.*

Hotel Metro
$$ Midtown West

With its Art Deco style, decent-sized rooms, and slew of free amenities, the Metro, just a block from the Empire State Building, is one of Manhattan's best values. The rooms are outfitted with smart retro furnishings, playful fabrics, and fluffy pillows. Though on the small side, the marble bathrooms are lovely and have shower stalls big enough for two. The two-room family suite has a second bedroom in lieu of a sitting area; families on tighter budgets can opt for a roomy double/double. The comfy, fire-lit library/lounge area off the lobby, where complimentary buffet breakfast is laid out and the coffeepot's on all day, is a popular hangout. The well-furnished rooftop terrace boasts a breathtaking view of the Empire State Building and makes a great place to order up room service.

See map p. 108. 45 W. 35th St. (between Fifth and Sixth avenues). One block north of the Empire State Building. ☎ *800-356-3870 or 212-947-2500. Fax: 212-279-1310.* www.hotelmetronyc.com. *Subway: B, D, F, V, N, R to 34th Street. Parking: $17 nearby. Rack rate: $165–$250 double. Rates include continental breakfast. AE, DC, DISC, MC, V.*

Hotel Newton
$ Upper West Side

On the burgeoning northern extreme of the Upper West Side, the Newton is a budget hotel that seems to be a notch above in almost every category. The lobby is small but tasteful, and the rooms are generally large, with good, firm beds, a work desk, and a sizable new bathroom, plus roomy closets in most (a few of the cheapest rooms have wall racks only). Some rooms are big enough to accommodate families with two doubles or two queen beds. The suites feature two queen beds in the bedroom, a sofa in the sitting room, plus niceties like a microwave, minifridge, and iron, making them well worth the few extra dollars. This AAA-approved hotel is impeccably kept. The 96th Street express subway stop is just a block away, providing convenient access to the rest of the city, and the Key West Diner next door is a favorite for huge, cheap breakfasts.

See map p. 111. 2528 Broadway (between 94th and 95th streets). ☎ *888-HOTEL58 or 212-678-6500. Fax: 212-678-6758.* www.newyorkhotel.com. *Subway: 1, 2, 3, 9 to 96th Street. Parking: $20 nearby. Rack rates: $95–$160 double. Children under 15 stay free in parent's room. AE, DC, DISC, MC, V.*

Larchmont Hotel
$ Greenwich Village

On a beautiful tree-lined block in a quiet residential part of Greenwich Village, you find this wonderful European-style hotel. And maybe that's why it has a loyal European following. Each bright guest room is tastefully done in rattan and outfitted with a writing desk, a mini-library of books, an alarm clock, a washbasin, and a few extras that you normally have to pay a lot more for, such as cotton bathrobes, slippers, and ceiling fans. Every floor has two shared bathrooms (with hair dryers) and a small, simple kitchen. The Larchmont is a great choice if you're on a budget and don't mind sharing a bathroom. And if you're looking for a trendy downtown base that's close to some of the city's best shopping, dining, and sightseeing (and your choice of subway lines are just a walk away), you can't do much better than the Larchmont Hotel.

See map p. 107. 27 W. 11th St. (between Fifth and Sixth avenues). ☎ *212-989-9333. Fax: 212-989-9496.* www.larchmonthotel.com. *Subway: A, C, E, F, V to West 4th Street. (use 8th Street exit); F to 14th Street. Parking: $18 nearby. Rack rates: $90–$125 double. Rates include continental breakfast. Children under 13 stay free in parent's room. AE, MC, V.*

Le Marquis
$$$ Midtown East

This lovely boutique property is one of the better options in the residential Murray Hill neighborhood. The lobby, with blue-glass light fixtures and cherry wood, is stunning. In the back is a wonderful living room–style lounge that you're meant to really enjoy. It boasts a 40-inch flat-screen TV, books, board games, and sofas. The guest rooms aren't huge, but the space is used efficiently with custom furnishings that include armoires and good-sized work desks. All rooms have platform beds with goose down and Frette linens, DVD/CD/MP3 players, plush terry robes, and Aveda toiletries. Most rooms only have showers, but double-wide stalls and luxurious rain-shower heads make these rooms more desirable than those with standard tub/shower combos. At press time, a restaurant in the hotel was in the works.

See map p. 108. 12 E. 31st St. (between Fifth and Madison avenues). ☎ *866-MAR-QUIS or 212-889-6363. Fax: 212-889-6699.* www.lemarquisny.com. *Subway: B, D, F, V, N, R to 34th Street. Parking: $35. Rack rates: $199–$399 double. AE, DC, DISC, MC, V.*

Le Parker Meridien
$$$$ Midtown West

With its central location, incredible amenities like the 17,000 square-foot fitness center with a rooftop pool, and three excellent restaurants, Le Parker Meridien just about has it all. The gorgeous, always bustling lobby also serves as a public space, and elevators with televisions that continuously show Tom & Jerry and Rocky & Bullwinkle cartoons and Charlie Chaplin shorts are a wonder for the kids. The spacious hotel rooms, though a bit on the IKEA side, have a fun feel to them with hidden drawers and swirling television platforms, inventively exploiting an economical use of space. The slate and limestone bathrooms are large but unfortunately come only with a shower. **Norma's** serves one of the best breakfasts in the city, and many, myself included, have rated the burgers at **Burger Joint** as the best in the city. A stay at Le Parker Meridien is definitely a New York experience in itself.

See map p. 108. 118 W. 57th St. (between Sixth and Seventh avenues). One block from Carnegie Hall. ☎ *800-543-4300 or 212-245-5000. Fax: 212-307-1776.* www.parker meridien.com. *Subway: N, R, B, Q to 57th Street. Parking: $40. Rack rates: $370–$680 double. Pets accepted. AE, DC, DISC, MC, V.*

The Library Hotel
$$$ Midtown East

I'm usually very suspicious of theme hotels, but this one, located a block from the main branch of the New York Public Library, is an exception. Each of the ten guestroom floors are dedicated to one of the ten major categories of the Dewey Decimal System. When I visited the hotel I was appropriately booked into the "Geography and Travel" room. There I was greeted with books, such as *Barcelona,* by Robert Hughes, and *Bella Tuscany,* by Frances Mayes. The most disappointing thing about all those books is that I was only staying one night and didn't have the chance to read any of them. Still, there was something about having them by my bed — they give off a soothing aura that I found comforting. Or maybe it was just the comfy rooms, which come in three categories: petite (really small), deluxe, and junior suite; and feature mahogany built-ins, generous desks, and immaculate marble bathrooms. The public spaces feature a reading room where wine and cheese and a complimentary breakfast are served daily, and a writer's den with a fireplace, flat screen TV, and a rooftop terrace.

See map p. 108. 299 Madison Ave. (at 41st Street). ☎ *877-793-7323 or 212-983-4500. Fax: 212-499-9099.* www.libraryhotel.com. *Subway: 4, 5, 6, 7, S to 42nd Street/ Grand Central. Parking: $28 nearby. Rack rates: $295–$425 double. Rates include continental breakfast buffet, all-day snacks, and weekday wine and cheese. AE, DC, MC, V.*

The Lucerne
$$ Upper West Side

This magnificent 1903 landmark building that was recently transformed into a luxury boutique hotel is a triumph on many levels. The Lucerne best captures the feel of the Upper West Side, and you won't do better if you want to stay in this very special neighborhood. Service here is impeccable, especially for a moderately priced hotel. The rooms are all comfortable and big enough for kings, queens, or two doubles with attractive bathrooms complete with travertine counters. Some of the rooms have views of the Hudson River. The suites are extra special here and include kitchenettes, stocked minifridges, microwaves, sitting rooms with sofas and extra televisions. The highly-rated restaurant, **Nice Matin,** offers room service or eat-in breakfast, lunch, and dinner. Or you may want to skip room service and order take-out from nearby Zabar's or H&H Bagels.

See map p. 111. 201 W. 79th St. (at Amsterdam Avenue). One block from the Museum of Natural History. ☎ *800-492-8122 or 212-875-1000. Fax: 212-579-2408.* www. newyorkhotel.com. *Subway: 1, 9 to 79th Street. Parking: $25 nearby. Rack rates: $140–$270 double. Children under 16 stay free in parent's room. AE, DC, DISC, MC, V.*

The Mark
$$$$$ Upper East Side

Just a block separates the Mark from its chief hotel rival (the Carlyle) on that coveted stretch of Upper East Side real estate that comprises the boutiques of Madison Avenue and Museum Mile. Both feature impeccable service and comfort, but the Carlyle is more of a white-gloved grande dame, while the Mark prides itself on its motto, "no jacket, no tie, no attitude." But that doesn't mean the Mark is one of those ultra-trendy, shallowly-hip downtown hotels; it's surprisingly and happily quite traditional. All the rooms are spacious, with high ceilings, and decorated in soft tones that give them a warm, homey feel. The suites vary in size and some have terraces, dining areas, and French doors. The bathrooms on the top floors have been newly renovated in marble, but I prefer the look of the familiar white and black tile bathrooms on the lower floors. Off the small lobby is the intimate, cozy, and very popular **Mark's Bar,** and Mark's restaurant, also off the lobby, is an underrated pleasure.

See map p. 111. 25 E. 77th St. (between Madison and Fifth avenues). One block from Central Park. ☎ *800-THEMARK or 212-744/4300. Fax: 212-744-2749.* www.mandarin oriental.com/themark. *Subway: 6 to 77th Street. Parking: $45. Rack rates: $545–$695 double. AE, DC, MC, V.*

The Melrose Hotel
$$$ Upper East Side

Formerly a women-only hotel, men now can also enjoy staying at this lovely old building with its twin Deco towers that stand out majestically amongst the glass and steel of the Upper East Side. From a dorm-size petite room to a stately, sprawling tower suite, the range of rooms and the corresponding

Country in the city

If you're looking for an alternative to the quintessential huge New York hotel or if you want a taste of urban hominess where you may actually meet your innkeeper, you have a number of options to consider.

On the steep end of the economic scale, but definitely worth the price if authentic 19th century Victorian romance is what you're seeking, is the fabulous **Inn at Irving Place**, 56 Irving Place (between 17th and 18th streets), (☎ 800-685-1447 or 212-533-4600; www.innatirving.com). (See the "Midtown Hotels" map.) Located in a 170-year-old townhouse, rates range from $325 to $495. The 12 rooms are all named after late 19th century or early 20th century New Yorkers, many inspired by the works of Edith Wharton and Henry James. Complimentary breakfast is served each morning in Lady Mendl's parlor, where, if the weather is nippy, you can find a comforting fire roaring.

Breakfast prepared by culinary students at the New School is one of the highlights of the **Inn on 23rd**, 131 W. 23rd St. (between Sixth and Seventh avenues), (☎ 877-387-2323 or 212-463-0330; www.innon23rd.com). (See the "Midtown Hotels" map.) Each of the inn's 14 rooms, which range in price from $179 to $359, were distinctly decorated by the personable owners, Annette and Barry Fisherman, with items they've collected from their travels over the years.

The first home of the Gay Men's Health Crisis, an 1850 brownstone in the heart of Chelsea, is now the charming **Colonial House Inn**, 318 W. 22nd St. (between Eighth and Ninth avenues), (☎ 800-689-3779 or 212-243-9669; www.colonialhouseinn.com). (See the "Midtown Hotels" map.) This 20-room, four-story walk-up caters to a largely gay and lesbian clientele, but everybody is welcome, and straight couples are a common sight. Some rooms have shared bathrooms; deluxe rooms have private bathrooms, and some have working fireplaces. The inn has a roof deck with a clothing optional area. Breakfast is included in the rates, which range from $80 to $125 for a shared bathroom or $125 to $140 for a deluxe.

On the increasingly popular yet still residential Upper West Side is the aptly named **Country Inn the City**, 270 W. 77th St. (between Broadway and West End avenue), (☎ 212-580-4183; www.countryinnthecity.com). (See the "Uptown Hotels" map.) This 1891 townhouse has only four rooms, but all are spacious, quaintly decorated, and come with full kitchens. Rates range from $150 to $210 and include breakfast items stocked in your refrigerator. But you're on your own here in many respects. You won't find a resident innkeeper, and a maid only services your room every few days. Still, if you're the independent sort, the inn's charm makes it an excellent choice.

rates can also be considered eclectic. You can spend as little as $150 a night or as much as $1,700. All rooms, no matter what size, are well kept, offer plenty of light, and are equipped with all the basic amenities. Standard and superior rooms come with small workstations, while the magnificent (and very expensive) tower suites come with terraces. **The Library Bar** in the lobby serves light snacks throughout the day, and the hotel has a "Sign and Dine" program with some highly rated local restaurants. A few blocks from

Bloomingdales, Madison Avenue, and Central Park, The Melrose is a nice mid-range alternative to other more pricey hotels in the area.

See map p. 111. 140 E. 63rd St. (at Lexington Avenue). Three blocks from Bloomingdales. ☎ *800-MELROSE or 212-838-5700. Fax: 212-888-4271.* www.melrose hotel.com. *Subway: F to Lexington Avenue. Parking: $40. Rack rates: $239–$399 double. AE, DC, MC, V.*

The Michelangelo
$$$$ Midtown West

This Italian-owned hotel offers a very welcome dose of Italian hospitality in the heart of midtown Manhattan. As soon as you enter the spacious, beautiful lobby adorned with Italian marble, you feel as if the rapid-fire sight-and-sound assault of Times Square is thousands of miles away. Off the lobby is a nice lounge where coffee and cappuccino are served all day and a complimentary breakfast comprised of pastries and fruit is offered each morning. The rooms come in multiple sizes and are curiously decorated in three different styles: Art-Deco, country French, and neoclassical. I prefer the country French but whatever the style, the good-sized rooms include marble foyers, Italian fabrics, king beds, and two television sets (one in the bathroom). The bathrooms are well maintained and feature deep whirlpool bathtubs. Service is helpful and friendly, which creates a relaxed and casual atmosphere rare in so many New York hotels.

See map p. 108. 152 West 51st St. (between Sixth and Seventh avenues). ☎ *800-237-0990 or 212-765-1900. Fax: 212-541-6604.* www.michelangelohotel.com. *Subway N, R to 49th Street. Valet parking: $38. Rack rates: $295–$535. AE, DC, MC, V.*

The Muse
$$$$ Midtown West

You know that the Muse is something different the moment you step beyond the avowedly modern exterior into the warmly contemporary, mahogany-paneled lobby. Management has done away with the traditional front desk in favor of sit-down concierge service that makes everyone feel like an extra-special, warmly welcomed guest. An attentive bellman will familiarize you with your well-equipped room. In keeping with the hotel's emphasis on "anticipatory service," everything is designed with comfort and functionality in mind. Plusses include plump featherbeds, CD players, cordless phones, business cards personalized with your name and in-house direct-dial line, and handsome, well-outfitted baths.

See map p. 108. 130 W. 46th St. (between Sixth and Seventh avenues). ☎ *877-692-6873 or 212-485-2400. Fax: 212-485-2900.* www.themusehotel.com. *Subway: B, D, F, V to 42nd Street. Parking: $43. Rack rates $229–$399. AE, DC, DISC, MC, V.*

The Peninsula–New York
$$$$$ Midtown East

Once you get beyond admiring the beautiful 1905 landmark building where the Peninsula is housed, you no longer marvel at the past, but are amazed at the state-of-the-art future offered here in the way of service and amenities. The decor is a rich mix of Art Nouveau, vibrant Asian elements, and contemporary art. Every room boasts storage space that is the envy of most New Yorkers and incredible marble bathrooms where a tub-level panel allows you to control the speaker system, answer the phone, and in some rooms, control the bathroom TV. That's part of the hotel's high tech features, which also include a room-wide speaker system and mood lighting; an executive workstation with desk-level inputs, fax, and dual-line speakerphones; a bedside panel for everything, from climate controls to the DO NOT DISTURB sign; even a door-side weather display. A tri-level rooftop health club with a pool may motivate you to get some exercise, or you can stay up on the roof for a cocktail at the spectacular Pen Top Bar.

See map p. 108. 700 Fifth Ave. (at 55th Street). ☎ *800-262-9467 or 212-956-2888. Fax: 212-903-3949.* www.peninsula.com. *Subway: E, F to Fifth Avenue. Valet parking: $45. Rack rates: $590–$750 double. Children under 12 stay free in parent's room. Pets accepted. AE, DC, DISC, MC, V.*

Plaza Athénée
$$$$$ Upper East Side

If money is no object and you don't want to stray too far from Madison Avenue shopping, this elegant, sophisticated hideaway is for you. Antique furniture, hand-painted murals, and the Italian marble floor that adorns the exquisite lobby give the Plaza Athénée a distinctly European feel. Service here is as good as it gets with personalized check-in and an attentive staff. The rooms come in a variety of shapes and sizes, but all are high-ceilinged and spacious with entrance foyers that give them a residential feel. The suites have so much closet space that this New Yorker, used to miniscule apartment closets, was very envious. The marble bathrooms are outfitted with thick robes made exclusively for the hotel; put one on and you may never want to take it off. The lush lounge is appropriately called **Bar Seine** and is a welcome spot for a pre-dinner cocktail. It's not the most technologically advanced hotel — the televisions are old and the rooms don't have VCRs or DVD players. You don't come to the Plaza Athénée for the high-tech life, however; you come to escape it.

See map p. 111. 37 E. 64th St. (between Madison and Park avenues). ☎ *800-447-8800 or 212-734-9100. Fax: 212-772-0958.* www.plaza-athenee.com. *Subway: F to Lexington Avenue. Parking: $48. Rack rates: $495–$675 double. AE, DC, MC, V.*

Red Roof Inn
$ Midtown West

Manhattan's first and only Red Roof Inn offers welcome relief from Midtown's high-priced hotel scene. Both the rooms and bathrooms are more spacious than you may find at most hotels in the category. The high-ceilinged lobby also has an elegant feel, again unusual for a budget hotel. What's more, in-room amenities are better than most competitors', and furnishings are fresh, brand-new, and comfortable. Located very close to the Empire State Building and Herald Square, on a street in Manhattan's

Little Korea, the smell of Korean barbecue permeates the air, which can be good or bad, depending on how you feel about Korean barbecue. Complimentary continental breakfast adds to the good value.

See map p. 108. 6 W. 32nd St. (between Broadway and Fifth Avenue). Two blocks south of the Empire State Building. ☎ *800-567-7720 or 800-RED-ROOF or 212-643-7100. Fax: 212-643-7101.* www.applecorehotels.com *or* www.redroof.com. *Subway: B, D, F, V, N, R to 34th Street. Parking: $22. Rack rates: $109–$300 double. Rates include continental breakfast. Children 13 and under stay free in parent's room. AE, DC, DISC, MC, V.*

The Regency
$$$$$ **Midtown East**

The Regency has been a haven for celebrities and those who aspire to celebrity status for years, but even if you aren't on the cover of a magazine, a stay at the Regency may make you feel like you are. The guestrooms are all huge, featuring king beds or two doubles, a large marble writing desk with an ergonomic chair, and a small eating table. The bathrooms, though not enormous, are equipped with terrycloth robes and a small television. Suites are typically grandiose, ranging from a 450-square-foot executive with two bathrooms and French doors to a grand suite with two bedrooms and two marble bathrooms. The Regency, despite its elegance, is a surprisingly good choice for kids; children under 18 stay free when sharing a room with their parents; rollaway beds are an additional $25 for the stay. The hotel's restaurant, **540 Park Avenue,** is one of the great power breakfast spots in the city while **Feinstein's at The Regency** is considered the gold standard when it comes to cabaret.

See map p. 111. 540 Park Ave. (at 61st Street). One block east of Barney's, and one block west of Bloomingdale's. ☎ *212-759-4100. Fax: 212-826-5674.* www.loewshotels. com. *Subway: 4,5,6, N, R to 59th Street. Parking: $49. Rack rates: $419–$499 doubles. Pets accepted. AE, DC, MC, V.*

The Ritz-Carlton New York, Battery Park
$$$$ **Financial District**

Located on the extreme southern tip of Manhattan, you can't get further downtown than this. And if you don't mind being away from most of the action, no options are better than this one. Not only do you get typically excellent Ritz service, but you also get amazing views of New York Harbor from most guest rooms. You can even use one of the hotel telescopes for close-ups of Lady Liberty. This modern, Art Deco–influenced high-rise is different in style than the English countryside look of most Ritz-Carlton hotels, but that's where the differences end. Here you find the full slate of comforts and services typical of Ritz-Carlton, from Frette-dressed feather beds to the chain's signature Bath Butler, who will draw a scented bath for you in your own deep soaking tub. Standard rooms are all very large and have huge bathrooms, while suites are bigger than most city apartments. The **Rise Bar** on the 14th floor is a special place for a cocktail and a sunset.

See map p. 107. 2 West St. Across the street from Battery Park. ☎ 800-241-3333 or 212-344-0800. Fax: 212-344-3801. www.ritzcarlton.com. *Subway: 4, 5 to Bowling Green. Valet parking: $50. Rack rates: $350–$490 double. AE, DC, DISC, MC, V.*

The Ritz-Carlton New York, Central Park
$$$$$ Midtown West

Not only does this Ritz own one of the best locations in the city, on Central Park South overlooking Central Park, but it also, despite the incredible luxuriousness, manages to maintain a homey elegance that does not intimidate you with stuffy service or an over-abundance of style. Rooms are spacious and decorated in traditional, English countryside-style. Suites are larger than most New York City apartments, and rooms facing Central Park come with telescopes. The marble bathrooms are also oversized and feature a choice of bathrobes — terry or linen — and extravagant Frederic Fekkai bath amenities. For families who can afford the very steep prices, the hotel is extremely kid-friendly. Suites have sofa beds, and cribs and rollaway beds can be brought in. Adults can enjoy the *New York Times* three-star-winning restaurant **Atelier** and the Switzerland-based **La Prairie Spa**.

See map p. 108. 50 Central Park South (at Sixth Avenue). Across the street from Central Park. ☎ 212-308-9100. Fax: 212-207-8831. www.ritzcarlton.com. *Subway N, R, B, Q to 57th Street. Parking: $50. Pets accepted. Rack rates: $650–$975 double. AE, DC, DISC, MC, V.*

Swissôtel New York, The Drake
$$$ Midtown East

This regal hotel has presided over Park Avenue since 1929, and over 75 years later, that classic New York grace remains, now coupled with 21st century technology. The grand lobby is a welcome gathering place for guests, while the spacious and high-ceilinged guest rooms are a luxurious refuge. Every room boasts an extra-large work desk, a club chair or other comfy seating area, and thoughtful touches, like plush robes and an umbrella in the closet for rainy days. The large suites also feature a wet bar with minifridge; some also have entertainment centers, terraces, or other special features. Service and facilities are first rate. Parisian chocolatier Fauchon operates a large, elegant boutique off the lobby that features a tea salon and sparkling glass cases displaying a gorgeous array of chocolates and sweet treats flown in daily.

See map p. 108. 440 Park Ave. (at 56th Street). ☎ 888-737-9477 or 212-421-0900. Fax: 212-371-4190. www.swissotel.com *or* www.raffles.com. *Subway: 4, 5, 6, N, Q, R, W to 59th Street. Pets welcome. Rack rates: $239–$625 double. AE, DC, DISC, MC, V.*

Sofitel New York
$$$ Midtown West

The block of 44th Street between Fifth and Sixth avenues is known as "Hotel Row," and some of the hotels there are historic and extremely elegant. The soaring Sofitel is the newest addition to the block and, in my opinion, the best of the bunch. Thanks to the hotel's entrance and the warm, inviting lobby with check-in tucked off to the side, it feels like you're entering a "grande dame" hotel and not one that is no more than five years old. That's one of the reasons the hotel is so special. The designers have successfully melded modern new-world amenities with European old-world elegance. The rooms are spacious and ultra-comfortable, adorned with art from New York and Paris. The lighting is soft and romantic, and walls and windows are soundproofed. Suites are extra-special, equipped with king beds, two televisions, and pocket doors separating the bedroom from the sitting room. Bathrooms in all rooms are magnificent with separate showers and soaking tubs. A unique gift shop called **Le Petit Bijou** features hard-to-find fun French products, including perfumes and cosmetics, and a stylish French restaurant called **Gaby** bakes delicious croissants for breakfast.

See map p. 108. 45 W. 44th St. (between Fifth and Sixth avenues). One block east of Times Square. ☎ *212-354-8844. Fax: 212-782-2480.* www.sofitel.com. *Subway: B, D, F, V to 42nd Street. Parking: $42. Pets accepted. Rack rates: $229–$429 double. AE, DC, MC, V.*

The Stanhope Park Hyatt New York
$$$$ Upper East Side

Located across from the Metropolitan Museum of Art, The Stanhope is a more than worthy complement to that grand edifice. This elegant, grand dame built in 1926 has been expertly run for the past five years by the Park Hyatt group, providing ultra-attentive service without being stuffy or overbearing. The rooms are all huge and designed in an old-world European style. Bathrooms are also roomy and equally elegant with Italian marble and European fabrics. Suites are even more luxurious and come as large as two bedrooms. The lobby is small with very little seating, but you can find a cozy, clubby reading room off the lobby where coffee is available every morning and an intimate lobby bar that is a popular refuge for many Fifth Avenue residents. To add to the hotel's already romantic feel, every spring and fall, cabaret performer Steve Ross becomes the resident singer and pianist. And with the Met, Guggenheim, Whitney, Cooper Hewitt, and Frick museums all within walking distance, you can't do better if museum-going is your thing.

See map p. 111. 995 Fifth Ave. (at 81st Street). Across the street from the Metropolitan Museum of Art. ☎ *800-233-1234 or 212-774-1234. Fax: 212-517-0088.* www.stanhope park.hyatt.com. *Subway: 6 to 77th Street. Parking: $48. Rack rates: $299–$549 doubles. AE, DC, DISC, MC, V.*

Trump International Hotel & Tower
$$$$$ Upper West Side

From the outside, it's just your typical tall, dark, not very attractive Trump monolith, but spend a night or two inside and you'll immediately forgive and forget the Donald's hokey grandiose taste in design. Experience services like your own Trump Attaché, which is a personal concierge who provides comprehensive services; take advantage of facilities like a 6,000-square-foot health club with a lap pool and full service spa; or order room service from the hotel's signature restaurant, the four-star **Jean Georges**. Enjoy the hotel's impeccable service and first-class facilities from a lovely, yet surprisingly understated high-ceilinged room with floor-to-ceiling windows, some that offer incredible views of Central Park. You also get sumptuous bathrobes, telescopes for taking in the view, and marble bathrooms with Jacuzzi tubs.

See map p. 111. 1 Central Park West (at 60th Street). Across from Central Park. ☎ *888-44-TRUMP or 212-299-1000. Fax: 212-299-1150.* www.trumpintl.com. *Subway: A, B, C, D, 1, 9 to 59th Street/Columbus Circle. Parking: $42. Rack rates: $525–$575 double. AE, DC, DISC, MC, V.*

Thirty Thirty
$$ Midtown East

Formerly the Martha Washington women's hotel, Thirty Thirty is now a hip, budget option for those looking for style and value. The design-conscious tone is set in the loft-like, industrial-modern lobby. Rooms are mostly on the smallish side, but they do the trick for those who intend to spend their days out on the town rather than holed up here. Configurations are split between twin/twins (great for friends), queens, and queen/queens (great for triples, budget-minded quads, or shares who want more spreading-out room). Nice features include cushioned headboards, firm mattresses, two-line phones, nice built-in wardrobes, and spacious, nicely tiled bathrooms. A few larger units have kitchenettes, great if you're staying in town for a while, as you can appreciate the extra room and the fridge. No room service, but delivery is available from nearby restaurants.

See map p. 108. 30 E. 30th St. (between Madison and Park avenues). ☎ *800-497-6028 or 212-689-1900. Fax: 212-689-0023.* www.thirtythirty-nyc.com. *Subway: 6 to 28th Street. Parking: $35, 1 block away. Rack rates: $115–$145 double. AE, DC, DISC, MC, V.*

Travel Inn
$ Midtown West

Though it's a bit too close to the busy, exhaust-choked Lincoln Tunnel, the Travel Inn makes up for its location with extras like a huge outdoor pool and sundeck, a sunny and up-to-date fitness room, and absolutely free parking (with in-and-out privileges!). The interior is clean and reminiscent of a chain motel, but for these prices, you get very good-sized rooms that are comfortably furnished, with extra-firm beds and work desks; even the smallest double is sizable and has a roomy bathroom, and double/doubles make great affordable shares for families. Bathrooms are basic yet clean and fresh-looking. This spot is close to Times Square, many Off-Broadway theaters, and the interesting dining options of nearby Hell's Kitchen.

See map p. 108. 515 W. 42nd St. (just west of Tenth Avenue). ☎ *888-HOTEL58 or 800-869-4630 or 212-695-7171. Fax: 212-967-5025.* www.newyorkhotel.com.

Subway: A, C, E to 42nd Street/Port Authority. Free self-parking. Rack rates: $125–$250 double. Children under 16 stay free in parent's room. AE, DC, DISC, MC, V.

The Westin New York at Times Square
$$$ Midtown West

This high-tech, high-style high-rise has a surprisingly warm and quirky personality. The warmth comes from the inside, from the extra-attentive staff, but the quirkiness is outside, realized in the building's odd, wavy exterior. The 10-color, mostly copper and blue glass edifice looks more like a transplant from Miami Beach than something familiar to the New York City terrain. Though style is big here, there's plenty of substance, too. The rooms are spacious — the Club Rooms and Suites are the biggest. All rooms feature the same amenities, including Westin's truly celestial Heavenly Bed — a custom Simmons Beautyrest pillow-top mattress set dressed in layer upon layer of fluffy down and crisp white linen — and the signature Heavenly Bath, featuring the luxurious two-head shower. The hotel is located on very busy Eighth Avenue, taking up the block between 42nd and 43rd streets; rooms facing 42nd Street and Eighth can be loud.

See map p. 108. 270 W. 43rd St. (at Eighth Avenue). ☎ 800-WESTIN-1 or 888-627-7149 or 212-201-2700. Fax 212-201-2701. www.westinnewyork.com. *Subway: A, C, or E to 42nd Street. Parking: $38. Rack rates: $199–$539 double. AE, DC, DISC, MC, V.*

Waldorf=Astoria and the Waldorf Towers
$$$$ Midtown East

This massive one-square-block Art Deco masterpiece is not only a hotel icon, but a genuine New York City landmark and the epitome of old-school elegance. The lobby is so big and grand, it's reminiscent of Grand Central Station, including having it's own signature clock. With over 1,000 rooms, the pace can be hectic, but after you're in your room, all airy with high ceilings, traditional décor, comfortable linens and beds, and spacious marble bathrooms, you quickly forget about that hectic pace and chill out. If you crave more luxury, book a room on the **Astoria** level, which features huge suites, deluxe bathroom amenities, access to the clubby Astoria Lounge for breakfast or afternoon hors d'oevres, and free entry to the hotel's fitness club (others pay a fee); or for even more opulence, try a suite in the **Waldorf Towers** where most rooms are bigger than New York City apartments. One of three bars in the hotel, **Sir Harry's Bar** (off the lobby) is the main gathering spot for a pre- or post-dinner cocktail, but even better is the **Bull & Bear** with its signature round mahogany bar, classic original cocktail creations, and celebrated steaks.

See map p. 108. 301 Park Ave. (between 49th and 50th streets). ☎ 800-WALDORF or 800-774-1500 or 212-355-3000. Fax: 212-872-7272 (Astoria) or 212-872-4799 (Towers). www.waldorfastoria.com *or* www.waldorf-towers.com. *Subway: 6 to 51st Street. Parking: $45. Rack rates: Waldorf=Astoria, $229–$485 double; Waldorf Towers, $329–$625 double. Children under 18 stay free in parent's room. AE, DC, DISC, MC, V.*

Wall Street Inn
$$ Financial District

This seven-story hotel is ideal for those Wall Street businesspeople who want a Lower Manhattan location without corporate blandness. But it's also a good choice for visitors not working on Wall Street. The lovely early American interiors boast a pleasing freshness. The hotel is warm, comforting, and serene, and the friendly, professional staff offers the kind of personalized service you won't get from a chain. Rooms aren't huge, but the bedding is top-quality and all the conveniences are at hand. Vacationers who don't mind the weekend quiet of Wall Street can find amazing deals once the execs go home; check the Web site for rates.

See map p. 107. 9 S. William St. (at Broad Street). ☎ *212-747-1500. Fax: 212-747-1900.* www.thewallstreetinn.com. *Subway: 2, 3 to Wall St.; 4, 5 to Bowling Green. Parking: $35–$40 nearby. Rack rates: $249–$450 double. Rates include continental breakfast. AE, DC, DISC, MC, V.*

Runner-Up Hotels

The Algonquin

$$$ Midtown West   This turn-of-the-20th-century hotel has a grand literary tradition as headquarters for the acerbic Dorothy Parker and her famed Round Table. The rooms are smallish but have a pampered, old-world feel. *See map p. 108. 59 W. 44th St. (between Fifth and Sixth avenues). (Steps from Times Square, the Theater District, Grand Central Terminal, and Rockefeller Center.)* ☎ *888-304-2047 or 212-840-6800. Fax: 212-944-1419.* www.algonquinhotel.com.

Belvedere Hotel

$$ Midtown West   The rooms here have kitchenettes, and some come with Nintendo, making this Theater District hotel an excellent and affordable choice for families. *See map p. 108. 319 W. 48th St. (between Eighth and Ninth avenues).* ☎ *888-468-3558 or 212-245-7000. Fax: 212-245-4455.* www.newyorkhotel.com.

Hotel Beacon

$$ Upper West Side   With a kitchenette in every room, double beds in most rooms, and great deals on one- and two-bedroom suites, the Beacon on the Upper West Side is one the best values in town, especially for families. *See map p. 111. 2130 Broadway (at 75th Street).* ☎ *800-572-4969 or 212-787-1100. Fax: 212-724-0839.* www.beaconhotel.com.

The Iroquois

$$$ Midtown West   Just a few steps from Times Square and on famed Hotel row, this 1923 building is now one of the best small luxury hotels of the world. *See map p. 108. 49 West 44th St. (between Fifth and Sixth avenues).* ☎ *212-840-3080. Fax 212-719-0006.* www.iroquoisny.com.

The Mansfield

$$$ **Midtown West**   This inviting hotel has a warm, romantic atmosphere and a great location. Check the Web site or call for special promotions, which can make this an amazing deal. *See map p. 108. 12 W. 44th St. (between Fifth and Sixth avenues). (Between Rockefeller Center and the New York Public Library.)* ☎ *800-255-5167 or 212-944-6050. Fax: 212-764-4477.* www.mansfield hotel.com.

The Novotel

$$ **Midtown West**   This 480-room hotel features excellent bargains and spectacular views of Times Square and the Hudson River. The glass-enclosed Café Nicole in the 7th-floor lobby is one of the best spots to watch both the dropping of the ball on New Year's Eve and the Macy's Thanksgiving Day Parade. *See map p. 108. 226 West 52nd St. at Broadway.* ☎ *800-668-6835 or 212-315-0100. Fax: 212-765-5369.* www.novotel.com.

The Plaza Hotel

$$$$ **Midtown West**   This landmark hotel is almost as famous as the Statue of Liberty, and although you can find better options at this price range, if you want the cachet of staying in a landmark, and in a great location, head for The Plaza. *See map p. 108. 768 Fifth Ave. (between 58th and 59th streets on Central Park South).* ☎ *800-441-1414 or 212-759-3000. Fax: 212-759-3167.* www.fairmont.com.

Tribeca Grand Hotel

$$$$ **TriBeCa**   The high-style luxury of the building is a perfect mesh with the trendy, ultra-hip neighborhood where it is located. *See map p. 107. 2 Avenue of the Americas (between White and Walker streets, 1 block north of Franklin Street).* ☎ *877-519-6600 or 212-519-6600. Fax: 212-519-6700.* www.tribeca grand.com.

W New York–Union Square

$$$$ **Gramercy Park**   The magnificent 1911 Guardian Life building overlooking Union Square combines beaux arts grandeur with sleek W modernism to produce terrific results. *See map p. 108. 201 Park Ave. South (at the northeast corner of Union Square).* ☎ *212-253-9119. Fax: 212-253-9229.* www.whotels.com.

Washington Square Hotel

$ **Greenwich Village**   Tiny but clean, well-outfitted rooms with private bathrooms in a great location at bargain prices that include breakfast make this one of the best budget deals downtown. *See map p. 107. 103 Waverly Place (between Fifth and Sixth avenues, off Washington Square, the center of the Village).* ☎ *800-222-0418 or 212-777-9515. Fax: 212-979-8373.* www.wshotel.com.

Index of Accommodations by Neighborhood

Upper West Side

Country Inn the City ($$)
Excelsior Hotel ($$)
Hotel Beacon ($$)
Hotel Newton ($)
The Lucerne ($$)
Trump International Hotel and
    Tower ($$$$$)

Upper East Side

The Carlyle ($$$$$)
The Mark ($$$$)
Melrose Hotel ($$$)
Plaza Athénée ($$$$$)
The Stanhope Park Hyatt
    New York ($$$$)

Midtown East

Affinia Dumont ($$$)
The Benjamin ($$$$)
Habitat Hotel ($)
Le Marquis ($$$)
The Library ($$$)
The Peninsula ($$$$$)
Swissôtel The Drake ($$$)
Thirty Thirty ($$)
The Waldorf=Astoria and
    Waldorf Towers ($$$)

Midtown West

The Algonquin ($$$)
Belvedere Hotel ($$)
Broadway Inn ($$)
Casablanca Hotel ($$)
Doubletree Guest Suites
    Times Square ($$$)
Herald Square Hotel ($)

Hotel Metro ($$)
Iroquois Hotel ($$$)
Le Parker Meridien ($$$$)
The Mansfield ($$$)
The Michelangelo ($$$$)
The Muse ($$$$)
Novotel New York ($$)
The Plaza Hotel ($$$$)
Red Roof Inn ($)
The Ritz-Carlton New York,
    Central Park ($$$$$)
Sofitel ($$$)
Travel Inn ($)
Westin New York at Times Square ($$$)

Chelsea/Flatiron District/ Gramercy Park

Chelsea Lodge ($)
Colonial House Inn ($)
Gershwin Hotel ($)
Hotel Giraffe ($$$$)
Inn at Irving Place ($$$$)
Inn on 23rd Street ($$$)
W New York–Union Square ($$$$)

Greenwich Village/SoHo

Larchmont Hotel ($)
Washington Square Hotel ($$)

TriBeCa/Financial District/ South Street Seaport

Cosmopolitan Hotel–Tribeca ($)
The Ritz-Carlton New York,
    Battery Park ($$$$)
Tribeca Grand ($$$$)
Wall Street Inn ($$)

Index of Accommodations by Price

$$$$$ ($450 and up)

The Carlyle (Upper East Side)
The Mark (Upper East Side)
Plaza Athénée (Upper East Side)

The Ritz-Carlton New York, Central
    Park (Midtown West)
The Peninsula (Midtown East)
Trump International Hotel and Tower
    (Upper West Side)

$$$$ ($350–$450)

The Benjamin (Midtown East)
Hotel Giraffe (Flatiron District)
Le Parker Meridien (Midtown West)
The Inn at Irving Place
  (Gramercy Park)
The Michelangelo (Midtown West)
The Muse (Midtown West)
The Plaza (Midtown East)
The Ritz-Carlton New York, Battery
  Park (Financial District)
The Stanhope Park Hyatt New York
  (Upper East Side)
Tribeca Grand (TriBeCa)
W New York–Union Square
  (Gramercy Park)
The Waldorf=Astoria and Waldorf
  Towers (Midtown East)

$$$ ($250–$350)

Affinia Dumont (Midtown East)
The Algonquin (Midtown West)
Doubletree Guest Suites Times Square
  (Midtown West)
The Inn on 23rd Street (Chelsea)
The Iroquois (Midtown West)
Le Marquis (Midtown East)
The Library (Midtown East)
The Mansfield (Midtown West)
Melrose Hotel (Upper East Side)
Novotel New York (Midtown West)
Sofitel (Midtown West)

Swissôtel Drake (Midtown East)
Westin New York at Times Square
  (Midtown West)

$$ ($150–$250)

Belvedere Hotel (Midtown West)
Broadway Inn (Midtown West)
Casablanca (Midtown West)
Country Inn the City
  (Upper West Side)
Excelsior Hotel (Upper West Side)
Hotel Beacon (Upper West Side)
Hotel Metro (Midtown West)
The Lucerne (Upper West Side)
Novotel New York (Midtown West)
Thirty Thirty (Midtown East)
Wall Street Inn (Financial District)

$ ($85–$150

Chelsea Lodge (Chelsea)
Colonial House Inn (Chelsea)
Cosmopolitan Hotel–Tribeca
  (TriBeCa)
Habitat Hotel (Midtown East)
Hotel Newton (Upper West Side)
Gershwin Hotel (Flatiron District)
Larchmont Hotel (Greenwich Village)
Red Roof Inn (Midtown West)
Travel Inn (Midtown West)
Washington Square Hotel
  (Greenwich Village)

Chapter 10

Dining and Snacking in New York City

. . . .

In This Chapter

▶ Scoring a reservation at a hot restaurant
▶ Finding out about your dining options
▶ Getting the most out of your food budget
▶ Listing the top New York City restaurants

. . . .

Y ou can't do better than New York for the dining possibilities;
the city is bursting with restaurants of every type and category.
You could eat out every night of the year and still have a mountain of
restaurants to climb before you've been to them all. And over the past
few years, the restaurant scene in New York has become as vibrant and
as high profile as it ever was. Chefs are as famous as supermodels and
rock stars, and when a new restaurant opens, the pomp and circum-
stance sometimes equals the opening of a major Broadway show. What
I'm trying to say is that eating out in New York is a very big deal —
something many New Yorkers take seriously.

Although I'm intrigued by the food-mania that has gripped Gotham,
maybe we've taken it a bit too far (as we always seem to). Food and
eating should not be taken *too* seriously. I'm not completely down on
it, however. The upside of this mania has been an increase in quality
restaurants.

The variety of restaurants in New York is staggering; from American
to multi-ethnic, from a simple diner to an elegant four-star palace. All
that variety can be intimidating, but it shouldn't be. You know what
you like; now you just need to know where to find it.

Getting the Dish on the Local Scene

Unless the restaurant you're interested in doesn't take reservations,
it always pays to make a reservation, especially if your party is bigger
than two. You've got nothing to lose by calling ahead. If you're booking

dinner on a weekend night, it's a good idea to call a few days in advance if you can. And if you're really set on visiting one very special restaurant, let's say Chanterelle, call well in advance, preferably before you even arrive in the city.

If you've tried and still can't get a reservation for the dates you want, try for an early dinner, between 5 and 6 p.m., or a later one, after 9 p.m. That's all you may get offered anyway, so if, for example, your heart is set on dining at Babbo while you're in town, you may have to take what's offered.

Most top places start taking reservations 30 days in advance, so if you want to eat at a hot restaurant at a popular hour — Saturday at 8 p.m., say, at Jean-Georges — mark your calendar and start dialing 30 days prior at 9 a.m. If you're booking a holiday dinner, call even earlier. Many of the top restaurants require you to leave a credit card number when making a reservation, and if you don't show up, they penalize you with a service charge.

Smoking

Since the tough new no-smoking laws were imposed in 2003, basically you can't light up in any restaurant anywhere in the city — with the exception of some outdoor spaces.

Other restaurant sources

The best online restaurant sources are:

- ✔ **Citysearch** (www.citysearch.com): Runs a restaurant page that's updated weekly as part of its comprehensive offerings, including reader reviews.

- ✔ **New York Metro** (www.newyorkmetro.com): The online arm of weekly *New York* magazine.

- ✔ **New York Today** (www.nytoday.com): The *New York Times'* arts and lifestyle site where you can access a database of the paper's very influential restaurant reviews.

- ✔ **Village Voice** (www.villagevoice.com): Especially good for the cheap eats reviews by Robert Sietsema.

The best online source for the serious foodie is www.chowhound.com, a national Web site with message boards in local areas, including New York, where you can make an inquiry about a certain restaurant, type of food, or location, and within a few hours, you may have five or more very informative responses.

The *Zagat Survey* (www.zagat.com), though far from my favorite source because its reviews are often popularity contests, is still a good online database; consider using it as a starting point. The guide, which has made a name for itself by rating restaurants based on extensive diner surveys, maintains a searchable database. It is, however, now charging a fee to access the online information, which, with all the other better online options available, is not worth it (in my opinion). Better just to buy the book.

And if you do want a book reference to have on hand while you're in the city, I recommend the colorful, reviewer-written *Time Out New York: Eating & Drinking* guide, which I find to be more comprehensive, candid, and descriptive than Zagat's. If you don't feel the need for a big ol' book, stop at any newsstand for a copy of the slick weekly *Time Out New York;* the "Eat Out" section includes listings for *TONY*'s 100 Favorite Restaurants in every issue, as well as coverage of new openings and dining trends. Weekly *New York* magazine also maintains extensive restaurant listings in the "Cue" section at the back of the magazine.

Trimming the fat from your budget

Yes, prices in New York are high, but you can eat well without spending a lot of money if you follow a few simple rules — and you never need to sacrifice quality. The best and most famous restaurants are expensive, but you don't need to pay through the nose if you keep these tips in mind.

- ✓ **Go for the prix fixe menu at top restaurants.** Usually, the best deals are at lunch, when many of the best restaurants in New York offer a special deal — a three-course meal for $20.

- ✓ **They get you with the drinks.** You may find yourself saying this after you look at your check. And it's true; that's where restaurants make their money. If you insist on a bottle of wine with dinner, then it's gonna cost you. If you can do without (believe me, food tastes just as good without a $60 bottle of wine), then have your wine at happy hour before dinner.

- ✓ **Eat at ethnic restaurants.** Most authentic ethnic restaurants are in the $ category. (See the table below.)

- ✓ **Skip the national fast-food chains and go for local food.** It may be fast, but it's not as cheap as advertised, and with so many good, inexpensive local restaurants, you really have no excuse for eating at a national fast food chain while in New York.

- ✓ **Order takeout.** Thousands of takeout places all over Manhattan deliver to hotel rooms for free, and they offer food more varied and far less expensive than room service. (Don't forget to tip the delivery person.)

- ✓ **Avoid eating in the big tourist centers like Times Square and Rockefeller Center.** Not only are food prices jacked up in these areas, it's usually not very good. Try to plan your meals and snacks for before or after you visit the big tourist sights, or in adjacent neighborhoods, rather than busy hubs of visitor activity.

For the listings below I offer two price indicators for each restaurant: a number of dollar signs, which gives you an idea of what a complete meal

Great fixed-price deals at top restaurants

New York's popular **Restaurant Week,** held every January and June, pioneered the idea of offering prix fixe (fixed price) lunches at a price mirroring the digits of the current year ($20.04 in 2004, $20.05 in 2005, and so on). Happily, some of the best restaurants in New York have adopted the idea; even better, several have extended the offer throughout the year, making it possible to have a superior culinary experience for an affordable price year-round. Check with individual restaurants to see if they offer a prix fixe lunch special.

costs; and the price range of the entrees on the menu. Those two pieces of information can help you choose a place that's right for you and your budget.

One dollar sign ($) means inexpensive, and five dollar signs ($$$$$ — the maximum) means extravagant. The symbols reflect what one person can expect to pay for an appetizer, entree, dessert, one drink, tax, and tip. Here's a more complete key to the dollar-sign ratings that I use in this chapter:

Dollar Sign(s)	*Price Range*
$	= Under $25
$$	= $25–$35
$$$	= $35–$50
$$$$	= $55–$70
$$$$$	= Over $70

Our dollar signs give you a rough idea of how much a meal will cost, but don't use them as the only factor in your decision; restaurants may offer prix fixe meals or other deals that aren't reflected in their price rankings.

As you peruse the listings, check the maps in this chapter to pinpoint a restaurant's location. The indexes at the end of this chapter can help you select a restaurant by location, cuisine, or price.

New York's Best Restaurants

Aix
$$$$ **Upper West Side**   **MODERN FRENCH**

This smartly designed, airy, and comfortable tri-level restaurant offers some surprisingly fresh twists on the traditional cuisine of Provence. Take a classic dish like the vegetable soup pistou; add fresh raw sardines, and it not only works, it enhances the soup's flavor greatly. The only mistake I encountered on the menu was the bland gnocchi with Jerusalem artichoke and black truffle cream. Desserts are adventurous and may not be for everyone, but it's not often you have the chance to experience Provence salad (sugared green tomatoes and celery topped with mint sorbet) or a licorice pannacotta. Despite the crowds, Aix's service is personable; waitresses in dowdy brown uniforms are cheerfully helpful, but the restaurant is loud, so don't expect intimacy.

See map p. 140. 2398 Broadway (at 88th Street). ☎ 212-874-7400. www.aixnyc.com. *Reservations highly recommended. Subway: 1, 9 to 86th Street. Main courses: $14–$28. AE, MC, V. Open: Sun–Thurs 5:30–10:30 p.m., Fri–Sat 5:30–11 p.m.*

Angelica Kitchen
$ East Village   ORGANIC VEGETARIAN

You don't have to be a vegetarian or vegan to enjoy the delicious fare served here. Angelica Kitchen offers a cheese-free onion soup that matches any French restaurant's and many excellent fruit-based desserts as well. Try the "daily seasonal creation" or the lunch or dinner special, with soup, salad, homemade bread, and spread — the cornbread is outstanding. One specialty is the Dragon Bowl: a healthy helping of rice or noodles and vegetables (a little of everything).

See map p. 136. 300 E. 12th St. (between First and Second avenues). ☎ 212-228-2909. Reservations accepted for parties of 6 or more on Mon–Thurs. Subway: L/N/ Q/R/W/4/5/6 train to 14th Street/Union Square stop, walk east on 14th Street to Second Avenue, turn right, and turn left on 12th Street. Main courses: $7–$15. No credit cards. Open: Daily 11:30 a.m.–10:30 p.m.

Aquavit
$$$$ Midtown West   SCANDINAVIAN

A clamoring for Scandinavian food in New York never existed before Aquavit arrived. The fact that the food is prepared by the immensely talented chef Marcus Samuelsson may have made Aquavit all the rage. Or maybe the incredible food tastes even better because it's served in a magnificent townhouse, in a dining room complete with birch trees and an indoor waterfall. I daydream about the herring plate: four types of herring accompanied by a tiny glass of Aquavit, a distilled liquor not unlike vodka that's flavored with fruit and spices, and a frosty Carlsberg beer. The smorgasbord is a specialty as well: three types of herring, smoked salmon, gravlax, shrimp, and Swedish meatballs with lingonberries. If you can't get into the main dining room or you want a more affordable option, upstairs is a moderately priced cafe.

At press time I heard disturbingly strong murmurs that Aquavit was closing at this location. Check the Web site below for more information.

See map p. 138. 13 W. 54th St. (between Fifth and Sixth avenues). ☎ 212-307-7311. www.aquavit.org. *Reservations recommended. Subway: E, F to Fifth Avenue. Cafe: Main courses $9–$20; 3-course fixed-price meal $20 at lunch, $32 at dinner.*

Main dining room: Fixed-price meal $35 at lunch, $65 at dinner ($39 for vegetarians); 3-course pre-theater dinner (5:30–6:15 p.m.) $39. Tasting menus: $48 at lunch, $85 at dinner ($58 for vegetarians). Supplement for paired wines: $25 at lunch, $35 at dinner. AE, DC, MC, V. Open: Daily noon–2:30 p.m. and 5:30–10:30 p.m.

Atelier
$$$$$ Midtown West   FRENCH

Housed in The Ritz-Carlton New York, Central Park, the dining room is so elegant you may want to tread lightly in fear that even a bit of heavy breathing may shatter the delicate ambience. Once seated, note that the food, in both taste and preparation, matches that elegant mood. Start with bluefin tuna or diver scallops tartare seasoned in Osetra caviar; then follow up with spiced venison medallions with huckleberry jus. On a final, sweet note, end with a creation of rice crispies, peanut ice cream, chocolate, and condensed milk cappuccino. The wine list offers more than 1,000 varieties, and the sommelier helps pair your wine with your meal. At these prices, Atelier is not your everyday dining experience, but the staff seems to know that and provides extra-attentive service.

See map p. 138. 50 Central Park South (at Sixth Avenue). ☎ 212-521-6125. Reservations recommended. Subway: N, R, W to 57th Street. Lunch: 3-course prix fixe $35, 4-course $45. Dinner: 3-course prix fixe $72. Chef tasting menu: $128. Seasonal tasting menu: $95. AE, MC, V. Open: Mon–Sat noon–2 p.m., 6:30–10 p.m.; Sunday brunch: 10:30 a.m.–2:30 p.m., 6:30–8:30 p.m. Jackets required for men at dinner.

Babbo
$$$$ Greenwich Village   NORTHERN ITALIAN

Celebrated television chef "Molto" Mario Batali has a number of restaurants in New York, but Babbo is his centerpiece. The feeling here is relaxed and comfortable, and the service is smart and friendly. The menu, as is Batali's trademark, is adventurous, and here he has reinvented the notion of antipasti with such starters as fresh anchovies beautifully marinated in lobster oil and warm tripe "alla parmigiana." The pastas are equally creative; try the spicy lamb sausage in delicate clouds called mint love letters. The *secondi* menu features such wonders as tender fennel-dusted sweetbreads; smoky grilled quail in a gamey but heavenly fig and duck liver vinaigrette; and spicy two-minute calamari, a paragon of culinary simplicity. The sommelier can help you choose from the unusual but excellent wine list, all Italian and well priced. You need to book ahead — preferably well ahead, like before you leave home — to guarantee a comfortable table.

See map p. 136. 110 Waverly Place (just east of Sixth Avenue). ☎ 212-777-0303. www.babbonyc.com. Reservations highly recommended. Subway: A, C, E, F, B, D to 4th Street (use 8th Street exit). Main courses: pastas $17–$21 (most under $21); meats and fish $23–$29. AE, MC, V. Open: Mon–Sat 5:30–11:30 p.m., Sun 5–11 p.m.

Downtown Dining

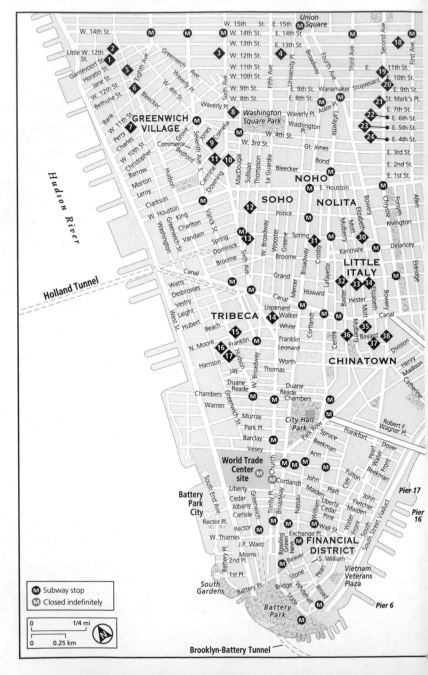

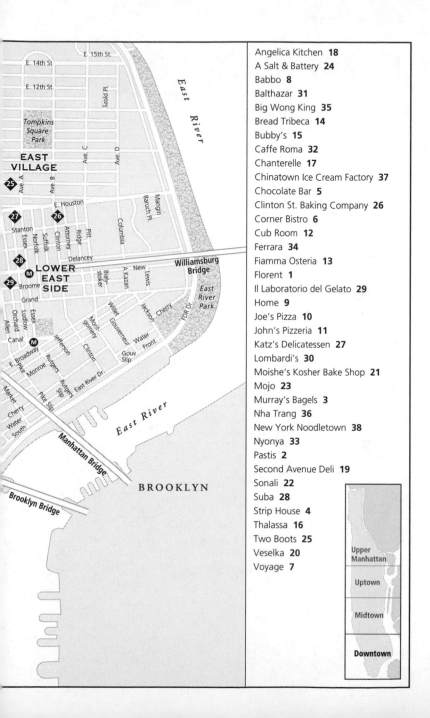

Angelica Kitchen **18**
A Salt & Battery **24**
Babbo **8**
Balthazar **31**
Big Wong King **35**
Bread Tribeca **14**
Bubby's **15**
Caffe Roma **32**
Chanterelle **17**
Chinatown Ice Cream Factory **37**
Chocolate Bar **5**
Clinton St. Baking Company **26**
Corner Bistro **6**
Cub Room **12**
Ferrara **34**
Fiamma Osteria **13**
Florent **1**
Il Laboratorio del Gelato **29**
Home **9**
Joe's Pizza **10**
John's Pizzeria **11**
Katz's Delicatessen **27**
Lombardi's **30**
Moishe's Kosher Bake Shop **21**
Mojo **23**
Murray's Bagels **3**
Nha Trang **36**
New York Noodletown **38**
Nyonya **33**
Pastis **2**
Second Avenue Deli **19**
Sonali **22**
Suba **28**
Strip House **4**
Thalassa **16**
Two Boots **25**
Veselka **20**
Voyage **7**

Midtown Dining

Afghan Kebab House **4**
Aquavit **30**
Atelier **33**
Biltmore Room **13**
Blue Smoke **21**
Burger Joint **32**
Buttercup Bakery **27**
Carmine's **9**
Carnegie Deli **2**
Churrascaria Plataforma **6**
Cold Stone Creamery **11**
Curry in a Hurry **22**
db Bistro Moderne **24**
Dos Caminos **20**
Eleven Madison Park **18**
Ess-A-Bagel **17, 28**
F&B Gudtfood **16**
Grand Sichuan International **14**
Hallo! Berlin **5**
Island Burgers and Shakes **4**
John's Pizzeria **10**
Joseph's **25**
Mandoo Bar **23**
Mickey Mantle's **34**
Molyvos **1**
Murray's Bagels **15**
Norma's **31**
Pampano **26**
P.J. Clarke's **31**
Prime Burger **29**
rm **35**
Sapporo **7**
Siam Inn **3**
Tamarind **18**
Uncle Jack's Steakhouse **12**
Virgil's Real BBQ **8**

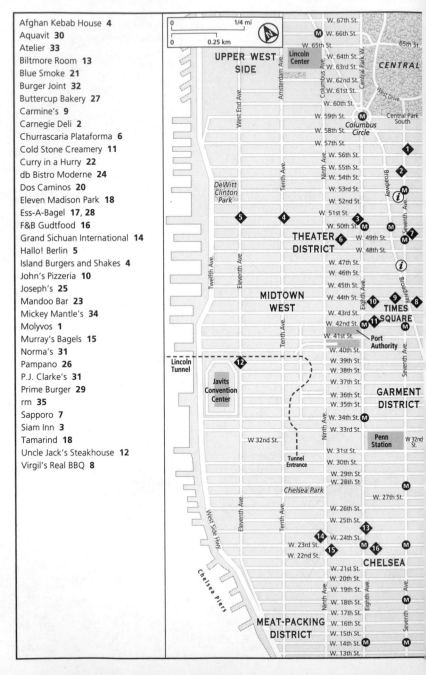

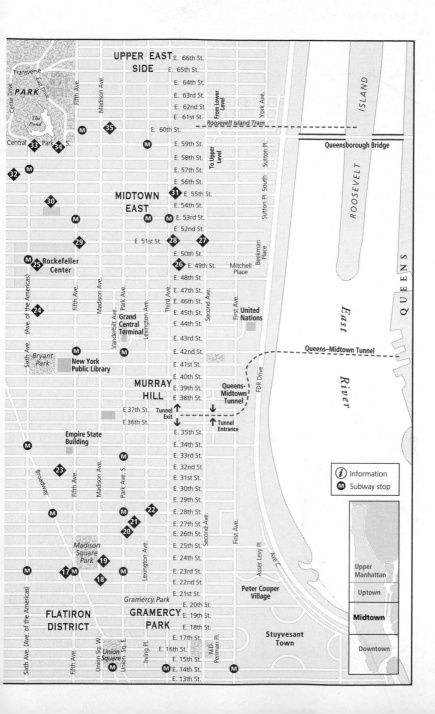

UPPER EAST SIDE

E. 66th St.
E. 65th St.
E. 64th St.
E. 63rd St.
E. 62nd St.
E. 61st St.
E. 60th St.
E. 59th St.
E. 58th St.
E. 57th St.
E. 56th St.
E. 55th St.
E. 54th St.
E. 53rd St.
E. 52nd St.
E. 51st St.
E. 50th St.
E. 49th St.
E. 48th St.
E. 47th St.
E. 46th St.
E. 45th St.
E. 44th St.
E. 43rd St.
E. 42nd St.
E. 41st St.
E. 40th St.
E. 39th St.
E. 38th St.
E 37th St.
E 36th St.
E. 35th St.
E. 34th St.
E. 33rd St.
E. 32nd St.
E. 31st St.
E. 30th St.
E. 29th St.
E. 28th St.
E. 27th St.
E. 26th St.
E. 25th St.
E. 24th St.
E. 23rd St.
E. 22nd St.
E. 21st St.
E. 20th St.
E. 19th St.
E. 18th St.
E. 17th St.
E. 16th St.
E. 15th St.
E. 14th St.
E. 13th St.

Transverse
PARK
Center Drive
East Drive
The Pond
Central Park S.

Fifth Ave.
Madison Ave.
Park Ave.

MIDTOWN EAST

Rockefeller Center
Sixth Ave. (Ave. of the Americas)
Fifth Ave.
Madison Ave.
Vanderbilt Ave.
Lexington Ave.
Third Ave.
Second Ave.
First Ave.

Grand Central Terminal

Bryant Park
New York Public Library

MURRAY HILL

Empire State Building

Broadway
Madison Avenue
Park Ave. S.

Madison Square Park

FLATIRON DISTRICT

Sixth Ave. (Ave. of the Americas)
Fifth Ave.
Union Sq. W
Union Sq. E.
Irving Pl.

Union Square

GRAMERCY PARK

Gramercy Park

N.D. Perlman Pl.

From Lower Level
Roosevelt Island Tram
To Upper Level

York Ave.
Sutton Pl.
Sutton Pl. South
Beekman Place
Mitchell Place
First Ave.
Second Ave.

Queensborough Bridge

ISLAND

ROOSEVELT

QUEENS

East River

United Nations

Queens–Midtown Tunnel

FDR Drive

Queens–Midtown Tunnel

Tunnel Exit
Tunnel Entrance

Asser Levy Pl.
Ave. C

Peter Cooper Village

Stuyvesant Town

(i) Information
Ⓜ Subway stop

Upper Manhattan
Uptown
Midtown
Downtown

33 34 35 32 30 31 29 28 27 26 25 24 23 22 21 20 19 18 17

Uptown Dining

Absolute Bagels **1**
Aix **4**
Artie's Delicatessen **8**
Barney Greengrass,
  the Sturgeon King **5**
Big Nick's Burger Joint **11**
Café des Artistes **15**
Carmine's **3**
Celeste **6**
'Cesca **13**
Cold Stone Creamery **23**
Crumbs **12**
Daniel **21**
Flor de Mayo **2**
E.J.'s Luncheonette **9**
Good Enough to Eat **7**
Gray's Papaya **14**
H&H Bagels **10**
Jean-Georges **18**
John's Pizzeria **20**
Papaya King **22**
Rosa Mexicano **17**
Sal & Carmine's **2**
Serendipity 3 **19**
Tavern on the Green **16**

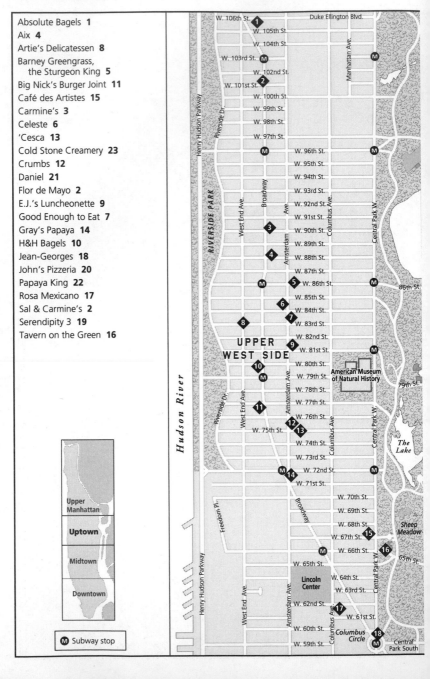

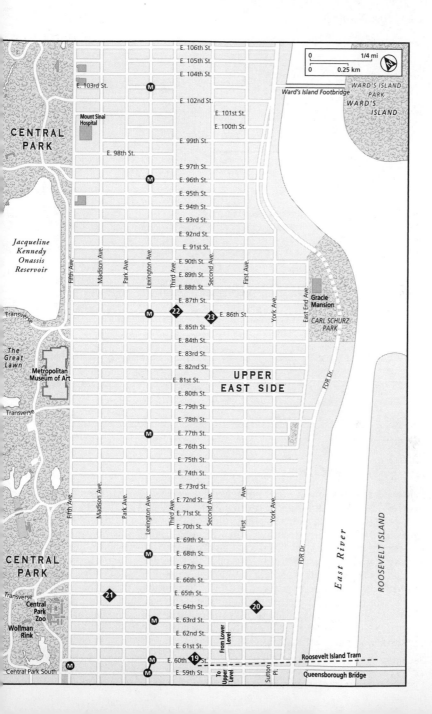

Brooklyn Dining

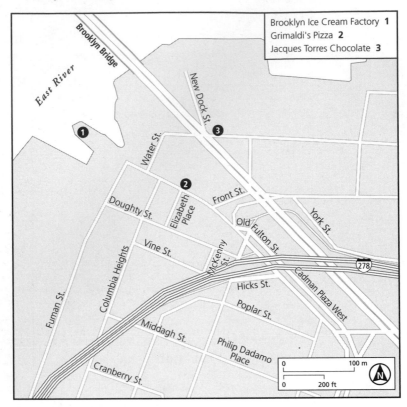

Brooklyn Ice Cream Factory **1**
Grimaldi's Pizza **2**
Jacques Torres Chocolate **3**

Balthazar
$$$ SoHo   FRENCH BISTRO

You want the authentic Parisian brasserie experience without flying to France? Visit the stunningly gorgeous Balthazar. The classic French bistro fare, ranging from steak frites and grilled calf's liver to a duck shepherd's pie and a brook trout with honey mustard glaze, is surprisingly affordable and excellently prepared. The expansive raw bar offerings are beautifully displayed and make a worthy splurge. That's the good news. The bad news is that this is the loudest restaurant I've ever been in, so practice sign language if you plan to converse while dining. The long mirrored bar is a hopping spot unto itself that attracts beautiful people galore. To diminish the noise levels somewhat, come during the off hours — for breakfast, lunch, or a midday meal. The adjacent boulangerie sells fresh-baked breads, desserts, and sandwiches to go.

See map p. 136. 80 Spring St. (at Crosby Street, 1 block east of Broadway).
☎ *212-965-1785. Reservations highly recommended (some walk-ins accepted).*

Subway: 6 to Spring Street; N, R to Prince Street. Main courses: $11–$20 at lunch, $12–$32 at dinner. AE, MC, V. Open: Mon–Thurs 7:30 a.m.–1:30 a.m., Fri–Sat 7:30 a.m.–2:00 a.m., Sun 7:30 a.m.–midnight.

The Biltmore Room
$$$$ Chelsea ASIAN FUSION

The name Biltmore Room conjures up a retro, noirish feel, but besides the dazzling decor (much of it salvaged from the old Biltmore Hotel), there's nothing retro or noirish about the food here. Start with an original cocktail like "The Way of the Dragon," with vodka, lime juice, honey, mint, and a blast of hot pepper, and you know you're onto something unique. Fiery is a good word to describe much of the cuisine, especially the Tataki of Blue Fin Tuna starter, with a tear-inducing cayenne pepper oil that is balanced by cucumber ginger sorbet. For those who are heat-shy, try the crisp squash blossoms stuffed with crab in a mild mango chili dipping sauce. The main dishes also display an Asian influence, especially the excellent Indian-spiced wild king salmon and the Thai-marinated free-range chicken. For dessert, those passionate about chocolate are not disappointed by the warm chocolate tort, while the passion fruit souffle is worth the extra wait. Seating is not the most comfortable — you're close to your neighbors no matter where you're seated and don't expect whispered conversation — and the room can get very cacophonous. Know that going in, and you can enjoy the room's visual splendor while dining on the chef's innovatively tangy creations.

See map p. 138 290 Eighth Ave. (between 24th and 25th streets). ☎ 212-807-0011. Reservations recommended. C, E to 23rd Street. Main Courses: $27–$35. AE, MC, V. Open: Mon–Thurs 6–10:30 p.m., Fri–Sat 6–11:30 p.m.

Blue Smoke
$$ Flatiron District BARBECUE/SOUTHERN

From New York restaurant impressario (Union Square Cafe, Gramercy Tavern) Danny Meyer comes this effort to reproduce the barbecue he grew up on in St. Louis. The ribs I tasted, which come in three varieties (Memphis baby backs, salt-and-pepper dry rubbed, and St. Louis style) were all tender to the bone, but the St. Louis variety, glazed in a mild barbecue sauce, was the clear winner. Though the meats are the attraction here, the side dishes are as good as I've tasted anywhere, especially the collard greens, speckled with bits of pork, and the slow-cooked green beans, oozing with flavor. The house Blue Smoke ale is the perfect hearty complement to the tangy food. This heartland barbecue joint, in typical Meyer fashion, is perfectly run.

See map p. 138 116 E. 27th St. (between Park and Lexington avenues). ☎ 212-447-7733. www.bluesmoke.com. Reservations suggested. Subway: 6 to 28th Street. Main courses: $10–$22. AE, DC, DISC, MC, V. Open: Daily 11:30 a.m.– 11 p.m.; Late-night menu: Wed–Sat 11 p.m.–1 a.m.

Bread Tribeca
$$$ TriBeCa NORTHERN ITALIAN

It's about time a New York restaurant recognized the distinctive, seafood-rich cuisine of Liguria. And even better that the restaurant is the very good Bread Tribeca. Two staples of the region are done perfectly here: the *fritto misto*, a mixture of fried fish such as calamari, cod, and mussels along with wedges of vegetables; and *zuppa de pesce*, assorted seafood in a saffron-tomato sauce. The homemade pastas, another trademark of Ligurian food, are also excellent. Don't miss the *pansotti*, ravioli-like dumplings served with a walnut sauce, and the *taglierini*, a spaghetti-like pasta accompanied by pesto with haricots verts and potatoes. A wood-burning oven turns out excellent thin-crust pizzas and roasted meats. The breads are superb, especially a baguette slathered with a remarkable sardine, tomato, and peperoncino mixture. Most of the tables are communal so if the restaurant is crowded don't expect intimacy. The 50-inch television above the bar is often a distraction, not a complement, to the food.

See map p. 136. 301 Church St. (at Walker Street). ☎ *212-334-8282. Reservations recommended. Subway: A, C, E to Canal Street. Main courses: $13–$23. AE, DC, DISC, MC, V. Open: Daily 11:30 p.m.–5 p.m., Sun–Thurs 5:30 p.m.–11 p.m., Fri–Sat 5:30 p.m.–12 a.m.*

Bubby's
$$ TriBeCa AMERICAN

Brave the lines to get in, squeeze into one of the close tables, try to block out the loud noise, and as soon as you begin to eat Bubby's comfort food, you immediately forget all that discomfort. Whether it's the slow-cooked pulled-pork barbecue; the magnificent, lighter than air meatloaf; or the buttermilk fried half chicken; coupled with sides like collard greens, sautéed spinach, macaroni and cheese, and baked beans, Bubby's dishes define comfort. Save room for the desserts, especially the homemade pies; one taste of the chocolate peanut butter pie immediately brings on a flood of happy childhood flashbacks. Breakfast is big here and lasts well into the middle of the day. Brunch is a big thing in trendy TriBeCa and on weekends the waits can get very lengthy. Celebrities need comfort too, and you may spot one or two at Bubby's seeking anonymity and down-home chow.

See map p. 136. 120 Hudson St. (at N. Moore Street). ☎ *212-219-0666.* www. bubbys.com. *Reservations recommended for dinner (not accepted for brunch). Subway: 1, 9 to Franklin Street. Main courses: $2–$7 at breakfast, brunch, and lunch, $9–$19 at dinner. AE, DC, DISC, MC, V. Open: Mon–Thurs 8 a.m.–11 p.m., Fri 8 p.m.–midnight, Sat 9 a.m.–4:30 p.m. and 6 p.m.–midnight, Sun 9 a.m.–10 p.m.*

Café des Artistes
$$$$$ Upper West Side FRENCH

One of the oldest restaurants in Manhattan, Café des Artistes was established in 1917, and with its gorgeous "wood nymph" murals painted in the 1930s, it's still one of the most romantic restaurants in the city. The solid, French country food served is very expensive, but this is a place to splurge, to soak in not only the history but the romantic aura exuding from those murals. You don't find any fancy twists on French cooking here, and if they appear on the menu, stick with the old favorites, such as the starters like salmon five ways or snails; or entrées like Dover sole with brown butter sauce, roasted duck, or the challengingly hearty stew *pot au feu,* complete with marrow bone. For dessert, the chocolate bread pudding is a treat, while the hot fudge Napoleon is truly, as described by my waiter, a "killer." The waiters here have been around the block a few times, so service is refreshingly old school. The restaurant does a brisk, pre-Lincoln Center business, so if you want intimacy and romance (the main reason to come here), reserve before or after the rush.

See map p. 140. One West 67th St. (at Central Park West). ☎ *212-877-3500.* www.cafenyc.com. *Reservations strongly recommended. Subway: 1, 9 to 66th Street. Main courses: $18–$26 for lunch, $29–$42 for dinner. AE, DC, DISC, MC, V. Open: Lunch: Mon–Fri noon–3 p.m. Brunch: Sat 11 a.m.–3 p.m., Sun 10 a.m.–3 p.m. Dinner: Mon–Sat 5:30 p.m.–12:30 a.m., Sun 5:30 p.m.–11 p.m. Jackets preferred.*

Carmine's
$$ Upper West Side   FAMILY-STYLE SOUTHERN ITALIAN

This fun, family-style Upper West Side institution will not let you go home hungry. Portions are huge here, and though big often means bad, it doesn't at Carmine's. Remarkably, the restaurant turns out better pasta and entrees than most 20-table Italian restaurants. I've never had pasta here that wasn't *al dente* and the marinara sauce is as good as any I've had in Manhattan. For starters, the daily salads are always fresh and the mountainous platter of fried calamari perfectly tender. Rigatoni marinara and ziti with broccoli are pasta standouts, and the best meat entrees include veal parmigiana, broiled porterhouse steak, and the remarkable chicken *scarpariello* (chicken pan broiled with a lemon-rosemary sauce). The tiramisu is pie-size, thick and creamy, and bathed in Kahlúa and Marsala. Order half of what you think you need. Don't expect intimate conversation here; in fact, ear plugs may be in order. Unless you come early, expect to wait. Carmine's also has an outlet in Times Square.

See map p. 138. 2450 Broadway (between 90th and 91st streets). ☎ *212-362-2200.* www.carminesnyc.com. *Reservations recommended before 6 p.m.; accepted for 6 or more after 6 p.m. Subway: 1, 2, 3, 9 to 96th Street. Family-style main courses: $15–$49 (most $23 or less). AE, DC, DISC, MC, V. Open: Tues–Sat 11:30 a.m.–midnight; Sun–Mon 11:30 a.m.–11 p.m.*

Celeste
$$ Upper West Side   ITALIAN

I'm wary of fancy, trendy Italian restaurants that can't hold a candle to my late *nonna's* (Italian for "grandmother") magnificently simple cooking. Tiny, but charming Celeste, however, dispels my wariness with some delicious simple creations of its own. Celeste has its own wood-burning pizza oven, which churns out thin-crusted, simple-but-delicious pizzas. The "fritti" (fried) course here is unique; the fritto misto de pesce (fried mixed seafood) is delectable, but the fried zucchini blossoms (something my *nonna* did so well), usually available in the summer and fall, are amazing. The fresh pastas are better than the dried pasta; I never thought the fresh egg noodles with cabbage, shrimp, and sheep's cheese would work, but the combination is delicious. Not on the menu but usually available are plates of rare, artisanal Italian cheeses served with homemade jams. Though the main courses are also good, stick with the pizzas, antipasto, frittis, and pastas. For dessert, try the gelato; the pistachio was the best I've ever had in New York. The restaurant has been "discovered," so go early or late or expect a wait.

See map p. 140. 502 Amsterdam Ave. (between 84th and 85th streets). ☎ *212-874-4559. Reservations not accepted. Subway: 1, 9 to 86th Street. Pizza: $10–$12; main courses: $10–$16. No credit cards. Open: Mon–Sat 5–11 p.m., Sun noon–3:30 p.m.*

'Cesca

$$$$ Upper West Side   ITALIAN COUNTRY

With the opening of 'Cesca on the Upper West Side in late 2003, another gem was added to the neighborhood's dining crown. It's not easy to describe the Italian food served in 'Cesca; it's like nothing many New Yorkers have experienced before. Where else have you had roasted sardines paired with a "soft" egg? With a roaring wood-burning oven used to roast everything from oysters to peppers, this place is as rustic as it gets. Imagine yourself in an Italian farmhouse where you're served slow-cooked meats, like pork shank with the fat cooked off and the meat falling from the bone or a hearty potato gnocchi with tender braised duck. Try to save room for the equally interesting desserts, like honey goat milk gelato or fresh figs with fig gelato. Service is friendly and informal, and the restaurant is spacious and comfortable with a large bar area complete with long tables where you snack on marinated olives, *fritto misto,* or spicy parmigiana fritters, while sipping unusual Italian wines. At press time, 'Cesca is the most popular restaurant on the Upper West Side, so call well ahead for reservations.

See map p. 140. 164 W. 75th St. (at Amsterdman Avenue). ☎ *212-787-6300. Reservations highly recommended. Subway: 1, 2, 3, 9 to 72nd Street. Main courses: $16–$28. AE, DC, MC, V. Open: Tues–Thurs 5–11 p.m., Fri–Sat 5–11:30 p.m., Sun 5–10 p.m.*

Chanterelle

$$$$ TriBeCa   CONTEMPORARY FRENCH

If you want the royal treatment as you dine on excellent and innovative French cuisine, you can't do better than Chanterelle. The dining room is simple but beautiful, with a pressed-tin ceiling, widely spaced large tables, comfortable chairs, and gorgeous floral displays; the restaurant also boasts a superb modern art collection. Expect knowledgeable service; your waiter will have no trouble answering any questions you have about the menu. The seasonal menu changes every few weeks, but one signature dish appears on almost every menu: a marvelous grilled seafood sausage. Cheese lovers should opt for a cheese course — the presentation and selection can't be beat. The wine list is superlative, though expensive. Chanterelle is a place to celebrate.

See map p. 136. 2 Harrison St. (at Hudson Street). ☎ *212-966-6960.* www.chanterelle nyc.com. *Reservations recommended well in advance. Subway: 1, 9 to Franklin Street. Fixed-price lunch: $38; à la carte lunch: $19.50–$26.50; 3-course fixed-price dinner: $84; tasting menu: $95 ($155 with wines). AE, DC, DISC, MC, V. Open: Mon 5:30–11 p.m.; Tues–Sat Noon–2:30 p.m. and 5:30–11 p.m.*

Charles' Southern Style Kitchen
$ Harlem   SOUL FOOD

Nothing fancy about this place, just a brightly lit, 25-seater on a not very attractive block in upper Harlem. But you don't come here for fancy; you come for soul food at its simplest and freshest. And you better come hungry. The $11 all-you-can-eat buffet features crunchy, moist pan-fried chicken, ribs in a tangy sauce with meat falling off the bone, smoky stewed oxtails in a thick brown onion gravy, macaroni and cheese, collard greens with bits of smoked turkey, black-eyed peas, and cornbread warm and not overly sweet. Hours, however, can be erratic, so call ahead before you make the trek.

2841 Eighth Ave. (between 151st and 152nd streets). ☎ *877-813-2920 or 212-926-4313. Subway: D to 145th Street. All-you-can-eat buffet: $11. No credit cards. Open: Mon 4 p.m.–midnight, Tues–Sat noon–4 a.m.*

Churrascaria Plataforma
$$$ Midtown West   BRAZILIAN

If you're an Atkins addict, you'll love this colorful, upscale, all-you-can-eat Brazilian rotisserie. A large selection of teasers like octopus stew, paella, and carpaccio at the phenomenal salad bar may tempt you to fill up too quickly, but hold out for the never-ending parade of meats. Roving servers deliver beef (too many cuts to mention), ham, chicken (the chicken hearts are great, trust me), lamb, and sausage — more than 15 delectable varieties — and traditional sides like fried yucca, plantains, and rice until you can't eat another bite. The service is friendly and generous, and the cavernous room is *loud.* The ideal accompaniment to the meal is a pitcher of Brazil's signature cocktail, the *caipirinha* (a margarita-like blend of limes, sugar, crushed ice, and raw sugarcane liquor); Plataforma's caipirinhas are some of the best in town. A new outlet with the same menu recently opened in SoHo.

See map p. 138. 316 W. 49th St. (between Eighth and Ninth avenues). ☎ *212-245-0505.* www.churrascariaplataforma.com. *Reservations recommended. Subway: C, E to 50th Street. All-you-can-eat fixed-price: $28 at lunch, $39 at dinner; half-price for children ages 5–10. AE, DC, DISC, MC, V. Open: Daily noon–midnight.*

Cub Room
$$$$ SoHo   AMERICAN

Try dragging yourself from the Cub Room's inviting lounge and bar scene to the very attractive dining room; you'll be very happy you did. Not because you needed to get away from all the beautiful people socializing at the bar, but because now you get to chow on chef Benjamin Grossman's delectable creations. The menu changes seasonally, but whatever the season, the signature Cub Steak, a butter-roasted filet, is a must. If steak's not your thing, explore the fish options; I had a very good sauteed red snapper in a orange-brown butter emulsion. Another worthy signature dish is the *pâté de campagne,* an unforgettable homemade rustic pâté that's chunky with bits of pork. Service is friendly but not over-solicitous.

See map p. 136. 131 Sullivan St. (at Prince Street). ☎ 212-677-4100. Reservations recommended. Subway: C, E to Spring Street. Main courses: $24–$30. AE, DC, MC, V. Open: Mon–Fri noon–10 p.m, Sat–Sun 11 a.m.–10 p.m.

Daniel
$$$$$ Upper East Side   FRENCH COUNTRY

Many reasons explain why Daniel (Daniel Boulud's signature restaurant) is a *New York Times* four-star winner: the luxurious decor, the comfortable seating, the impeccable, white-gloved service — but the best reason is Boulud's faultless classic country French cooking. The menu is heavy with game dishes in elegant but unfussy preparations, plus Daniel signatures like black sea bass in a crisp potato shell, with tender leeks and a light Syrah sauce. Excellent starters include foie gras terrine with fennel confit and dried apricot compote, and rosemary and blood orange glazed endive. Sublime entrees include spit-roasted and braised organic guinea hen with black truffle butter, or chestnut-crusted venison with sweet potato purée. But you can't really go wrong with anything here. The wine list is terrific and, divided between seasonal fruits and chocolates, the desserts are uniformly excellent. *Tip:* You can dine in the lounge and sample the same food without the formality (jacket-and-tie for men is not enforced in the lounge).

See map p. 140. 60 E. 65th St (between Madison and Park avenues). ☎ 212-288-0033. www.danielnyc.com. Reservations required. Subway: 6 to 68th Street. 3-course fixed-price dinner: $88; tasting menus: $120–$160. Main courses: $34–$38 in bar and lounge. AE, MC, V. Open: Mon–Sat 5:45–11 p.m. (lounge until 11:30 p.m.). Jacket and tie required for men in main dining room.

db Bistro Moderne
$$$$ Midtown West   FRENCH BISTRO

Compared to Daniel Boulud's signature and formal restaurant **Daniel** (see listing earlier in this chapter), db Bistro Moderne is as casual as a burger joint. But casual means the models who dine here wear Armani T-shirts while digging into burgers that cost $29. Okay, so it's not your typical coffee-shop burger. Boulud's famous creation is made with minced sirloin, foie gras, preserved black truffle, and braised short ribs on a Parmesan onion roll. So casual may mean many things, but here it does not mean cheap. Despite the silly burger excess, the food is, like all Boulud's ventures, outstanding — especially bistro favorites such as bouillabaisse, coq au vin, and frogs' legs.

See map p. 138. 55 W. 44th St. (between Fifth and Sixth avenues). ☎ 212-391-2400. Reservations required. Subway: B, D, F, Q to 42nd Street. Lunch entrees: $26–$28;

pre-theater 3-course prix fixe: $39; dinner entrees: $27–$31. AE, DC, MC, V. Open: Lunch Mon–Sat noon–2:30 p.m., dinner daily 5:45–11 p.m.

Dos Caminos
$$$ Flatiron District MEXICAN

This upscale Mexican restaurant is the rage of the Flatiron district (and SoHo, where a sister branch opened recently). Guacamole is made at your table with all the fresh ingredients, but it lacked the spice I would have liked. The fish tacos, made with red snapper in a soft taco with fresh coleslaw, are outstanding, as are the many ceviches, especially *pulpito* (baby octopus). The Mexican standard, chicken *mole en poblano,* is very good, though not worth the steep price (almost $20). In general, stay away from the traditional offerings and explore the more innovative dishes, such as chipotle-tamarind glazed mahi mahi, ancho-seared big-eyed tuna, and ten-chile barbecued baby back ribs; such dishes — and those sublime tequilas — are what sets Dos Caminos apart from your local *taqueria.*

See map p. 138. 373 Park Ave. South (between 26th and 27th streets). ☎ *212-294-1000. Reservations recommended. Subway: 6 to 28th Street. Main courses: $17–$24. AE, DISC, MC, V. Open: Sun 11:30 a.m.–11 p.m., Tues–Thurs 11:30 a.m.–midnight, Fri–Sat 11:30 a.m.–1 a.m.*

Eleven Madison Park
$$$$ Flatiron District FRENCH CONTINENTAL

This immense, high-ceilinged restaurant housed in the lobby of the Art Deco Met-Life building is a marvel and one of my favorites in Manhattan. Before you can even take in the grandeur of the place, the waitstaff, working with the efficient precision of a secret service unit, is upon you, almost before you even have to ask. The French-infused country cooking specializes in hearty fare, including organ meats, such as the almond-crusted calf's brain; crisped pig's feet; prime-aged *côte de boeuf;* and an incredible sautéed skate wing. All the desserts are wonderful, especially the amazing chocolate soufflé (not on the menu, but order it with your meal so it's ready for your dessert); you may even consider skipping the entrees and getting right to dessert. The excellent tasting menu (choose five or seven courses) lets you sample much of what the restaurant has to offer.

See map p. 138. 11 Madison Ave. (at 24th Street). ☎ *212-889-0905. Reservations recommended. Subway: N, R, 6 to 23rd Street. À la carte lunch: $15–$24; dinner main courses: $23–$31; tasting menu of 5–7 courses: $60–$80. AE, DC, DISC, MC, V. Open: Lunch Mon–Sat 11:30 a.m.–2 p.m., dinner Mon–Thurs 5:30–10:30 p.m., Fri–Sat 5:30–11 p.m., Sun 5:30–10 p.m.*

Fiamma Osteria
$$$$ SoHo MODERN ITALIAN

This beautifully designed four-floor restaurant with mirrors galore, lustrous red walls, leather chairs, and a glass elevator serves modern Italian food so good it surpasses the stylish decor. Start with an antipasti of grilled octopus in an olive vinaigrette sprinkled with ceci beans and cooled by chopped mint leaves, and then move on to a pasta or two; the *agnolini* (braised oxtail and beef shank ravioli) and the *tortelli* (buffalo milk ricotta tortelli) are both outstanding. The *orata* (grilled *daurade* with cranberry beans in a Manilla clam broth) and the *nodino* (seared veal chop with sage and sweet and sour cipollini onions) are scrumptious main courses. Fiamma is blessed to have the services of pastry chef extraordinaire Elizabeth Katz; her dessert creations are really second to none, especially her torta (dark chocolate praline cake layered with hazelnut brittle and gianduja gelato). The extensive wine list features over 400 bottles, mostly Italian with a number of good offerings by the glass. Dinner is a scene, so don't expect intimacy, but lunch, with a similar menu, is a much more relaxed option.

See map p. 136. 206 Spring St. (between Sixth Avenue and Sullivan Street). ☎ *212-653-0100. Reservations recommended. Subway: C, E to Spring Street. Main courses: $21–$32. AE, DISC, MC, V. Open: Lunch Mon–Sat noon–2:30 p.m.; Dinner Mon–Thurs 5:30–11 p.m., Fri–Sat 5:30–midnight, Sun 5:30–11 p.m.*

Florent
$$ Greenwich Village DINER/FRENCH BISTRO

One of the great, late-night dining spots in Manhattan, Florent (open nearly 24-hours) is French bistro dressed up as a '50s-style diner. After the clubs close, Florent gets busy, and tables are tightly packed, almost uncomfortably so in some cases. This place has a real sense of humor (check out the menu boards above the bar) and a CD catalog full of the latest indie sounds, all adding to the hipster fun. The food's good, too; the grilled chicken with herbs and mustard sauce is a moist and flavorful winner, as is the French onion soup crowned with melted Gruyère. You can always pick from diner faves like burgers and chili, in addition to Gallic standards like *moules frites* (mussels and fries), and the comfort food specialties, such as chicken potpie.

See map p. 136. 69 Gansevoort St. (2 blocks south of 14th Street and 1 block west of Ninth Avenue between Greenwich and Washington streets). ☎ *212-989-5779. www.restaurantflorent.com. Reservations recommended for dinner. Subway: A, C, E, L to 14th Street. Main courses: $4.50–$14.50 at brunch and lunch, $8–$20.50 at dinner (most less than $15). No credit cards. Open: Mon–Thurs 9 a.m.–5 a.m., Fri–Sun 24 hours.*

Grand Sichuan International
$ Chelsea SZECHUAN

Finally, a Szechuan restaurant that doesn't alter its standards to appease those with an aversion to the heat of chili peppers. The food here is intensely spiced the way Szechuan food should be. And the heat doesn't compromise the flavors, which remain complex and strong, especially in such top choices as Szechuan wontons in red oil, Chairman Mao's pork with chestnuts, and my favorite, boneless whole fish with pine nuts in a modified sweet-and-sour sauce. The house bean curd in spicy sauce is another winner and so hot its best washed down with a cold beer.

Eating around the world on one island

Not many cities can offer you a sampling of all the world's cuisines. In New York, just about every variety of ethnic food is available. The following is a food tour of Manhattan, where you can circle the island and experience no less than 14 different ethnic cuisines. And the best part is that all these ethnic restaurants won't wear out your wallet.

Start your tour in Chinatown where, obviously, you can choose from countless Chinese restaurants. One of my favorite Chinese restaurants in Chinatown is **New York Noodletown**, 28½ Bowery at Bayard Street (☎ 212-349-0923), where, as advertised, the noodles, especially in soups, are the specialty. (See the "Downtown Dining" map.) But the seafood is fantastic too — try the salt-baked squid for a really special treat. Another favorite is **Big Wong King** 67 Mott St. (☎ 212-964-0540).

But you can find more than Chinese restaurants in Chinatown; witness the happy existence of many Vietnamese restaurants, including my favorite **Nha Trang**, 87 Baxter St. between Canal and Bayard streets (☎ 212-233-5948). (See the "Downtown Dining" map.) At Nha Trang, I can't resist the meal-sized *pho* noodle soup.

With the increasing encroachment of Chinatown upon what was formerly Little Italy's turf, the neighborhood north of Canal Street, made so famous in movies such as *The Godfather*, has lost much of its appeal. More importantly, the quality restaurants are gone. Though many Italian restaurants still exist (especially along Mulberry Street) I can't recommend any of them in good conscience.

Sadly, Canal Street has become a tourist trap with waiters trying to lure customers off the streets by waving menus at them. I do, however, recommend the very appetizing combination of dinner in Chinatown at an Asian restaurant followed by coffee and a pastry at one of Little Italy's *pasticcerie*. My favorite is **Caffe Roma**, 385 Broome St. on the corner of Mulberry (☎ 212-226-8413). (See the "Downtown Dining" map.) The cannolis (try the chocolate-covered) and tiramisu are spectacular here, and it's open 8 a.m. to midnight daily. Another spot you may want to try is **Ferrara**, 195 Grand St. between Mott and Mulberry streets (☎ 212-226-6150). (See the "Downtown Dining" map.) Founded in 1892, the pasticceria claims to be America's first espresso bar. Cafe seating is available so you can enjoy instant sweet-tooth gratification. Ferrara is open daily from 8 a.m. to midnight (to 1 a.m. on Saturday).

The good cheap ethnic eats are not easy to find around Times Square, but even in that American mall-like neighborhood, if you search hard enough, you can find something. When I find myself hungry in Times Square, I head to **Sapporo**, 152 W. 49th St. at Seventh Avenue (☎ 212-869-8972), the Japanese noodle shop where the constant din of the mostly Japanese diners slurping at huge bowls of Ramen (noodle soups) is the best evidence of Sapporo's authenticity. (See the "Midtown Dining" map.)

Ninth Avenue in the '40s and '50s, also known as Hell's Kitchen, is probably the most diverse for ethnic dining. And each year that diversity is celebrated in the Ninth Avenue Food Festival. We may have had our difficulties with Afghanistan the past few years, but that hasn't stopped me from frequenting any of the numerous branches of the

(continued)

(continued)

Afghan Kebab House. The original is at 764 Ninth Ave. between 51st and 52nd streets (☎ 212-307-1612), and it features large portions of spit-roasted kebabs served with amazing basmati rice and fresh, flat Afghan bread. (See the "Midtown Dining" map.)

For a taste of Germany, **Hallo! Berlin**, 402 W. 51st St. just west of Ninth Avenue (☎ 212-541-6248), offers the best *wurst* in the city. And with a cold mug of German beer, the combination is hard to beat. (See the "Midtown Dining" map.)

The Hell's Kitchen neighborhood is also an enclave of Thai restaurants. My favorite is **Siam Inn**, 854 Eighth Ave. between 51st and 52nd streets (☎ 212-757-4006), where I always order the incredible *Gai Yang*, barbecued Thai chicken. (See the "Midtown Dining" map.)

On the Upper West Side, you can find numerous Hispanic restaurants: Mexican, Cuban, Dominican, and Peruvian to name just a few of the variations. The neighborhood is also the home of that curious combination of cuisines: Cuban/Chinese. The best Cuban/Chinese is **Flor de Mayo**, at 2651 Broadway between 100th and 101st streets (☎ 212-663-5520), where my usual meal is a bowl of wonton soup, followed by a big plate of yellow rice and black beans. (See the "Uptown Dining" map.)

Harlem is home to some great soul food (see listing for **Charles' Southern Style Kitchen** earlier in this chapter for the best of the best in soul), but Harlem is also where you can find a number of very good African restaurants. And all of them are incredibly inexpensive. I favor the Senegalese **La Marmite** at 2264 Frederick Douglass Ave. between 120th and 121st streets (☎ 212-666-0653). My favorite is their couscous with lamb chop and *poisson grille*, whole fried fish served with tomato, onions, and a fiery sauce.

East Harlem is known as El Barrio or Spanish Harlem because it became the home of so many who immigrated from the island of Puerto Rico. For the best taste of Puerto Rican cuisine in El Barrio, try **La Fonda Boricua**, 169 E. 106th St. between Third and Lexington avenues (☎ 212-410-7292).

Many Mexican immigrants are moving into East Harlem now, and, as a result, a number of excellent and inexpensive Mexican restaurants have opened. I like **El Paso Taqueria**, 1642 Lexington Ave. between 103rd and 104th streets, where the tacos come in numerous varieties, including *lengua res* (beef tongue) and *tripas* (tripe).

Two enclaves where you can sample cheap, good Indian and Pakistani cuisine are the Murray Hill area of Lexington Avenue in the upper 20s and East 6th Street between First and Second avenues. (Many of the Indian restaurants don't serve liquor, but they may allow you to bring your own alcoholic beverages in, which can save you some money. Call ahead or ask before you go into one of them).

Murray Hill is so packed with East Asian restaurants that it's called Curry Hill. Many of the Curry Hill restaurants are popular with cab drivers because they (the restaurants, not the cabbies!) are cheap and fast — especially the aptly named **Curry in a Hurry** at 119 Lexington Ave. between 28th and 29th streets (☎ 212-683-0900). (See the "Midtown Dining" map.)

The other Indian enclave in the East Village is called "Little India." Here you can find at least a dozen Indian restaurants in that little block, and all of them clamor for your business by stationing hawkers waving menus at you and trying to convince you that theirs is better than the competition's. Of the many I've sampled, my favorite is **Sonali,** 326 E. 6th St. (☎ 212-505-7515). (See the "Downtown Dining" map.)

Finally, if you've had enough of exotic, spicy food but still want something ethnic, try out the English-themed **A Salt & Battery,** 80 Second Ave. between 4th and 5th streets (☎ 212-254-6610), where you can eat authentic British fish and chips out of a greasy brown paper bag. (See the "Downtown Dining" map.)

See map p. 138. 229 Ninth Ave. (at 24th Street). ☎ *212-620-5200. Reservations accepted for parties of 3 or more. Subway: C, E to 23rd Street. Main courses: $3.25–$14. AE, DC, MC, V. Open: Daily 11:30 a.m.–1 p.m.*

Home
$$ Greenwich Village CONTEMPORARY AMERICAN

This cozy restaurant is as homey as it sounds, in attitude and menu. The dinner menu changes regularly, but signature dishes such as the rich, creamy blue cheese fondue with rosemary toasts; an excellent cumin-crusted pork chop on a bed of homemade barbecue sauce; a filleted-at-your-table brook trout accompanied by sweet potatoes, apples, and sage; and moist roasted chicken with a side of spicy onion rings are all worthy of their signature status. For dessert, Home's chocolate pudding is legendary. Breakfast and weekend brunch are great times to visit, too, with fluffy pancakes and excellent egg dishes. The interesting wine list boasts a large selection of local bottles from Long Island's North Fork. Heated year-round, the lovely garden is most charming in warm weather; book an outside table well ahead.

See map p. 136. 20 Cornelia St. (between Bleecker and W. 4th streets). ☎ *212-243-9579. Reservations recommended. Subway: A, C, E, F, B, D to W. 4th Street. (use W. 3rd Street exit). Main courses: $8–$12 at breakfast and lunch, $14–$18 at dinner. AE, DISC, MC, V. Open: Mon–Fri 9 a.m.–4 p.m. and 5–11 p.m., Sat 10:30 a.m.–4:30 p.m. and 5:30–11 p.m., Sun 10:30 a.m.–4:30 p.m. and 5:30–10 p.m.*

Island Burgers and Shakes
$ Midtown West GOURMET BURGERS/SANDWICHES

This aisle-sized diner glows with the wild colors of a California surf shop. Service is minimal and tables are tiny, but the food is topnotch. A small selection of sandwiches and salads are on hand, but as the name implies, folks come here for the Goliath-size burgers — either beef hamburgers or, the specialty of the house, *churrascos* (flattened grilled chicken breasts). Innovation strikes with the more than 40 topping combinations. Although Island Burgers doesn't serve fries, they do have very tasty dirty potato chips.

See map p. 138. 766 Ninth Ave. (between 51st and 52nd streets). ☎ 212-307-7934. www.island.citysearch.com. Reservations not accepted. Subway: C, E to 50th Street. Sandwiches and salads: $6.50–$9. No credit cards. Open: Sun–Thurs noon– 10:30 p.m., Fri–Sat noon–11:30 p.m.

Joseph's
$$$$$ Midtown West   SEAFOOD

You'd be hard-pressed to find seafood fresher and in more varieties than what is served at this sleek, tri-level Rockefeller Center restaurant. Maybe that's because Joseph's is affiliated with the famous seafood purveyor, Citarella's. Although pasta and meat options are on the menu, stick with the fish. The crab cake appetizer, stuffed full with fresh lump crab meat, and the oysters (whatever is available that day) are great starters. The black cod entree with a miso glaze served with bok choy and a shrimp and onion broth is buttery and full of flavor, and you can't go wrong with any of the whole grilled fish options offered daily and prepared simply with olive oil, salt, and pepper. Desserts are typically decadent, especially the devil dog — a very upscale variation of what you used to see in your lunchbox at school. The restaurant is in the heart of expense-account land and is very busy at lunch — and also very pricey. Still, if you want seafood as fresh as it gets in a stylish setting, Joseph's is the choice.

See map p. 138. 1240 Sixth Ave. (at 49th Street). ☎ 212-332-1515. Reservations recommended. Subway: B, D, F, V to 47th/50th Street. Main courses: $26–$40. AE, DC, MC, V. Open: Mon–Fri 11:30 a.m.–2:15 p.m. and 5:30 p.m.–12 a.m., Sat 5:30 p.m.–12 a.m.

Jean-Georges
$$$$$ Upper West Side   FRENCH

What can be said about the immense culinary skills of master chef Jean-Georges Vongerichten that hasn't already be said? And here, at his signature restaurant, those skills are best showcased. French and Asian touches mingle with a new passion for offbeat harvests, like lamb's quarters, sorrel, yarrow, quince, and chicory. Young garlic soup with thyme and a plate of sautéed frogs' legs makes a great beginning. Muscovy duck steak with Asian spices and sweet-and-sour jus is carved table-side while the lobster tartine with lemongrass, pea shoots, and a broth of fenugreek receives a final dash of spices seconds before you dig in. If the chestnut soup is on the menu, don't miss it. The wine list is also excellent, with a number of unusual choices in every price range. Be aware: They have a tendency to jack up the prices for holiday meals. And reserve before you leave home to guarantee a table.

See map p. 140. In the Trump International Hotel & Tower, 1 Central Park West (at 60th Street/Columbus Circle). ☎ 212-299-3900. www.jean-georges.com. Reservations required well in advance. Subway: A, B, C, D, 1, 9 to 59th Street/ Columbus Circle. Main courses: $26–$42. AE, DC, MC, V. Open: Dining room: Mon–Fri noon–3 p.m. and 5:30–11 p.m., Sat 5:30–11:30 p.m. Jacket required for men; tie optional.

Mandoo Bar
$ Midtown West   KOREAN

When you think of Korean food, you probably think of barbecue at your table. Not so at Mandoo Bar, where the specialty is *mandoo,* or dumplings. In the heart of New York's Koreatown, find the two women in the window lovingly rolling and stuffing fresh mandoo and you know you've arrived. Because of the constant preparation, the dumplings are incredibly fresh and stuffed with a variety of ingredients. The restaurant offers many options, including Mool Mandoo (the basic white dumpling filled with pork and vegetables), Kimchee Mandoo (steamed dumplings with potent kimchee, Korean spiced cabbage, tofu, pork, and vegetables), and Goon Mandoo (a pan-fried dumpling filled with pork and vegetables). You really can't go wrong with any of these dumplings, so sample them all with a Combo Mandoo. Soups are also special here; try the beef noodle in a spicy, sinus-clearing broth. The seats are nothing more than wooden benches here, so Mandoo Bar is more suited for quick eats rather than a lingering meal. This makes it perfect for nearby Empire State Building touring and/or shopping in Herald Square after lunch.

See map p. 138. 2 W. 32nd St. (just west of Fifth Avenue). ☎ *212-279-3075. Reservations not accepted. Subway: B, D, F, N, Q, R, V, W to 34th Street/Herald Square. Main courses: $6–$14. AE, DC, MC, V. Open: Daily 11:30 a.m.–11 p.m.*

Mojo
$$ East Village   ECLECTIC LATIN

It's hard to define the cuisine served at Mojo, but it isn't hard to say that however defined, the food is very good. What makes this small, East Village find tough to describe are the unusual pairings of dishes that feature Latin ingredients combined with Southern specialties, like catfish with chipolte mayo, tacos filled with short ribs, hanger steak rubbed with chiles, grilled apple blue cheese quesadillas with smoked bacon, and macaroni and cheese with oven dried tomatoes and chorizo. Even the desserts, like the Mexican brownie with pecan graham crust and cinnamon ice cream, and the cocktails, like "Johnny's Mommy" (a mix of Jack Daniels with ginger beer), reflect this fusion. Who cares about labels anyway; the culinary creations at Mojo work and that's really all that matters. Arrive early or, with only 28-tables available, be prepared to dull the wait by enjoying numerous inventive cocktails.

See map p. 136. 309 E. 5th St. (at Second Avenue). ☎ *212-539-1515.* www.mojony. com. *Subway: F to Second Avenue or 6 to Astor Place. Main courses: $11–$19. AE, DC, MC, V. Open: Sun–Wed 6 p.m.–11 p.m., Thurs 6 p.m.–midnight, Fri–Sat 6 p.m.–2 a.m.*

Molyvos
$$$$ Midtown West   GREEK

Molyvos serves some of the best simple, unpretentious traditional Greek food you can find in the city, albeit at upscale prices. But if you like Greek food, Molyvos is worth the splurge. Start with the cold mezedes: an assortment of familiar appetizers like the spreads *tzatziki, melitzanosalata,* and *taramosalata,* and a terrific vegetable *dolmades,* grape leaves filled with rice, raisins, and pine nuts. Move on to a sampling of hot mezedes like spinach pie or an appetizer of grilled octopus. I often daydream about Molyvos's traditional entrees, like rabbit *stifado,* a rabbit stew that tastes even better than chicken; lamb *yuvetsi,* lamb shanks baked in a clay pot with orzo, cheese, and tomatoes; or a whole fish roasted in Molyvos's wood-burning grill. Many very good Greek wines and, even better, dozens of ouzos, are available. The chocolate baklava for dessert is the perfect ending to your meal.

See map p. 138. 871 Seventh Ave. (between 55th and 56th streets). ☎ *212-582-7500. Reservations recommended. Subway: N, R to 57th St.; B, D, E to Seventh Avenue. Main courses: $13–$24.50 at lunch (most less than $20), $19.50–$29.50 at dinner (most less than $25). AE, DC, DISC, MC, V. Open: Daily noon–midnight.*

Nyonya
$ Chinatown MALAYSIAN

One of the few Malaysian restaurants in Manhattan (and also one of the best) is Chinatown's Nyonya. This spacious, bustling restaurant designed like a south Asian tiki hut offers efficient and friendly service, but it's the huge portions of exotic, spicy food that's the real treat. Coconut milk–, curry–, and chile pepper–laden dishes are staples of Malaysian cuisine, and they're the norm at Nyonya. The Malaysian national dish, *roti canai* (an Indian pancake with a curry chicken dipping sauce), is outstanding. The noodle soups are meals in themselves; *prawn mee* (egg noodles, shredded pork, large shrimp in a spicy shrimp broth) is sinus-clearing, and the curry spare ribs are nothing short of spectacular. Even the drinks and desserts are exotic, including *sooi pooi* drink (sour plum) and *pulut hitam* dessert (creamy black glutinous rice with coconut milk). But vegetarians beware: There's not much on the menu for you here; most dishes are prepared in either a meat or fish broth.

See map p. 136. 194 Grand St. (between Mulberry and Mott streets). ☎ *212-334-3669. Subway: 6 to Spring Street. Noodle soups: $4–$6, main dishes: $5–$16. No credit cards. Open: Sun–Thurs 11 a.m.–11:30 p.m., Fri–Sat 11 a.m.–midnight.*

Pampano
$$$$ Midtown East MEXICAN SEAFOOD

Because I usually prefer my Mexican food simple and cheap, good expensive Mexican food is, in my mind, a contradiction in terms. Pampano, however, and the things it does with Mexican ingredients, especially seafood, has made me reconsider my bias. Set in a lovely, lush townhouse, seating here is much more comfortable than I'm used to, which is a bonus. But even if I were seated on a hard bench, the ceviches here would taste spectacular. For a rare and very special treat, try a lobster taco — you won't find that at your local taqueria. Of the entrees, it's difficult to order anything but the fantastic *pampano adobado,* sautéed pompano with creamy black rice, roasted garlic, and chile guajillo sauce; but you won't suffer too much if you settle for the very memorable pan-fried baby red snapper in a *chile de arbol* sauce. Save room for chocolate flan for dessert and maybe a cleansing shot of one of the restaurant's many excellent tequilas.

See map p. 138. 209 E. 49th St. (at Third Avenue). ☎ 212-751-4545. Reservations recommended. Subway: E, V to Lexington Avenue/53rd or 6 to 51st Street. Main courses: $21–$26. AE, DC, MC, V. Open: Mon–Fri 11:30 a.m.–3 p.m., Sun–Tues 5–10 p.m., Wed–Sat 5–11 p.m.

Pastis
$$ Greenwich Village   FRENCH BISTRO

Located in the meatpacking district, this French bistro packs in the crowds at all hours of the day to eat classic bistro fare and to be seen, not necessarily in that order. Tables are ridiculously close together and, whether you want to or not, you get the scoop on your neighbor's sex life. If that's not your thing, dine early or come for weekday breakfast or lunch, when things are quieter. If you can take your eyes off the beautiful crowd, study the menu and look for standouts, such as fricassees of monkfish, skate au *beurre noir* (literally, "black butter," but the sauce is brown), or the classic steak frites with a rich béarnaise. Bottles are pricey, but plenty of good, affordable wines are available by the carafe. Don't miss the crêpes Suzettes for dessert.

See map p. 136. 9 Ninth Ave. (at Little W. 12th Street). ☎ 212-929-4844. www.pastisny.com. Reservations recommended. Subway: A, C, E to 14th Street. Main courses: $13–$22. AE, MC, V. Open: Sun–Thurs 9 a.m.–5 p.m. and 6 p.m.–1 a.m., Fri–Sat 9 a.m.–5 p.m. and 6 p.m.–3 a.m.

Peter Luger Steakhouse
$$$$ Brooklyn   STEAKS

You want the best steak in New York? You gotta cross the Williamsburg Bridge into Brooklyn to find it. It's definitely worth the search. And you don't even need a jacket and tie. In fact, you can come to Peter Luger's any way you want, just come hungry and bring cash (no credit cards here). This century-old institution is porterhouse heaven. The first-rate cuts — the only ones this 113-year-old institution serves — are dry-aged on the premises and come off the grill dripping with fat and butter, crusty on the outside and pink within. If you really want to be foolish, you can order sole or lamb chops, but why bother? The $5.95 Peter Luger burger, however, served only at lunch, is a little known treasure. As sides go, the German fried potatoes are crisp and delicious, and the creamed spinach is everything it should be.

178 Broadway (at Driggs Avenue), Williamsburg, Brooklyn. ☎ 718-387-7400. www.peterluger.com. Reservations essential; call a month in advance for weekend bookings. Subway: J, M, Z to Marcy Avenue. (Or take a cab.) Main courses: $5–$20 at lunch, $20–$32 at dinner. No credit cards (Peter Luger accounts only). Open: Mon–Thurs 11:45 a.m.–9:45 p.m., Fri–Sat 11:45 a.m.–10:45 p.m., Sun 12:45–9:45 p.m.

P.J. Clarke's
$$ **Midtown East** **AMERICAN**

This 120-year-old saloon/restaurant is a New York institution; it's a late-night hangout for politicians, actors, and athletes. Also an institution is the P.J Clarke hamburger, curiously priced at $8.10 and nothing more than a slab of chopped meat cooked to order on a bun — the hamburger is a simple masterpiece. Try it with P.J.'s home fries or onion rings. Salads also are a good accompaniment to the beef, particularly the tomato, red onion, and blue cheese salad. If meat isn't your thing, visit the raw bar. Beer, the drink of choice here, comes in mugs, but pints are available if you ask. Amidst the steel and glass skyscrapers of Third Avenue, P.J. Clarke's is a welcome relief.

See map p. 138. 915 Third Ave. (at 55th Street). ☎ *212-317-1616.* www.pjclarkes.com. *Subway: E, V to Lexington Avenue. Main courses: $8–$21. AE, MC, V. Open: Daily 11:30 a.m.–4 a.m.*

Rosa Mexicano
$$$$ **Upper West Side** **MEXICAN**

You can choose from two branches of this popular New York Mexican eatery, but it's the spacious Lincoln Center location, designed by David Rockwell and highlighted by a 30-foot-high blue tile waterfall adorned with hundreds of sculpted divers, that is a marvel. Rosa Mexicano originated the now common experience of guacamole prepared at your table using the freshest ingredients. But why, when a gringo asks for it to be prepared spicy, does he always get the toned-down version? In my opinion, as long as they serve those deservedly famous frozen pomegranate magaritas to quell the heat, they won't get complaints about the guacamole being too spicy. The ceviche starter with citrus-marinated mahi-mahi had the bite the guacamole was missing, but the entrees, with the exception of the delicious *Enchiladas de Jaiba* (corn tortillas filled with lump crabmeat topped with pumpkin seeds and tomatillo sauce), are a bit overly ambitious and, as a result, bland.

See map p. 140. 61 Columbus Ave. (at 62nd Street). ☎ *212-977-9700. Reservations recommended. Main courses: $13–$18 for lunch, $17–$25 for dinner. AE, DC, DISC, MC, V. Subway: A, B, C, D, 1, 9 to Columbus Circle. Open: Lunch daily noon–3 p.m., dinner Tues–Sat 5–10:30 p.m.*

rm
$$$$$ **Midtown East** **SEAFOOD**

With seafood just about as fresh as Joseph's (see listing earlier in this chapter) — minus the formality of Joseph's and plus the immense culinary talent of owner/chef Rick Moonen — rm is currently the best seafood restaurant in Manhattan. Shaped a bit like the inside of a yacht, rm is comprised of three adjoining rooms, but if you can snag a seat in the rear under the skylight, you're extra lucky. The restaurant offers a three-course prix

Family-friendly restaurants

Although it's always smart to call ahead to make sure a restaurant has kids' menus and high chairs, you can count on the following restaurants to be especially accommodating (and find more info on each restaurant from the alphabetical list in this chapter). You and the kids may consider **Florent**, **Artie's Delicatessen**, and, for a Brazilian-style party, **Churrascaria Plataforma**. And don't forget pizzerias — **John's Pizzeria** and **Lombardi's** especially.

Choose from some of these other great options for the whole family:

✔ **Bubby's**: Even the pickiest kid can find something on this menu.

✔ **Carmine's**: This rollicking, family-style Italian restaurant was created with kids in mind. You won't have to worry about them making too much noise here.

✔ **Good Enough to Eat**: Kids love the comfort food, like macaroni and cheese, pizza, and great desserts.

✔ **Mickey Mantle's** (42 Central Park South, between Fifth and Sixth avenues, ☎ 212-688-7777): As a player, the Mick had a reputation for being testy with autograph hounds and children, but he more than made up for it in retirement when he opened his extremely kid-friendly restaurant, located just across the street from Central Park. (See the "Midtown Dining" map.)

✔ **Serendipity 3**: Kids love this whimsical restaurant and ice-cream shop, which serves up a huge menu of American favorites, followed by colossal ice-cream treats.

✔ **Tavern on the Green** (Central Park West and W. 67th Street, ☎ 212-873-3200): Your kids will be wowed by the Central Park setting, and the children's menu makes them easy and affordable to feed. What's more, if the little ones get rambunctious, you can just take them outdoors to blow off a little steam. (See the "Uptown Dining" map.)

✔ **Virgil's Real BBQ**: This raucous Times Square barbecue joint is possibly one of the loudest restaurants in New York, so the kids will fit right in.

fixe meal, but the best way to sample the chef's genius is to go for one of the four- or six-course kitchen tastings, in which Moonen takes what is freshest off the boat and works his magic with it. You may want to try the pan-seared rouget, poached Florida snapper, Chatham cod, or local striped bass. If you desire, the knowledgeable sommelier will pair each course with the perfect accompanying wine. The service is very helpful in guiding you through each course, yet it's happily pretension-free; no white gloves here.

See map p. 138 33 E. 60th St. (between Park and Madison avenues). ☎ 212-319-3800. Reservations recommended. Subway: N, R, 4, 5, 6 to 59th Street. Lunch: $32 prix fixe. Dinner: $63 prix fixe and $75 for 4-course tasting menu, $100 for 6-course tasting menu. AE, DISC, DC, MC, V. Open: Mon–Fri noon–2 p.m., Mon–Sat 5:30–10 p.m.

Strip House
$$$$ Greenwich Village   STEAKHOUSE

For titantic portions of perfectly charred and seasoned red meat in a bur-
lesque-like setting (complete with semi-nude, old-time stripper photos that
adorn the red velvet walls, roomy burgundy banquettes, and a steady flow
of lounge music), visit the appropriately named Strip House. As soon as
one of those steaks lands on your table, the semi-nudes quickly take a
backseat to the enjoyable task in front of you: devouring that meat. The
signature strip steak still brings back fond memories, and you really can't
go wrong with either the filet mignon or the porterhouse for two, carved
at your table. The sides here are innovative variations on the standards:
creamed spinach with black truffles, French fries with herbs and garlic,
and, best of all, the crisp goose fat potatoes. They sound scary, but they're
worth the indulgence. Desserts are monumental — especially the multi-
layered chocolate cake — so have your waiter bring extra forks for sharing. With the exception of those few previously mentioned banquettes,
seating is tight so don't expect intimacy.

See map p. 136. 13 E. 12th St. (between University Place and Fifth Avenue). ☎ *212-
328-0000.* www.theglaziergroup.com. *Reservations recommended. Subway:
L, N, R, Q, 4, 5, 6, to 14th Street/Union Square. Main courses: $22–$40. AE, DC, DISC,
MC, V. Open: Mon–Thurs 5–11 p.m., Fri–Sat 5–11:30 p.m., Sun 5–10 p.m.*

Suba
$$$$ Lower East Side   SPANISH

With its eclectic, almost surreal design and innovative Latin cuisine, Suba
is a sensual delight. Walking past the suave cocktail and tapas lounge and
down the steel staircase to your table in the "grotto," a dining room surrounded by an illuminated pool, you think you have stepped onto the set
of the 1960s Peter Sellers movie, *The Party.* The place is definitely groovy,
but I wouldn't describe the food that way, especially the wonderful tapas,
ceviches, and appetizers. The grilled sardines with red cabbage, beans,
and guacamole, and a sliver of spicy chipotle sauce are a standout, but the
absolute best appetizer is the salty, flavorful Serrano ham with goat cheese
and quince paste layered on a black pepper tuiles. Entrees, though not
the strength here, feature a delicate melding of flavors, such as a chipotle-
marinated tuna with an aioli on top of a pumpkin cake. Candles on the
tables come in handy — you need them to read the menu in the dimly lit
dining room. Or better yet, ask the very helpful and knowledgeable waiters to order for you. Late at night, a DJ spins Latin and world music, and
on Sundays you can enjoy live Flamenco dancing.

See map p. 136. 109 Ludlow St. (at Delancey Street). ☎ *212-982-5714. Reservations
suggested. Subway: F to Delancey Street. Main courses: $18–$25. AE, DISC, DC, MC, V.
Open: Sun–Wed 6 p.m.–1 a.m., Thurs 6 p.m.–2 a.m., Fri–Sat 6 p.m.–4 a.m.*

Tamarind
$$$ Flatiron District INDIAN

Inexpensive Indian restaurants, like inexpensive Mexican restaurants, abound in Manhattan so much so that it's often not worth splurging on a more upscale restaurant when you can get the same quality food at a cheaper price. In Tamarind's case, innovative and flavorful variations on the old standards served flawlessly in a sleek, gallery-like setting make the splurge most definitely worth it. Adjacent to the bar is a glassed-in cubicle where you can watch the chefs work the tandoor ovens. Just about anything that comes out of those ovens is spectacular. The incredible breads, *Bhel Poori,* and the assorted crisps and noodles with sweet and sour chutneys make great starters, especially when accompanied by an Indian beer. But try not fill up on the bread and starters and save room for entrees like the *Jhinga Angarey* (jumbo prawns marinated in yogurt and chiles). If you venture from the tandoor, try the lamb *pasanda* (apricot-filled grilled lamb in a cashew and saffron sauce) or Tamarind swordfish marinated in tamarind chutney and fenugreek leaves. You can also choose from a number of vegetarian options here; the Raji vegetarian Thali, an assortment of tandoori salad, lentils, vegetables, chutneys, and relishes, is a treat. Desserts are also special here; try the *gujjia,* a samosa filled with semolina, raisins, cashews, and coconut.

See map p. 138. 41-43 E. 22nd St. (between Broadway and Park Avenue). ☎ *212-674-7400. Reservations recommended. Subway: N, R 23rd Street, or 6 to 23rd Street. Main courses: $11–$30. AE, DC, MC, V. Open: Daily 11:30 a.m.–3 p.m. and 5:30–11:30 p.m.*

Thalassa
$$$$ TriBeCa GREEK

You can't find many dishes better than a simply prepared, grilled whole fish seasoned Greek-style with lemon, olive oil, and garlic. Thalassa, where the seafood offerings are staggering, does that simple dish as well as anyone. But at Thalassa you may also have the option of sampling fresh langoustines from Scotland, monstrous shrimp from Mexico, or a number of different oyster selections. They prepare whatever is fresh off the boat. The grilled octopus, a Greek staple, is perfectly done here and served with a red wine vinaigrette, while the dover sole entree, again simply prepared with olive oil, sea salt, and a hint of lemon, is faultless. The large restaurant is comfortable and has a huge wine cellar stocked with some very good Greek wines.

See map p. 136. 197 Franklin St. (between Greenwich and Hudson streets). ☎ *212-941-7661.* www.thalassanyc.com. *Reservations recommended. Subway: 1, 9 to Franklin Street. Lunch: $20 prix fixe. Dinner $30 prix fixe. Main courses: dinner $14–$28. AE, DC, DISC, MC, V. Open: Mon–Thurs 12–2:30 p.m. and 6–11 p.m., Fri–Sat 6–midnight, Sun 5–10 p.m.*

Uncle Jack's Steakhouse
$$$$ Midtown West STEAKHOUSE

Like so many other steakhouses, Uncle Jack's is testosterone-fueled. Portions are monstrous, décor is plush and bawdy with huge banquettes, it boasts a lively bar with a large variety of single malt scotches, and two private party rooms with helpful tuxedoed waiters are available. But don't let all that "manliness" deter you from enjoying the excellent cuts of meat. Steaks are dry-aged for 21 days, and that seems perfect for the tender 28-ounce T-Bone, big enough for two big men. The 48-ounce porterhouse, Uncle Jack's signature dish, is large enough for a family. The restaurant also features chops; the thick-cut pork chop marinated for 24 hours in Jack Daniels holds its own against the steak and seafood. And the baked clams appetizer is as good as I've had at many Italian restaurants. Desserts are, of course, mammoth, but find room to at least share the spectacular pecan pie.

See map p. 138. 440 Ninth Ave. (at 34th Street). ☎ *212-244-0005.* www.uncle jacks.com. *Reservations recommended. Subway: A, C, E, to 34th Street. Main courses: $37–$75, most steaks: $37. AE, DC, DISC, MC, V. Open: Mon–Sat noon–midnight.*

Virgil's Real BBQ
$$$ Midtown West   BARBECUE/SOUTHERN

The pickings are slim in Times Square for decent, value-priced food, so my suggestion for the best bet in the immediate area is Virgil's. The "theme" is Southern barbecue, and the restaurant, sprawling with dining on two levels, is made to look and feel like a Southern roadhouse with good ole boy decorations on the walls and blues on the soundtrack. But forget the gussied-up theme stuff and enjoy the surprisingly authentic smoked meats, especially the spice-rubbed ribs, which are slow cooked and meaty. Or you can try the smoked slices of Owensboro lamb or the Texas beef brisket. For starters, the corn dogs with poblano mustard are something New Yorkers rarely have the pleasure of experiencing, and the barbecue nachos — tortilla chips slathered with melted cheese and barbecued pulled pork — are a meal in themselves. Desserts are what you would expect from a restaurant emulating a Southern theme: big and sweet. Try the homemade ice cream sandwich made with the "cookie of the day." Virgil's is a great place to bring the kids; they can make as much noise as they want here and no one will notice.

See map p. 138. 152 W. 44th St. (between Sixth and Seventh avenues). ☎ *212-921-9494.* www.virgilsbbq.com. *Reservations recommended. Subway: 1, 2, 3, 7, 9, N, R to 42nd Street/Times Square. Sandwiches: $6–$11, main courses and barbecue platters: $13–$26. AE, DC, DISC, MC, V. Open: Sun–Mon 11:30 a.m.–11 p.m., Tues–Sat 11:30 a.m.–midnight.*

Voyage
$$$$ Greenwich Village   SOUTHERN/ASIAN

As its name implies, the theme of this wonderful restaurant is travel. And the food here, by just subtly touching on the spices and styles of a region, takes you to many different culinary destinations all in one sitting. The appetizer of truffled scallops combined with grits and redeye gravy was a revelation never before sampled on my own journeys to the American

South, while the phenomenal entree of roasted cod served in a bath of cilantro and coconut broth and accompanied ingeniously by samosas was obviously inspired by India, yet like nothing I've had in an Indian restaurant. Voyage has an extensive wine list, but skip the wine and order one of the talented bartender's signature cocktails. I had an island rum punch that was as good as I've had on any island. Tables are a bit too close together, but don't let that — or the somewhat disconcerting black-and-white photographs on the walls of cigar-chomping Cuban men — distract you from enjoying your dining expedition.

See map p. 136. 117 Perry St. (at Greenwich Street). ☎ *212-255-9191. Reservations recommended. Subway: 1, 9 to Christopher Street. Main courses: $14–$24. AE, MC, V. Mon–Wed 5–11 p.m., Thurs–Sat 5–midnight.*

Dining and Snacking on the Go

New York is a city where everyone is constantly on the move. The pace feels like you have just 15 minutes before your curtain goes up, the game begins, or the tour starts. More often than not, you don't have time to sit down to a leisurely dinner. We're well aware of the rush here in New York, which is why you can find so many quick and tasty eats.

Breakfast

I'm going to be honest: I think brunch is for suckers. I mean, what is it but a slightly fancier version of breakfast at inflated prices — and it's usually not served until after 11:00 a.m. . . . and only on weekends! Talk about scams. I'll take breakfast over brunch any day — *especially* on weekends. Some of my favorite restaurants for breakfast — not to be confused with brunch — include:

✔ **Clinton St. Baking Company**, 4 Clinton St. at Houston Street (☎ 646-602-6263). The blueberry pancakes with maple butter and the buttermilk biscuit egg sandwich are worth braving the morning lines. Or wait until the lines subside and have them for lunch and dinner — they're served all day. Opens at 8 a.m. daily. (See the "Downtown Dining" map.)

✔ **EJ's Luncheonette,** 447 Amsterdam Ave. between 81st and 82nd streets (☎ 212-873-3444). The best of the retro-diners, EJ's banana-pecan pancakes are so good you may want to return and have them again for dinner. Opens at 8:30 a.m. daily. (See the "Uptown Dining" map.)

✔ **Good Enough to Eat,** 483 Amsterdam Ave. between 83rd and 84th streets (☎ 212-496-0163). Waiting on line for breakfast is another of my pet peeves, and the wait for breakfast at this Upper West Side institution on the weekends is ridiculous and should be avoided. So go during the week when you can gorge on pumpkin French toast, a "Wall Street" omelet, baked honey-mustard glazed ham with Vermont cheddar, or "Peter Paul" pancakes filled with Belgian chocolate chips, coconut, and topped with roasted coconut. Opens weekdays at 8 a.m., weekends at 9 a.m. (See the "Uptown Dining" map.)

✔ **Big Wong King,** 67 Mott St. between Canal and Bayard streets (☎ 212-964-1452). No eggs. No coffee. No pancakes. Can this be breakfast? You bet it can. Not much is more satisfying in the morning than a hot bowl of *congee* (rice porridge with either pork, beef, or shrimp), accompanied by a fried cruller and tea served in a glass. Big Wong is a breakfast favorite among the residents of Chinatown. Opens daily at 8:30 a.m. (See the "Downtown Dining" map.)

✔ **Veselka,** 144 Second Ave. at 9th Street (☎ 212-228-9682). The Greek diner may be extinct in Manhattan, but this Ukrainian diner lives on. And we're all very grateful, because New York just would not be the same without Veselka's buckwheat pancakes and cheese blintzes. Open 24 hours. (See the "Downtown Dining" map.)

✔ **Norma's At Le Parker Meridien hotel,** 118 W. 57th St. between Sixth and Seventh avenues (☎ 212-708-7460). Norma's is a glorious ode to comfort food. It's pricey but worth it for classics done with style and creativity. Open weekdays at 6:30 a.m., weekends at 7 a.m. (See the "Midtown Dining" map.)

Bagels

We take our bagels seriously here in New York, and I admit to being a bagel snob. I like mine moist, not too big, and without too much adornment. Here, in my estimation, is a list of places to find New York's best bagels, which, of course, are the world's best.

✔ **Absolute Bagels.** 2708 Broadway between 107th and 108th streets (☎ 212-932-2105). Their egg bagels, hot out of the oven, are perfectly-sized and melt in your mouth. (See the "Uptown Dining" map.)

✔ **Ess-A-Bagel,** 359 First Ave. at 21st Street (☎ 212-260-2252; www. ess-a-bagel.com) and 831 Third Ave. between 50th and 51st streets (☎ 212-980-1010). These are a little too hefty for my taste, but they have a very loyal following, so I must acknowledge Ess-a-Bagel's worthiness. (See the "Midtown Dining" map.)

✔ **H&H Bagels,** 2239 Broadway at 80th Street (☎ 212-595-8003; www. handhbagel.com) and 639 W. 46th St. at 12th Avenue (☎ 212-595-8000). For years my undisputed favorite bagel, but in their arrogance, they raised their prices to $1 per bagel, and, as is usually the case, the quality declined as well. But it's still an excellent bagel. Take-out only. (See the "Uptown Dining" map.)

✔ **Murray's Bagels,** 500 Sixth Ave. between 12th and 13th streets (☎ 212-462-2830) and 242 Eighth Ave. at 23rd Street (☎ 646-638-1334). There's nothing like a soft, warm bagel to begin your day, and Murray's does them beautifully. (See the "Downtown Dining" and "Midtown Dining" maps.)

Pizza

Hear this Chicago: Your deep-dish pizza abominations have nothing on the delectable thin-crusted New York variety. And even though the quality of pizza in the city — due to the very troubling proliferation of Domino's, Pizza Hut, and other fast-food pizza chains — has noticeably declined, this is still where you can find the best pizza anywhere west of Italy.

So when pizza is what you seek, search out the real deal and don't be tempted by the sad, soggy imitations that seem to litter every block. You can find the best pizza in the city at:

- ✔ **Grimaldi's Pizza,** 19 Old Fulton St. between Front and Water streets (☎ 718-858-4300). At the foot of the Brooklyn Bridge in Brooklyn, the pizza made by the Grimaldis, who have made pizzas in New York for almost 100 years, is cooked in a coal-oven and features a crisp, thin crust; homemade mozzarella; and a rich, flavorful sauce. If you need incentive to walk across the Brooklyn Bridge, Grimaldi's is it. (See the "Brooklyn Dining" map.)

- ✔ **John's Pizzeria,** 278 Bleecker St. near Seventh Avenue South (☎ 212-243-1680). Thanks to recent expansion, you can now choose from one of three John's locations in Manhattan. The quality has been diluted somewhat, but not enough not skip this favorite. Thin-crusted and out of a coal oven with the proper ratio of tomato sauce to cheese, John's is worthy of its loyal following. The original Bleecker Street location is the most old-world romantic and my personal favorite. Also at 260 W. 44th St. between Broadway and Eighth Avenue (☎ 212-391-1560) and 408 E. 64th St. between York and First avenues (☎ 212-935-2895). (See the "Downtown Dining," "Midtown Dining," and "Uptown Dining" maps.)

- ✔ **Lombardi's,** 32 Spring St. between Mulberry and Mott streets (☎ 212-941-7994). Claiming to be New York's oldest pizzeria (circa 1905), Lombardi's still uses a generations-old Neapolitan family pizza recipe. The coal-oven kicks out perfectly cooked pies, some topped with ingredients such as pancetta, homemade sausage, and my favorite, fresh-shucked clams. A garden in the back makes Lombardi's even more inviting during warm weather. (See the "Downtown Dining" map.)

- ✔ **Patsy's Pizzeria,** 2287 First Ave. between 117th and 118th streets (☎ 212-534-9783). The coal oven here has been burning since 1932, and although the neighborhood in East Harlem where Patsy's is located has had its ups and downs, the quality of pizza at this place has never wavered. Try the marinara pizza: a pie with fresh marinara sauce, but no cheese (the pie is so good that you won't miss the mozzarella). Unlike at the other pizzerias mentioned here, you can order by the slice at Patsy's.

With the exception of Patsy's, most of the pizzerias I've listed are not the place to go for a quick slice. Unfortunately, it's tough to find a good "slice" of pizza anywhere in New York. If a slice is all you want, a few of my top choices include:

- ✔ **Sal & Carmine's,** 2671 Broadway between 100th and 101st streets. (See the "Uptown Dining" map.)

- ✔ **Joe's Pizza,** 7 Carmine St. at Sixth Avenue. (See the "Downtown Dining" map.)

- ✔ **Two Boots,** 42 Ave. A between 3rd and 4th streets, and four other Manhattan locations. (See the "Downtown Dining" map.)

Hamburgers and hot dogs

While most of the country in the 1960s and '70s was being inundated with Golden Arches every few miles, New York proudly held out. But then in the 1980s, the arches came, and now, just like everywhere else in the world, the Golden Arches are here to stay. But that doesn't mean that you should settle for what's conveniently familiar when you can find so many better, and even cheaper, options that aren't affiliated with national fast food chains. Instead, check out any of New York's best burger joints listed below.

- ✔ **Big Nick's Burger Joint,** 2175 Broadway at 77th Street (☎ 212-362-9238). Be careful you don't get singed as you enter Big Nick's, where the griddle is perilously close to the entrance and burgers are always frying. Trying to decide whether you want your burger with buffalo meat, turkey, or ground beef is one problem; the other is what you want on it, because at Big Nick's, the options are dizzying. (See the "Uptown Dining" map.)

- ✔ **Burger Joint in the Le Parker Meridien Hotel,** 118 W. 57th St. between Sixth and Seventh avenues (☎ 212-245-5000). This clever addition to the Le Parker Meridien Hotel is hidden off the lobby by a red curtain, but word has spread about the perfect $4.50 hamburgers sold at this real joint where it's just burgers, fries, and beer. (See the "Midtown Dining" map.)

- ✔ **Corner Bistro,** 331 W. 4th St. at Hudson Street (☎ 212-242-9502). This aged dark-wood tavern and neighborhood hangout is always mentioned as a top contender for New York's best hamburger. Try it and decide for yourself. (See the "Downtown Dining" map.)

- ✔ **Prime Burger,** 5 E. 51st St. between Fifth and Madison avenues (☎ 212-759-4729). Located across from St. Patrick's Cathedral, this no-frills coffeeshop serves juicy burgers and is a welcome refuge in this high-priced neighborhood. (See the "Midtown Dining" map.)

What's better than a New York City hot dog from a cart on the street? How about two New York City hot dogs from a cart on the street? Better yet, skip the cart and head to the Upper West Side **Gray's Papaya,** 2090

Broadway at 72nd Street (☎ 212-799-0243), for one of the cheapest meals on the planet, the "recession special": $2.45 for two beef dogs and a fruit drink. And the good thing is that at Gray's, there's always a recession. (See the "Uptown Dining" map.)

If you're on the Upper East Side and yearn for a hot dog fix, head to **Papaya King,** 179 E. 86th St. (☎ 212-369-0648), the poor man's Gray's Papaya. (See the "Uptown Dining" map.)

When a hot dog with just mustard and sauerkraut does not suffice and you want something more exotic, visit **F&B Gudtfood** in Chelsea at 269 W. 23rd St. between Seventh and Eighth avenues (☎ 646-486-4441), where the hot dogs are made with pork, beef, chicken, salmon, and tofu, and the toppings include items like feta cheese, guacamole, and hummus. (See the "Midtown Dining" map.)

New York delicatessens

New York delis are all about pastrami and attitude. And New York has plenty of both. Some of the best delis include:

✔ **Artie's Delicatessen,** 2290 Broadway between 82nd and 83rd streets (☎ 212-579-5959). This new kid on the deli block can hold its own on the playground with the big boys, thank you very much, especially in the wiener department. (See the "Uptown Dining" map.)

✔ **Barney Greengrass, the Sturgeon King,** 541 Amsterdam Ave. between 86th and 87th streets on the Upper West Side (☎ 212-724-4707). This unassuming, daytime-only deli has become legendary for its high-quality salmon (sable, gravlax, Nova Scotia, kippered, lox, pastrami — you choose), whitefish, and sturgeon (of course). (See the "Uptown Dining" map.)

✔ **Carnegie Deli,** 854 Seventh Ave. at 55th Street (☎ 800-334-5606 or 212-757-2245). Even big eaters may be challenged by mammoth sandwiches with names like "Fifty Ways to Love Your Liver" (chopped liver, hard-boiled egg, lettuce, tomato, and onion). (See the "Midtown Dining" map.)

✔ **Katz's Delicatessen,** 205 E. Houston St. at Ludlow Street (☎ 212-254-2246). The tour buses line up outside Katz's for good reason: This old-world deli is the city's best. But be prepared to wait or try to hit it in the off hours. (See the "Downtown Dining" map.)

✔ **Second Avenue Deli,** 156 Second Ave. at 10th Street (☎ 800-NYC-DELI or 212-677-0606). This is the best kosher choice in town. (For all you goyim out there, that means no milk, butter, or cheese is served.) And Second Avenue doesn't bow to tourism — it's the real deal. The dishes are true New York classics: gefilte fish, matzo ball soup, chicken livers, potato knishes, nova lox, and eggs. (See the "Downtown Dining" map.)

Sweet Treats

As all of you are my witnesses, I now stand and confess my addiction: I am a sugar addict. I cannot end a meal without a decadently sweet fix. Be it ice cream, cake, cookies, or candy, I'm like that spoiled girl in the movie *Willie Wonka and the Chocolate Factory*. You know, "I want the world . . . I want the whole world," as long as the major ingredient is sugar. Fortunately, I live in New York, and thus I can fulfill my constant sweet cravings. So if you suffer as I do, look for some of New York's best sweet sources to help get you through the day.

Ice cream

For the best ice cream in New York, you have to travel across the Brooklyn Bridge to the **Brooklyn Ice Cream Factory,** Fulton Ferry Landing Pier in Brooklyn (☎ 718-246-3963), where everything is freshly made, including the hot fudge for your sundae. (See the "Brooklyn Dining" map.) For original, exotic flavors, like Green Tea, Red Bean, and Almond Cookie — perfect complements to a spicy Asian meal in Chinatown — head to the **Chinatown Ice Cream Factory,** 65 Bayard St. between Mott and Elizabeth streets (☎ 212-608-4170). (See the "Downtown Dining" map.) Jon Snyder, owner of the curiously named **Il Laboratorio del Gelato,** 95 Orchard St. between Broome and Delancey streets (☎ 212-343-9922; www.laboratoriodelgelato.com), uses only the freshest ingredients to create sweet magic in his laboratory. (See the "Downtown Dining" map.)

A new entry into the New York ice cream market is the Arizona-based **Cold Stone Creamery** at 253 W. 42nd St. between Seventh and Eighth avenues (☎ 212-398-1882) and 1651 Second Ave. at 86th Street (☎ 212-249-7080; www.coldstonecreamery.com). The super-rich ice cream here is mixed on a frozen granite stone and made into creations like "mud pie mojo," "coconut cream pie," and the irresistible "German chocolate cake." (See the "Midtown Dining" and "Uptown Dining" maps.)

Serendipity 3, 225 E. 60th St. between Second and Third avenues (☎ 212-838-3531), serves regular meals, but why bother when you can go right to the restaurant's signature dish: the Frozen Hot Chocolate, a slushy version of everybody's cold-weather favorite. (See the "Uptown Dining" map.)

Mmmm . . . hot chocolate

Although the second coming of the Ice Age could not deter me from seeking out ice cream, some people, inexplicably, feel that ice cream is best eaten in hot weather. The winter alternative to ice cream is hot chocolate, and at some bakeries and candy stores, the hot chocolate is so rich and so good that the next time you have to succumb to one of those packages of Swiss Miss, you'll find yourself spitting the vile swill across the room.

At **Jacques Torres Chocolate,** 60 Water St. in Brooklyn (☎ 718-875-9772; www.mrchocolate.com), the lines on winter weekends begin forming at 9 a.m. Customers wait for hot chocolate perfected by the former pastry chef of the restaurant Le Cirque. You can choose from many varieties, but the most popular is the hot chocolate with allspice, cinnamon, sweet ancho chile peppers, and hot chipotle peppers. (See the "Brooklyn Dining" map.)

The Chocolate Bar, 48 Eighth Ave. between Jane and Horatio streets (☎ 212-366-1541; www.chocolatebarnyc.com), features not only hot chocolate, but chocolate tea, and if you can't live without the stuff in the middle of August, Iced Chocolate as well. (See the "Downtown Dining" map.) Both Jacques Torres and The Chocolate Bar also make sinfully delicious chocolates to accompany your chocolate beverage. And if that doesn't get you through the day, nothing will.

Baked goods

For something sweet to go with that hot chocolate, New York has no shortage of bakeries. The baked goods at the **Buttercup Bakery,** 973 Second Ave. between 51st and 52nd streets (☎ 212-350-4144), live up to the store's mouth-watering name. And besides incredible cakes and pies, the Buttercup makes the best banana pudding in town. (See the "Midtown Dining" map.)

In the East Village, **Moishe's Kosher Bake Shop,** 115 Second Ave. between Sixth and Seventh streets (☎ 212-505-8555), bakes fresh challah and babka daily, but I go for the perfect black-and-white cookies. (See the "Downtown Dining" map.) On the Upper West Side, you can't find better cupcakes (in such flavors as Oreo cookie, Heath Bar, and Coconut) than at **Crumbs,** 221½ Amsterdam Ave. between 75th and 76th streets, (☎ 212-712-9800). (See the "Uptown Dining" map.)

Index of Establishments by Neighborhood

Lower East Side

Clinton St. Baking Company $
Il Laboratorio del Gelato $
Katz's Delicatessen $
Suba $$$$

East Village

A Salt & Battery $
Angelica Kitchen $
Moishe's Kosher Bake Shop $
Mojo $$
Second Avenue Deli $
Sonali $
Two Boots Pizza $
Veselka $

Greenwich Village

Babbo $$$$
The Chocolate Bar $
Corner Bistro $
Home $$
Joe's Pizza $
John's Pizzeria $
Murray's Bagels $
Strip House $$$$
Voyage $$$$

Meatpacking District/Chelsea

Biltmore Room $$$$
F&B Gudtfood $
Florent $$
Grand Sichuan International $
Murray's Bagels $
Pastis $$

Gramercy/Flatiron District/Union Square

Blue Smoke $$
Dos Caminos $$$
Eleven Madison Park $$$$
Ess-A-Bagel $
Tamarind $$$

Midtown East

Buttercup Bakery $
Curry In A Hurry $
Ess-A-Bagel $

rm $$$$$
Pampano $$$$
P.J. Clarke's $$
Prime Burger $

Midtown West/Theater District

Afghan Kebab House $
Aquavit $$$$
Atelier $$$$$
Burger Joint $
Carmine's $$$
Carnegie Deli $
Cold Stone Creamery $
Churrascaria Plataforma $$$
db Bistro Moderne $$$$
Hallo! Berlin $
Island Burgers and Shakes $
Joseph's $$$$$
John's Pizzeria $
Molyvos $$$$
Mickey Mantle's $$$
Norma's $$
Sapporo $
Siam Inn $
Uncle Jack's Steakhouse $$$$
Virgil's Real BBQ $$$

Koreatown/Herald Square

Mandoo Bar $

Upper East Side

Cold Stone Creamery $
Daniel $$$$$
John's Pizzeria $
Papaya King $
Serendipity 3 $$

Upper West Side

Absolute Bagels $
Aix $$$$
Artie's Delicatessen $$
Barney Greengrass,
    the Sturgeon King $$
Big Nick's Burger Joint $
Café des Artistes $$$$$
Carmine's $$
Celeste $$
'Cesca $$$$

Crumbs $
EJ's Luncheonette $
Flor de Mayo $
Gray's Papaya $
Good Enough to Eat $
H&H Bagels $
Jean-Georges $$$$$
Rosa Mexicano $$$$
Sal & Carmine's$
Tavern on the Green $$$$

Harlem
Charles' Southern Style Kitchen $
El Paso Taqueria $
La Fonda Boricua $
La Marmite $
Patsy's Pizzeria $

Brooklyn
Brooklyn Ice Cream Factory $
Grimaldi's Pizza $
Jacques Torres Chocolate $

Index of Establishments by Cuisine

Afghan
Afghan Kebab House (Midtown West, $)

African
La Marmite (Harlem, $)

American
Bubby's (TriBeCa, $$)
Burger Joint (Midtown West, $)
Cub Room (SoHo $$$$)
EJ's Luncheonette (Upper West Side, $)
Good Enough To Eat
    (Upper West Side, $)
Mickey Mantle's (Midtown West, $$$)
Norma's (Midtown West, $$)
P.J. Clarke's (Midtown East, $$)
Prime Burger (Midtown East, $)
Serendipity 3 (Upper East Side, $$)
Tavern on the Green (Upper
    West Side $$$$)

Asian Fusion
Biltmore Room (Chelsea, $$$$)
Nyonya (Chinatown, $)

Bakeries
Buttercup Bakery (Midtown East, $)
The Chocolate Bar (Greenwich Village $)
Crumbs (Upper West Side, $)
Jacques Torres Chocolate (Brooklyn, $)

Brazilian
Churrascaria Plataforma (Times
    Square & Midtown West, $$)

Breakfast
Absolute Bagels (Upper West Side, $)
Balthazar (SoHo, $$)
Barney Greengrass, the Sturgeon King
    (Upper West Side, $)
Bubby's (TriBeCa, $$)
Columbia Bagels (Upper West Side)
Clinton St. Baking Company
    (Lower East Side $)
EJ's Luncheonette (Upper West Side, $)
Ess-A-Bagel (Midtown East,
    Flatiron District, $)
Florent (Meatpacking District, $)
Good Enough To Eat (Upper
    West Side, $)
Home (Greenwich Village, $$)
Katz's Delicatessen (Lower
    East Side, $)
Murray's Bagels (Greenwich Village,
    Chelsea $)
Norma's (Midtown West, $$)
Pastis (Meatpacking District, $$)
Veselka (East Village, $)

British
A Salt & Battery (East Village, $)

Chinese

Grand Sichuan International (Chelsea $)
Big Wong King (Chinatown, $)
New York Noodletown (Chinatown, $)

French

Aix (Upper West Side, $$$$)
Atelier (Midtown West, $$$$$)
Balthazar (SoHo, $$)
Café des Artistes (Upper West Side, $$$$$)
Chanterelle (TriBeCa, $$$$)
Daniel (Upper East Side, $$$$$)
db Bistro Moderne (Midtown West, $$$$)
Eleven Madison Park (Flatiron District, $$$$)
Florent (Meatpacking District, $$)
Jean-Georges (Upper West Side, $$$$$)
Pastis (Meatpacking District, $$)

German

Hallo! Berlin (Midtown West $)

Gourmet Sandwiches/Deli/TakeOut

Absolute Bagels (Upper West Side, $)
Artie's Delicatessen (Upper West Side, $$)
Barney Greengrass, the Sturgeon King (Upper West Side, $$)
Carnegie Deli (Midtown West, $$)
Ess-A-Bagel (Midtown East, $)
Gray's Papaya (Upper West Side, $)
Island Burgers and Shakes (Midtown West, $)
Katz's Delicatessen (Lower East Side, $)
Murray's Bagels (Greenwich Village, Chelsea, $)
Second Avenue Deli (Lower East Side, $)

Greek

Molyvos (Midtown West, $$$$)
Thalassa (TriBeCa, $$$$)

Hamburgers

Big Nick's Burger Joint (Upper West Side, $)
Burger Joint (Midtown West, $)

Corner Bistro (Greenwich Village, $)
Prime Burger (Midtown East, $)

Hot Dogs

F&B Gudtfood (Chelsea, $)
Gray's Papaya (Upper West Side, $)
Papaya King (Upper East Side, $)

Indian

Curry in a Hurry (Midtown East, $)
Sonali (East Village, $)
Tamarind (Flatiron District, $$$)

Italian

Babbo (Greenwich Village, $$$$)
Bread Tribeca (TriBeCa, $$$)
Caffe Roma (Little Italy, $)
Carmine's (Times Square, Upper West Side, $$)
'Cesca (Upper West Side, $$$$)
Celeste (Upper West Side, $$)
Ferrara (Little Italy, $)
Fiamma Osteria (SoHo, $$$$,)

Ice Cream

Brooklyn Ice Cream Factory (Brooklyn, $)
Chinatown Ice Cream Factor (Chinatown, $)
Cold Stone Creamery (Upper East Side, Midtown West, $)
Il Laboratorio del Gelato (Lower East Side, $)
Serendipity 3 (Upper East Side, $$)

Japanese

Sapporo (Midtown West, $)

Jewish Deli

Artie's Delicatessen (Upper West Side, $$)
Barney Greengrass, the Sturgeon King (Upper West Side, $$)
Carnegie Deli (Midtown West, $$)
Katz's Delicatessen (Lower East Side, $)
Second Avenue Deli (Lower East Side, $$

Korean

Mandoo Bar (Midtown West, $)

Latin American/Hispanic

Flor de Mayo (Upper West Side, $)
La Fonda Boricua (Harlem, $)
Mojo (East Village, $$)
Suba (Lower East Side, $$$$)

Mexican

Dos Caminos (Flatiron District, $$$)
El Paso Taqueria (Harlem, $)
Pampano (Midtown East, $$$)
Rosa Mexicano (Upper West Side, $$$$)

Pizza

Grimaldi's Pizza (Brooklyn, $)
Joe's Pizza (Greenwich Village, $)
John's Pizzeria (Times Square &
    Midtown West, Greenwich Village,
    Upper East Side, $)
Lombardi's (SoHo/Little Italy, $)
Patsy's Pizzeria (Harlem, $)
Sal & Carmine's (Upper West Side, $)

Ukrainian

Veselka (East Village, $)

Scandinavian

Aquavit (Midtown West, $$$$)

Seafood

Joseph's (Midtown West, $$$$$)
rm (Midtown East, $$$$)

Soul Food

Charles' Southern Style Kitchen
    (Harlem, $)

Southern/Barbecue

Blue Smoke (Flatiron District, $$)
Virgil's Real BBQ (Times Square, $$$,)
Voyage (Greenwich Village, $$$$)

Steaks

Peter Luger Steakhouse
    (Brooklyn, $$$$)
Strip House (Greenwich Village, $$$$)
Uncle Jack's Steakhouse
    (Midtown West, $$$$)

Thai

Siam Inn (Midtown West, $)

Vegetarian

Angelica Kitchen (East Village, $)

Vietnamese

Nha Trang (Chinatown, $)

Index of Establishments by Price

$$$$$

Atelier (Midtown West)
Café des Artistes (Upper West Side)
Daniel (Upper East Side)
Jean-Georges (Upper West Side)
Joseph's (Midtown West)
rm (Midtown East)

$$$$

Aix (Upper West Side)
Aquavit (Midtown West)
Babbo (Greenwich Village)

Biltmore Room (Chelsea)
'Cesca (Upper West Side)
Chanterelle (TriBeCa)
Cub Room (SoHo)
db Bistro Moderne (Midtown West)
Eleven Madison Park (Flatiron District)
Molyvos (Midtown West)
Pampano (Midtown East)
Peter Luger (Brooklyn)
Rosa Mexicano (Upper West Side)
Strip House (Greenwich Village)
Tavern on the Green (Upper West Side)
Thalassa (TriBeCa)

Uncle Jack's Steakhouse
(Midtown West)
Voyage (Greenwich Village)

$$$

Balthazar (SoHo)
Bread Tribeca (TriBeCa)
Churrascaria Plataforma
(Theater District)
Dos Caminos (Flatiron District)
Mickey Mantle's (Midtown West)
Tamarind (Flatiron District)
Virgil's Real BBQ (Midtown West)

$$

Artie's Delicatessen (Upper West Side)
Barney Greengrass, the Sturgeon King
(Upper West Side)
Blue Smoke (Flatiron District)
Bubby's (TriBeCa)
Carmine's (Upper West Side,
Midtown West)
Carnegie Deli (Midtown West)
Celeste (Upper West Side)
Florent (Meatpacking District)
Home (Greenwich Village)
Mojo (East Village)
Pastis (Meatpacking District)
P.J. Clarke's (Midtown East)
Second Avenue Deli (East Village)
Serendipity 3 (Upper East Side)

$

Absolute Bagels (Upper West Side)
Afghan Kebab House (Midtown West)
Angelica Kitchen (East Village)
A Salt & Battery (East Village)
Big Nick's Burger Joint (Upper
West Side)
Big Wong King (Chinatown)
Brooklyn Ice Cream Factory (Brooklyn)
Burger Joint (Midtown West)
Buttercup Bakery (Midtown East)
Charles' Southern Style Kitchen
(Harlem)
Chinatown Ice Cream Factory
(Chinatown)

The Chocolate Bar (Greenwich Village)
Clinton St. Baking Company
(Lower East Side)
Cold Stone Creamery (Midtown West,
Upper East Side)
Corner Bistro (Greenwich Village)
Crumbs (Upper West Side)
Curry in a Hurry (Midtown East)
EJ's Luncheonette (Upper West Side)
El Paso Taqueria (Harlem)
Ess-A-Bagel (Midtown East,
Gramercy Park)
F&B Gudtfood (Chelsea)
Flor de Mayo (Upper West Side)
Good Enough to Eat (Upper West Side)
Grand Sichuan International (Chelsea)
Gray's Papaya (Upper West Side)
Grimaldi's Pizza (Brooklyn)
Hallo! Berlin (Midtown West)
H&H Bagels (Midtown West,
Upper West Side)
Il Laboratorio del Gelato
(Lower East Side)
Island Burgers and Shakes
(Midtown West)
Jacques Torres Chocolate (Brooklyn)
Joe's Pizza (Greenwich Village)
John's Pizzeria (Greenwich Village,
Upper East Side, Midtown West)
Katz's Delicatessen (Lower East Side)
La Fonda Boricua (Harlem)
La Marmite (Harlem)
Lombardi's (SoHo)
Mandoo Bar (Midtown West)
Murray's Bagels (Greenwich
Village, Chelsea)
Nha Trang (Chinatown)
New York Noodletown (Chinatown)
Nyonya (Chinatown)
Papaya King (Upper East Side)
Patsy's Pizzeria (Harlem)
Prime Burger (Midtown East)
Sal & Carmine's (Upper West Side)
Sapporo (Midtown West)
Siam Inn (Midtown West)
Sonali (East Village)
Two Boots (East Village)
Veselka (East Village)

Part IV

Exploring New York City

The 5th Wave   By Rich Tennant

"It's a play in 2 Acts. The middle Act is about to start now."

In this part . . .

*H*ow do you get to Carnegie Hall? Practice . . .and the N/R/W train! Here's where I go over the top attractions, guided tours, the shopping scene, and specific itineraries that guarantee a good time no matter how long your visit lasts.

Use these handy Post-It® Flags to mark your favorite pages.

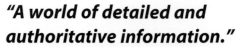

Chapter 11

New York's Top Sights

. . . .

In This Chapter

▶ Honing in on New York City's top sights
▶ Finding the best attractions to match your interests
▶ Taking a guided tour by bus, boat, or on foot

. . . .

*1*t's taken me years to get around to seeing many of the sights I'm recommending that you visit during the week or few days you're here. To get in as much as possible in the time you have, consider these pointers:

✔ **Visit the more popular museums and attractions as early as possible before lines begin to form.** Check the hours of the attraction and do your best to be there at or near the time the attraction opens to avoid wasting time waiting on lines.

✔ **Plan each half day so that the sights you want to see are close by.** For example: Visit the World Trade Center site early because you don't have to worry about times of operation. Then walk over to Wall Street and the Financial District, take in one of the lower Manhattan museums, and then either walk or take a subway to Chinatown for lunch.

✔ **Consider a guided bus tour or a Manhattan island cruise.** Most are around three hours long, and you get a good overview of the city's attractions. After the tour is done and you've seen all the major landmarks, you can spend more of your time concentrating on what interests you, which may include something you saw during your tour.

✔ **Buy tickets in advance.** Some attractions, like the Empire State Building, sell tickets online. They may be slightly more expensive, but if you're looking to save time from waiting on a line, the few dollars may be worth it. Purchasing a **CityPass** (see the sidebar "Save time and money with CityPass" later in this chapter) saves you both money *and* ticket-buying time.

Downtown Attractions

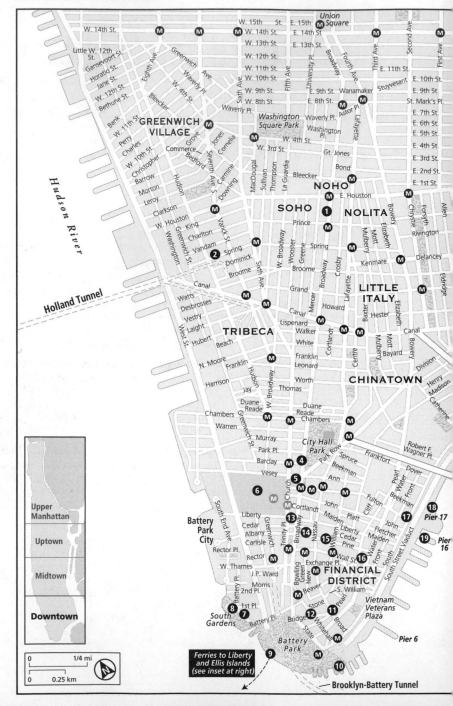

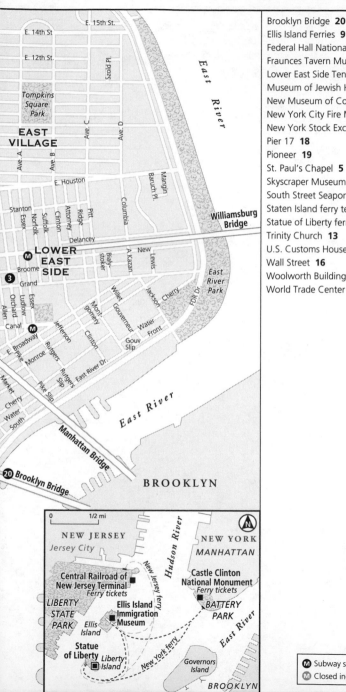

Brooklyn Bridge **20**
Ellis Island Ferries **9**
Federal Hall National Memorial **15**
Fraunces Tavern Museum **11**
Lower East Side Tenement Museum **3**
Museum of Jewish Heritage **8**
New Museum of Contemporary Art **1**
New York City Fire Museum **2**
New York Stock Exchange **14**
Pier 17 **18**
Pioneer **19**
St. Paul's Chapel **5**
Skyscraper Museum **7**
South Street Seaport and Museum **17**
Staten Island ferry terminal **10**
Statue of Liberty ferry terminal **9**
Trinity Church **13**
U.S. Customs House **12**
Wall Street **16**
Woolworth Building **4**
World Trade Center site **6**

Midtown Attractions

American Folk Art Museum **22**
Bateaux New York **6**
Bryant Park **12**
Carnegie Hall **1**
Chelsea Piers **7**
Chrysler Building **15**
Circle Line **4**
Empire State Building **11**
Flatiron Building **10**
Grand Central Station **14**
Gray Line Tours **2**
Intrepid-Sea-Air-Space Museum **3**
Madison Square Garden **8**
Museum of Modern Art **21**
Museum of Television & Radio **20**
New York Public Library **13**
New York Waterways **5**
Radio City Music Hall **17**
Rockefeller Center **18**
St. Patrick's Cathedral **19**
Sony Wonder Technology Lab **23**
Union Square Park **9**
United Nations **16**

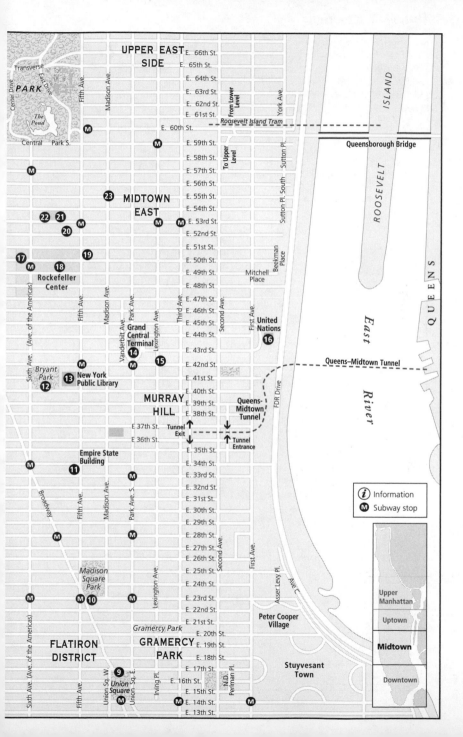

UPPER EAST SIDE

E. 66th St.
E. 65th St.
E. 64th St.
E. 63rd St.
E. 62nd St.
E. 61st St.
E. 60th St.

Transverse

PARK

The Pond

Central Park S.

Fifth Ave.
Madison Ave.
Fifth Ave.

From Lower Level

Roosevelt Island Tram

York Ave.

ISLAND

E. 59th St.
E. 58th St.
E. 57th St.
E. 56th St.
E. 55th St.
E. 54th St.
E. 53rd St.
E. 52nd St.
E. 51st St.
E. 50th St.
E. 49th St.
E. 48th St.
E. 47th St.
E. 46th St.
E. 45th St.
E. 44th St.
E. 43rd St.
E. 42nd St.
E. 41st St.

To Upper Level

Sutton Pl.

Queensborough Bridge

ROOSEVELT

Sutton Pl. South

Beekman Place

Mitchell Place

MIDTOWN EAST

Rockefeller Center

Grand Central Terminal

New York Public Library

Bryant Park

Sixth Ave. (Ave. of the Americas)
Fifth Ave.
Madison Ave.
Vanderbilt Ave.
Park Ave.
Lexington Ave.
Third Ave.
Second Ave.
First Ave.

United Nations

East River

QUEENS

Queens–Midtown Tunnel

MURRAY HILL

E. 40th St.
E. 39th St.
E. 38th St.
E. 37th St.
E. 36th St.
E. 35th St.
E. 34th St.
E. 33rd St.
E. 32nd St.
E. 31st St.
E. 30th St.
E. 29th St.
E. 28th St.
E. 27th St.
E. 26th St.
E. 25th St.
E. 24th St.
E. 23rd St.
E. 22nd St.
E. 21st St.
E. 20th St.
E. 19th St.
E. 18th St.
E. 17th St.
E. 16th St.
E. 15th St.
E. 14th St.
E. 13th St.

Queens–Midtown Tunnel

Tunnel Exit

Tunnel Entrance

FDR Drive

Empire State Building

Broadway
Fifth Ave.
Madison Ave.
Park Ave. S.

Madison Square Park

Gramercy Park

FLATIRON DISTRICT

GRAMERCY PARK

Sixth Ave. (Ave. of the Americas)
Union Sq. W.
Union Square
Union Sq. E.
Irving Pl.
N.D. Perlman Pl.

Peter Cooper Village

Stuyvesant Town

Second Ave.
First Ave.
Asser Levy Pl.
Avenue C

ⓘ Information
Ⓜ Subway stop

Upper Manhattan

Uptown

Midtown

Downtown

Uptown Attractions

American Museum of Natural
   History **2**
Asia Society **11**
Central Park Zoo **12**
Children's Museum of Manhattan **1**
Cooper-Hewitt National Design
   Museum **6**
The Frick Collection **10**
Guggenheim Museum **7**
Lincoln Center **4**
The Metropolitan Museum of Art **8**
Museum of the City of New York **5**
New-York Historical Society **3**
Whitney Museum of American Art **9**

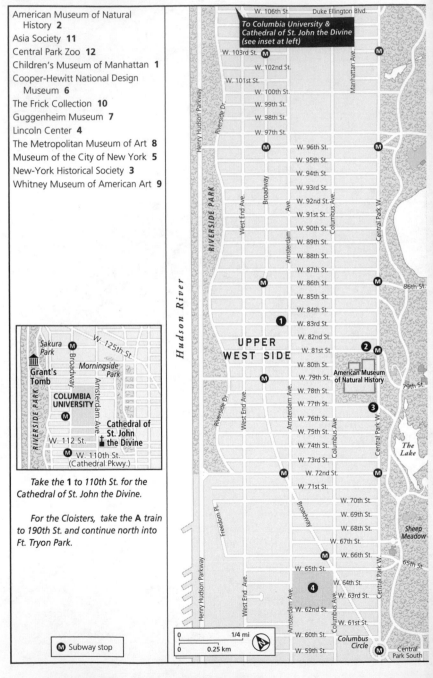

To Columbia University &
Cathedral of St. John the Divine
(see inset at left)

UPPER
WEST SIDE

American Museum
of Natural History

Sakura
Park
Grant's
Tomb
Morningside
Park
COLUMBIA
UNIVERSITY
Cathedral of
St. John
the Divine
W. 112 St.
W. 110th St.
(Cathedral Pkwy.)

*Take the **1** to 110th St. for the
Cathedral of St. John the Divine.*

*For the Cloisters, take the **A** train
to 190th St. and continue north into
Ft. Tryon Park.*

The
Lake

Sheep
Meadow

Columbus
Circle

Central
Park South

0   1/4 mi
0   0.25 km

Ⓜ Subway stop

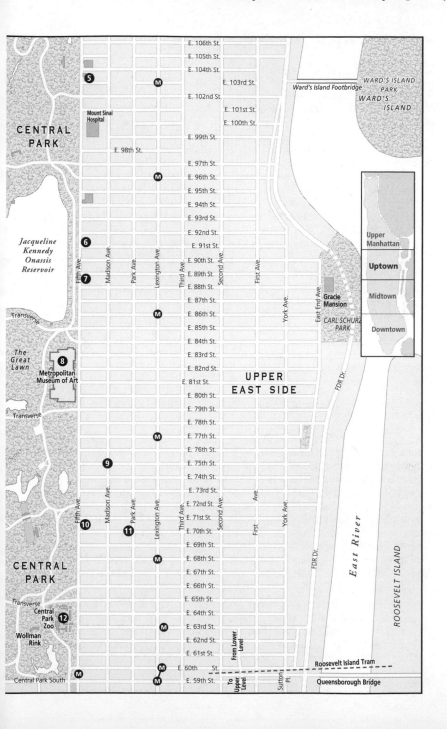

New York City's Top Sights

American Museum of Natural History
Upper West Side

You need at least two hours to take in even a small sampling of this vast museum, which spans four city blocks. In addition to special exhibitions, the museum features an astonishing permanent collection of taxidermic wildlife (including a famous herd of African elephants); an enormous exhibition dedicated to biodiversity; interactive exhibits for kids; and displays of gems, dinosaur fossils, and meteorites, among other treasures. It also has an IMAX theater. The planetarium — a huge sphere housed in a glass box several stories tall — is part of the **Rose Center for Earth and Space.** The top half of the sphere houses the state-of-the-art Space Theater, which airs a breathtaking space show; the bottom half houses the Big Bang, a multisensory re-creation of the first moments of the universe.

See map p. 182. Central Park West (between 77th and 81st streets). ☎ *212-769-5100.* www.amnh.org. *Subway: B/C train to 81st Street/Museum of Natural History stop, then walk south along the front to the entrance. Bus: M10 (north/south bus running on Central Park West, Eighth Avenue uptown, and Seventh Avenue downtown), and M79 (crosstown bus running on 79th Street) stop right at the museum. Suggested admission: $12 adults, $7 children ages 2–12 (free under 2), $9 seniors and students. Museum admission plus Space Show: $19 adults, $11.50 children, $14 seniors and students. Open: Daily 10 a.m.–5:45 p.m., Fri 10 a.m.–8:45 p.m. The museum is fully accessible to wheelchairs and the hearing impaired.*

Bronx Zoo Wildlife Conservation Park
The Bronx

With more than 4,000 animals living on 265 acres, the Bronx Zoo is not only the largest metropolitan animal park in the United States, it's also one of the city's best attractions. Visit any of the numerous exhibits scattered throughout the zoo; the best is the **Wild Asia Complex,** a zoo within a zoo that includes **Jungle World,** an indoor re-creation of Asian forests, and the **Bengali Express Monorail** (open May–Oct), which takes you on a narrated ride high above free-roaming Siberian tigers, Asian elephants, Indian rhinoceroses, and other non-native New Yorkers. You can also visit the **Congo Gorilla Forest,** home to those inquisitive gorillas and other African rainforest animals. Also located within the zoo are a **Children's Zoo** (open Apr–Oct), **Butterfly Zone,** camel rides, and the **Skyfari** aerial tram (each an extra $2 charge).

Fordham Road and Bronx River Parkway, the Bronx. ☎ *718-367-1010.* www.wcs.org/zoos. *Subway: 2 to Pelham Parkway, and then walk west to the Bronxdale entrance. Bus: Liberty Lines' BxM11 express bus. Admission: $8 adults, $6 seniors, $5 children ages 2–12.. Open: Nov–Mar daily 10 a.m.–4:30 p.m. (extended hours for Holiday Lights late Nov–early Jan), Apr–Oct Mon–Fri 10 a.m.–5 p.m., Sat–Sun 10 a.m.–5:30 p.m. Discounted admission Nov–Mar, free Wed year-round. Nominal additional charges may be applied for some exhibits.*

Save time and money with CityPass

The **New York CityPass** (☎ 208-787-4300; www.citypass.net) gives you admission to seven major attractions in the city: the American Museum of Natural History, Circle Line Harbor Cruise, Empire State Building Observatory, Intrepid Sea-Air-Space Museum, Guggenheim Museum, and Museum of Modern Art (MOMA). The pass costs $45 ($39 for children ages 12–17), almost 50 percent less than the $85 you pay if you purchase each ticket separately. You can buy the CityPass online, at the first attraction you visit, or at one of the Ticket Axis electronic kiosks maintained by NYC & Company (at the Visitor Information Center at 810 Seventh Ave. between 52nd and 53rd streets, NY Skyride on the second floor of the Empire State Building, Intrepid Sea-Air-Space Museum, Circle Line, Museum of American Financial History, Museum of the City of New York, Brooklyn Museum of Art, New York Hall of Science in Queens, and New York Botanical Gardens in the Bronx). Note that the CityPass is good for only nine days, and it doesn't include admission to the NY Skyride show on the second floor of the Empire State building or the Space Show at the Hayden Planetarium.

 ## Brooklyn Bridge
Downtown

With sweeping views of lower Manhattan, Brooklyn, and the New York Harbor, the walk across the historic stone-and-steel Brooklyn Bridge is one of my favorite New York activities. Crossing takes between 20 and 40 minutes each way, depending on how long you linger to enjoy the views. You can sit on the benches along the way if you need a break or just want to stop for a bit to try to comprehend that you're really in New York and that this is not a movie set.

 The perfect complement to your stroll over the Brooklyn Bridge is a stop for delicious homemade ice cream at the **Brooklyn Ice Cream Factory** ☎ **718-246-3963,** located in the shadow of the bridge at the Fulton Ferry Fire Boat House on the river. The ice cream fortifies you for your return stroll into Manhattan.

See map p. 178. Sidewalk entrance to the Manhattan end of the bridge is on Park Row just across from City Hall, south of Chambers Street. Subway: 4/5/6 train to Brooklyn Bridge/City Hall; exit across the street from the entrance. Bus: M1 (north/south bus running down Broadway and up Center Street/Lafayette/Park and Madison avenues), although traffic congestion makes the subway a better choice.

 ## Central Park
Upper West Side, Upper East Side

This 843-acre refuge in the middle of the city, is one of New York's most glorious wonders. (See the map "Central Park" for location details.) Throughout the year, but especially in nice weather, Central Park is a sanctuary for New

Central Park

Alice in Wonderland Statue **15**
Balto Statue **21**
The Bandshell **19**
Belvedere Castle **7**
Bethesda Terrace &
  Bethesda Fountain **17**
Boathouse Cafe **12**
Bow Bridge **9**
Carousel **27**
Central Park Zoo **24**
Charles A. Dana
  Discovery Center **1**
Cleopatra's Needle
  (The Obelisk) **10**
Conservatory **14**
Conservatory Garden **1**
The Dairy Information Center **26**
Delacorte Clock **23**
Delacorte Theater **8**
Diana Ross Playground **5**
Hans Christian Andersen
  Statue **13**
Harlem Meer **1**
Hecksher Ball Fields **29**
Hecksher Playground **30**
Henry Luce
  Nature Observatory **7**
Imagine Mosaic **18**
Jacqueline Kennedy Onassis
  Reservoir **3**
Lasker Rink and Pool **1**
Loeb Boathouse **16**
The Mall **20**
North Meadow Ball Fields **2**
Pat Hoffman Friedman
  Playground **11**
The Pool **2**
Rustic Playground **22**
Shakespeare Garden **9**
Spector Playground **4**
Swedish Cottage
  Marionette Theatre **6**
Tavern on the Green **28**
Tisch Children's Zoo **24**
Wollman Rink **25**

ⓘ Information
Ⓜ Subway stop

0 _____ 1/5 mile
0 _____ 200 meters

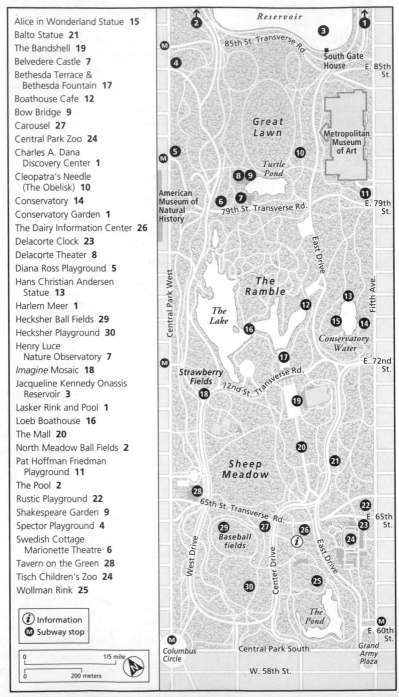

Yorkers and visitors looking for a green escape from the pace and tone of the city streets. Here you can spend hours strolling (or biking) miles of paths that wind through acres of landscaped fields and rolling hills. The park offers pleasures for kids of all ages — you and your children may enjoy taking a boat ride on the lake (call **Loeb Boathouse, ☎ 212-517-2233,** for rental information), skating around Wollman Rink just north of the pond (**☎ 212-439-6900**), or visiting the polar bears and other animals in Central Park Zoo. In the summer, the park plays host to Shakespeare in the Park and SummerStage (see Chapter 14), a series of free concerts. For information about tours of the park, flip to "Seeing the city on special-interest tours" and "Faring well with free walking tours" later in this chapter.

 Even though the park has the lowest crime rate of any of the city's precincts, keep your wits about you, especially in the more remote northern end. It's a good idea to avoid the park after dark, unless you're heading to one of the restaurants for dinner or to a SummerStage or Shakespeare in the Park event.

See map p. 186. From 59th to 110th streets (between Fifth Avenue and Central Park West, the continuation north of Eighth Avenue). Information Center: ☎ 212-310-6600. www.centralparknyc.org. *Subway: A/B/C/D/1/9 train to 59th Street/Columbus Circle stop for the southwest main entrance, N/R/W train to Fifth Avenue/59th Street stop for the southeast main entrance. Buses run along both sides of Central Park and make several stops; the M10 runs up and down Central Park West, and the M1, M2, M3, and M4 run south down Fifth Avenue on the east side of the park (they go north on Madison Avenue). Open: 24 hours.*

 ## Chrysler Building
Midtown East

Number 405 Lexington Avenue is one of the most stunning buildings in New York or any other city. Topped by a shiny steel needle, with triangular windows that are illuminated at night, it looks like something out of Oz. Steel sculptures are poised on its battlements like gargoyles. The building was designed by William Van Alen; finished in 1930, it enjoyed the title of world's tallest building until 1931, when the Empire State Building was completed. The observation deck is no longer open to the public, but be sure to visit the lobby — an Art Deco *tour de force* in chrome, wood, and marble.

See map p. 180. 405 Lexington Ave. (at 42nd Street). Subway: 4/5/6/7/S train to 42nd Street/Grand Central stop, follow the exit signs for Lexington Avenue, pass the barrier, and take the passage in front of you toward the right,which brings you right inside the Chrysler at the lower level. If you miss this exit, go up to street level and cross the street walking east. Bus: M104 from the Upper West Side (runs down Broadway and crosses town at 42nd Street) and M42 across town on 42nd Street; both stop right in front of the building. On the east side and from downtown, take the M101, M102, or M103 (running up Third Avenue and down Lexington Avenue). Open: Mon–Fri 8 a.m.–6 p.m.

The Cloisters
Upper West Side

Located at the north end of Manhattan in Fort Tryon Park, this museum is constructed from portions of medieval and early Renaissance European cloisters that were shipped across the Atlantic. The Cloisters houses an important collection of medieval art, including stained glass, metalwork, sculpture, and an impressive series of unicorn tapestries. The gardens that hug one side of the complex authentically reproduce the herbs, flowers, and other plants found in a typical medieval cloisters. Both the museum and the gardens have a commanding view of the Hudson River and the New Jersey Palisades. If you choose to get here by bus, consider that although the bus takes you right to the museum and offers a scenic, interesting ride, the ride is a long one (up to an hour or more, depending on where you start, as compared to 30 to 45 minutes on the subway). The subway is a good alternative; it takes you right to the entrance of Fort Tryon Park.

See map p. 189. At the north end of Fort Tryon Park, 1 block north of West 190th Street. ☎ *212-923-3700.* www.metmuseum.org. *Subway: A train to 190th Street stop, and then take the elevator to street level (don't walk up the long ramp — it takes you out of your way). Once outside, you see the park entrance; walk north along Fort Washington Avenue to the entrance of Fort Tryon Park and follow the signs along the path north to the Cloisters. Bus: The M4 (north/south bus running on Madison Avenue, 110th Street, Broadway, Fort Washington Avenue uptown, and Fifth Avenue downtown) is very convenient and stops right at the museum; if you're in a hurry, you can take the subway and then catch the bus for the last part of the run. Suggested admission: $12 adults, $7 seniors and students, free for children under 13 when accompanied by an adult; fee includes admission to the Metropolitan Museum. Open: Tues–Sun 9:30 a.m.–5:15 p.m.; Nov–Feb closes at 4:45 p.m.*

Ellis Island
Downtown

From its opening in 1892 to its closing in 1954, more than 12 million immigrants, including my own ancestors, entered America through the Registry Hall on Ellis Island. After a $160 million restoration in the 1980s, it reopened as a museum dedicated to the history of immigration. An enormous pile of luggage and other personal items (children's dolls, hairbrushes, clothing, and the like) remind visitors of the huddled masses who passed through here. Other exhibits illustrate how these immigrants changed the demography of the United States. And the American Immigrant Wall of Honor remembers more than half a million people who came to the U.S. in search of a better life. Ellis Island offers an optional audio tour (narrated by Tom Brokaw) and a documentary film called *Island of Hope, Island of Tears*. Note that a round-trip ferry ticket to Ellis Island includes a trip to Liberty Island, the site of the Statue of Liberty.

See map p. 178. In New York Harbor. ☎ *212-363-3200 for general information, 212-269-5755 for ticket and ferry information.* www.statueoflibertyferry.com *or* www.nps.gov/elis. *Transport: Ferry from Battery Park. Subway to ferry ticket*

Harlem & Upper Manhattan

0 — 1/2 mi
0 — 0.5 km

New York
Botanical
Garden
Bronx Zoo

Ⓜ Subway stop

ATTRACTIONS ●
Abyssinian Baptist Church **4**
Cathedral of St. John
  the Divine **10**
The Cloisters **1**
Schomburg Center for Research
  in Black Culture **5**
Yankee Stadium **2**

DINING AND NIGHTLIFE ◆
Apollo Theater **7**
Charles' Southern Style
  Kitchen **3**
El Paso Taqueria **12**
La Fonda Boricua **11**
La Marmite **8**
Lenox Lounge **6**
Patsy's Pizzeria **9**

booth: 4/5 train to Bowling Green stop, and then walk through the park heading south; the ticket booth is a little fortress at the edge of the trees by the promenade. Bus to ticket booth: M1 (running down Fifth/Park Avenue/Broadway), M6 (running down Broadway), or M15 (running down Second Avenue). Admission: Ferry plus Statue of Liberty and Ellis Island $8 adults, $3 children ages 3–17 (free under 3), $6 seniors. Open: Daily 10:30 a.m.–5 p.m. (extended hours in summer). Ferries run from Manhattan about every 30 minutes, in winter 10:30 a.m.–3:30 p.m. and in summer 9 a.m.–4:30 p.m. Tickets are sold only until an hour before the last ferry departs. Note that if you want to visit both Ellis Island and the Statue of Liberty, you can't take the last ferry; taking the last ferry enables you to visit only one of the two attractions. Due to security restrictions, no backpacks, luggage, or coolers are allowed.

Empire State Building
Midtown East

You can't see King Kong dangling from the top of the Empire State Building as he did in the 1933 version of *King Kong,* but you can get one of the best views of Manhattan from this 1,472-foot Art Deco structure — that is, if visibility is good the day you go. You can find a visibility rating posted in the lobby of the building, and you should take the rating seriously — zero visibility means that you really won't see a thing except clouds and fog. The observatory is on the 86th floor and has both an outdoor and an indoor viewing area. Huge lights glow in the top of the building and are lit up in different colors at night in honor of various holidays. On the second floor is the **NY Skyride** (☎ 212-279-9777), a simulated aerial tour of New York, which is worth seeing if you can't go for the real thing.

Lines to visit the observation deck can be horrible at the concourse-level ticket booth, so be prepared to wait — or purchase advance tickets online using a credit card at www.esbnyc.com. You pay slightly more — tickets were priced $1 higher on the Web site at press time — but it's well worth it, especially if you're visiting during busy seasons, when the line can be shockingly long. You're not required to choose a time or date for your tickets in advance; they can be used on any regular open day. However, order them well before you leave home, because only regular mail shipping is free. Expect them to take 7 to 10 days to reach you (longer if you live out of the country). Overnight delivery adds $15 to your total order. With tickets in hand, you're allowed to proceed directly to the second floor — past everyone who didn't plan as well as you did!

See map p. 180. Fifth Avenue at 34th Street. ☎ 212-736-3100. www.esbnyc.com. Subway: B/D/F/N/Q/R/V/W train to 34th Street/Herald Square, walk east on 34th Street, and turn right on Fifth Avenue to the entrance. Bus: M2/M3/M4/M5 run down Fifth Avenue and stop right in front of the entrance. Admission to observation deck: $10 adults, $9 seniors, $5 children under 12, free for children under 6. Open: Mon–Thurs 10 a.m.–12 a.m., Sat–Sun 9:30 a.m.–12 a.m. For security reasons, no backpacks or large parcels are allowed, and visitors are required to present a photo ID. You can buy tickets online with a surcharge at the Web site.

Grand Central Station
Midtown East

Even if you're not catching one of the Metro-North commuter trains, make Grand Central part of your itinerary. Finished in 1913 and beautifully renovated in 1998, this Beaux Arts masterpiece features a 12-story vibrant blue ceiling on which the stars of the zodiac are traced in 24-karat gold and a central kiosk over which the landmark brass clock is perched. Aside from the gorgeous main concourse, Grand Central offers a very good dining concourse on the lower level; top restaurants including **Michael Jordan's The Steakhouse,** the famous **Oyster Bar & Restaurant** (a glitzy bar), and **Campbell Apartment**; and a gourmet food market, **Grand Central Market.** You can enjoy a free guided tour of the terminal given by the Municipal Art Society (12:30 p.m. Wednesdays; ☎ 212-935-3960).

See map p. 180. Main entrance on 42nd Street at Park Avenue. Subway: S/4/5/6/7 train to 42nd Street/Grand Central stop. Bus: M1/M2/M3/M4 running up Madison Avenue and M101/M102/M103 running down Lexington Avenue take you right there. Open: 24 hours.

 ## Intrepid Sea-Air-Space Museum
Midtown West

The *USS Intrepid,* an aircraft carrier that saw active duty in World War II, is the focal point of this large naval museum and is now a National Historic Landmark. On deck, you find 40 aircraft from various periods on display. Some of the other vessels moored here are the submarine *Growler,* the naval destoyer *USS Edson,* the A-12 Blackbird (the world's fastest spy plane), and the newest addition, a retired British Airways Concorde jet. For the kids, this is like an educational amusement park with thrill rides like the naval flight simulator. Memorabilia and naval displays are housed below decks.

See map p. 180. Pier 86, Hudson River at 46th Street, west of Twelfth Avenue. ☎ 212-245-0072. www.intrepidmuseum.org. *Subway: A/C/E train to 42nd Street/Port Authority Bus Terminal stop, and then continue west on 42nd Street for 4 blocks, or change to the bus. Bus: M42 crosstown bus running on 42nd Street or, even better, the M50 crosstown bus running west on 49th Street and east on 50th Street. Admission: $14.50 adults; $10.50 seniors, students, youth under 18, and veterans; $7.50 children under 11; $2 children under 6; free for children under 2; $5 extra for simulator rides. Open: Daily 10 a.m.–5 p.m., Summer Sat–Sun 10 a.m.–7 p.m., Winter closed Mon. Last admission is 1 hour before closing time.*

 ## Metropolitan Museum of Art
Upper East Side

As the largest museum in the Western Hemisphere, the Met has something for everyone, from its world-famous Egyptian collection to its massive holdings of European and American masterpieces to its beautiful sculpture garden. Highlights also include the Asian collection, the collection of musical instruments, and the armor collection. And kids love the costume displays on the lower level. You're not going to get all of this in only one visit, so try to narrow your focus before you go. Tours of various parts of the collection are conducted several times an hour; you also can take a self-guided audio tour or a "highlights" tour. For schedules, check the tour bureau in the Great Hall or call ☎ 212-570-3930.

See map p. 182. On the edge of Central Park at Fifth Avenue and 82nd Street. ☎ 212-535-7710. www.metmuseum.org. *Subway: 4/5/6 train to 86th Street stop, walk 3 blocks west to Fifth Avenue, turn left, and walk along the park to the entrance. Bus: M1/M2/M3/M4 up Madison and down Fifth Avenue. Suggested admission: $12 adult, $7 seniors and students, free for children under 12 when accompanied by an adult; fee includes admission to the Cloisters. Open: Tues–Sun 9:30 a.m.–5:30 p.m., Fri–Sat 9:30 a.m.–9 p.m, "Holiday Mondays" 9:30 a.m.–5:30 p.m. No strollers allowed on Sun.*

Museum of Modern Art (MOMA)
Midtown West

After a major three-year renovation and temporary residence in Queens, this mecca of modern art returned to its original location — a bigger (630,000 square-feet) and better facility — in November 2004. At MOMA, you find a world-reknowned permanent collection, including works of Fauvism, Cubism, Futurism, Surrealism, German Expressionism, and Abstract Expressionism, among other schools. The new facility includes a six-story gallery building that houses the museum's main collection and an atrium-like lobby where you can view the distinctive Sculpture Garden from above.

See map p. 180. 11 West 53rd St. ☎ 212-708-9480. www.moma.org. *Subway: E, F to Fifth Avenue. Admission: $12 adults, $8.50 seniors and students, free for children under 16 when accompanied by an adult; pay what you wish on Fri 4:30–8:15 p.m. You can purchase tickets on the Web site. Open: Sat–Tues and Thurs 10:30 a.m.–5:45 p.m., Fri 10:30 a.m.–8:15 p.m., closed Wed.*

Rockefeller Center
Midtown West

This complex of 18 buildings includes the GE building, a 70-story Art Deco tower. The entertainment ranges from the outdoor skating rink to Radio City Music Hall, where the Rockettes perform. Call ☎ 212-247-4777 for backstage tours, and see Chapter 14 for more information. You can tour the NBC Studios (call ☎ 212-664-3700), where NBC's "Today" show tapes. Show up with your "We [heart] You, Matt!" sign and you may get on TV. A multitude of stores and restaurants are located under the center's concourse. For a self-directed tour, pick up a map at 30 Rockefeller Center; if you prefer a guided tour, call ☎ 212-664-3700. During the holiday seasons, you can expect huge crowds to gather and gaze upon the famous Christmas tree and the skaters on the rink, located below at Rockefeller Plaza (☎ 212-332-7654) — expect very long lines on weekends to enjoy the latter. Rink admission is $7.50–$9 for adults and $6–$6.75 for children; skate rental is $4. The rink is open from mid-October to mid-March.

See map p. 180. Between Fifth and Sixth avenues and from 48th to 51st streets. Promenade main entrance between 49th and 50th streets on Fifth Avenue.

☎ *212-332-6868.* www.rockefellercenter.com. *Subway: B/D/F/V train to 47th–50th streets/Rockefeller Center lets you out on the Sixth Avenue side of the complex. Bus: M1/M2/M3/M4/M5 down Fifth Avenue or M5/M6/M7 up Sixth Avenue.*

Solomon R. Guggenheim Museum
Upper East Side

Frank Lloyd Wright designed this famous museum, whose swirling, shell-like shape resembles a . . . hmmm, I'm not really sure; I'll let you decide. Inside, the exhibition space curves in a spiral; you can take an elevator to the top and work your way down if you don't want to make the hike up. Exhibits are constantly changing. The museum's addition, the Tower Galleries, holds the permanent collection of 19th- and 20th-century art, which includes works by the Impressionists and founding modernists, including Picasso. Free tours of the museum are available; check the Web site for special events like films, concerts, and lectures that may be on the schedule.

The Guggenheim has a branch museum in SoHo, at 575 Broadway at Prince Street (☎ 212-423-3500). The SoHo branch houses continually changing exhibits of postmodern art, with an emphasis on multimedia works.

See map p. 182. 1071 Fifth Ave. at 89th Street. ☎ *212-423-3500.* www.guggenheim.org. *Subway: 4/5/6 train to 86th Street stop, walk 3 blocks west to Fifth Avenue, turn right, and walk 2 blocks north to the entrance. Bus: The bus is a good idea because it brings you closer: Take the M1/M2/M3/M4 up Madison and walk 1 block west (it goes south on Fifth), or take the M86 crosstown on 86th Street. Admission: $15 adults, $10 seniors and students, free for children under 12 when accompanied by an adult; pay what you wish on Fri 6–8 p.m. Open: Sun–Wed 10 a.m.–5:45 p.m., Fri–Sat 10 a.m.–8 p.m. Closed Thurs.*

Staten Island Ferry
Downtown

You can't beat the price of this attraction — it's free. And not only do you get an hour-long excursion (round-trip) in New York Harbor, but you get beautiful views of the Statue of Liberty. You also get to mingle with commuters: people who take this ferry everyday to work in Manhattan. Your journey also provides great views of Ellis Island, the Verrazano Narrows Bridge, and Governor's Island. Returning from Staten Island, you can enjoy that very famous view of the lower Manhattan skyline.

See map p. 178. Departs from the Whitehall Ferry Terminal at the southern tip of Manhattan. ☎ *718-815-BOAT.* www.ci.nyc.ny.us/html/dot. *Subway: N, R to Whitehall Street; 4, 5 to Bowling Green; 1, 9 to South Ferry (ride in the first 5 cars). Admission: free ($3 for car transport on select ferries). Open: 24 hours; ferries run Mon–Fri every 20–30 min., less frequently on off-peak and weekend hours.*

Statue of Liberty
Downtown

Lady Liberty is one of the grandest symbols of what New York and America stand for. And it's for that reason that the interior and base of the Statue were closed for security measures after the terrorist attacks of September 11, 2001. But in the summer of 2004, access, albeit still somewhat limited (you can't climb to the Statue's crown), was once again permitted. Now you can explore the Statue of Liberty Museum, peer into the inner structure through a glass ceiling near the base of the Statue, and enjoy views from the observation deck on top of the 16-story pedestal. Whether you choose to wander the grounds or just get a look via the Staten Island Ferry, Circle Line Cruise, or on your way to Ellis Island, the Statue of Liberty is a must-see.

See map p. 178. On Liberty Island in New York Harbor. ☎ 212-363-7620 for general information, 212-269-5755 for ticket and ferry information. www.statueofliberty ferry.com. *Transport: Ferry from Battery Park. Subway to ferry ticket booth: 4/5 train to Bowling Green stop, and then walk through the park heading south; the ticket booth is a little fortress at the edge of the trees by the promenade. Bus to ticket booth: M1 (running down Fifth/Park Avenue/Broadway), M6 (running down Broadway), or M15 (running down Second Avenue). Admission: Ferry plus Statue of Liberty and Ellis Island $10 adults, $4 children ages 3–17 (free under 3), $8 seniors. Open: Daily 10:30 a.m.–5 p.m. (extended hours in summer). Ferries from Manhattan run about every 30 minutes in winter 10:30 a.m.–3:30 p.m., in summer 9 a.m.–4:30 p.m. Tickets are sold only until an hour before the last ferry. Note that if you want to visit both Ellis Island and the Statue of Liberty, you can't take the last ferry; taking the last ferry enables you to visit only one of the two attractions. Due to security restrictions, no backpacks, luggage, or coolers are allowed.*

Times Square
Midtown West

Times Square celebrated its 100th anniversary in 2004, and in those 100 years, the famed thoroughfare has undergone numerous transformations. Most recently Times Square has evolved into a sort of New York theme park. As a result, for New Yorkers, Times Square is a place we go out of our way to avoid. The crowds, even by New York standards, are stifling; the restaurants, mostly national chains, aren't very good; the shopping, also mostly national chains, is unimaginative; and the attractions, like Madame Tussaud's New York wax museum, are kitschy. It's like Times Square has evolved into the New York version of Las Vegas. And why would New York aspire to be like Las Vegas? Still, you've come all this way; you've got to at least take a peek, if only for the amazing neon spectacle of it.

Most of the Broadway theaters are in the immediate vicinity of Times Square, so plan your visit around your show tickets. For your pre-dinner meal, walk two blocks west to Ninth Avenue, where you can find a number of relatively inexpensive, good restaurants. If you're here with the kids, the Ferris wheel in the Toys 'R' Us store makes a visit to Times Square worthwhile.

See map p. 180. At the intersection of Broadway and Seventh Avenue, between 42nd and 44th streets. Subway: 1/2/3/7/N/Q/R/S/W train to Times Square/42nd Street stop. Bus: M6/M7 down Seventh Avenue or M104/M10 down Broadway offer a perfect view of Times Square.

United Nations
Midtown East

A guided one-hour tour of the United Nations headquarters examines the history and purpose of the U.N. and takes you through the General Assembly Hall and the Security Council Chamber. You also can walk through the grounds and a beautiful garden (the rose garden is fantastic) that offers a view of the East River, Roosevelt Island, and Brooklyn. The grounds feature many sculptures that member states have given the U.N., like the symbolic pistol with a knot in the barrel , a gift from the government of Luxembourg.

See map p. 180. United Nations Plaza (on First Avenue between 42nd and 48th streets; visitor entrance at 46th Street). ☎ *212-963-8687. Subway: 4/5/6/7/S train to Grand Central/42nd Street stop, walk east on 42nd Street to First Avenue, turn left, and walk to the visitor entrance at 46th Street. Bus: Much more convenient than the subway; take the M15 down Second Avenue and up First Avenue, the M104 down Broadway and 42nd Street, or the M42 crosstown on 42nd Street. Admission: Free to the park and lobby; guided tour $8.50 adults, $5 children, $6 students, $7 seniors. Children under 5 are not allowed on the guided tours. Open: 9:30 a.m.–4:45 p.m.; tours every 30 minutes 9:30 a.m.–4:15 p.m.; no tours on weekends in Jan and Feb. Reservations required only for non-English tours (French, Spanish, Russian, or Chinese).*

Wall Street and the Stock Exchange
Downtown/Wall Street

On weekdays, Wall Street offers a glimpse into the teeming world of finance that characterizes lower Manhattan. This is where it all started; it's the historical heart of the city and its financial center today. See the skyscrapers — many among the first ever built — and throngs of people who inhabit this world. While you're here, visit the Stock Exchange, its interactive information center (☎ 212-656-3000), and the Museum of American Financial History (26 Broadway at Wall Street). The Stock Exchange building, which dates from 1903, is a classical temple for dollar worship; from the observation gallery, you can watch the world's largest stock frenzy in action. Closed to the public for security reasons, the gallery is scheduled to reopen in the future, but at press time, no date has been set. Call the information center to find out if tourist visits to the exchange have resumed. If they have, get there early if you want to avoid a long wait in line; admission is free, but you need admission tickets, which are given out starting at 9 a.m.

See map p. 178. Wall Street runs between Broadway and South Street. New York Stock Exchange: 20 Broad St. at Wall Street. ☎ *212-656-3000. Subway: 4/5 train to Wall Street stop, or N/R to Rector Street, and then walk east across Broadway to Wall Street. Bus: M1/M6 down Broadway and up Trinity Place. Admission: Free. Open: Call for information.*

World Trade Center site (Ground Zero)
Downtown

The World Trade Center occupied 16 acres in lower Manhattan and was a sprawling office complex of more than 12 million square feet, including the two spectacular 110-story Twin Towers. On September 11, 2001, two planes crashed into the towers. The towers collapsed soon afterward, and the search began for the nearly 3,000 victims of this terrorist attack. A vast, empty crater now marks the spot where the World Trade Center once stood.

The Wall of Heroes has been erected on the Church Street side of the now barren site. On the wall are the names of those who lost their lives that day and the history of the site, including photos of the construction of the World Trade Center in the late 1960s and details about how, after it opened in 1972, it changed the New York skyline and downtown. A walk along the Wall of Heroes remains a painfully moving experience.

After much discussion, designer Daniel Libeskind's Freedom Tower proposal was chosen for construction on the former WTC site, and, in an open competition with over 5,000 entries from over 63 nations and 49 states, a design for a memorial commemorating the tragic events of 9/11 was chosen. The winner is titled Reflecting Absence and features two large cascading pools set 30 feet into the footprints of the Twin Towers; the names of the victims of the attack are listed around the pools. But it will be years before either the Tower or the memorial are unveiled.

See map p. 178. Broadway at Fulton Street. Subway: 1/2/4/5/A/C/J/M/Z train to Fulton Street/Broadway Nassau stop, and then walk west on Fulton. Bus: M1 and M6 run down Broadway, letting you off at the entrance to the platform. Open: Daily 24 hours. Admission: Free.

Yankee Stadium
The Bronx

Next to the Coliseum in Rome, you're not going to find many sports arenas in more famous than the House That Ruth Built. The Yankees play from April until October (and, because they seem to be in the playoffs most years, mostly through October). Tickets, which range in price from $8 to $80, are tough to snag, but if you plan in advance (and even if you don't), you should be able to score a seat by going through a broker or scalping (be careful of forgeries) the day of a game. (For more information about admission to Yankees' games, see "The New York Sports Scene" later in this chapter.

If your visit to New York falls during the off-season, you can still check out Yankee Stadium by taking the Yankee Stadium Tour, which runs year-round. The **Insider's Tour of Yankee Stadium** (☎ 718/579-4531) is the official tour of the House That Ruth Built and takes you onto the field, to Monument Park, and into the dugout. You even visit the press box and take a peek inside the clubhouse. Tours are offered daily at 10 a.m., except for on New Year's Day, during Opening Day preparations (and usually during the three weeks prior), on weekends when the team is at home, and on weekdays when a home day game is scheduled. If you're timing allows you to catch a tour, plan to arrive by 9:40 a.m. Tickets for the one-hour, basic **Classic Tour** are $12 for adults and $6 for kids 14 and under. No reservations are required; all you need to do is show up at the ballpark's press gate just before tour time, but it's still a good idea to call ahead and confirm.

See map p. 189. 161st and River Avenue, Bronx. ☎ *718-293-6000.* www.yankees. com. *Subway: 4, B, C to 161st Street. Bus: BX6, BX13, BX55 to 161st Street and Grand Concourse, walk two blocks to the Stadium.*

Finding More Cool Things to See and Do

After you've seen the top sights, check out these additional attractions.

Other excellent museums

The Met and MOMA (see "New York City's Top Sights" earlier in this chapter) are probably New York's best-known art museums, but many, many others are available for you to explore.

American Folk Art Museum
Midtown West

This stunning structure opened in 2001 and immediately garnered accolades for not only its architecture but also for the collections of American folk art that are housed in it. In 2004, one of my favorite exhibits, "The Perfect Game: America Looks at Baseball" opened. In addition to the collections and exhibits, you can also peruse an outstanding book/gift shop.

See map p. 180. 45 W. 53rd St. (between Fifth and Sixth avenues). ☎ *212-265-1040.* www.folkartmuseum.org. *Subway: E, V to Fifth Avenue. Admission: $9 adults, $7 seniors and students, free for children under 12; free to all Fri 6–8 p.m. Open: Tues–Thurs and Sat–Sun 10:30 a.m.–5:30 p.m., Fri 10:30 a.m.–7:30 p.m.*

The Frick Collection
Upper East Side

This museum features the splendid collection of tycoon Henry Clay Frick and is housed in his Gilded Age mansion, more or less as he organized it. The painting collection includes works by old masters of the 16th and 17th centuries, including Tiziano (also known as Titian), Vermeer, Rembrandt, and El Greco, as well as 19th-century artists, including Turner and Whistler. The furnishings and ceramic collections are also worth seeing. Enjoy some fantastic art and see how the cultured aristocracy of Old New York lived. Allow at least two hours.

See map p. 182. 1 E. 70th St. (at Fifth Avenue). ☎ *212-288-0700.* www.frick.org. *Subway: 6 train to Hunter College/68th Street stop, walk west to Fifth Avenue, and then walk 2 blocks north. Admission: $12 adults, $8 seniors and students (children under 10 not admitted, children under 16 admitted only with an adult); admission includes audio guide. Open: Tues–Sat 10 a.m.–6 p.m., Sun 1–6 p.m.*

Brooklyn Museum of Art
Brooklyn

New York's second largest museum after the Met, the Brooklyn Museum of Art is housed in a beautiful Beaux Arts building and has a collection that includes major Egyptian and African art; in fact, it lays claim to the largest collection of Egyptian artifacts in the world after London and Cairo. The museum also contains important 19th-century American and European paintings; 28 period rooms, some of them rescued from now-demolished historic buildings; and an important sculpture collection, including a rich Rodin gallery. The museum has built a reputation for dynamic temporary exhibitions as well. Recent ones have included a stunning watercolor retrospective, an exhibit of the Romanov treasures, and the controversial, Giuliani-boycotted show "Sensation," which presented cutting-edge artwork from Britain. You're not going to have any trouble getting here because the museum has its own subway stop. Allow at least three hours.

On the first Saturday of every month, The Brooklyn Museum of Art runs a program from 5 to 11 p.m. that includes free admission to the museum and a slate of live music, films, dancing, curator talks, and other entertainment that can get pretty esoteric — think karaoke, lesbian poetry, silent films, experimental jazz, and disco. As only–in–New York events go, **First Saturday** is a good one — you can always count on a full slate of cool.

200 Eastern Pkwy. (at Washington Avenue). ☎ *718-638-5000.* www.brooklynart. org. *Subway: 1/2 train to Eastern Parkway/Brooklyn Museum stop. Suggested admission: $6 adults, $3 students and seniors, free for children under 12. Open: Wed–Fri 10 a.m.–5 p.m., Sat–Sun 11 a.m.–6 p.m.; first Sat of each month 11 a.m.–11 p.m.*

Cooper-Hewitt National Design Museum
Upper East Side

Part of the Smithsonian Institution, the Cooper-Hewitt is housed in the Carnegie Mansion, built by steel magnate Andrew Carnegie in 1901. Some 11,000 square feet of gallery space is devoted to changing exhibits that are invariably well conceived, engaging, and educational. Shows are both historic and contemporary in nature. Many installations are drawn from the museum's own vast collection of industrial design, drawings, textiles, wall coverings, books, and prints. On your way in, note the fabulous Art Nouveau–style copper-and-glass canopy above the entrance. And be sure to visit the garden, which is ringed with Central Park benches from various eras.

See map p. 182. 2 E. 91st St. (at Fifth Avenue). ☎ *212-849-8400.* www.si.edu/ndm. *Subway: 4, 5, 6 to 86th Street. Admission: $10 adults, $7 seniors and students, free for children under 12; free to all Fri–9 p.m. Open: Tues–Thu 10 a.m.–5 p.m., Fri 10 a.m.–9 p.m., Sat 10 a.m.–6 p.m., Sun noon–5 p.m.*

Museum of Television & Radio
Midtown West

Have you ever wanted to travel back in time and "be there" during an unforgettable TV or radio moment — to watch the first moon landing, hear Orson Welles's *War of the Worlds* radio broadcast, or see the first ever *Sesame Street* program? Now you can. The Museum of Television & Radio has more than 100,000 radio and television programs in its permanent collection, almost all of which are available for your viewing or listening pleasure. The museum is actually more like a library; instead of wandering from one exhibit to the next, you "check out" recordings or videotapes and play them in audiovisual cubicles — anything from Sid Caesar to vintage cartoons to your favorite commercials from childhood. Several theaters and listening rooms can accommodate large groups for special screenings. "Exhibits" are thematic documentaries that cover topics as diverse as "horror on TV" and "the history of presidential campaign advertising" (on second thought, maybe those two topics aren't so diverse after all). It's best to go during the day, during the week; on evenings and weekends, the crowds make it hard to get a viewing booth.

See map p. 180. 25 W. 52nd St. (between Fifth and Sixth avenues). ☎ *212-621-6800, 212-621-6600.* www.mtr.org. *Subway: E/V train to 53rd Street/Fifth Avenue stop. Admission: $10 adults, $8 seniors and students, $5 children under 13. Open: Tues–Sun 12:30–6 p.m., Thurs 12:30–8 p.m.*

New Museum of Contemporary Art
SoHo

This museum is famous for its exhibitions of contemporary art, focusing on innovative art and artists. The permanent collection includes work by artists from around the world, ranging from installations to video, painting, and sculpture. On the ground floor is the **Zenith Media Lounge,** dedicated to digital art and interactive art projects. The whole ground floor is open to the public free of charge.

See map p. 178. 583 Broadway (between Houston and Prince streets). ☎ *212-219-1222.* www.newmuseum.org. *Subway: N/R train to Prince Street stop; F/V/S train to Broadway-Lafayette Street stop; or 6 train to Bleecker Street stop, and then walk west to Broadway. Admission: $6 adults, $3 seniors and students, free for children under 18; free to all Thurs 6–8 p.m. Open: Tues–Sun 12–6 p.m., Thurs 12–8 p.m.*

Whitney Museum of American Art
Upper East Side

The big show here is the Whitney Biennial (in even-numbered years), which highlights the good, the bad, and the ugly in contemporary art. The Whitney also has a spectacular permanent collection of modern American art, including works by Hopper, O'Keefe, and others. Allow at least three hours.

See map p. 182. 945 Madison Ave. (at 75th Street). ☎ *212-570-3676.* www.whitney.org. *Subway: 6 train to 77th Street stop. Admission: $12 adults, $9.50 students and* *seniors, free for children under 12; pay what you wish Fri 6–9 p.m. Open: Tues–Sun 11 a.m.–6 p.m.; Fri 11 a.m.–9 p.m.*

For culture & history buffs

Asia Society
Upper East Side

This museum was founded in 1956 by John D. Rockefeller, who donated 285 masterpieces of Asian art that form the core of the society's permanent collection. Its exhibits have expanded to include art, films, and performances. Allow at least two hours.

See map p. 182. 725 Park Ave. (at 70th Street). ☎ *212-517-ASIA.* www.asiasociety. org. *Subway: 6 train to 68th Street/Hunter College stop, walk 2 blocks north, turn left, and walk 1 block west to Park Avenue. Admission: $7 adults, $5 seniors, free for children under 16. Open: Tues–Sun 11 a.m.–6 p.m., Fri 11 a.m.–9 p.m.*

Fraunces Tavern Museum
Downtown

This is where Washington bade farewell to his officers at the end of the American Revolution. This 1907–built tavern is an exact replica of the original 1717 tavern. It's now a museum and a restaurant serving George's favorites.

See map p. 178. 54 Pear St. (near Broad Street). ☎ *212-425-1778.* www.fraunces tavernmuseum.org. *Subway: N, R to Whitehall Street; 2, 3 to Wall Street. Admission: $3 adults, $2 students and seniors. Open: Mon–Fri 10 a.m.–4:45 p.m.*

Lower East Side Tenement Museum
Downtown

This five-story tenement was the home of over 10,000 people from 25 countries between 1863 and 1935. Now it's a museum and a National Trust for Historic Preservation. The tenement museum tells the story of the great immigration boom of the late 19th and early 20th centuries, when the Lower East Side was considered the "Gateway to America." The only way to see the museum is by guided tour and you can choose from four different ones; the best is the 45-minute Confino Family Apartment Tour, on weekends only. To insure a spot on a tour, purchase your tickets early at ☎ **800-965-4827.**

See map p. 178. Visitors' Center at 90 Orchard St. (at Broome Street). ☎ *212-431-0233.* www.tenement.org. *Subway: F to Delancey Street; J, M, Z to Essex Street. Admission: tenement and walking tours $9 adults, $7 seniors and students; Confino Apartment $9 adults, $7 seniors and students. Open: Tenement tours depart every 40 minutes Tues–Fri 1 p.m.–4 p.m., Sat–Sun every half hour 11 a.m.–4:45 p.m.; Confino Apartment tour Sat–Sun hourly noon–3 p.m.; Walking tour Apr–Dec Sat–Sun 1 and 2:30 p.m.*

Museum of the City of New York
Upper East Side

Learn about the city's history through displays packed with information. A number of decorative objects related to New York are on display, including a collection of Tiffany glassware. Allow at least an hour for your visit.

See map p. 182. 1220 Fifth Ave. (at 103rd and 104th streets). ☎ 212-534-1672. www. mcny.org. Subway: 6 train to 103rd Street stop, and then walk west toward Central Park. Suggested admission: $7 adults; $4 seniors, students, and children; $12 for families. Open: Wed–Sat 10 a.m.–5 p.m., Sun noon–5 p.m.

Museum of Jewish Heritage—A Living Memorial to the Holocaust
Downtown

This spare six-sided building with a six-tier roof, alluding to the Star of David and the six million people murdered in the Holocaust, recounts the unforgettable horror yet tenacious renewal of Jews from the late 19th century to the present. Through objects, photographs, documents, and videotaped testimonies, the museum tells a very powerful story of survival and faith.

See map p. 178. 36 Battery Place (at First Place), Battery Park City. ☎ 212-968-1800. www.mjhnyc.org. Subway: 4, 5 to Bowling Green. Admission: $10 adults, $7 seniors, $5 students, free for children under 5. Check Web site for $2-off admission coupon (available at press time). Open: Sun–Wed 10 a.m.–5:45 p.m., Thurs 10 a.m.– 8 p.m., Fri and eves of Jewish holidays 10 a.m.–3 p.m.

New-York Historical Society
Upper West Side

This museum sits across the street from the American Museum of Natural History. If you have time, try to spend an hour or two in this museum that features American history, culture, and art with a special focus on New York. On the fourth floor, you can find the Henry Luce III Center for the Study of American Culture, a gallery and study facility with displays of objects, such as paintings, sculpture, Tiffany lamps, textiles, and furniture.

See map p. 182. 2 W. 77th St. (at Central Park West). ☎ 212-873-3400. www. nyhistory.org. Subway: B, C to 81st Street; 1, 9 to 79th Street. Admission: $8 adults, $5 seniors and students, free for children 12 and under. Open: Tues–Sun 11 a.m.–6 p.m.

Schomburg Center for Research in Black Culture
Harlem

One of the largest collections of African-American materials in the world can be found at this branch of the New York Public Library. The Exhibition Hall, the Latimer/Edison Gallery, and the Reading Room host changing exhibits related to black culture, such as "Lest We Forget: The Triumph over Slavery" and "Masterpieces of African Motherhood." A rich calendar of talks and performing arts events is also part of the continuing program. Make an appointment for a guided tour so you can see the 1930s murals by Harlem Renaissance artist Aaron Douglas; it's worth your while. Academics and others interested in a more complete look at the center's holding can preview what's available online.

See map p. 189. 515 Malcolm X Blvd. (Lenox Avenue between 135th and 136th streets).
☎ *212-491-2200.* www.nypl.org. *Subway: 2, 3 to 135th Street. Admission: Free. Open: Gallery Tue–Sat 10 a.m.–6 p.m., Sun 1—5 p.m.*

Notable New York City architecture

You can walk the city streets with your eyes skyward and your mouth open in awe over some of the magnificent structures scattered throughout the city. The Empire State Building and the Chrysler Building are two of the most famous buildings in New York and are also top sights (see their listings earlier in this chapter). But you may want to gawk at some of these other structures too.

Flatiron Building
Flatiron District

The Flatiron Building (its original name was the Fuller Building) takes its name from its unusual triangular shape. Built in 1902, it was one of the first skyscrapers in Manhattan. Although only 20 stories tall, it's one of the most recognized and unique buildings in the city. Now, the area surrounding the building, which features a number of publishing houses, modeling agencies, and dot-com companies, has been named after the building and is known as the "Flatiron" district.

See map p. 180. 175 Fifth Ave. (where Fifth Avenue and Broadway cross at 23rd Street). Subway: N/R train to 23rd Street stop. Bus: M6 and M7 down Broadway or M2/M3/M5 down Fifth Avenue for a magnificent view of the building; the buses stop right there, too.

New York Public Library
Midtown West

With its white Cornithian columns, allegorical statues, and the world-famous lion sculptures (their names are Patience and Fortitude) at the entrance, the New York Public Library is one of the country's finest examples of Beaux Arts architecture. Oh, and you can find a lot of good books inside to peruse, too. A book- or publishing-related exhibit is usually scheduled at the library. A Gutenberg Bible is currently on display until August 2005.

See map p. 180. Fifth Avenue and 42nd Street. ☎ *212-869-8089 (exhibits and events) or 212-661-7220 (library hours).* www.nypl.org. *Subway: B, D, F, V to 42nd St.; S, 4, 5, 6, 7 to Grand Central/42nd Street. Admission: Free to all exhibits. Open: Thurs–Sat 10 a.m.–6 p.m., Tues–Wed 11 a.m.–7:30 p.m.*

Skyscraper Museum
Financial District

This museum features those structures that you've craned your neck to get a good look at, and it's the first of its kind. After years of seeking a permanent home, the Museum finally opened in 2004 in the 38-story Skidmore, Owings & Merrill tower that also houses the Ritz-Carlton New York, Battery Park. The new space comprises two galleries: one housing a permanent exhibition dedicated to the evolution of Manhattan's commercial skyline, the other available for changing shows.

See map p. 178. 2 West St., Battery Park City. ☎ *212-968-1961.* www.skyscraper. org. *Subway: 4, 5 to Bowling Green. Admission: $5 adults, $2.50 children and seniors. Open: Wed–Sun noon–6 p.m.*

U.S Customs House
Downtown

This 1907 National Historic Landmark houses the **National Museum of the American Indian,** George Gustav Heye Center. The granite structure features giant statues carved by Daniel Chester French (of Lincoln Memorial fame); the statues lining the front personify Asia (pondering philosophically), America (bright-eyed and bushy-tailed), Europe (decadent, whose time has passed), and Africa (sleeping). Inside, the airy oval rotunda, designed by Spanish engineer Raphael Guastavino, was frescoed by Reginald Marsh to glorify the shipping industry (and, by extension, the Customs office once housed here).

See map p. 178. 1 Bowling Green (between State and Whitehall streets). ☎ *212-514-3700.* www.nmai.si.edu. *Subway: 4, 5 to Bowling Green; N, R to Whitehall. Admission: Free. Open: Daily 10 a.m.–5 p.m.*

Woolworth Building
Downtown

Completed in 1913, the Woolworth was the tallest building in the world for a time. Designed by famous architect Cass Gilbert, the Gothic tower is known for its beautifully decorated interior and exterior. Mr. Woolworth paid $15.5 million cash for the structure, and it shows. Besides the stunning exterior, this building — once known as "The Cathedral of Commerce" — has gorgeous mosaic ceilings, a marble staircase, and statues of people involved in the building's construction.

See map p. 178. 233 Broadway (at Park Place). Subway: 1/2 train to Park Place stop or 4/5/6 train to Brooklyn Bridge/City Hall stop, and then walk west across the park. Admission: Free. Open: Daily 9 a.m.–5 p.m.

Beautiful places of worship

New York is a city known for its religious tolerance. Places of worship for just about every denomination are everywhere, and many are housed in remarkable structures worth checking out even if religion is not want you came to New York to get.

Abyssinian Baptist Church
Harlem

This Baptist church, founded in 1808 by African-American and Ethiopian merchants, is the most famous of Harlem's 400-plus houses of worship. The chamber of commerce has declared the church a "Living Treasure." Come for Sunday morning services at 9 and 11 a.m. to get a sample of the Harlem gospel tradition.

See map p. 189. 132 Odell Clark Place (West 138th Street, between Adam Clayton Powell Boulevard and Lenox Avenue). ☎ *212-862-7474.* www.abyssinian.org. *Subway: 2, 3, B, C to 135th Street.*

Cathedral of St. John the Divine
Upper West Side

Towering over Amsterdam Avenue near the edge of Harlem is an unlikely sight: the largest Gothic cathedral in the world. The cathedral, begun in 1892, is still only two-thirds complete; the towers, transcepts, choir roof, and other aspects remain unfinished. The architects and builders have continually employed Gothic engineering, stone-cutting, and carving techniques. Numerous chapels throughout the cathedral commemorate various ethnic groups and traditions. A tour ($3) is offered at 11 a.m. Tuesday through Saturday and at 1 p.m. on Sunday. You can visit the towers on the first and third Saturdays of the month. Three services per day are held during the week (7:15 a.m., 12:15 p.m., and 5:30 p.m.), and four are held on Sunday (8 a.m., 9 a.m., 11 a.m., and 7 p.m.).

The cathedral hosts numerous concerts, including dance, choir, and classical music performances. But by far the most unforgettable special event is the **Blessing of the Animals,** held in early October as part of the Feast of St. Francis of Assisi. A procession of critters — everything from dogs and cats to camels and elephants — parades through the church; each is blessed in honor of St. Francis, the patron saint of animals. Call **212-316-7540** for tickets; advance reservations are necessary for this popular event.

See map p. 189. 1047 Amsterdam Ave. (between 110th and 113th streets). ☎ *212-316-7540. Subway: 1/9 train to Cathedral Parkway (110th Street) stop, and then walk 1 block east to Amsterdam Avenue. Bus: M11 (running up Tenth/Amsterdam Avenue and down Columbus/Ninth Avenue). Suggested admission: $2 adults, $1 seniors and children under 18. Open: Mon–Sat 7 a.m.–6 p.m., Sun 7 a.m.–7 p.m.*

St. Patrick's Cathedral
Midtown East

St. Patrick's, the largest Catholic cathedral in the United States, features Gothic spires, beautiful stained-glass windows, and an impressive white marble facade. Mass is held eight times a day Sunday through Friday and five times a day on Saturday. It's a calm island in a busy thoroughfare, located across from Rockefeller Center and next door to Saks Fifth Avenue.

See map p. 180. Fifth Avenue between 50th and 51st streets. ☎ *212-753-2261. Subway: B/D/F/V train to 47–50 streets/Rockefeller Center, and then walk west to Fifth Avenue. Bus: M1/M2/M3/M4/M5 down Fifth Avenue; or M1/M2/M3/M4 up Madison Avenue. Open: Sun–Fri 7 a.m.–8:30 p.m., Sat 8 a.m.–8:30 p.m.*

Trinity Church
Downtown

This Wall Street house of worship — with neo-Gothic flying buttresses, beautiful stained-glass windows, and vaulted ceilings — was designed and consecrated in 1846. The historic Episcopal church stood strong while office towers crumbled around it on September 11, 2001; however, an electronic organ has temporarily replaced the historic pipe organ, which was damaged by dust and debris. The gates to the historic church currently serve as an impromptu memorial to the victims of the September 11, 2001, terrorist attack, with countless tokens of remembrance left by both locals and visitors alike.

Also part of Trinity Church is **St. Paul's Chapel** at Broadway and Fulton Street, New York's only surviving pre-Revolutionary church and a transition shelter for homeless men until it was transformed into a relief center after September 11; it returned to its former duties in mid-2002.

See map p. 178. At Broadway and Wall Street. ☎ *212-602-0800, 212-602-0872, or 212-602-0747 for concert information.* www.trinitywallstreet.org. *Subway: 4, 5 to Wall Street. Admission and tours: Free, $2 suggested donation for noonday concerts. Open: Museum: Mon–Fri 9–11:45 a.m. and 1–3:45 p.m., Sat 10 a.m.–3:45 p.m., Sun 1–3:45 p.m. Services: Mon–Fri 8:15 a.m., 12:05 p.m., and 5:15 p.m. (additional Healing Service Thurs at 12:30 p.m.), Sat 8:45 a.m., Sun 9 and 11:15 a.m. (also 8 a.m. Eucharist service at St. Paul's Chapel, between Vesey and Fulton streets).*

Especially for kids
New York has plenty of attractions that you can enjoy with your children, and some of the city's top sites, like the Bronx Zoo, Central Park, and the Intrepid Sea-Air-Space Museum (see "New York City's Top Sights," earlier in this chapter), appeal especially to kids. Check out these other kid-friendly attractions.

The Children's Museum of Manhattan
Upper West Side

Designed for children ages 2 to 12, this museum is strictly hands-on. That means your kids can touch just about anything. This museum offers five floors of fun, including a media center where you can produce your own TV show; an early-childhood center, especially for children 4 and under; and a reading center for quiet time. The museum features special exhibits, such as an interactive tour of the human body. Allow at least two hours.

See map p. 182. 212 W. 83rd St. (between Broadway and Amsterdam avenues). ☎ *212-721-1234.* www.cmom.org. *Subway: 1/9 train to 79th Street stop, walk north* *on Broadway to 83rd, and turn right. Admission: $7 adults and children, $4 seniors, free for children under 2.. Open: During the school year, Mon, Wed, Thurs 1:30–5:50 p.m., Fri–Sun 10 a.m.–5 p.m.; in the summer, Wed–Sun 10 a.m.–5 p.m.*

New York Aquarium/Wildlife Conservation Park
Brooklyn

The oldest aquarium in operation in the United States (since 1896), the New York Aquarium is huge, covering over 14 acres by the sea at Coney Island. It houses more than 350 species and 8,000 specimens, including beluga (white) whales and sharks. The top attraction is always the dolphin show, held at the Aquatheater from May through October.

Surf Avenue and West 8th Street, Brooklyn. ☎ *718-265-FISH.* www.nyaquarium. com. *Subway: D/B train to West 8th Street/NY Aquarium stop, and then take the pedestrian bridge directly to the aquarium. Admission: $11 adults, $7 seniors and children under 12, free for children under 2. Open: Mon–Fri 10 a.m.–5 p.m., Sat–Sun 10 a.m.–5:30 p.m.*

New York City Fire Museum
SoHo

Housed in a three-story 1904 firehouse, the former quarters of FDNY Engine Co. 30, this museum houses one of the country's most extensive collections of fire-service memorabilia from the 18th century to the present. Displays range from vintage fire marks to fire trucks (including the last-known example of a 1921 pumper) to the gear and tools of modern firefighters. Best of all, real firefighters are almost always on hand to share stories and fire-safety information with kids. The retail store sells authorized FDNY logo wear and souvenirs. Call ahead for details on scheduling a guided tour.

See map p. 178. 278 Spring St. (between Varick and Hudson streets). ☎ *212-691-1303.* www.nycfiremuseum.org. *Subway: C, E to Spring Street. Admission: $4 adults, $2 seniors and students, $1 children under 12. Open: Tues–Sat 10 a.m.–5 p.m., Sun 10 a.m.–4 p.m.*

New York Transit Museum
Brooklyn

Housed in a real (decommissioned) subway station, this recently renovated underground museum is a wonderful place to spend an hour or so. The museum is small but very well done, with good multimedia exhibits exploring the history of the subway from the first shovel full of dirt scooped up at groundbreaking (March 24, 1900) to the present. Kids can enjoy the interactive elements and the vintage subway cars, old wooden turnstiles, and beautiful station mosaics of yesteryear. This museum is a minor but remarkable tribute to an important development in the city's history.

Boerum Place and Schermerhorn Street, Brooklyn. ☎ *718-694-5100.* www.mta. info/museum. *Subway: A, C, to Hoyt Street; F to Jay Street; M, R to Court Street; 2,*

3, 4, 5 to Borough Hall. Admission: $3 adults, $1.50 seniors and children 3–17 (free for seniors Tues noon–4 p.m.). Open: Mon–Fri 10 a.m.–4 p.m., Sat–Sun noon–5 p.m.

South Street Seaport and Museum
Downtown

The whole Seaport neighborhood is an important historical landmark that has been progressively restored, in part by the South Street Seaport Museum and in part by private businesses. This attraction offers a look at commerce in the past and in the present. The Seaport's cobbled streets and restored brick buildings house many interesting shops and pubs, and two huge warehouses from the days when sailing ships ruled trade now contain indoor shopping complexes and fine restaurants. On the waterside, the museum has completed the restoration of a number of historical ships that you can visit, including the *Peking,* an enormous four-master built of steel; the *Ambrose,* a lightship; and *Lettie G. Howard,* a fishing schooner. Still under restoration are the *Ellen McAllister,* a large tugboat, and the *Marion M.,* a wood-hulled chandlery lighter. Two of the restored ships, the schooner *Pioneer* and the *W. O. Decker,* a cute wooden tugboat, take people out for tours of the harbor from May through October.

At Pier 17 of the Seaport, on the third floor of the building there, two rows of deck chairs line the south terrace and overlook the water. These chairs are a great place to relax and take in the view of Brooklyn, the bridges, and New York Harbor. On weekends, though, the seats fill up fast.

Also an historical landmark of the Seaport — but not part of the Seaport Museum — is the **Fulton Fish Market** (at South Street and Fulton Street; ☎ 212-669-9416). Though it's rumored to be relocating, at press time it was still operating daily here from 12 a.m. to 9 p.m. If you'd like something fishy, you can schedule a (quite impressive) guided tour (first and third Thursdays of every month at 6 a.m.; for $10) by calling to make a reservation. Otherwise, just go for the morning outdoor fish market across the street.

See map p. 178. From Pearl Street to the East River; the heart of the Seaport being between John Street and Peck Slip. ☎ 212-SEAPORT. www.southstreet seaport.com. Museum: 12 Fulton St. (between Water and South streets). ☎ 212-748-8725. www.southstseaport.org. Subway: 1/2/4/5/A/C/J/M/Z train to Fulton Street/Broadway Nassau stop; walk east on Fulton and you'll be right in the middle of it all. Bus: M15 (down Second Avenue and up First) stops at Fulton and Water streets. Museum admission: $5. Open: Wed–Mon 10 a.m.–5 p.m.; April–Sept closes at 6 p.m.

New York City for teens

Let's not underestimate the interests of teenagers; I know many who are much more adult than I am. On the other hand, I know a few who tend toward the infantile. So what appeals to both adults and kids, probably also appeals to teens. Still, don't forget these options that may go over well with the teens.

American Museum of the Moving Image
Queens

Is there a teenager who doesn't like going to the movies? I don't think so, which is why this movie lovers' museum is perfect for teens. "Behind the Screen," the museum's major exhibit, is a two-floor installation that takes you step–by–step through the process of moviemaking. The museum houses more than 1,000 artifacts, from technological gadgetry to costumes, and interactive exhibits where you can try your own hand at sound-effects editing or create your own animated shorts, among other simulations. Teens also love the popular "BLIP: Arcade Classics from the Museum Collection" exhibit of vintage, playable video games. The museum is close to a working studio complex where many movies and TV shows are filmed. Woody Allen and Martin Scorsese have made movies in the neighborhood, so if you're lucky, you may even happen upon a real movie being made. "Insiders' Hour" tours are offered every day at 2 p.m.

35th Avenue at 36th Street, Astoria, Queens. ☎ *718-784-0077.* www.ammi.org. *Subway: R to Steinway Street; N to Broadway. Admission: $10 adults, $7.50 seniors and college students, $5 children 5–18. Open: Tues–Fri noon–5 p.m., Sat–Sun 11 a.m.–6 p.m. (evening screenings Sat–Sun at 6:30 p.m.).*

Chelsea Piers
Chelsea

Jutting out into the Hudson River on four huge piers between 17th and 23rd streets is a terrific multifunctional recreational facility. Among the many sports' venues within this 30-acre complex are basketball courts, bowling alleys, a roller rink, ice rink, a 30-foot indoor climbing wall, batting cages, a golf driving range, beach volleyball courts, and a 25-yard indoor pool.

See map p. 180. On the Hudson River between Battery Park and 23rd Street. ☎ *212-336-6666.* www.chelseapiers.com. *Subway: C/E train to 23rd Street stop, and then walk west to the river. Bus: M11 running up Tenth Avenue and down Ninth Avenue, M14 running east-west on 14th Street, or M23 running east-west on 23rd Street. Open: Contact individual venues for hours.*

Sony Wonder Technology Lab
Midtown East

Welcome to an interactive technology wonderland! Here you and your kids can explore the history of technology by enjoying three floors of gadgets, robots, and video. Thankfully, the staff limits the number of people who can use the facility at one time to avoid total chaos. Plan on staying for at least two hours. The Lab is fully wheelchair accessible.

See map p. 180. 550 Madison Ave. (entrance on 56th Street). ☎ *212-833-8100 or TTY 212-833-6532.* www.sonywondertechlab.com. *Subway: E/F train to Fifth Avenue/53rd Street stop, walk 1 block east to Madison, turn north, walk up to 56th Street, and turn left. Bus: M1, M2, M3 and M4 buses run along Fifth Avenue (traveling downtown) and Madison Avenue (traveling uptown). Admission: Free, but reservations are strongly recommended. Open: Tues–Sat 10 a.m.–6 p.m., Sun 12–6 p.m., Thurs 10 a.m.–8 p.m.*

Fun for TV fans

With all the sitcoms and talk shows based in New York, the city often feels like one big set. If applauding on cue is what you'd like to do while you're visiting the city, check out these major shows where you can do just that.

One TV show you won't need a ticket for is *The Today Show.* All you have to do to see Matt, Katie, and Al is get up early and join the crowd outside the Rockefeller Center studio on 49th Street between Fifth and Sixth avenues. (The show schedules more out-of-doors segments in warmer weather, including the Friday Summer Concert Series.) You have a good chance of getting on camera if:

- ✔ You're holding up a creative sign.

- ✔ You want to propose to your significant other on the air.

- ✔ You show up and stick around during some *really bad* weather.

 For the shows listed here, it's a good idea to arrange for tickets as far in advance of your trip as possible — I'm talking six months or more. Tickets are always free. For more information about getting tickets to TV tapings, contact NYC & Company at ☎ 212-484-1222, www.nyc visit.com.

- ✔ *The Daily Show with Jon Stewart:* Comedy Central's half-hour humor and news show tapes Monday through Thursday at 5:45 p.m.; the studio is at 513 W. 54th St. Request tickets in advance by phone (☎ 212-586-2477), or call Monday through Thursday between 11 a.m. and 4 p.m. for last-minute cancellations.

- ✔ *Late Night with Conan O'Brien:* Conan tapes Tuesday through Friday at 5:30 p.m. (ticket holders should arrive an hour early). No one under 16 is admitted. Send a postcard with your request to NBC Studios/*Late Night,* 30 Rockefeller Plaza, New York, NY 10112, or call ☎ 212-664-3056 Monday through Friday between 9 a.m. and 5 p.m. Standby tickets are distributed on the day of show at 9 a.m. on the 49th Street side of 30 Rockefeller Plaza; get there early if you want to get a seat.

- ✔ *The Late Show with David Letterman:* Dave's is the hardest TV ticket in town to score. Write *at least* nine months in advance with your ticket request; each person is allowed only two tickets, and multiple requests are discarded. Send a postcard with your name, address, and day and evening phone numbers to *Late Show* Tickets, Ed Sullivan Theater, 1697 Broadway, New York, NY 10019 (☎ 212-247-3054). You must be 18 years or older to attend. You also can fill

out a form on the Web site (www.cbs.com/latenight/lateshow)
to be put on a list for last-minute cancellation tickets (last-minute in
this case being three months or sooner). Standby tickets are available *only* by phone, starting at 11:00 a.m. on taping day; call ☎ 212-
247-6497. The line is answered until the tickets are gone. Tapings
are Monday through Thursday at 5:30 p.m. (arrive by 4:15 p.m.),
with an additional show taped Thursday evening at 8:00 p.m.
(arrive by 6:45 p.m.).

✔ **MTV's *Total Request Live:*** An endless parade of music stars drops
by the second-floor glassed-in studio to chat, sing songs, and wave
to the adoring throngs that jam the sidewalk below. For tickets
to sit in the studio audience, call ☎ 212-398-8549 or e-mail
TRLcasting@mtvstaff.com.You must be between 16 and 24 to
attend. If you want to take your chances on the day of the show,
join the crowd on the traffic island across from 1515 Broadway at
44th Street in Times Square, weekdays at 3:30 p.m. Staff members
sometimes roam the crowd asking trivia questions, and correct
answers land you a standby ticket.

✔ ***Saturday Night Live:*** *SNL* has enjoyed a resurgence, making tickets
harder than usual to obtain. Tapings are Saturday at 11:30 p.m.
(arrive by 10:00 p.m.), with a dress rehearsal at 8:00 p.m. (arrive
by 7:00 p.m.). No one under 16 is admitted. Ticket requests are
processed only during the month of August; send a postcard
with your request (to arrive during August *only*) to NBC Studios/
Saturday Night Live, 30 Rockefeller Plaza, New York, NY 10112
(☎ 212-664-3056 for information). Tickets are awarded by lottery.
For standby tickets, arrive *no later than* 7:00 a.m. on taping day (and
wait under the NBC Studios marquee at the 49th street entrance
of 30 Rockefeller Plaza). You may choose a standby ticket for the
8:00 p.m. dress rehearsal or for the 11:30 p.m. live show. Only one
ticket is issued per person.

Don't forget to stop by the **Museum of Television & Radio.** See the listing
in the section "More Cool Things to See and Do" earlier in this chapter.

The New York Sports Scene

You can get a real feel for New Yorkers when you watch their hometown
teams. Sitting in the bleachers or nosebleed seats at Yankee Stadium or
at Madison Square Garden is a (cheap) thrill, and the minor league teams
are a hit in the big city.

Yankees & Mets: Major leaguers

With two baseball teams in town, you can catch a game almost any day
from opening day in April to the beginning of the playoffs in October.
(Don't bother trying to get subway series tix, though — they're the
hottest seats in town. Ditto for Opening Day or any play-off game.)

The Amazin' **Mets** play at **Shea Stadium** in Queens (Subway: 7 to Willets Point/Shea Stadium). For tickets (which ran $12–$43 for regular-season games in the 2004 season) and information, call the Mets Ticket Office at ☎ **718-507-TIXX**, or visit www.mets.com.

The Bronx Bombers, a.k.a. the **Yankees,** haven't won a World Series in three years — that only means they're overdue to win their 27th championship in 2004. The Yanks play at the House That Ruth Built, otherwise known as **Yankee Stadium** (Subway: C, D, 4 to 161st Street/Yankee Stadium). For tickets ($8–$80 in 2004), contact **Ticketmaster** (☎ 212-307-1212 or 212-307-7171; www.ticketmaster.com) or Yankee Stadium (☎ **718-293-6000**; www.yankees.com). Most of the expensive seats (field boxes) are sold out in advance to season ticket holders. You can often purchase these very same seats from scalpers, but you'll pay a premium for them. Bleacher seats (the cheapest) are sold the day of the game.

Down on the farm in New York: The minors

The **Brooklyn Cyclones,** the New York Mets' A-level farm team, and the **Staten Island Yankees,** the Yanks' junior leaguers, both play in sparkling, picturesque stadiums. What's more, with bargain-basement ticket prices (which topped out at $8 for the Cyclones, $10 for the Yanks in the 2004 season), these teams offer a great way to experience baseball in the city for a fraction of the major-league hassle and cost. Both teams have already developed a rabidly loyal fan base, so it's a good idea to buy your tickets for the 2005 summer season in advance.

The Cyclones have been a major factor in the revitalization of Coney Island; **Keyspan Park** sits right off the legendary boardwalk. For Cyclones info and tickets, call ☎ **718-449-8497** or visit www.brooklyncyclones.com (Subway: F, N, Q, W to Stillwell Avenue/Coney Island).

The SI Yanks play at the **Richmond County Bank Ballpark,** just a five-minute walk from the Staten Island Ferry terminal (Subway: N, R to Whitehall Street; 4, 5 to Bowling Green; 1, 9 to S. Ferry). To reach the SI Yanks, call ☎ **718-720-9200** or go online to www.siyanks.com.

The city game: Basketball

Though the New Jersey Nets are rumored to be moving (possibly) to Brooklyn, two pro teams now play in New York at **Madison Square Garden** (Seventh Avenue between 31st and 33rd streets; ☎ 212-465-6741 or www.thegarden.com; 212-307-7171 or www.ticketmaster.com for tickets; Subway: A, C, E, 1, 2, 3, 9 to 34th Street). MSG is the home court for Stephon Marbury, Allen Houston, Penny Hardaway, and the rest of the **New York Knicks** (☎ 877-NYK-DUNK or 212-465-JUMP; www.nyknicks.com). It's also the home court for the **New York Liberty** (☎ 212-465-6080; www.nyliberty.com), who electrify fans each summer with their tough-playing defense and All-Stars like Becky Hammon, Vickie Johnson, and Tari Phillips. In September of 2004, because MSG was otherwise occupied (with the Republican Convention), the Liberty played at Radio City Music Hall, only the second time a major sporting event has taken place at that great theater. (See the "Midtown Attractions" map.)

You hockey puck: NHL action

The **New York Rangers** also play at Madison Square Garden (Seventh Avenue between 31st and 33rd streets; ☎ **212-465-6741,** www.newyork rangers.com or www.thegarden.com; Subway: A, C, E, 1, 2, 3, 9 to 34th Street). The Rangers have been going through tough times, but tickets are hard to get nevertheless, so plan well ahead; call ☎ **212-307-7171,** or visit www.ticketmaster.com for online orders.

Seeing New York by Guided Tour

If your time is limited and you want an overview of the city's highlights, a guided tour is the way to go. Also, because New York has tours for just about every interest, you're sure to find one that fits your needs. Below I've listed some of the best tours in the city.

If you decide to take a group tour, ask about group size when you call to reserve your spot. Generally, you want as small a group as possible to minimize the time required to get organized and move around.

Seeing the city by tour bus

Several companies offer very general city sightseeing tours, many on double-decker buses. These tours are fine for seeing the sights and orienting yourself to the city, but don't expect too much from the running commentary.

- ✔ **Gray Line New York Tours (☎ 800-669-0051** or 212-397-2600; www.graylinenewyork.com) offers daily escorted bus tours ($75 adults, $55 children; total time 8½ hours) that include lunch, a one-hour harbor cruise, and admission to the Empire State Building. Gray Line also offers daily hop-on/hop-off tours (on double-decker buses) organized around three loops — uptown, downtown, and a night loop — including about 50 stops ($49 adults, $39 children; total time three hours per loop, but tickets for the uptown and downtown loops are valid for 48 hours). You also can try out a number of mini-packages, such as helicopter and harbor tours. The daily "Essential New York" tour includes the three loops on the double-decker bus tour, plus a harbor cruise, admission to the Empire State Building, and a one-day FunPass MetroCard ($72 adults, $51 children; total time three hours per loop plus one hour for the cruise). You can buy tickets at the visitor center at 777 Eighth Ave. between 47th and 48th streets. (See the "Midtown Attractions" map.)

- ✔ **New York Double-Decker Tours (☎ 877-693-3253** or 718-361-6079; www.nydecker.com) also offers daily hop-on/hop-off tours on double-decker buses. The complete tour costs $48 for adults and $25 for children (tickets are valid for 48 hours). It's cheaper than the Gray Line tour but has fewer possibilities: The circuit is organized in only two loops, uptown and downtown, for a total of about 40 stops, and no nighttime loop. You can purchase tickets from the dispatcher at any of the tour's stops or from the driver and guide on the bus.

Although they aren't tour buses, **public buses** crisscross the city. If having a tour guide isn't essential, consider taking advantage of the $1.50 tour that the buses afford. Try the M1 all the way down Fifth Avenue from Museum Mile to 42nd Street; then change to the M104 and go across to Times Square, up Broadway through the Theater District, past Lincoln Center, and on to the Upper West Side. Or stay on the M1 all the way to City Hall and Battery Park.

Cruising around the island

✔ **Circle Line** (☎ 212-563-3200; www.circleline.com) offers the famous "Full Island Cruise," which sails around Manhattan in three hours (daily March to December; $25 adults, $12 children, $20 seniors). The cruise leaves from Pier 83 at West 42nd Street and Twelfth Avenue. You see Manhattan from both sides, go under the George Washington Bridge, and pass down through Hell Gate, the murky, swirling spot where the East River and the Harlem River meet. Departing from the same location, Circle Line also offers a shorter cruise, which goes back and forth around the lower half of Manhattan and lasts two hours (daily March to December; $20 adults, $10 children, $17 seniors); and a Harbor Lights cruise, also a two-hour cruise (at dusk, call for precise schedule; $20 adults, $10 children, $17 seniors). From Pier 16 at the South Street Seaport, Circle Line has a one-hour Liberty cruise to see the Lady and the harbor (daily March to December; $13 adults, $7 children, $11 seniors). Allow up to 45 minutes for ticketing and boarding.

To get to Pier 83 via the subway, take the A/C/E train to Port Authority or the N/Q/R/S/1/2/3/7 to Times Square, and then take the M42 bus westbound on 42nd Street or walk west to Twelfth Avenue. To reach Pier 16, take the 1/2/4/5/A/C/J/M/Z train to the Fulton Street/Broadway Nassau stop and then walk east to the Seaport. (See the "Midtown Attractions" map.)

✔ **New York Waterways** (☎ 800-533-3779; www.nywaterway.com), the nation's largest privately held ferry service and cruise operator, also does the 35-miles around Manhattan, but does it on faster catamaran boats, passing by all the same sights as the Circle Line in only two hours. They also offer a staggering amount of different sightseeing options, including a very good 90-minute New York Harbor Cruise, Romantic Twilight Cruise, Friday Dance Party Cruise, and Baseball Cruises to Mets and Yankee games. The two-hour Manhattan cruise goes around the island from Pier 78 at West

38th Street and Twelfth Avenue and from Pier 17 at the South Street Seaport (daily May to November from Pier 38, weekends May to September from Pier 17; $24 adults, $12 children, $19 seniors). The 90-minute harbor cruise departs from Pier 78 only and circles around the lower part of Manhattan and up the East River (daily year-round, but on a reduced schedule in January and February, so call for info; $19 adults, $9 children, $16 seniors).

To reach Pier 78, take the free shuttle (blue, red, and white; it stops at regular city bus stops and you hail it as a cab) that runs along 57th, 49th, 42nd, and 34th streets and up and down Twelfth Avenue; or take the hotel bus that runs twice a day (call for route and schedule). To get to Pier 17, take the 1/2/4/5/A/C/J/M/Z train to the Fulton Street/Broadway Nassau stop and then walk east to the Seaport. (See the "Midtown Attractions" map.)

✔ **Bateaux New York** (☎ 866-211-3806; www.bateauxnewyork.com) offers gourmet lunch and dinner cruises under a glass dome: The ship has a glass top with a special anti-fog system and is climate controlled, making the evening cruises quite romantic. The three-hour dinner cruise sails down the Hudson River and around to the East River and back, passing by the Statue of Liberty (daily; $102.87 weekdays, $116.89 weekends). Jackets and ties required. Board 30 minutes before departure from Pier 61 at Chelsea Piers. Via the subway, take the A/C train to the 23rd Street stop and then the westbound M23 bus on 23rd Street. (See the "Midtown Attractions" map.)

✔ **Spirit Cruises** (☎ 866-211-3805 or 212-727-2789; www.spiritcruises.com) runs year-round cabaret-style cruises, including a two-hour lunch cruise (with a narrated tour of the harbor and a buffet lunch; ranging from $29.95 weekdays January through March up to $43.95 weekends April through December) and a three-hour dinner sunset cruise (with live music and a buffet; from $52.95 weekdays January through March up to $83.95 Saturdays April through December). Prices include taxes and service. Cruises board 30 minutes before departure from Pier 61 at Chelsea Piers. To get there via the subway, take the A/C train to the 23rd Street stop and then take the westbound M23 bus on 23rd Street.

Flying high with helicopter tours

If you can afford it, a helicopter tour is something you absolutely shouldn't miss! For a breathtaking tour, try **Liberty Helicopters** (☎ 212-967-6464; www.libertyhelicopters.com), which offers several packages from $56 up to $162. Liberty runs several tours every day, and reservations are only necessary for groups of three people or more. The helicopters can hold up to six people. Note that tours are very short — from about 10 minutes to about 25 minutes. The tours start both from the VIP Heliport at West 30th Street and 12th Avenue and from the Downtown Manhattan Heliport at Pier 6 and the East River (four blocks south of Wall Street).

To get to the VIP Heliport by subway, take the A/C/E train to Penn Station, and then walk (or take the M34 crosstown bus) four blocks west on 34th Street, turn left on Twelfth Avenue, and walk two blocks south. To reach the Downtown Manhattan Heliport, take the 1/9 train to South Ferry, walk northeast on South Street for approximately four blocks to the Vietnam Veterans Memorial, and turn right toward the water.

You will be asked to present identification before boarding a helicopter tour, so make sure you have your driver's license or passport with you.

Broadening your mind with architectural and historical tours

✔ **The Municipal Art Society** (☎ **212-439-1049** or 212-935-3960; www.mas.org) offers excellent historical and architectural walking tours aimed at individualistic travelers. Each tour is led by a highly qualified guide who gives insight into the significance of buildings, neighborhoods, and history. Topics range from the urban history of Greenwich Village to "Williamsburg: Beyond the Bridge" to an examination of the "new" Times Square. Weekday walking tours are $12; weekend tours are $15. Reservations may be required depending on the tour, so it's best to call ahead. A full schedule is also available online.

✔ **NYC Discovery Tours** (☎ 212-465-3331) offers more than 70 tours of the Big Apple, divided into five categories: neighborhood (including "Central Park" and "Brooklyn Bridge and Heights"); theme (such as "Gotham City Ghost Tour" and "Art History NYC"); biography ("John Lennon's New York"); tavern/food tasting; and American history and literature ("The Charles Dickens Tours"). Tours are about two hours long and cost $13 per person (more for food tastings).

✔ **Joyce Gold History Tours of New York** (☎ 212-242-5762; www.nyctours.com) features weekend walking tours of neighborhoods all over Manhattan, going everywhere from Harlem to Wall Street. Gold teaches New York City history at New York University and the New School. Tours are conducted on weekends from March to December and cost $12.

✔ **Adventures on a Shoestring** (☎ 212-265-2663) is one of the earliest entrants into the booming walking tour market. Host Howard Goldberg has provided unique views of New York since 1963, exploring New York with a breezy, man-of-the-people style. Tours focus on behind-the-scenes views of neighborhoods. A variety of Greenwich Village tours emphasize the haunted, the picturesque, and the historic; the Historic Roosevelt Island tour includes taking the Roosevelt Island Tram. He even does theme walks, such as "Marilyn Monroe's Manhattan" and a "Salute to Katherine Hepburn." Tours are a bargain at $5 for 90 minutes and are given 12 months a year, rain or shine.

Seeing the city on special-interest tours

✔ **Bike the Big Apple** (☎ 877-865-0078; www.toursbybike.com) offers guided half-day, full-day, and customized bike tours through a variety of city neighborhoods, including the fascinating but little-explored Upper Manhattan and Harlem. You don't have to be an Ironman candidate to participate; tours are designed for the average rider with an emphasis on safety and fun. Shorter (approximately 2½ hours) and longer versions (around 5 hours) are available. Tours are offered year-round; prices run from $69 to $89 and include a bike and all gear.

✔ **Harlem Spirituals Tours** (☎ 800-660-2166 or 212-391-0900; www.harlemspirituals.com) offers a variety of tours of Harlem, including gospel tours, jazz tours, and soul-food tours. Tours leave from the office at 690 Eighth Ave. between 43rd and 44th streets. The Sunday Gospel tour costs $30 for adults and $27 for children ($70 for adults and $60 for children with brunch included); call or check the Web site for the prices of other tours.

✔ **Hidden Jazz Haunts** (☎ 718-606-8842), hosted by New York Jazz expert Gordon Polatnick, is the real deal for jazz buffs. Polatnick's tours are small (2 to 10 people), and he bases the destinations on the jazz interests of his clients. If you're into Bebop, he shows you Minton's Playhouse, the still-standing but now defunct jazz club that was the supposed birthplace of bop. From there he takes you to other, active Harlem clubs that he feels embody Minton's Bebop spirit. If you're into the Bohemian Village scene, he takes you to clubs that represent that era. The tour is five hours and costs $100, including transportation, music charges, two drinks, and guide service.

✔ **NoshWalks** (☎ 212-222-2243; www.noshwalks.com) guide Myra Alperson knows the all the best food in New York City and where to find it. Alperson leads adventurous— and hungry — walkers to some of the city's most delicious neighborhoods. Highlights include the Uzbek, Tadjik, and Russian markets of Rego Park, Queens, and the Dominican coffee shops of Washington Heights in upper Manhattan. Tours are conducted on Saturdays and Sundays, leaving around 11 a.m. The preferred means of transportation is subway. The tours generally last around three hours and are $15, not including the food you undoubtedly buy on the tour. Space is limited, so book well in advance.

Faring well with free walking tours

✔ **Big Apple Greeter** (☎ 212-669-8159 or 212-669-2896; www.bigapplegreeter.org) is a nonprofit organization with a staff of volunteer New Yorkers who take you around their beloved neighborhoods for three or four hours on a free tour. For schedule and tour information, call Monday through Friday from 9 a.m. to 5 p.m., or check out the company's Web site. Make sure to book your spot at least a week in advance.

✔ **Wall Street Walking Tour** (☎ **212-606-4064;** www.downtownny.com) is a free 90-minute tour offered every Thursday and Saturday at noon, rain or shine. This guided tour explores the vivid history and amazing architecture of the nation's first capital and the world center of finance. Stops include the New York Stock Exchange, Trinity Church, Federal Hall National Monument, and many other sites of historic and cultural importance. Tours meet on the steps of the U.S. Customs House at 1 Bowling Green (Subway: 4, 5 to Bowling Green). Reservations are not required (unless you're a group), but you can call to confirm the schedule.

✔ **Central Park Conservancy** (☎ **212-360-2726**) offers a slate of free walking tours of the many nooks and crannies of Central Park. Call for schedules.

Chapter 12

Shopping in New York City

- -

In This Chapter

▶ Surveying the shopping scene
▶ Knowing the big names
▶ Discovering the best shopping neighborhoods
▶ Finding the most interesting stores

- -

*Y*ou have to ask yourself two potentially tough questions when you come to New York: Did you come here to see the sights, like the Empire State Building or the Statue of Liberty? Or did you really come here to hit the stores and explore all the city's amazing shopping possibilities, in essence, to give your credit card a major workout? Only you know the answer to those questions and if your answers involve your credit card, when it comes to shopping, you can't do better than New York. This chapter gives you a starting point from which you can begin your New York shopping adventure.

Surveying the Shopping Scene

First, you need to know that regular shopping hours don't really exist in New York. Most department stores are open Monday through Saturday 10 a.m. to 6 p.m. and Sunday noon to 5 p.m., with a late-night Thursday (and often Monday) until 8 p.m. However, the open hours of other stores, shops, and boutiques vary widely, and the only way to know them for certain is to call the store you want to visit.

Sales tax in New York is 8.65 percent for most goods, although some luxury goods, such as cigars, are taxed at a higher rate.

 If you're on the hunt for a specific item that we don't mention in this chapter, two excellent resources for shopping information are the weekly magazines New York (www.nymetro.com), which spotlights "sample" sales (see sidebar "Scoring at the sample sales," later in this chapter), and *Time Out New York* (www.timeoutny.com).

Knowing the Big Names

Shopaholics, I'm sure the names that follow are all very familiar to you, but for the many others (also known as the non-shopping afflicted), this list helps you get to know some of the biggest and best-known of the New York stores.

✔ **Barneys:** This store sets the tone for upscale chic for both men and women. 660 Madison Ave. at 61st Street (☎ 212-826-8900; www. barneys.com. Subway: N/R/W train to Fifth Avenue/59th Street stop). (See the "Uptown Shopping" map.) Downtown, **Barneys Co-Op** has blossomed into a real fashion hotspot with its own strong identity, sisterly but separate from the chic Barneys New York Madison Avenue headquarters. 236 W. 18th St. between Seventh and Eighth avenues (☎ 212-593-7800; Subway: 1, 9 to 18th Street).

Twice a year, Barney's hosts their famous **warehouse sale** in their warehouse facility in Chelsea. Prices change daily, so markdowns are 50–80 percent off the original retail prices on all clothing and gifts. If you're planning a shopping trip to the city, keep your eyes open and your ear to the ground to find out when these sales occur. 255 W. 17th St. between Seventh and Eighth avenues.

✔ **Bergdorf Goodman** and **Bergdorf Goodman Men:** Bergdorf's represents the pinnacle of exclusive shopping, with prices to match. 745 Fifth Ave. at 58th Street (main store) and 754 Fifth Ave. at 57th Street (men's store) (☎ 212-753-7300; www.bergdorfgoodman. com. Subway: N/R/W train to Fifth Avenue/59th Street stop). (See the "57th Street Shopping" map.)

✔ **Bloomingdales:** Ever hear of Bloomies? If not, move on to the next chapter. This store has just about anything you could want. You may want to survey the store first, sans credit card, before going in for the kill. 1000 Third Ave. at 59th Street (☎ 212-705-2000; www. bloomingdales.com. Subway: 4/5/6 train to 59th Street stop or N/R/W train to Lexington Avenue/59th Street stop). (See the "Midtown Shopping" map.)

✔ **The Disney Store:** Just try walking past one of these stores with your kids in tow; it's impossible not to step inside and absorb the Wonderful World of Disney products. The original store is at 711 Fifth Ave. at 55th Street (☎ 212-702-0702; Subway: E/V train to Fifth Avenue/53rd Street stop), with branches at 210 W. 42nd St. at Seventh Avenue (☎ 212-221-0430), 39 W. 34th St. between Fifth and Sixth avenues (☎ 212-279-9890), and 141 Columbus Ave. at 66th Street (☎ 212-362-2386). (See the "Midtown Shopping" and "57th Street Shopping" maps.)

✔ **Henri Bendel:** The store is gorgeous and so are the goods inside — super stylish and expensive stuff for women with a flair for the funky and frilly. 712 Fifth Ave. between 55th and 56th streets (☎ 212-247-1100; Subway: N, R to Fifth Avenue). (See the "57th Street Shopping" map.)

Downtown Shopping

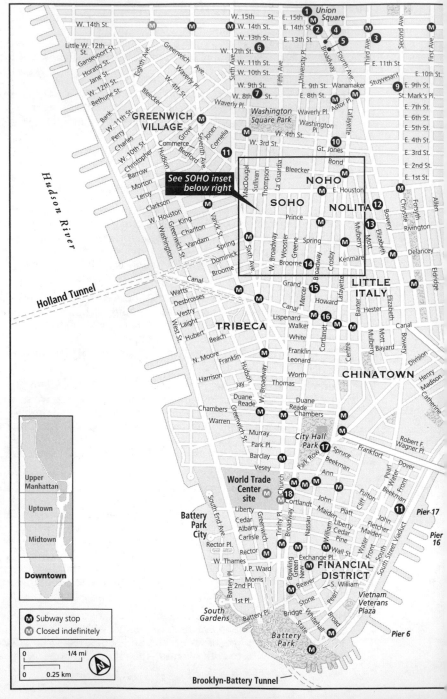

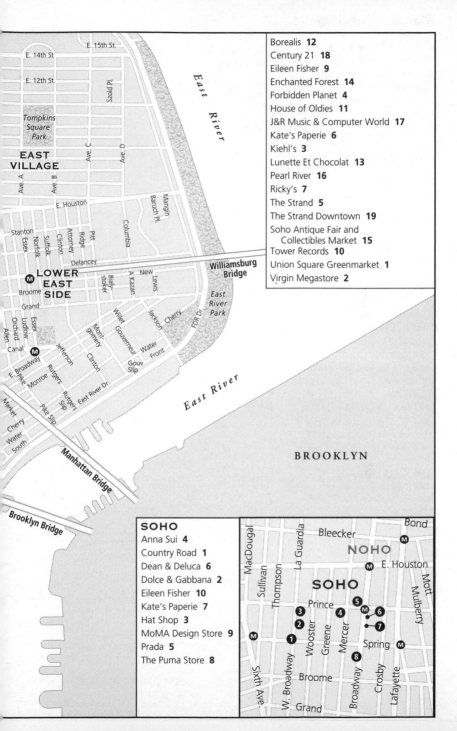

Borealis **12**
Century 21 **18**
Eileen Fisher **9**
Enchanted Forest **14**
Forbidden Planet **4**
House of Oldies **11**
J&R Music & Computer World **17**
Kate's Paperie **6**
Kiehl's **3**
Lunette Et Chocolat **13**
Pearl River **16**
Ricky's **7**
The Strand **5**
The Strand Downtown **19**
Soho Antique Fair and
    Collectibles Market **15**
Tower Records **10**
Union Square Greenmarket **1**
Virgin Megastore **2**

SOHO
Anna Sui **4**
Country Road **1**
Dean & Deluca **6**
Dolce & Gabbana **2**
Eileen Fisher **10**
Kate's Paperie **7**
Hat Shop **3**
MoMA Design Store **9**
Prada **5**
The Puma Store **8**

Midtown Shopping

Annex Antique Fair & Flea Market **29**
Bloomingdales **12**
Books of Wonder **31**
Brooks Brothers **39**
B&H Photo & Video **6**
Cartier **16**
Coliseum Books **22**
Colony Music Center **1**
The Disney Store **4, 28**
Drama Book Shop **5**
Dylan's Candy Bar **11**
Eileen Fisher **17, 30**
Foot Locker **25**
Gucci **13**
H&M **15, 27**
Jazz Record Center **8**
Lord & Taylor **23**
Lush **34**
Macy's **24**
Manhattan Mall **26**
Metropolitan Museum of Art
   Store **19, 24**
Mysterious Bookshop **9**
NBA Store **14**
New York Transit Museum Store **21**
Old Navy **7**
Rizzoli **10**
Saks Fifth Avenue **18**
Toys "R" Us **3**
Union Square Greenmarket **33**
Virgin Megastore **2**

57th Street Shopping
(see map on p. 230)
Bergdorf Goodman **2**
Chanel **6**
Christian Dior **7**
The Disney Store **10**
Fendi **9**
Henri Bendel **11**
Hermes **5**
Laura Biagiotti **1**
Louis Vuitton **3**
Niketown **4**
Tiffany & Co. **8**

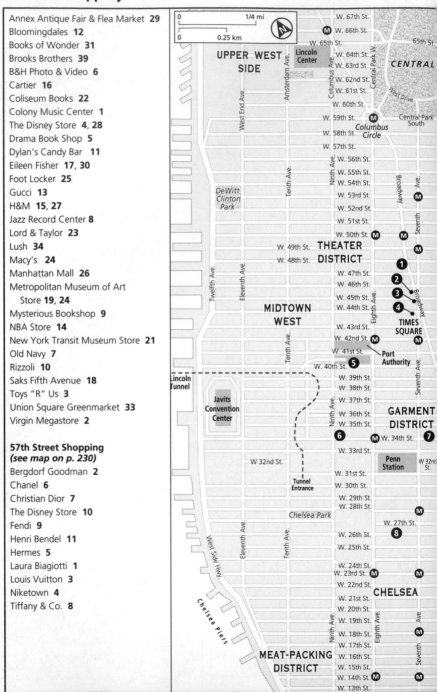

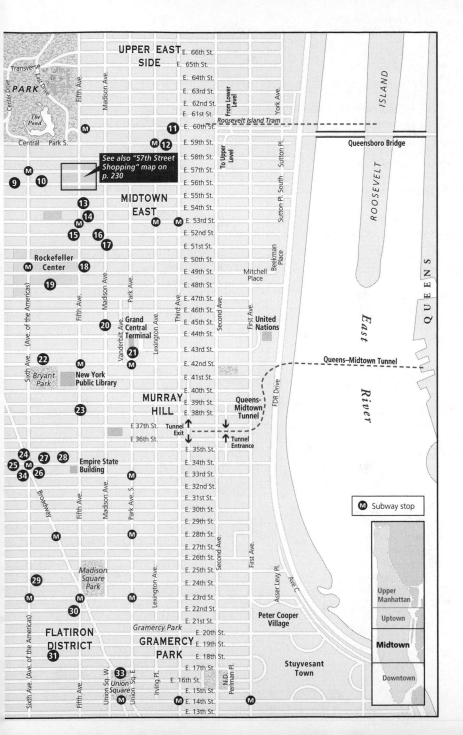

UPPER EAST SIDE
E. 66th St.
E. 65th St.
E. 64th St.
E. 63rd St.
E. 62nd St.
E. 61st St.
E. 60th St.

Transverse
PARK
The Pond
Central Park S.

Fifth Ave.
Madison Ave.
York Ave.

ISLAND

From Lower Level
Roosevelt Island Tram

⑪ E. 60th St.
⑫ E. 59th St.

Queensboro Bridge

See also "57th Street Shopping" map on p. 230

⑨ ⑩

To Upper Level
Sutton Pl.
Sutton Pl. South

E. 58th St.
E. 57th St.
E. 56th St.
E. 55th St.

MIDTOWN EAST
⑬
⑭
⑮ ⑯
⑰

ROOSEVELT

E. 54th St.
E. 53rd St.
E. 52nd St.
E. 51st St.
E. 50th St.
E. 49th St.

Beekman Place
Mitchell Place

Rockefeller Center ⑱
⑲

QUEENS

E. 48th St.
E. 47th St.
E. 46th St.
E. 45th St.
E. 44th St.
E. 43rd St.
E. 42nd St.

Sixth Ave. (Ave. of the Americas)
Fifth Ave.
Madison Ave.
Park Ave.
Vanderbilt Ave.
Lexington Ave.
Third Ave.
Second Ave.
First Ave.

⑳ Grand Central Terminal
㉑

United Nations

East River

Queens–Midtown Tunnel

㉒
New York Public Library
Bryant Park

MURRAY HILL
㉓

Queens-Midtown Tunnel

E. 41st St.
E. 40th St.
E. 39th St.
E. 38th St.
E. 37th St. Tunnel Exit
E. 36th St.

FDR Drive

Tunnel Entrance

E. 35th St.
E. 34th St.
E. 33rd St.
E. 32nd St.
E. 31st St.
E. 30th St.
E. 29th St.
E. 28th St.
E. 27th St.
E. 26th St.
E. 25th St.
E. 24th St.
E. 23rd St.
E. 22nd St.
E. 21st St.
E. 20th St.
E. 19th St.
E. 18th St.
E. 17th St.
E. 16th St.
E. 15th St.
E. 14th St.
E. 13th St.

㉔ ㉗ ㉘
㉕
㉞ ㉖
Empire State Building

Broadway
Fifth Ave.
Madison Ave.
Park Ave. S.

㉙

Madison Square Park

㉚
FLATIRON DISTRICT
㉛

Sixth Ave. (Ave. of the Americas)

Gramercy Park

GRAMERCY PARK

Lexington Ave.
Second Ave.
First Ave.

Asser Levy Pl.

Peter Cooper Village

Stuyvesant Town

N.D. Perlman Pl.

㉝
Union Square
Union Sq. W.
Union Sq. E.
Irving Pl.

Ⓜ Subway stop

Upper Manhattan

Uptown

Midtown

Downtown

Uptown Shopping

Barney's **7**
Bulgari **11**
Calvin Klein **6**
Dolce & Gabbana **13**
Fairway **3**
Giorgio Armani **10**
Hermes **8**
I.S. 44 Flea Market **2**
Moschino **12**
Polo/Ralph Lauren **15**
Prada **14**
The Shops at Columbus Circle **5**
Tower Records **4**
Valentino **9**
Zabar's **1**
Zitomer **16**

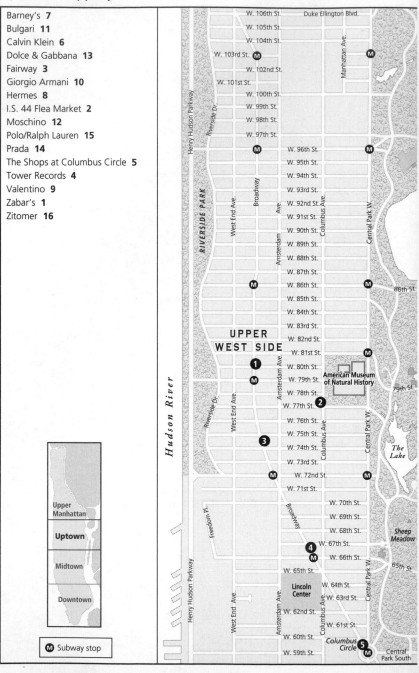

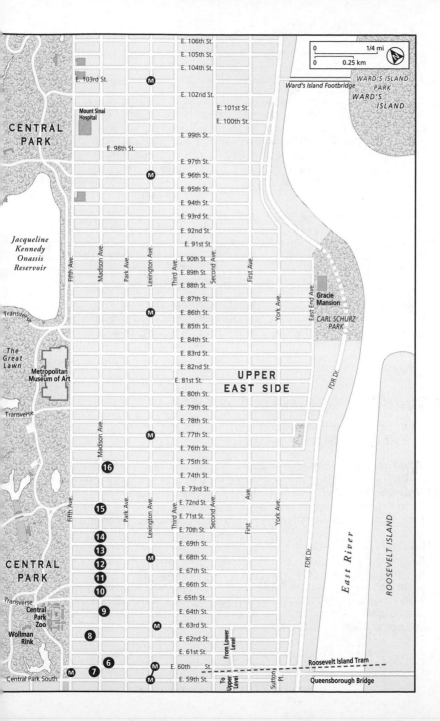

✔ **Lord & Taylor:** L&T is, in it's own way, retro-chic; kind of the anti-dote to those boutiques in SoHo and NoLiTa. The holiday windows are always a treat. 424 Fifth Ave. at 39th Street (☎ 212-391-3344; www.lordandtaylor.com. Subway: B/D/F/V train to 42nd Street stop or 7 train to Fifth Avenue stop). (See the "Midtown Shopping" map.)

✔ **Macy's:** Macy's has something for every taste and every price range. The annual floral show in its great hall is a special event as is the thrill of meeting Santa — just like Natalie Wood did in *Miracle on 34th Street*. The annual Thanksgiving Day parade ends here. Herald Square where West 34th Street, Sixth Avenue, and Broadway meet (☎ 212-695-4400; www.macys.com. Subway: B/D/F/N/Q/R/V/W train to 34th Street stop). (See the "Midtown Shopping" map.)

✔ **Saks Fifth Avenue:** If you only have time to stop in one department store while you're in town, Saks is the one. Smaller and more lavish than some of the other department stores, Saks best typifies New York verve and spirit. 611 Fifth Ave. at 50th Street (☎ 212-753-4000; www.saksfifthavenue.com. Subway: E/V train to Fifth Avenue/53rd Street stop). (See the "Midtown Shopping" map.)

✔ **Tiffany & Co.:** Tiffany's, as in *Breakfast at Tiffany's*. You can ogle the jewels, housewares, and other shoppers just like Audrey Hepburn did in the classic movie. 727 Fifth Ave. at 57th Street (☎ 212-755-8000; www.tiffany.com. Subway: N/R/W train to Fifth Avenue/59th Street stop). (See the "57th Street Shopping" map.)

Shopping in Open-Air Markets

New York hosts some great outdoor farmers' markets, flea markets, and street fairs — weather permitting, of course.

New York has greenmarkets at different locations throughout the city on different days, but the biggest and the best is the **Union Square Greenmarket.** You can find pickings from upstate and New Jersey farms, fresh fish from Long Island, homemade cheese and other dairy products, baked goods, plants, and organic herbs and spices. It's a true New York scene with everyone from models to celebrated chefs poring over the bounty. The Union Square Greenmarket is open all year but is at its peak August through October when the local harvest — tomatoes, corn, greens, grapes, peppers, and apples — flourishes. The Greenmarket is set up on the west and north sides of the square, between 14th and 17th streets, every Monday, Wednesday, Friday, and Saturday year-round from 6 a.m. to 6 p.m. Go early for the best selection. (See the "Downtown Shopping" map.)

Antiques are big in New York, and the locals love to browse and (some-times) stumble upon real treasures in several markets.

✔ The **Annex Antique Fair & Flea Market,** on Sixth Avenue at 25th Street, is probably the most famous market of its type. It has furniture, but also a lot of bric-a-brac, and it's open Saturday and Sunday from 9 a.m. to 5 p.m. (See the "Midtown Shopping" map.)

✔ The **SoHo Antique Fair and Collectibles Market,** on Grand Street at Broadway, also has furniture and accessories. It's open Monday through Saturday from 9 a.m. to 5 p.m. (See the "Downtown Shopping" map.)

✔ The **I.S. 44 Flea Market,** on Columbus Avenue between West 76th and 77th streets, specializes in secondhand clothes, antiques, and jewelry; it's open on Sundays from 10 a.m. to 6 p.m. (See the "Uptown Shopping" map.)

On weekends from spring to fall, you can catch a major New York enterprise called the Street Fair. The Street Fair is a generic fair; the food, clothes, and crafts sold by vendors are the same at every fair, and if you've seen one, you've seen them all. Still, New Yorkers cram the streets when they're held, and not only can you find some good items at very low prices, the fairs are fun for people-watching. Look for listings in the magazines *Time Out New York* and *New York.*

New York's sidewalks are also home to a plethora of (usually illegal) street vendors. And they don't succumb to bad weather. Indeed, at the first sign of rain, men selling umbrellas magically appear on almost every corner! Don't spend more than $3 for an umbrella unless you're absolutely desperate. These "umbrella men" and other street vendors operate year-round, working the streets and subway stations of the most popular neighborhoods. Other vendors sell everything from socks to "pre-owned" Rolex watches. Sometimes you can find bargains, but it's

Scoring at the sample sales

A bargain-hunter's dream, sample sales are events at which New York fashion designers sell — at *deep* discounts — discontinued styles, overstocks, and the sample outfits they create to show to store buyers (hence the name "sample sales"). How great are the deals? It's entirely possible to get a $300 dress from a big-name designer for $45 or less. Because the sales aren't widely publicized and may last anywhere from two days to a week, you have to hunt around to get the inside scoop. The weekly magazines *Time Out New York* and *New York* publish lists of upcoming sales; you also can try the Web sites www.nysale.com, www.dailycandy.com, and www.inshop.com for information.

Bring cash; credit cards are rarely accepted. You have more to choose from if you fit what designers call an "average" size — a U.S. 8 or 10 for women, a 40 for men. Items are sold as-is, so try things on before you buy.

best to approach these enterprises with extreme skepticism. The thousands of street vendors who offer gold jewelry and watches at cheap prices are selling fake goods, of course — with the exception of the occasional vendor of stolen merchandise. You can find fake Rolexes and other phony big-name watches for as little as $25 if you bargain, even less for smaller models or if you buy more than one. These pieces usually keep good time, but even if they don't, you obviously won't be getting a warranty with your purchase. Other hotbeds for imitation (or knock-off) designer goods and poor quality, bootleg DVDs are the stall shops along Canal Street in Chinatown — see the following section for more information.

Discovering the Best Shopping Neighborhoods

Zones for great shopping exist throughout New York. Some, however, are better than others. And new zones seem to sprout every year, so you're hard-pressed not to find good shopping no matter where you happen to be. What follows are the best neighborhoods, as of this writing, for shopping.

Madison Avenue

If you can find any bargains on Madison Avenue, let me know, and I'll investigate that very rare phenomena. No, you won't score any deals here; the stores in this neighborhood are some of the most expensive in town. But that doesn't mean you can't have fun window-shopping and dreaming about winning the lottery.

Uptown

High fashion (and high prices) is what you find in the stores on Madison Avenue between 57th and 78th streets. (If you can't find some of these stores on the "Uptown Shopping" map, check out the "Midtown Shopping" map.) Here you can find **Barney's** (see the "Knowing the Big Names" section earlier in this chapter) and some other high-end emporiums. To catch everything, start at one end and walk the length of this swanky strip. Take the 6 train to the 77th Street stop and walk south; or take the 4/5/6 train to the 59th Street stop or the N/R train to Lexington Avenue stop and walk north. I've mentioned only a few of my favorite stores along this strip; you're sure to find others along the way.

Along Madison Avenue, you find top European fashion designers' shops, such as the ultra-elegant **Giorgio Armani,** 760 Madison Ave. at 65th Street (☎ 212-988-9191), and his younger and less expensive line, **Emporio Armani,** 601 Madison Ave. at 60th Street (☎ 212-317-0800); the sometimes-outrageous **Moschino,** 803 Madison Ave. at 68th Street (☎ 212-639-9600); the trendy Italian designer **Dolce & Gabbana,** 825 Madison Ave. at 69th Street (☎ 212-249-4100); and the famous **Valentino,** 747 Madison Ave. at 65th Street (☎ 212-772-6969).

American designers are represented, too. Browse **Calvin Klein,** 654 Madison Ave. at 60th Street (☎ 212-292-9000); **Eileen Fisher,** 521 Madison Ave. at 53rd Street (☎ 212-759-9888); and **Polo/ Ralph Lauren** and **Polo Sport,** 867 Madison Ave. at 72nd Street (☎ 212-606-2100), among others.

If you're in search of fine Italian shoes and leather, visit **Prada,** 841 Madison Ave. between 69th and 70th streets (☎ 212-327-4200). Don't forget to stop by **Bulgari,** 783 Madison Ave. at 67th Street (☎ 212-717-2300), the big name in Italian jewelry, to see what the ladies in Monte Carlo are wearing around their necks this year.

Fifth Avenue and 57th Street

From classic department stores to flagship "brand" stores like Disney, you'll find a lot of variety (except in price, which is usually high) on luxury items, jewelry, clothing and accessories in this area.

Midtown

Elegant shopping is the order of the day in this area, centered on Fifth Avenue south of 59th Street and East 57th Street up to Lexington Avenue. (See the "Midtown Shopping" and "57th Street Shopping" maps.) This is the area where you can find a number of big stores like **Bloomingdales, Tiffany & Co., Bergdorf Goodman, The Disney Store,** and **Saks Fifth Avenue** (see "Knowing the Big Names" earlier in this chapter). To get here, take the subway to one of the nearby stops: the E/V train to the Fifth Avenue/53rd Street stop, the N/R/W train to the Fifth Avenue/59th Street stop, or the 4/5/6 train to the 59th Street stop. From any of these starting points, you can explore north and south on Fifth Avenue and east and west on 57th Street.

Stores on this stretch include those of some top European haute couture designers, such as **Christian Dior,** 21 E. 57th St. between Fifth and Madison avenues (☎ 212-931-2950); **Chanel,** 15 E. 57th St. between Fifth and Madison avenues (☎ 212-355-5050); **Gianni Versace,** 647 Fifth Ave. at 54th Street (☎ 212-317-0224); and **Laura Biagiotti,** 4 W. 57th St. at Fifth Avenue (☎ 212-399-2533). The high-end names for accessories and shoes are here also, including **Ferragamo,** 725 Fifth Ave. at 56th Street (☎ 212-759-3822); **Gucci,** 685 Fifth Ave. between 53rd and 54th streets (☎ 212-826-2600); **Hermés,** 11 E. 57th St. between Fifth and Madison avenues (☎ 212-751-3181); **Louis Vuitton,** 1 E. 57th St. at Fifth Avenue (☎ 212-758-8877); and **Fendi,** 720 Fifth Ave. at 56th Street (☎ 212-767-0100).

Among the other big names in this area is **Niketown,** 6 E. 57th St. at Fifth Avenue (☎ 212-891-6453), the five-floor shoe and clothing emporium that appears to be one giant "Just Do It" commercial. As you enter, check out the five-story screen that unfurls periodically to show a video montage of Nike's ultra-famous pitchmen and -women. A few blocks down on

57th Street Shopping

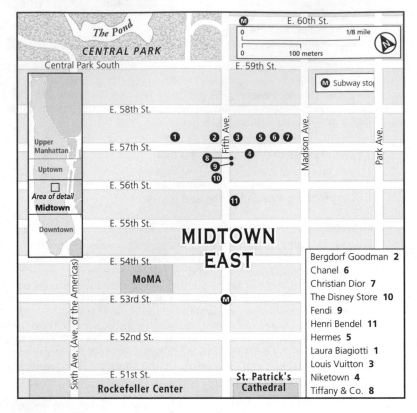

Fifth Avenue is **The NBA Store,** 666 Fifth Ave. at 52nd Street (☎ 212-515-NBA1), where, in addition to all sorts of NBA and WNBA merchandise, you may catch a player appearing for an in-store signing.

SoHo, NoHo, and NoLiTa

Head downtown for the edgy, the alternative, the hip, the tacky, and the cheap (though sometimes it costs a lot of money to look cheap). (See the "Downtown Shopping" map.)

Downtown

We all moan that SoHo is too trendy; I mean, who really wants to shop where off-duty supermodels shop? Okay, don't answer that one. Despite the complaints, SoHo remains one of the best shopping neighborhoods in the city; it's the epicenter of cutting-edge fashion where you can definitely find something unique to show off to your friends back home.

NoLiTa and NoHo are two of the shopping zones of the moment. And the "moment" has lasted for more than a few years now and doesn't seem to be fading. Here you can find tiny boutiques specializing in high-quality fashion and design. Don't expect cheap here, and if you're an early bird, do your shopping somewhere else first; most shops don't put out the welcome mat before 11 a.m.

SoHo is loosely bordered by Grand Street to the south, Avenue of the Americas (Sixth Avenue) to the west, Broadway to the east, and Houston to the north, forming a quadrangle. Here's my suggested plan of attack: Enter the quadrangle at one of the four corners and walk up and down or left and right (pretend that you're hoeing a field). Take the A/C/E train to the Canal Street stop, the C/E to the Spring Street stop, the N/R train to the Canal Street or Prince Street stop, the 6 train to the Bleecker Street or Spring Street stop, or the F/V/S train to the Broadway/Lafayette Street stop.

Designer boutiques include American **Anna Sui,** 113 Greene St. (☎ 212-941-8406), and **Todd Oldham,** 123 Wooster St. (☎ 212-226-4668); French **Tehen,** 91 Greene St. (☎ 212-925-4788); Australian **Country Road,** 411 W. Broadway (☎ 212-343-9544); and Italian **Dolce & Gabbana,** 434 W. Broadway (between Prince and Spring streets) (☎ 212-965-8000). **The Hat Shop,** 120 Thompson St. between Prince and Spring streets (☎ 212-219-1445), is a full-service milliner for women that also features plenty of off-the-rack toppers. The same street also features shoe stores galore — high-end home design and housewares boutiques add to the appeal. **The Puma Store,** 521 Broadway (☎ 212-334-7861) offers an amazing array of Puma athletic shoes made especially for non-athletes.

Rizzoli, 454 W. Broadway (☎ 212-674-1616), a bookstore synonymous with elegance, is also in the area; shop here for unusual editions and extravagant art books. **Kate's Paperie,** 561 Broadway (☎ 212-941-9811) features paper products; stationery, note paper, cards, and paper toys so scrumptious you may be tempted to eat them. Just kidding.

NoLiTa and NoHo are on the east side of Broadway and Lafayette from SoHo. You find smaller buildings, smaller shops, and a less hyped atmosphere in these neighborhoods. Interesting boutiques dot the tree-lined streets; the best streets to start your exploring are Elizabeth and Prince. **Borealis,** 229 Elizabeth St. between Prince and East Houston streets (☎ 917-237-0152), sells beautiful designer jewelry. **Lunette Et Chocolat,** 25 Prince St. between Elizabeth and Mott streets (☎ 212-925-8800), translates, I think, to eyewear and chocolate. Here you can ponder your choice of frames while having a chocolate crepe at the garden cafe in the rear. Now that's the kind of shopping I like.

Herald Square & The Garment District

You can actually find some bargains around here, along with an actual mall. (See the "Midtown Shopping" map.)

Midtown

This area is dominated by the self-proclaimed, "Biggest Department Store in the World": **Macy's.** But you can also find **Lord & Taylor** here (see "Knowing the Big Names," earlier in this chapter). But it's because of Macy's and Lord & Taylor that the area has attracted other big names like **Old Navy**, 150 W. 34th St. (☎ 212-594-0049), where you can outfit your extended family at bargain-basement prices; discounter **H&M**, 1328 Broadway at 34th Street (☎ 212-564-9922); and the mega-sneaker emporium, **Foot Locker**, 120 W. 34th St. (☎ 212-629-4419). At Sixth Avenue and 33rd Street is the **Manhattan Mall** (☎ 212-465-0500), where you can find mall standards like Radio Shack and LensCrafters.

Chinatown & The Lower East Side

The heart of Chinatown's commercial zone runs along Canal Street, from West Broadway to the Bowery. (See the "Downtown Shopping" map.) Here, interspersed with more fruit, vegetable, and fish markets than you can imagine, you pass store after store — most merely hallway-sized stalls — selling "designer" sunglasses, watches, and handbags (think Gucci, Coach, Louis Vuitton, and kate spade, for example), as well as bootleg CDs and DVDs of just released movies. The film quality of these bootlegs is so bad that you feel like you're watching a movie through a screen door. No matter what you find here, don't expect quality; still, it can be fun to browse, and after you get a sense of the prices, haggle a bit.

Existing alongside this extravaganza of fake merch is the *other* Chinatown, where you can find quirky, one-of-a-kind Asian-inspired gifts at bargain-basement prices. **Mott Street,** south of Canal Street, has a stretch of knick-knack and housewares shops that sell everything from lacquered jewelry boxes and toys to embroidered silk pajamas and pottery dinnerware. If you prefer one-stop shopping, try **Pearl River,** 477 Broadway at Grand Street (☎ 212-431-4770), a department store complete with a waterfall and specializing in all things Chinatown — food, music, movies, clothing, and more.

The Lower East Side's main shopping is on Orchard Street, now known as the **Historic Orchard Street Shopping District,** which basically runs from Houston to Canal along Allen, Orchard, and Ludlow streets, spreading outward along both sides of Delancey Street. The bargains aren't quite what they used to be, but prices on leather bags, shoes, luggage, and fabrics on the bolt are still quite good. Be prepared for the hard sell and don't worry about saying no.

Before you browse, stop into the **Lower East Side Visitor Center,** 261 Broome St. between Orchard and Allen streets, (☎ 866-224-0206 or 212-226-9010; Subway: F to Delancey Street.), for a shopping guide that includes vendors both old-world and new. Or you can preview the list online at www.lowereastsideny.com.

They say it's not a mall . . .

But what else would you call it? The new **Shops at Columbus Circle,** located in the Time Warner Center, features not only some of the biggest (and most expensive) names in retail, but it also offers shopping with a view of Central Park. The mall, located just off the southwest corner of Central Park, is two city blocks long and four stories high. But the picturesque view doesn't really matter to serious shoppers who are setting their sights on the goods at retailers like **Williams Sonoma, A/X Armani Exchange, Coach, Hugo Boss, Joseph Abboud, Eileen Fisher, Thomas Pink,** and the massive 59,000-square-foot **Whole Foods Supermarket.** For more information about the Shops, you can check out the mall's Web site at www.shopsatcolumbus.com or call ☎ **212-823-6300.**

Other shopping areas

A host of other shopping zones exist all around Manhattan. If you're looking for something specific, chances are there's a part of town that sells nothing but what you want. The most famous is probably the **Diamond District,** a conglomeration of jewelry and gem stores along West 47th Street between Fifth and Sixth avenues (www.47th-street.com). If you're after **beads, crafts, and notions,** the area between 35th and 39th streets between Fifth and Sixth avenues is the place to go. In the Village, Bleecker Street between Sixth and Seventh avenues is home to a number of **used CD stores** (check out St. Mark's Place between Second and Third avenues as well).

 Teenagers and those striving for a younger look love the **shoes, clothing, and leather shops** that populate 8th Street from Second to Sixth avenues (east of Broadway, 8th Street becomes known as St. Mark's Place). Clothes and accessories for trendsters are also to be found on Seventh and Ninth streets.

Lower Manhattan & the Financial District

You won't find any major shopping zones in Lower Manhattan and the Financial District, but you will find a few excellent stores like **Century 21,** 22 Cortlandt St. (☎ 212-227-9092). This king of discount department stores is across the street from the World Trade Center site, along with the city's best electronics retailer, **J&R Music & Computer World,** Park Row (☎ 800-426-6067), which is a block-long emporium where you can find great prices on everything from cameras and computers to CDs and software.

The most concentrated shopping in this area is at the **South Street Seaport** (☎ 212/732-8257; www.southstreetseaport.com). Familiar names like Abercrombie & Fitch, Bath & Body Works, Brookstone, and the Sunglass Hut line Fulton Street, which is the Seaport's main cobbled drag; similar shops fill the levels at **Pier 17,** a waterfront barge-turned-shopping mall. There's nothing here you can't get anywhere else in

Manhattan, but come anyway — for the historic ambience and the wonderful harbor views.

The Best of New York Shopping A to Z

If your shopping intentions are less of the browsing variety, here are some of New York's specialized shopping options.

Beauty

✔ **Kiehl's:** More a cult than a store. Everyone from models to stockbrokers stop by this always-packed old-time apothecary. 109 Third Ave. between 13th and 14th streets (☎ 212-677-3171; www.kiehls.com. Subway: L, N, R, 4, 5, 6 to 14th Street/Union Square). (See the "Downtown Shopping" map.)

✔ **Ricky's:** This chain of funky drug stores also features a wide range of beauty products. If you're just dying for a multi-colored wig, rainbow-colored lipstick, glitter galore, and more than 80 kinds of hair brushes, and even edible undies, this is the store for you. At numerous locations, including 44 E. 8th St. at Greene Street (☎ 212-254-5247; www.rickys-nyc.com. Subway: N, R to 8th Street). (See the "Downtown Shopping" map.)

✔ **Lush:** This London-based handmade cosmetics store has a fanatical following for its gentle, sweet-smelling products (some vegan, some organic). They've just opened a store in New York in the shadow of Manhattan Mall. 1293 Broadway at 34th Street (☎ 212-564-9120; www.lush.com). (See the "Midtown Shopping" map.)

✔ **Zitomer:** This three-story drugstore is more a mini-department store than a pharmacy. They have their own very good line of cosmetics called **Z New York.** Big Apple lip gloss makes a wonderful souvenir — something you won't find in your local Walgreens. 969 Madison Ave. at 76th Street (☎ 212-737-2016; www.zitomer.com. Subway: 6 to 77th Street). (See the "Uptown Shopping" map.)

Books

✔ **Books of Wonder:** This store is so saccharin that you may think you've stepped onto the set of the children's television show, *Barney.* But just like they inexplicabley love Barney, kids also love this place. 16 W. 18th St. between Fifth and Sixth avenues (☎ 212-989-3270; www.booksofwonder.net. Subway: L, N, R, 4, 5, 6 to 14th Street/Union Square). (See the "Midtown Shopping" map.)

✔ **Coliseum Books:** This is my favorite book store in New York. Before there were Barnes and Noble superstores, there was Coliseum Books. The store is now at a new location opposite Bryant Park. 11 W. 42nd St. between Sixth and Fifth avenues (☎ 212-803-5890; www.coliseumbooks.com. Subway: B, D, F, V to 42nd Street). (See the "Midtown Shopping" map.)

✔ **Drama Book Shop:** This store has a resident theater company and in-house performance space. Offering thousands of plays, from translations of Greek classics to this season's biggest hits, the shop also offers books, magazines, and newspapers on the craft and business of the performing arts. 250 W. 40th St. between Eighth and Ninth avenues (☎ 212-944-0595; www.dramabookshop.com. Subway: A, C, E to 42nd Street). (See the "Midtown Shopping" map.)

✔ **Forbidden Planet:** Here's the city's largest collection of sci-fi, comics, and graphic-illustration books. The proudly geeky staff really knows what's what. 840 Broadway at 13th Street (☎ 212-473-1576; www.forbiddenplanetnyc.com. Subway: L, N, R, 4, 5, 6 to 14th Street/Union Square). (See the "Downtown Shopping" map.)

✔ **The Mysterious Bookshop:** This two-level shop, where the second floor is reached via a spiral staircase, is owned by mystery publisher Otto Penzler, and it's a great source for rare and collectible titles along with signed first editions. 129 W. 56th St. between Sixth and Seventh avenues (☎ 212-765-0900; www.mysteriousbookshop.com. Subway: F train to 57th Street). (See the "Midtown Shopping" map.)

✔ **The Strand:** A New York legend, The Strand is worth a visit for its staggering "eight miles of books" as well as its extensive inventory of review copies and bargain titles at up to 85 percent off list price. 828 Broadway at 12th St (☎ 212-473-1452; www.strandbooks.com. Subway: L, N, R, 4, 5, 6 to 14th Street/Union Square) **Strand Annex** at 95 Fulton St. between William and Gold streets (☎ 212-732-6070. Subway: 4, 5, 6 to Fulton Street). (See the "Downtown Shopping" map.)

Edibles

✔ **Dean & DeLuca:** This upscale gourmet store in the heart of SoHo is a symbol of that area's prosperity. The store features premier quality across the board at premium prices. A small cafe up front makes this place a great stop for a cappuccino break from SoHo shopping. 560 Broadway at Prince Street (☎ 212-226-6800; www.dean-deluca.com. Subway: N, R to Prince Street).

✔ **Dylan's Candy Bar:** Dylan (daughter of Ralph) Lauren is one of the co-owners of this new wonderland that would make Willy Wonka proud. Located across the street from Bloomingdale's, Dylan's stocks candy classics like Necco wafers, Charleston Chews, and both of my favorite childhood chewing gums: Black Jack and Gold Mine. 1011 Third Ave. at 60th Street (☎ 646-735-0078; www.dylanscandybar.com. Subway: 4, 5, 6, N, R to 59th Street). (See the "Midtown Shopping" map.)

✔ **Fairway:** You won't find a better all-in-one market in Manhattan. Here you can find the best and most modestly priced vegetables and cheeses in the city. Fairway also carries gourmet items you may find at Dean & Deluca, but at a fraction of the cost. The Harlem store is huge and features a walk-in freezer complete with down jackets provided for customers. 2127 Broadway between 74th and 75th streets (☎ 212-595-1888; www.fairwaymarket.com. Subway: 1, 2, 3, 9 to 72nd Street). Also at 2328 12th Ave. at 132nd Street (☎ 212-234-3883. Subway: 1, 9 to 125th Street). (See the "Uptown Shopping" map.)

✔ **Zabar's:** More than any other of New York's gourmet food stores, Zabar's is an institution. This giant deli sells prepared foods, packaged goods from around the world, coffee beans, fresh breads, and much more (no fresh veggies, though). You can also find an excellent — and well-priced — collection of housewares and restaurant-quality cookware. Prepare yourself for serious crowds. 2245 Broadway at 80th Street (☎ 212-787-2000; Subway: 1, 9 to 79th Street). (See the "Uptown Shopping" map.)

Electronics

✔ **B&H Photo & Video:** Looking for a digital camera at a good price? You really can't do any better than B&H, the largest camera store in the country. This camera superstore has everything from lenses to darkroom equipment. The store can be somewhat intimidating, but service is helpful. Just follow the signs to find whatever you're seeking. 420 Ninth Ave. at 34th Street (☎ 800-606-6969; www.bhphotovideo.com. Subway: A, C, E to 34th Street). (See the "Midtown Shopping" map.)

B&H closes early on Fridays (2 p.m.) and isn't open at all on Saturdays or major Jewish holidays.

✔ **J&R Music & Computer World:** This block-long, Financial District emporium is the city's top discount computer, electronics, small appliance, and office equipment retailer. Park Row at Ann Street, opposite City Hall Park (☎ 800-426-6027 or 212-238-9000; www.jandr.com. Subway: 2, 3 to Park Place; 4, 5, 6 to Brooklyn Bridge/City Hall). (See the "Downtown Shopping" map.)

Museum Stores

✔ **Metropolitan Museum of Art Store:** Treasures from the museum's collection have been reproduced as jewelry, china, and other objets d'art and sold in the museum's stores. The range of art books is dizzying, and upstairs is an equally comprehensive selection of posters and inventive children's toys. At numerous locations, including 1000 Fifth Ave. at 82nd Street (☎ 212-570-3894; www.metmuseum.org/store. Subway: 4, 5, 6 to 86th Street and Rockefeller Center). Also at 15 W. 49th St. (☎ 212-332-1360. Subway: B, D, F, V to 47th–50th streets/Rockefeller Center). (See the "Midtown Shopping" map.)

✔ **MoMA Design Store:** Across the street from the Museum of Modern Art is this terrific shop, whose stock ranges from museum posters and clever toys for kids to fully licensed reproductions of many of the classics of modern design. The SoHo store is equally fabulous. 44 W. 53rd St. between Fifth and Sixth avenues (☎ 212-767-1050; www.moma.org. Subway: E, F to Fifth Avenue; B, D, F, Q to 47th–50th streets/Rockefeller Center) Also at 81 Spring St. at Crosby Street (☎ 646-613-1367. Subway: 6 to Spring Street).

✔ **New York Transit Museum Store:** My four-year-old could spend hours here gazing at all this train stuff. Be the first in your neighborhood to own a pair of ancient New York City subway token cuff-links. Grand Central Terminal (on the main level, in the shuttle passage next to the Station Masters' office), 42nd Street and Lexington Avenue (☎ 212-878-0106. Subway: 4, 5, 6, 7, S to 42nd Street/Grand Central). Also at 1560 Broadway at 47th Street. (☎ 212-230-4901. Subway: 1, 9, to 50th Street); and Boerum Place at Schermerhorn Street, Brooklyn (☎ 718-694-5100. Subway 4, 5 to Borough Hall). (See the "Midtown Shopping" map.)

Music

✔ **Colony Music Center:** Housed in the legendary Brill Building, the Tin Pan Alley of '50s and '60s pop, this place has been around since 1948. You can find a great collection of Broadway scores and cast recordings; decades worth of recordings by pop song stylists both legendary and obscure; the city's best collection of sheet music (including some hard-to-find international stuff); and a great selection of original theater and movie posters. 1619 Broadway at 49th Street (☎ 212-265-2050; www.colonymusic.com. Subway: N, R to 49th Street; 1, 9 to 50th Street). (See the "Midtown Shopping" map.)

✔ **House of Oldies:** I skipped many a high school class to spend time in this musty old store searching for doo-wop recordings. The store has over one million vinyl records in stock in everything from R&B to surf music. So if vinyl oldies are your thing, House of Oldies is your dream come true. 35 Carmine St. at Bleecker (☎ 212-243-0500; www.houseofoldies.com. Subway: A, C, B, D, F, V to West 4th Street). (See the "Downtown Shopping" map.)

✔ **Jazz Record Center:** My friend the jazz buff from Paris swears by this place as the best to find rare and out-of-print jazz records. In addition to the extensive selection of CDs and vinyl (including 78s), the store also offers videos, books, posters, magazines, photos, and other memorabilia. 236 W. 26th St., 8th floor, between Seventh and Eighth avenues (☎ 212-675-4480; www.jazzrecordcenter.com. Subway: 1, 9 to 28th Street). (See the "Midtown Shopping" map.)

✔ **Tower Records:** Even though this mighty chain has filed for bankruptcy protection, it's still my favorite music superstore, and I'm pulling for its survival. Both main locations are huge multimedia superstores brimming with an encyclopedic collection of music — classical, jazz, rock, world, you name it. The downtown location has a "bargain annex" and the 66th St. store (across from Lincoln Center) has a breathtakingly huge and complete classical section.

692 Broadway at W. 4th Street (☎ 212-505-1500; www.tower records.com. Subway: N, R to 8th Street; 6 to Astor Place). Also at 1961 Broadway at 66th Street (☎ 212-799-2500. Subway: 1, 9 to 66th Street). (See the "Downtown Shopping" and "Uptown Shopping" maps.)

✔ **Virgin Megastore:** In the heart of Times Square, this *super* superstore bustles day and night. 1540 Broadway at 45th Street (☎ 212-921-1020; www.virginmega.com. Subway: N, R, 1, 2, 3, 7, 9 to Times Square/42nd Street). Also at 52 E. 14th St. at Broadway (☎ 212-598-4666. Subway: 4, 5, 6, N, R, L to 14th Street/Union Square). (See the "Midtown Shopping" and "Downtown Shopping" maps.)

Toys

✔ **Enchanted Forest:** This joyful SoHo shop overflows with stuffed animals and puppets, plus the kinds of simple but absorbing games that parents remember from the days before Sony PlayStation, like PickUp Sticks and Chinese Checkers. 85 Mercer St. between Spring and Broome streets (☎ 212-925-6677; www.sohotoys.com. Subway: N, R to Prince Street). (See the "Downtown Shopping" map.)

✔ **Toys "R" Us:** Sure, you have a Toys "R" Us in the mall back home. But does your "Toys" have its own full-scale Ferris wheel where your kids can ride for free? Don't miss it if you're traveling with kids. 1514 Broadway at 44th Street (☎ 800-869-7787. Subway: 1, 2, 3, 7, 9 to 42nd Street). (See the "Midtown Shopping" map.)

Chapter 13

Following an Itinerary: Five Great Options

. . . .

In This Chapter

▶ Exploring the best of New York in three, four, or five days

▶ Making the most of many museums

▶ Following the paths of history

. . . .

I've lived in New York for more than half my life, and I still haven't seen it all. That's not because I don't have the desire to see it all; it's just that in New York, you *can't* see it all. So if you feel a bit overwhelmed by all the options, I've laid out a few itineraries in this chapter that help you focus on your interests and use your time most efficiently, while giving you a good sampling of what New York has to offer. Remember, these are just my ideas — feel free to tailor these itineraries to suit your own schedule and taste.

New York in Three Days

Although your three-day visit may take place in the middle of the week, I'm writing this chapter as if your three days are part of a long weekend. Even if you're constantly on the move, you just can't cover all of New York in 72 hours. This itinerary enables you to get a taste of New York — just enough to make you want to come back for more. You're always welcome.

Day one

Okay, start with getting a big picture of Manhattan. The best way to do this is to take either a three-hour **Circle Line Cruise** or the two-hour **New York Waterways** (see Chapter 11) full-island cruise. Both encircle Manhattan from the water. You pass by the Statue of Liberty and Ellis Island, see the Lower Manhattan skyline, go up the East River where you cruise under the Brooklyn Bridge, view the United Nations, cruise around to the Hudson River where you pass the George Washington Bridge, and then head back to dock on the West Side piers.

The ride on both cruises is generally calm, but if you're like me and just looking at the water from a boat begins to turn your face an unpleasant shade of green, you may want to consider the land alternative: a double-decker bus tour. **Gray Line New York** (see Chapter 11) offers many tour options, but the one that passes most of the major attractions is the downtown loop. The tour takes approximately two hours and shows you Times Square, the Empire State Building, the Flatiron building, Rockefeller Center, Greenwich Village, the Lower East Side, and Chinatown.

If you're here for a three-day weekend, hold this tour for either Saturday or Sunday morning. The double-decker buses don't have special lanes, so they get stuck in traffic just like anything else on wheels. Traffic is light on Saturday and Sunday mornings, and you should cruise through the tour without any traffic hiccups.

You're deposited on the West Side Highway around 42nd Street after your morning tour (if you took the boat rather than the bus). Head over a couple of blocks to Ninth Avenue and have lunch at one of Hell's Kitchen's inexpensive ethnic restaurants. See Chapter 10 for some restaurant suggestions. After lunch you can walk east across 42nd Street to see many of the sights you couldn't view from the boat. You pass through the most famous crossroads in the world, 42nd and Broadway. Make your way through the crowds and continue east where you hit **Bryant Park;** if you see camera crews and tents in the park it means it's Fashion Week. On Fifth Avenue at 42nd is one of New York's great structures: the **New York Public Library.** As you walk further east between Park Avenue and Lexington Avenue, you see Grand Central Station, another of New York's architectural treasures, and at Lexington Avenue, the city's most magnificent Art Deco building, the **Chrysler Building.** Finally, make your way back to Fifth Avenue and walk eight blocks south to 34th Street. Look up — all the way to the top of the Empire State Building. You've got your tickets already (order them online before you leave), so you don't have to wait in line to get to the 86th-floor Observatory, and check out the view from the tallest building in New York.

You've done a lot of walking, so head back to your hotel and rest for a bit before setting out again. It's Friday night and that means museums are usually open late. You don't have time to hit them all, so I recommend **The Metropolitan Museum of Art** (see Chapter 11), where, not only will you be in one of the world's greatest museums, but on Friday (and Saturday) the Met's beautiful Great Hall Balcony Bar is open for cocktails with classical music from a string quartet. From May to October in good weather, the lovely open-air Roof Garden Cafe overlooking Central Park is also open.

After the museum and cocktails, you've got reservations at one of those four-star restaurants run by a chef you've seen on television and on the cover of a famous magazine. Now you can judge for yourself what all the fuss is about.

Day two

Make sure you have your hotel give you a wake-up call — you have plenty of time to sleep on the flight home. Head down to Chinatown in the morning and watch as the fish markets, and there are a lot of them, prepare the day's catch (some still flopping in the ice). Canal Street is the area's major thoroughfare, and by 11 a.m. on most days, especially on Saturdays, the sidewalk is absolutely teeming; so the earlier you get to Chinatown, the better. Have a late breakfast or early lunch at one of the neighborhood's great, cheap restaurants. (See Chapter 10 for tips.)

After eating, walk or get on the number 6 train at the Canal Street station and take it one stop downtown to the Brooklyn Bridge–City Hall stop. You're going to see New York's City Hall, but it's the **Brooklyn Bridge** that you want. If the weather is decent, follow the signs to the walkway that takes you across that truly amazing structure. Don't forget to turn around for numerous photo ops with the New York skyline behind you. After you reach Brooklyn and you've sufficiently worked off that meal in Chinatown, you deserve a reward; head down to the river's edge, under the Brooklyn Bridge, and buy yourself an ice cream at the **Brooklyn Ice Cream Factory** (see Chapter 10).

If you don't want to walk back across the bridge, take the C train at High Street back into Manhattan and get off at the Spring Street stop. At Spring Street you've entered the chic, fashion-conscious neighborhood known as **SoHo.** Traverse Spring Street and then up West Broadway to Prince Street. With all the designer boutiques and funky (but expensive) stores to explore, the going is going to be slow. You didn't forget your plastic, did you? Walking north across Houston, you enter Greenwich Village. You'll think you're in old Europe with the narrow streets, quaint brown-stones, and numerous cafes. Have a cappuccino at one of the cafes, or eat an early dinner (look for early-bird and prix-fixe specials!), and then head back to your hotel to freshen up. Tonight's the night you've got tickets to that Tony-award winning show on Broadway. This is also your chance to take a peek at the neon spectacle of Times Square. After the show, if you are still itching to move, hit one of the downtown dance clubs (see Chapter 15), or if you're hungry and just want a late bite, you have numerous options to choose from.

Day three

For some reason, you wake up and miss hearing the sounds of birds chirping like you hear back home. Not to worry — get on the subway and make your way to New York's green oasis, Central Park. But first pick up some bagels and coffee for a breakfast alfresco. For hints on where you can get the best bagels, see Chapter 10. The park is vast with much to explore (see Chapter 11 for ideas); then amble over to the **Museum of Natural History**, on Central Park West. The museum opens at 10 a.m.; if you get there much later on a Sunday, expect to wait on line. You won't be able to see this entire phenomenal museum, but make sure you see the dinosaurs or maybe the space show at the Rose Center for Earth and Space. (For more on what to see, head to Chapter 11.)

After the museum, you may still have time to catch a gospel service (assuming this is Sunday) in Harlem, which you can follow up with a soul food lunch (see Chapters 10 and 16). Or head across the park to the eastside and walk Museum Mile where you can see museums like the **Guggenheim,** the **Frick,** and the **Whitney** to name just a few (see Chapter 11). You won't have time to explore all of them, but find one that interests you and make it your afternoon destination.

Have a light dinner at one of the city's very good pizzerias or anywhere else you like and then cap off your whirlwind New York weekend listening to some live music at a club or relax in a cozy lounge. See Chapter 15 for tips on where to find them.

New York in Five Days

Compared to three days in New York, you're going to feel like five days is a lifetime — until all the things you want to do begin to add up and you realize even in five days you can't do it all. Don't worry, and try not to stress. Remember, you're never going to do it all. But the following five-day itinerary should help give you an idea of what you can do, and it will be plenty.

Day one

Start your day and your visit at the beginning — where the city was born: Manhattan's southern tip, New York's oldest and most historic precincts. Leave early to catch the morning's first ferry to the **Statue of Liberty** and **Ellis Island** (Chapter 11). This ride will take up most of your morning.

After you're back on the island, if you didn't arrange for tickets before you left home, pop over to the downtown **TKTS booth** at South Street Seaport (the line is usually shorter here than at the Times Square location) to pick up some discounted tickets for a **Broadway** or **Off-Broadway show** (something's always available for the evening or for tomorrow afternoon if you prefer a matinee; see Chapter 14).

By now, you're sure to need lunch, if you haven't succumbed to your hunger already. Do you want a leisurely meal or a quick snack? Check the options listed in Chapter 10. Or hop the subway over to Brooklyn (the A/C line will whisk you from Lower Manhattan over to the High Street stop in minutes) and stroll back to Manhattan over the majestic **Brooklyn Bridge.** The bridge and the views from it beg to be photographed, so if you have a traditional camera, make sure you have plenty of film and batteries; if you've made the leap into the digital age, make sure your batteries are charged and your memory card has plenty of space.

Or, if you prefer, use the time to enjoy one of Lower Manhattan's many historic or cultural attractions, such as the insightful and moving **Museum ͏ Jewish Heritage, a Living Memorial to the Holocaust;** surprisingly ͏ utive **Wall Street;** or the **National Museum of the American Indian,** housed in the stunning1907 Beaux Arts **U.S. Customs House,** which is worth a visit for the architecture alone. See Chapter 11 for more information on the city's best architecture.

Head back to your hotel to freshen up so you can enjoy a leisurely dinner at one of the city's hundreds of fantastic restaurants, see a Broadway show, or stop at a club for some dancing or just to listen to some jazz.

Day two

Spend the bulk of your day at one of the big museums: either the **Metropolitan Museum of Art** or the **American Museum of Natural History.** Both of these can easily fill a week of browsing, so you may want to begin with a Highlights Tour. Don't miss the dinosaurs or the Space Show at the Natural History Museum's **Rose Center for Earth and Space.**

After you've had enough of the museum, head into **Central Park** (Chapter 11) to see some of its many highlights; both museums sit on its fringe. You've worked up a big appetite with all that walking, so plan for another special dinner followed by the nightlife of your choice; the options are limitless.

Day three

Start your morning with a full-island cruise with either **Circle Line** (three hours) or **New York Waterways** (two hours), which circumnavigate Manhattan and offer a fascinating perspective on the island. If you're strapped for time, opt for the 1½-hour cruise that ferries you around New York Harbor and halfway up the East River.

Spend the afternoon roaming some of the city's downtown neighborhoods: **SoHo,** the winding 19th-century streets of **Greenwich Village,** and exotic **Chinatown.** Walk the prime thoroughfares, poke your head into shops, or park yourself at a street-side cafe and just watch the world go by. If you prefer to have a knowledgeable guide as you explore, schedule a **guided walking tour** (see Chapter 11 for a list of various tours, including free ones).

Stay downtown for the evening; catch dinner in a stylish (or authentically old-world) restaurant and follow dinner up with a trip to a cutting-edge dance club or model-laden cocktail lounge. (See Chapter 15 for recommendations.) Or if you've had enough of downtown, head back to your hotel and freshen up, then head uptown for dinner; maybe order up some down-home cooking in Harlem and wander over for some jazz at the **Lenox Lounge.**

Day four

Head over to Rockefeller Center and see if you can get on one of the early NBC Tours (for information on times, ticket prices and reservations, call ☎ 212-664-7174). Then make your way to the **Empire State Building** (flip to Chapter 11 for details) to see the view from the 86th-floor observation deck of New York's tallest building and ultimate landmark skyscraper.

After you're done, walk eight blocks to **Grand Central Terminal** (the walk is pleasant on a nice day) to admire that marvelous Beaux Arts monument to modern transportation. The dining concourse on the lower level gives you some very good lunch options.

Spend the afternoon browsing one or two of the Big Apple's brilliant smaller museums. Take in the **Frick Collection** or the **Whitney.** Or, if you prefer, use the afternoon to stroll up Madison Avenue and gawk, or exercise your credit line, at the staggeringly expensive shops.

Enjoy another evening at the theater, or catch a performance at **Lincoln Center, Carnegie Hall,** or one of the city's other terrific performing-arts institutions. Don't forget the innovative **Brooklyn Academy of Music;** it's easy to get to by subway with many of the major lines stopping nearby (see Chapter 14).

Day five

Use the morning to explore one of the major attractions you've missed thus far. If you spent day two at the Met, spend today at the **American Museum of Natural History.** Or go see Frank Lloyd Wright's iconic **Guggenheim Museum.** Tour the nerve center of international relations: the **United Nations.** Or, if you haven't seen **Central Park** yet, go now; you cannot leave New York without visiting it. If you've already done all the above, maybe today is the day you leave Manhattan for the Bronx and make a stop at the fabulous **Bronx Zoo.** Or head to Brooklyn for the sometimes-controversial **Brooklyn Art Museum** (see Chapter 11).

In the evening, celebrate the end of a great vacation with some live music. Flip to Chapter 15 for a rundown of the city's nightlife offerings. A night of jazz at the legendary **Village Vanguard,** or rock at **Arlene Grocery,** or maybe some klezmer music at the intimate club **Satalla,** makes a very festive close, as does a night of laughs at one of the city's legendary comedy clubs, such as **Carolines** or the **Comedy Cellar.** Or, for the ultimate in New York elegance, dress to the nines and opt for a night of champagne and cabaret at the venerable **Cafe Carlyle** or **Feinstein's at the Regency.** If you want the velvet rope experience, head to one of the city's hottest dance clubs. This is your last night, so make it memorable.

New York for Museum Mavens

You would easily need (at least) five days to see the many museums and galleries in New York. But even if you're a maven, that's a bit extreme. Here's my stress-free two-day museum itinerary.

Start at the busiest and most extensive museum, the **Metropolitan Museum of Art.** Plan to arrive at the museum around opening time

(9:30 a.m.) to avoid the crowds. Give yourself a minimum of two hours for your visit. Remember, the Met is closed on Mondays. From the Met, stroll up Museum Mile and try to decide if you want to go inside that funny-looking building called the **Guggenheim,** or head south from the Met to the **Frick** or the **Whitney** or any of the other fine museums in the area. But you won't have time to visit more than one before your hunger wins out. You can hit a branch of **El Paso Taqueria** on 97th Street, between Park and Lexington avenues, or take a taxi up to **Patsy's Pizzeria** on First Avenue and 116th Street for the best pizza in New York. See Chapter 10 for more restaurant information.

After lunch, head to 53rd Street, between Fifth and Sixth avenues, and visit the newly-renovated **Museum of Modern Art (MoMA)** (see Chapter 11). If you still have the time and energy, just up the street is the stunning **American Folk Art Museum** (also detailed in Chapter 11). If you're truly dedicated, you can try to make it to west Chelsea in time to hit the galleries there and then eat at one of the innumerable restaurants nearby.

After a night dreaming of gilded treasures, take the subway out to Brooklyn for part two of your museum-going adventure and the second-largest museum after the Met, the **Brooklyn Museum of Art.** You're in Brooklyn and you've got all morning so give yourself three hours at this wonderful museum.

Take the train back to Manhattan and, if you didn't get to Chelsea for a bit of gallery hopping, now's your chance. Or check out the **New Museum of Contemporary Art** in SoHo. In either neighborhood, you can visit galleries galore. For more information about museums in New York, see Chapter 11.

New York for Families with Kids

New York, despite its gritty reputation, is a wonderland for children. Start your family vacation at the great **Museum of Natural History.** Promising the little ones a peek at Barney, proceed directly to the fourth floor and the Dinosaur exhibit. Don't worry, after they view the real dinosaurs, they may forget all about that whiney purple one. After they've had enough dinosaurs, take the brood to the **Rose Center for Earth and Space,** whose four-story-tall planetarium sphere hosts the excellent Harrison Ford–narrated Space Show that will awe all of you. The museum is right across from Central Park, the perfect place for a picnic lunch with the family. Children can explore much in Central Park: playgrounds galore, boat rides, the Central Park Zoo, the Carousel, and ice-skating. To do it all takes a day in itself.

After lunch, take the C train at Central Park West and 81st Street downtown to Times Square, where the kids can gawk at all the lights, familiar stores, arcades, and junk food that the reinvented tourist zone has to offer. If you have little ones, take them to the **Toys "R" Us** superstore (see Chapter 12) where they can get a ride on the store's free indoor Ferris wheel. You're all probably famished by now, so treat the family to dinner at **Virgil's Real BBQ** or **Carmine's,** both extremely kid-friendly (see Chapter 10).

The next day, head over to the Hudson River piers in the West 40s and take either the three-hour **Circle Line** cruise around Manhattan or the 90-minute **New York Waterways** Harbor Cruise. Both offer a different perspective on some of the city's greatest attractions like the Statue of Liberty, Ellis Island, the Brooklyn Bridge, and the United Nations. After your time on the water, visit the retired aircraft carrier, the *USS Intrepid* at the **Intrepid Sea-Air-Space Museum** (see Chapter 11). At this astonishing museum, the kids (and you too!) can climb inside a replica Revolutionary War submarine, sit in an A-6 Intruder cockpit, and follow the progress of America's astronauts as they work in space.

For lunch, the pizza at **John's Pizzeria,** just off Times Square and not far from the Intrepid, can make any kid happy. After lunch work your way to 34th and Fifth and the **Empire State Building.** Because you've already bought tickets (see Chapter 11), you won't have to wait on line, and you and your family are quickly whizzed up to the 86th-floor observatory where you experience the same view King Kong had when he climbed to the top of the city's tallest building. From the observation deck, look downtown and tell the kids that is where they're going for dinner: to Chinatown where the constant commotion, street vendors, flopping fish, and all-around exotic feel may excite the children as much as it does you. After the excitement of the day you're all going to be famished and ready for a big, communal, and inexpensive dinner at one of Chinatown's many restaurants.

After dinner, take the 6 train uptown to 14th Street-Union Square where you will switch to the number 4 express train. Stay on the train until you come out of the tunnel and see the bright lights of Yankee Stadium. Your stop is 161st Street; **Yankee Stadium** — The House that Ruth Built — and you're here to see the most celebrated franchise in all sports play, the New York Yankees.

If you have another day with the family, take a poll from the kids on what they want to do. Return to Central Park? Head up to the Bronx Zoo? Visit a few museums like the New York Transit Museum, the Skyscraper Museum, or the Children's Museum? Check out South Street Seaport? Explore the activities of Chelsea Piers? Don't worry. With any of these choices, you can't go wrong.

It's always good to have a Plan B in case it rains. The weather may very well determine how much walking you can do (or want to do).

New York for History Buffs

The history of most cities is written in its neighborhoods. New York is no exception. Try out this itinerary and visit some of the city's historic neighborhoods to get a good feel for the character and growth of New York.

Start in Lower Manhattan, at the extreme southern tip of the island of Manhattan. At Battery Park, you can see **Castle Clinton,** completed in 1808. Just a short walk away is the gorgeous U.S. Customs House, built in 1907, which houses the **National Museum of the American Indian at the George Gustav Heye Center.**

 Though most of the lower Manhattan historic sights are within walking distance, the Alliance for New York offers free bus service on their **Downtown Connection** bus (see Chapter 8 for details).

Next on your walking/bus tour should be historic Wall Street and the **Federal Hall National Monument** (circa 1842), along with the famous statue of George Washington. Also on Wall Street is **Trinity Church,** built in 1846 and beautifully preserved.

For a taste of very modern and very tragic history, just a few blocks up from Trinity Church you can see the huge, soon-to-be-built upon open lot that, before September 11, 2001, was the site of the **World Trade Center.** Almost directly across the street and miraculously spared from the terrorist attacks is the **St. Paul's Chapel,** built in 1766 and part of the Trinity Church, where George Washington was a frequent worshiper.

From here, you want to get on one of those free buses and take it east to the **South Street Seaport and Museum** where the 18th- and 19th-century buildings lining the cobbled streets and alleyways have been impeccably restored. You can also hit the very modern mall-like shopping center and numerous restaurants here if you've had too much history or just want to take a lunch break.

After lunch, you can head to another historic downtown neighborhood, the Lower East Side, which is a tenement neighborhood where many immigrants — notably Eastern European Jews — settled back in the mid- to late-19th century. **Delancey Street** and historic **Orchard Street** are the main thoroughfares to explore. And to get the best taste of what life was like for the immigrants in the late 19th and early 20th centuries, visit the **Lower East Side Tenement Museum** (see Chapter 11). Then treat yourself to some great ice cream at **Il Laboratorio del Gelato** next door or head to Houston Street and **Katz's Delicatessen** for a genuine New York egg cream (see Chapter 10).

Take a break and rest a bit before heading out to your next neighborhood, **Greenwich Village.** The Village has always been the domain of the unconventional; the place for radical thinkers; the haunt of literary figures like Henry James, Eugene O'Neill, and Dylan Thomas. Artists like Edward Hopper and Jackson Pollack and the famous beatniks Allen Ginsberg, Jack Kerouac, and William Burroughs lived and hung out in Greenwich Village. Unlike other parts of the city, the Village is not laden with historical landmarks. Its landmarks are its streets, alleyways, and brownstone blocks.

The physical center of the Village is **Washington Square Park,** located in the heart of New York University, where along with some serious chess players, some entertaining street performers, and a few determined drug dealers, you can see the famous Washington Square Arch. The heart of beatnik society was centered on Bleecker and MacDougal Streets. Stop and have an espresso at one of the many cafes in the area; the people-watching doesn't get any better. The West Village around Christopher Street is the center of the pioneering gay community where you find some quaint boutiques and more cafes.

Dinnertime should be approaching, and maybe you've planned ahead and have reservations at **Babbo,** just a few blocks from Washington Square Park, or maybe you just want to try one of those **Corner Bistro** burgers. For more ideas on restaurants you may want to check out, see Chapter 10. No matter when you get out of dinner, the Village will still be buzzing with activity. You may want to hear some jazz at the venerable **Village Vanguard** club or catch a comedy show at the **Comedy Cellar** (see Chapter 16 for more on clubs and bars), or check out the Tower Records at 4th and Broadway (or its Bargain Annex right next to it).

Continue your historic neighborhood itinerary the next day on the Upper West Side. The Upper West Side has a history of liberalism and of being a home to musicians. It's only fitting that **Lincoln Center,** at 64th Street and Broadway, is the unofficial gateway to the Upper West Side.

From Lincoln Center cut over to Central Park West and you see the grandeur of that boulevard lined with beaux arts apartment houses, the oldest being the **Dakota,** built in 1884 on Central Park West and 72nd Street. The Dakota has the infamous distinction of being not only the location for the Roman Polanski film, *Rosemary's Baby*, but also where John Lennon, who lived there with Yoko Ono, was shot and killed. Other famous residents of the Dakota have included Leonard Bernstein, Lauren Bacall, and Judy Garland.

Walk west across 72nd Street to Broadway where you can see the area's other magnificent residence, the **Ansonia** at 73rd and Broadway. Musicians such as Caruso, Toscanini, and Igor Stravinsky, to name just a few, have called this building home.

If you're hungry, grab some lunch at **Zabar's** (see Chapter 10), the area's most famous restaurant, and take it either to Riverside Park for a picnic lunch overlooking the Hudson River or walk a few blocks east to Central Park. If you choose to go east, you may want to stop at the **New-York Historical Society** at Central Park West and 77th Street (see Chapter 11 for details). If you choose west, stroll up **Riverside Drive,** which, like Central Park West, features some of the city's most stately apartment houses.

After lunch head up to Harlem where the wealthiest New Yorkers lived in the late 19th and early 20th centuries. Many of the Harlem mansions still stand and are impeccably preserved. On 130th Street between Fifth and Lenox avenues, you can see a series of 28 redbrick townhouses, known as the **Astor Row Houses,** which date back to the early 1880s. On 139th

Street between Adam Clayton Powell Jr. and Frederick Douglass boulevards sits the impressive **Strivers' Row,** where hardly a brick has changed among the gorgeous neo-Italian Renaissance town houses that were built in 1890. After the original white owners moved out, these lovely houses attracted the cream of Harlem, "strivers" like Eubie Blake and W. C. Handy.

Handsome brownstones, limestone townhouses, and row houses are sprinkled atop **Sugar Hill,** 145th to 155th streets between St. Nicholas and Edgecombe avenues, named for the "sweet life" enjoyed by its residents. Finally, head up to 160th Street, east of St. Nicholas Avenue, to see Manhattan's oldest surviving house, the 1765-built **Morris-Jumel Mansion** (65 Jumel Terrace, ☎ 212-923-8008, www.morrisjumel.org; open Wed–Sun 10 a.m.–4 p.m. for tours).

All that history works up a major appetite, so stay in Harlem for dinner; you can't go wrong with the soul food buffet at **Charles' Southern Style Kitchen** (see Chapter 10 for a description).

Part V
Living It Up After Dark: New York City Nightlife

The 5th Wave   By Rich Tennant

"...and for our entree special, we're offering New York's famous foot-long Veal Oscar."

In this part . . .

Someone once sang that New York was the "city that never sleeps." And with such an embarrassment of nighttime riches to choose from, New York truly is an insomniac's dream. In the chapters that follow, I go over some of the venues for theater, dance, and music that you may want to visit. I also give you a roundup of clubs and bars where you can kick back and relax or dance the night away.

Chapter 14

Applauding the Cultural Scene

● ●

In This Chapter

▶ Finding out what's going on around the city
▶ Being theatrical (and where you can do it)
▶ Listening to all sorts of music
▶ Leaping from modern dance to ballet

● ●

*N*o other city rivals New York in the breadth and scope of the performing arts offered. From the incredible range of theater, opera,
dance, and symphony to live rock and jazz, the bounty is almost too
full. Your biggest problem is probably going to be choosing among the
many temptations.

Getting the Inside Scoop

For the latest, most comprehensive nightlife listings, from theater and
performing arts to live rock, jazz, and dance club coverage, *Time Out
New York* (www.timeoutny.com) is my favorite weekly source; a new
issue hits newsstands every Thursday. The free weekly *Village Voice*
(www.villagevoice.com), the city's legendary alterna-paper, is available late Tuesday downtown and early Wednesday throughout the
rest of the city. The arts and entertainment coverage couldn't be more
extensive, and just about every live music venue advertises its shows
here. Its competitor, the free weekly *New York Press* (www.nypress.
com) also offers extensive listings. The *New York Times* (www.ny
today.com) features terrific entertainment coverage, particularly in
the two-part Friday "Weekend" section. The cabaret, classical music,
and theater guides are particularly useful. Other great weekly sources
are *The New Yorker* (www.newyorker.com), in its "Goings on About
Town" section; and *New York* magazine (www.nymetro.com), whose
"Cue" features the latest happenings.

NYC/Onstage (☎ 212-768-1818; www.tdf.org) is a recorded service
providing complete schedules, descriptions, and other details on

theater and the performing arts. The focus is more toward theater, but NYC/Onstage is also a good source for chamber and orchestral music (including all Lincoln Center events), dance, opera, cabaret, and family entertainment.

A little research can get you an array of information and reviews of current shows. The *New York Times* is a good source for the scoop on big theater shows; the *Village Voice* and *New York Press* are strong on alternative culture. The listings in *New York* magazine, the *New Yorker,* and *Time Out New York* regularly offer information about both mainstream shows and those off the beaten path. The following Web sites also offer valuable theater information:

- ✔ **Applause:** www.applause-tickets.com

- ✔ **CitySearch New York:** www.newyork.citysearch.com

- ✔ **NYC & Company:** www.nycvisit.com

- ✔ **Ticketmaster:** www.ticketmaster.com

- ✔ **Theatermania:** www.theatermania.com

To get information by phone, call **Broadway Line** (☎ **888-BROADWAY** or 212-302-4111) or the **Off-Broadway Theater Information Center** (☎ **212-575-1423**), the two official theater resources in New York. You also can call **NYC/On Stage** (☎ **212-768-1818**) or **NYC & Company** (☎ **800-NYC-VISIT** or 800-692-8474).

Taking in New York Theater

New York's theater scene is second to none. With so much breadth and depth, and so many wide-open alternatives, just keeping up with it is exhausting as well as exhilarating, especially for theater buffs. Broadway, of course, gets the most ink and the most airplay, and deservedly so. Broadway is where you find the big stage productions, from crowd-pleasing warhorses like *The Lion King* to the phenomenally successful shows like *The Producers.* But smaller "alternative" theater has become popular both commercially and critically, too. With bankable stars on stage, crowds lining up for hot tickets, and hits popular enough to generate major-label cast albums, Off-Broadway isn't just for culture vultures.

Helping to assure the recent success of the New York theater scene is the presence of Hollywood stars like Hugh Jackman, Kevin Spacey, Glenn Close, Patrick Stewart, Liam Neeson, and Dame Judi Dench. But keep in mind that stars' runs on stage are often limited, and tickets for their shows tend to sell out fast.

If you hear that an actor you'd like to see is coming to the New York stage, don't put off your travel and ticket-buying plans. (The box office can tell you how long a star is contracted for a role.)

Theater District Theaters

Al Hirschfeld **19**	Ford Center for the Performing Arts **44**	New Victory **41**
Ambassador **11**		Palace **32**
American Airlines **45**	Gershwin **7**	Playwright's Horizons **48**
American Place **34**	Helen Hayes **40**	Plymouth **29**
Barrymore **26**	Imperial **18**	Richard Rogers **17**
Belasco **36**	John Golden **20**	Royale **24**
Booth **30**	Longacre **15**	Samuel Beckett **47**
Broadhurst **23**	Lunt-Fontanne **28**	St. James **22**
Broadway **4**	Lyceum **35**	Shubert **39**
Brooks Atkinson **16**	Majestic **21**	Stardust **8**
Circle in the Square **10**	Marquis **31**	Studio 54 **3**
City Center Stage **2**	Minskoff **38**	Town Hall **37**
Cort **33**	Mitzi E. Newhouse **1**	Virginia **5**
Douglas Fairbanks **49**	Music Box **25**	Vivian Beaumont **1**
Duffy **27**	Nederlander **43**	Walter Kerr **13**
Ethel Barrymore **14**	Neil Simon **6**	WestSide **46**
Eugene O'Neill **12**	New Amsterdam **42**	Winter Garden **9**

Culture for free: Shakespeare in Central Park

A New York institution since 1957, Shakespeare in the Park is as much a part of a New York summer as fireworks on the 4th of July. Shakespeare in the Park is the brainchild of the late Joseph Papp, former director of the Public Theater, who came up with the idea of staging two Shakespeare plays each summer at the open-air Delacorte Theater in Central Park. Best of all, and the reason Shakespeare in the Park has become an institution, is that the performances are free.

Budget cuts in the last few years have reduced the number of shows offered from two to one, usually a revival of a Shakespeare play featuring a large company, including at least one or more "names" from film and television. The production runs from the end of June to early August. Depending on the star power of the cast, tickets can be quite scarce. The production of *Much Ado About Nothing* in 2004 featured Jimmy Smits, Sam Waterston, and Kristen Johnson, among others. In years past, Morgan Freeman and Tracey Ullman have starred in *Taming of the Shrew,* Raul Julia in *Othello,* and Patrick Stewart in *The Tempest,* which later graduated to a successful Broadway run.

Summer 2004 featured a new program at the Delacorte: two weeks of musical performances called "Joe's Pub in the Park," an outdoor version of the artists featured at Joe's Pub, the intimate music venue at the Public Theater.

Roughly 1,800 tickets are distributed at the Delacorte on a first-come, first-served basis (only two per person) for the plays, starting at 1 p.m. on the day of each performance. But keep in mind that people start lining up at least two or three hours in advance, so bring a book or some refreshments and be prepared to wait. Tickets are also available between 1 and 3 p.m. on the day of the performance at the Public Theater, 425 Lafayette St., between Astor Place and East 4th Street in the East Village (the lines get long there, too).

For more information about Shakespeare in the Park, contact the Public Theater (☎ 212-539-8750; www.publictheater.org), or call the Delacorte at ☎ 212-861-7277.

Figuring out the Broadway basics

The terms **Broadway, Off-Broadway,** and **Off-Off-Broadway** refer to theater size, pay scales, and other details, not location — or, these days, even star wattage. Most of the Broadway theaters are in Times Square, around the thoroughfare the scene is named for, but not directly on it. Instead, you can find theaters dotting the side streets that intersect Broadway, mostly in the mid-40s between Sixth and Eighth avenues (44th and 45th streets in particular), but also running north as far as 53rd Street.

Off-Broadway, on the other hand, could be anything and anywhere. Off-Off-Broadway shows tend to be more avant-garde, experimental, and/or nomadic (and also have the cheapest ticket prices). Off- and Off-Off-Broadway productions tend to be based downtown, but pockets of performance spaces exist in Midtown and on the Upper West Side as well. Broadway shows tend to keep pretty regular **schedules.** Eight performances a week is the norm, with evening shows on Tuesday through Saturday, plus matinees on Wednesday, Saturday, and Sunday. Evening shows usually start at 8 p.m., while matinees are usually at 2 p.m. on Wednesday and Saturday, and 3 p.m. on Sunday, but schedules can vary, especially Off-Broadway. Shows usually start on the dot, or within a few minutes of starting time; if you arrive late, you may have to wait until after the first act to take your seat — so be on time and you won't miss any of the show.

Kids like theater, too!

And they have lots of venues and shows to choose from in New York City.

✔ The **New Victory Theater,** 229 W. 42nd St., between Seventh and Eighth avenues (☎ 646-223-3020; www.newvictory.org), is the city's first full-time, family-oriented performing arts center and has hosted companies ranging from the Trinity Irish Dance Company to the astounding Flaming Idiots, who juggle everything from fire and swords to bean-bag chairs.

✔ Called "the best children's theater in the country" by *Newsweek* magazine, The **Paper Bag Players** (☎ 212-663-0390; www.paperbagplayers.org), perform funny tales for children ages 4 to 9 in a set made from bags and boxes at Hunter College's Sylvia and Danny Kaye Playhouse, 68th Street between Park and Lexington avenues (☎ 212-772-4448). Shows are performed in the winter only, and if you can't make it to the Kaye, call the players to inquire whether they're staging other performances around town.

✔ **TADA! Youth Theater,** 15 W. 28th St., between Fifth Avenue and Broadway (☎ 212-252-1619; www.tadatheater.com), is a fun youth ensemble that performs musicals and plays with a multiethnic perspective for kids, teens, and their families.

✔ The **Swedish Cottage Marionette Theatre** (☎ 212-988-9093; www.centralpark.org) puts on marionette shows for kids at its 19th-century Central Park theater throughout the year. Reservations are a must.

✔ The "World Voices Club" of the **New Perspectives Theatre,** 750 Eighth Ave., between 46th and 47th streets (☎ 212-730-2030; www.newperspectivestheatre.org), has a different puppet show based on fables from different world cultures each month.

✔ Yes it's the same David Mamet who writes those hardboiled movies and plays, but he shows his softer side with acclaimed youth productions as part of his **Atlantic Theater Company,** 453 16th St., between Ninth and Tenth avenues (☎ 212-645-8015; www.atlantictheater.org), which Mamet co-founded with Academy Award–nominated actor William H. Macy.

Getting theater tickets

Ticket prices for Broadway shows vary dramatically. Expect to pay a lot for good seats; the high end for any given show is likely to be between $60 and $100 or more. The cheapest end of the price range can be as low as $20 or as high as $50, depending on the theater configuration. If you're buying tickets at the very low end of the available range, be aware that you may be buying obstructed-view seats. If all tickets are the same price or the range is small, you can pretty much count on all the seats being pretty good.

One of my many pet peeves is that despite having to pay so much for a show, the theaters haven't installed more comfortable seating (especially in the older theaters, which can date from the early 20th century, when people were *smaller*). I often feel like my knees are up to my chest at most of these theaters — and those are orchestra seats. Consider yourself forewarned.

Off-Broadway and Off-Off-Broadway shows tend to be cheaper than Broadway shows, with tickets often as low as $10 or $15. However, seats for the most established shows and those with star power can command prices as high as $50.

If you've already decided on a show to see before you leave for your trip, just have your credit card in hand and contact any of the following ticket agencies by phone or on the Web (you usually encounter a service fee in addition to the cost of the tickets).

Some of these theater and ticket organizations have lists of discounted shows, the latest theater news and reviews, and member bulletin boards where you can ask for recommendations. If you're planning to get to as many shows as you can, it's worth it to register with a service like Theatermania.com, Playbill.com, or Broadway.com to access discounts and subscribe their e-mail newsletters.

- **Applause:** www.applause-tickets.com; Also offers discounts

- **Broadway.com:** www.broadway.com; Also offers dinner packages and gift certificates

- **Manhattan Concierge:** ☎ 800-NY-SHOWS or 212-239-2591; www.manhattanconcierge.com; A ticket broker that can sell you good tickets to almost anything (including concerts and sporting events); expect to pay a service charge

- **Playbill.com:** www.playbill.com; The online presence of the company that distributes the familiar programs with the yellow logo in theaters; also offers packages, industry news, and photos and videos of shows

- **Tele-charge:** ☎ 800-432-7250 or 212-239-6200; www.telecharge.com

✔ **Theatermania:** ☎ **212-352-0255**; www.theatermania.com; An excellent source for Off- and Off-Off Broadway, as well as full-price and discounted Broadway tickets

✔ **Ticketmaster:** ☎ **212-307-4100**; www.ticketmaster.com

If you didn't buy your tickets in advance, you can buy same-day tickets at the following outlets:

✔ **TKTS** sells discounted (up to 50 percent) tickets as they become available from theaters. It has a booth in the Theater District (Broadway at 47th Street, open daily from 3–8 p.m., 10 a.m.–2 p.m. on Wed and Sat for matinees, and Sun from 11 a.m.–6:30 p.m.). A booth is also open downtown at Pier 17 at South Street Seaport (open Mon–Sat 11 a.m.–6 p.m. and Sat 11 a.m.–3:30 p.m.; at this location only, matinee tickets must be purchased the day before the show).

For the most up-to-date ticket information, consult www.tkts.com. Before you visit a physical ticket booth, keep in mind that long lines are the norm, and you're not guaranteed to get tickets for a specific show. Also note that tickets for a popular show may be available because the cast for that day changed, which is not the best scenario if you have your heart set on seeing a particular production or actor.

✔ For same-day advance tickets at regular prices for most shows, visit the two official booths run by the League of American Theaters and Producers: the **Broadway Ticket Center** inside the Times Square Visitors Center (Broadway at 46th Street; ☎ **888-BROADWAY** or 212-302-4111; open daily 8 a.m.–8 p.m.) and the **Off-Broadway Theater Information Center** (251 W. 45th St., between Broadway and Eighth Avenue; ☎ **212-575-1423**; open Tues–Thurs 12 –8 p.m., Fri–Sat 12 p.m.–10 p.m., Sun–Mon 12 –6 p.m.).

You also can get tickets after you arrive in the city by calling one of the telephone services listed earlier in this chapter, by asking the concierge at your hotel, or by using one of the numerous ticket brokers, whose listings you can find in newspapers and in the phone book. According to New York City law, these brokers are only supposed to charge a $5 fee or a 10 percent commission, whichever is less. However, New Jersey has no such law, and a lot of the brokers are based there. Ask about the fee up front, because tickets to a very hot show can go for as much as double or more the face value.

Another option is to call the box office of the theater where the show is playing to ask whether they have any tickets available, because they often do. Some long-running shows run special promotions, so it pays to inquire when you call. As a last resort, remember that a cheap way to get a seat is not to have one: Standing room is available at some theaters for about $20.

Catching a little pre-theater dinner

You want to eat before you go to the theater for a number of reasons. If you try to hold out until after the show ends, your hunger may distract you from the drama in front of you. You may end up thinking more about whether you want a steak or a taco during the performance. Also, you don't want to disturb other theatergoers with the rumblings emitting from your empty stomach. So plan to eat something before you go. Many restaurants in the Theater District have pre-theater prix-fixe specials, and all of them are expert at serving you quickly. Consider these suggestions.

- ✔ The Scandinavian restaurant, **Aquavit,** 13 W. 54th St., between Fifth and Sixth avenues (☎ **212-307-7311**), offers a three-course pre-theater prix-fixe dinner for $55. If you want a lighter meal, grab some herring and some Swedish meatballs at Aquavit's Cafe.

- ✔ Daniel Boulud's casual cafe, **db Bistro Moderne,** 55 W. 44th St., between Fifth and Sixth avenues (☎ **212-391-2400**), is the home of the famous $29 hamburger. If you don't want a hamburger made with ground short ribs and shaved black truffles, the restaurant also offers a three-course pre-theater dinner for $45.

- ✔ My favorite Greek restaurant, **Molyvos,** 871 Seventh Ave., between 55th and 56th streets (☎ **212-582-7500**), is the perfect place for a meal before a concert at nearby Carnegie Hall. The three-course pre-theater prix fixe at Molyvos is $34.50.

- ✔ My favorite Times Square restaurant, **Virgil's Real BBQ,** 152 W. 44th St., between 6th and 7th avenues (☎ **212-921-9494**), is just a short stroll from most Broadway theaters. Because of the pre-theater dining rush, reservations are an absolute must.

If you just want a quick, inexpensive, and good meal before your show, you may want to consider several options. You can't beat the Ramen noodles at **Sapporo,** 152 W. 49th St., just east of Seventh Avenue, where a meal won't cost you much more than $10. At the cozy, very good **Siam Inn,** 854 Eighth Ave., between 51st and 52nd streets, the Thai food is the best in the neighborhood.

Always inform the staff at sit-down restaurants that you have theater tickets, and they make sure you're out the door in time to make the opening curtain.

For more information on all the above restaurants, see Chapter 10.

Make the rounds of Broadway theaters at about 6 p.m., when unclaimed house seats are made available to the public. These tickets — reserved for VIPs, friends of the cast, the press, or industry professionals — offer great seats and are sold at face value. (If you're with someone, tell the salesperson that you don't have to sit together. Single seats are usually easier to come by than pairs at the last minute).

Also, note that **Monday** is often a good day to score big-name show tickets. Although most theaters are dark on that day, some of the most sought-after choices aren't. Locals are likely to stay at home on the first night of the workweek, so the odds of getting tickets are in your favor. Your chances of getting tickets are always better on weeknights or for Wednesday matinees, rather than on weekends (but do check and see if the Big Star is on, rather than the understudy).

Venues That Break the Mold

New York is blessed with a number of amazing venues to hear and see the performing arts. Some, like Lincoln Center and Carnegie Hall, are so famous that they're household names around the globe, while the Brooklyn Academy of Music, though not as famous worldwide, certainly should be.

The Lincoln Center for the Performing Arts

This celebrated complex, shown in the "Lincoln Center" map, extends over four blocks on the Upper West Side. It hosts an extraordinary range of productions, from opera to film to dance to classical music, in the following performance spaces:

- **Metropolitan Opera House** (☎ 212-362-6000; www.metopera.org) is home to the Metropolitan Opera Company (see the "Opera" section later in this chapter) and the American Ballet Theater (see "Dance" later in this chapter). It also showcases visiting ballet performers from around the world.

- **Avery Fisher Hall** (☎ 212-721-6500) is the seat of the New York Philharmonic (see "Classical Music" later in this chapter), but it also hosts many important seasonal musical events organized by Lincoln Center, such as Mostly Mozart, and concerts performed by students of the famed Juilliard School.

- **New York State Theater** is home to the New York City Opera (see "Opera") and the New York City Ballet (see "Dance").

- **Alice Tully Hall** (☎ 212-875-5000) hosts the Chamber Music Society of Lincoln Center (☎ 212-875-5788; www.chamberlinc.org). Jazz at Lincoln Center also holds events here, and other groups perform concerts here as well.

- **Walter Reade Theater** (☎ 212-875-5600) is home to the Film Society of Lincoln Center (www.filmlinc.com), which sponsors the New York Film Festival and other events.

- The **Juilliard School** (☎ 212-769-7406; www.juilliard.org) hosts many concerts — mostly classical but not only — as well as other performances. The quality is excellent and the prices are very attractive — many concerts are free. The maximum charge for a ticket is about $15. Check the bulletin board in the hall, or call for current productions. The school also sponsors many free outdoor concerts in the summer.

Lincoln Center

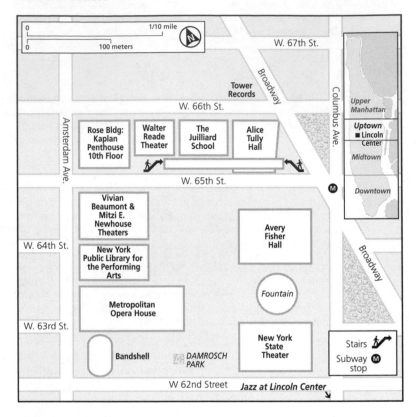

<ul>
<li>✔ Vivian Beaumont Theater (☎ 212-362-7600) is the city's northern-most Broadway theater and shares a building with Mitzi E. Newhouse Theater, an important off-Broadway establishment. They host a variety of shows. Together, they form the Lincoln Center Theater (www.lct.org).</li>
<li>✔ Frederick P. Rose Hall (☎ 212-258-9800; www.jazzatlincoln center.org) is the newest venue at Lincoln Center, giving a perma-nent home to Jazz at Lincoln Center, and celebrating its grand opening in the fall of 2004. Located at Broadway and 60th Street.</li>
</ul>

The Center also has two outdoor spaces: a central plaza with a huge fountain and Damrosch Park toward the back. In summer, the outdoor spaces host some great series, such as Midsummer Night's Swing in July and Lincoln Center Out-of-Doors in August, as well as many free concerts. Summer is the season of special series indoors, too — such as the JVC Jazz Festival, Mostly Mozart, and the Lincoln Center Festival — because it is the resident companies' time off.

To get the Center's calendar, check its Web site at www.lincolncenter. org, which also has links to each of the companies and organizations that belong to the Center. You also can send a self-addressed stamped envelope (or a label and a stamp) to **Lincoln Center Calendar,** 70 Lincoln Center Plaza, New York, NY 10023-6583, or call ☎ **212-546-2656** for information about the current shows.

If you want to use public transportation to get to the Center, take the 1/9 train to the 66th Street/Lincoln Center stop, or take one of the following buses: M104 (running east/west on 42nd Street, north on Sixth Avenue, and south on Broadway), M5 and M7 (running up Sixth Avenue and Broadway), or M66 (across town running west on 67th Street).

Carnegie Hall

Perhaps the world's most famous performance space, **Carnegie Hall** offers everything from grand classics to the music of Ravi Shankar. The **Isaac Stern Auditorium,** the 2,804-seat main hall, welcomes visiting orchestras from across the country and around the world. Many of the world's premier soloists and ensembles give recitals here. The legendary hall is both visually and acoustically brilliant; don't miss an opportunity to experience it if there's something on the schedule that interests you.

Also part of Carnegie Hall is the intimate 268-seat **Weill Recital Hall,** usually used to showcase chamber music and vocal and instrumental recitals. Carnegie Hall has also reclaimed the ornate underground 650-seat **Zankel Concert Hall,** which was occupied by a movie theater for 38 years.

Carnegie Hall is located at 881 Seventh Ave. at 57th Street. For schedule and ticket information, check the Web site at www.carnegiehall.org or call ☎ **212-247-7800.** Besides practice, practice, practice, another way to get to Carnegie Hall is by taking the N, Q, R, and W trains to 57th Street.

Brooklyn Academy of Music

The city's most renowned contemporary arts institution, **Brooklyn Academy of Music** is often at the forefront of cutting-edge theater, opera, dance, and music.

Like Lincoln Center, BAM sponsors many special series, including the prestigious Next Wave Festival in the fall, a showcase for experimental American and international artists; and DanceAfrica in spring, a choice of productions with an African heritage, ranging from traditional to modern. BAM also sponsors three youth series during the year and free outdoor concerts throughout the city in the summer.

BAM (☎ **718-636-4100;** www.bam.org) is at 30 Lafayette Ave. between Ashland Place and Felix Street; the BAM Majestic Theater is nearby at 651 Fulton St. between Ashland and Rockwell places. If you want to take public transportation, take the 2/4/5/Q train to the Atlantic Avenue stop or the M/N/R/W train to the Pacific Street stop. If you reserve tickets 24 hours in advance and pay $5, you can take the BAM bus from the Whitney Museum at Philip Morris, 120 Park Ave. at 42nd Street, which leaves one hour before scheduled performance time. The return bus makes several stops in Manhattan.

Other major concert spaces

Live music is always in the air in New York City; you just have to listen for it. Here are some other exceptional venues where you can hear and see a wide variety of the performing arts.

- ✔ **Radio City Music Hall,** 1260 Sixth Ave. at 50th Street (☎ 212-247-4777, www.radiocity.com), is a gorgeous venue to see a roster of renowned artists from crooner Tony Bennett to crossover salsa star Marc Anthony to retro '80s act Culture Club. (See the "Midtown Attractions" map on p. 180.)

- ✔ **Madison Square Garden,** Seventh Avenue at 32nd Street (☎ 212-465-6741; www.thegarden.com), proves that only the biggest stage is appropriate for the biggest names — The Who, Madonna, and Bruuuuuuuce (Springsteen, that is). Bring your binoculars — that speck on the stage really is a grizzled Keith Richard. Adjacent to the Garden is **The Theater at Madison Square Garden,** a smaller space that usually features popular but not cover-of-*People*-magazine famous musical acts. (See the "Midtown Attractions" map on p. 180.)

- ✔ **Town Hall,** 123 W. 43rd St. between Sixth and Seventh avenues (☎ 212-840-2824; www.the-townhall-nyc.org), is a lovely, medium-sized theater that hosts a wide range of events — everything from world music to modern dance to one-man shows to live ensemble performances of Garrison Keillor's *Prairie Home Companion* radio program.

- ✔ Harlem's legendary **Apollo Theater,** 253 W. 125th St. between Adam Clayton Powell and Frederick Douglass boulevards (☎ 212-531-5300; www.apolloshowtime.com), was the ultimate stage for musical legends like Smokey Robinson and The Miracles, the Temptations, and James Brown. These days, a steady stream of hip-hop and R&B acts perform at this beautifully restored theater; Wednesday night is the famous (and infamously unforgiving) Amateur Night. (See the "Harlem & Upper Manhattan" map on p. 189.)

- ✔ An Upper West Side institution, **Symphony Space,** 2537 Broadway at 95th Street (☎ 212-864-1414; www.symphonyspace.org), offers an eclectic mix of performing arts. The variety of shows at the **Peter Jay Sharp Theater** includes series by the World Music Institute as well as classical, rock, and blues and dance. Adjacent to the Peter Jay Sharp Theater is the **Leonard Nimoy Thalia Theater;** the film revival house that was known for its quirky sightlines was rescued by none other than Mr. Spock and has now been totally renovated.

Classical Music

The **New York Philharmonic** at Avery Fisher Hall in Lincoln Center, at Broadway and 64th Street (☎ 212-875-5656; www.nyphilharmonic.org), offers what many consider to be the city's best concerts. Ticket prices range from less than $35 to $70.

Carnegie Hall, at 57th Street and Seventh Avenue (☎ 212-247-7800; www.carnegiehall.org), is a gem in the crown of New York's music community. The price of a ticket depends on the performance; call or check the Web site for information. (See the "Midtown Attractions" map on p. 180.)

The **Brooklyn Academy of Music** hosts performances of outstanding quality, some of them experimental or cutting edge. Don't let the location of this famed venue dissuade you from going to one of its shows — it's quite easy to reach. See the section "Brooklyn Academy of Music" earlier in this chapter for specifics.

 Bargemusic, in Brooklyn at Fulton Ferry Landing just south of the Brooklyn Bridge, (☎ 718-624-2083 or 718-624-4061; www.bargemusic.org) is an internationally renowned recital room located, yes, on an actual

---

Dining after the show

It's a well-known fact that classical music and opera can make you quite hungry. The good news is that you are in New York and many restaurants are still open and serving full dinners past 10 or 11 p.m.

If you're in the Theater District and you don't mind being weighted down before bedtime, finish off an enormous (and exceptional) pastrami sandwich and a slice of cheesecake at the **Carnegie Deli,** 854 Seventh Ave., at 55th Street, (☎ 800-334-5606).

For most after-hours dining, you may want to head downtown. Two of the most popular spots are in the Meatpacking District in the West Village, and they're open into the wee hours. The funky Francophile diner **Florent,** 69 Gansevoort St., between Greenwich and Washington streets (☎ 212-989-5779), and the authentic bistro **Pastis,** 9 Ninth Ave., at Little W. 12th Street (☎ 212-929-4844) are excellent choices. Then there's the sexy, rollicking bistro **Balthazar,** 80 Spring St., at Crosby Street in SoHo (☎ 212-965-1785).

In the East Village, head to **Veselka,** 144 Second Ave., at 9th Street (☎ 212-228-9862), a comfortable and appealing diner offering Eastern European fare at rock-bottom prices, and **Katz's Delicatessen,** 205 E. Houston St., at Ludlow Street, (☎ 212-254-2246) for first-class Jewish deli eats served Friday and Saturday until 2:30 a.m. In Chinatown, many restaurants are open late or even all night. Of note is the great **New York Noodletown,** 28½ Bowery, at Bayard Street (☎ 212-258-9800), which is open until 3:30 a.m. nightly.

barge. This unusual venue boasts more than 100 first-rate chamber music performances a year. Three shows take place per week, on Thursday and Friday evenings at 7:30 p.m. and Sunday afternoon at 4 p.m. The musicians perform on a small stage in a cherry-paneled, fireplace-lit room accommo-dating 130 people. The music rivals what you can find in almost any other New York concert hall — and the panoramic view of Manhattan through the glass wall behind the stage can't be beat. Tickets are just $35 ($25 for students), or $40 for performances by larger ensembles. But reserve your tickets well in advance. To get to Bargemusic, take the 2/3 train to Clark Street or the A/C to High Street.

Opera

The **Metropolitan Opera Company,** housed at the Metropolitan Opera House at Lincoln Center, Broadway and 64th Street (☎ 212-362-6000; www.metopera.org), stages classic operas and is the world's premier opera company today. The sets are works of art, and the performers among the most famous in the world. Ticket prices range from $25 to $295.

The **New York City Opera,** in the New York State Theater at Lincoln Center, Broadway and 64th Street (☎ 212-870-5570; www.nycopera.com), stages less elaborate shows (but from the same classic repertoire) than the Metropolitan Opera Company, with lower ticket prices — seats range in price from $25 to $100.

Performances of the **Amato Opera Company,** 319 Bowery at 2nd Street (☎ 212-228-8200; www.amato.org), are likely to sell out quickly; the theater has only 100 seats, with an average ticket price of $20. Buy your tickets at least three weeks in advance to catch one of its performances of classic Italian and other opera.

Music Alfresco

With summer also comes the sound of music to Central Park, where the **New York Philharmonic** and the **Metropolitan Opera** regularly enter-tain beneath the stars; for the current schedule, call ☎ 212-360-3444, 212-875-5709, or 212-362-6000, or visit www.lincolncenter.org.

The most active music spot in the park is **SummerStage** (at Rumsey Playfield, mid-park around 72nd Street), which has featured everyone from the Godfather of Soul, James Brown, to cerebral hip hoppers DeLaSoul. Recent offerings have included concerts by Orchestra Baobab, Sugarhill Gang, Johnny Winter, and Jimmy Cliff; "Viva, Verdi!" festival performances by the New York Grand Opera; cabaret nights; and more. The season usually lasts from mid-June to early August. While some big-name shows charge admission, tickets aren't usually required; donations are warmly accepted, however. For the latest performance info, call the SummerStage hotline at ☎ 212-360-2777 or visit www.summerstage.org.

Additionally, most of the city's top museums offer free music and other programs after regular hours on select nights. The **Metropolitan Museum of Art** has an extensive slate of offerings each week, including live classical music and cocktails on Friday and Saturday evenings. You can have lots of fun at other museums as well, including the **Guggenheim,** whose weekend Worldbeat Jazz series is a big hit; the **American Museum of Natural History,** which features live jazz in the Hall of the Universe in the new Rose Center for Earth and Space; and the **Brooklyn Museum of Art,** which hosts the remarkably eclectic **First Saturday** program monthly.

Dance

The **New York City Ballet** (☎ 212-870-5570; www.nycballet.com) performs at the New York State Theater, sharing this space with the New York City Opera. The leading dance company in the world, it presents wonderfully staged productions featuring world-class dancers. New works of choreography use both classical and modern music. Their performance of *The Nutcracker* is a highlight of the Christmas season.

The **American Ballet Theater** (☎ 212-477-3030; www.abt.org) performs at the Metropolitan Opera House and shares its space with the Metropolitan Opera. The guest companies and dancers are of international renown in the world of dance.

City Center, 131 W. 55th St. between Sixth and Seventh avenues (☎ 877-247-0430; www.citycenter.org), hosts premier companies, such as the Alvin Ailey American Dance Theater, Twyla Tharp Company, and Martha Graham Company. Some of the world's leading choreographers have performed there. To get there, take the B, D, or E trains to Seventh Avenue.

The **Joyce Theater,** 175 Eighth Ave. at 19th Street (☎ 212-242-0800; www.joyce.org), boasts performances by the likes of the Erick Hawkins Dance Company and Meredith Monk. To get there, take the C or E train to 23rd Street or the 1 or 9 to 18th Street.

 Radio City Music Hall (see "Other major concert spaces" earlier in this chapter for contact details) is home to a longstanding tradition in New York that's popular with children of all ages and needs no introduction: the Rockettes. You can even take a Stage Door Tour guided by one of the famed leggy beauties!

Chapter 15

Hitting the Clubs and Bars

In This Chapter

▶ Listening to the music

▶ Laughing it up at the comedy clubs

▶ Quenching your thirst at the hottest bars

▶ Tripping the light fantastic at dance clubs

*T*he so-called serious cultural entertainment is covered in Chapter 14, so in this chapter, I dig into the less serious, but just as entertaining, entertainment options in New York City. Whether it's live jazz, rock, comedy, or cabaret; or if it's sweating on a dance floor, sipping a martini while lounging on a plush lounge couch, or just people-watching in a neighborhood pub, New York has plenty of choices for your evening's entertainment.

To find out what's happening and where, check out these print and online sources. The *Village Voice*, www.villagevoice.com, is a weekly free newspaper that has a very good calendar with listings of weekly entertainment. Rivaling the *Voice* in its listings is the weekly magazine, *Time Out New York,* www.timeoutny.com. A good source for information about bars and clubs is the annual book, *Shecky's New York Bar, Club, & Lounge Guide.* The Web site at www.sheckys.com is more current than the book, as is **Shecky's Bar Phone** at ☎ **212-777-BARS** or 212-777-2277, which offers up-to-the minute nightlife news.

It's About the Music

From punky bands at holes-in-the-wall with no cover charge to the world's greatest musicians in the new venue Jazz at Lincoln Center, you can find something for every taste every night of the week in New York.

All that jazz

People come from all over the world to experience jazz in New York at any of the city's many celebrated clubs. No matter when you come, you're guaranteed to find top talent playing at a city venue. The best of New York's jazz clubs include:

✔ **Birdland,** 315 West 44th St., between Eighth and Ninth avenues (☎ 212-581-3080; www.birdlandjazz.com).This legendary club is one of the city's premier jazz spots. The big room is spacious, comfy, and classy, with an excellent sound system and top-notch talent roster any night of the week. Expect lots of accomplished big bands and jazz trios, but you can't go wrong with the regular Sunday night show, starring Chico O'Farrell's smokin' Afro-Cuban Jazz Big Band. (See the "Midtown Arts & Nightlife" map.)

✔ **Blue Note,** 131 W. 3rd St., at Sixth Avenue (☎ 212-475-8592; www.bluenote.net). This Greenwich Village institution attracts some of jazz's biggest names. Lately the club has veered away from the harder edge in favor of the popular smooth jazz. Prices can be astronomical here. (See the "Downtown Arts & Nightlife" map.)

✔ **Jazz Standard,** 116 E. 27th St., between Park Avenue South and Lexington Avenue (☎ 212-576-2232; www.jazzstandard.net). With 150 tables, the Standard is one of New York's largest jazz clubs. But its size does not detract from the quality of the sound. Here you can hear straightforward, mainstream jazz by new and established musicians. (See the "Midtown Arts & Nightlife" map.)

✔ **Lenox Lounge,** 288 Malcolm X Blvd., Lenox Avenue between 124th and 125th streets (☎ 212-427-0253). The club's history includes past performances by such artists as Billie Holliday and Dinah Washington. Now, at this beautifully restored club, you just may hear the next Billie or Dinah. (See the "Harlem & Upper Manhattan" map on p. 189.)

✔ **Smoke,** 2751 Broadway, between 105th and 106th streets (☎ 212-864-6662; www.smokejazz.com). This intimate Upper West Side club is a welcome throwback to the informal clubs of the past. On weekends, covers never exceed $20, and the music is free Sunday through Thursday. (See the "Uptown Arts & Nightlife" map.)

✔ **The Village Vanguard,** 178 Seventh Ave. South (☎ 212-255-4037; www.villagevanguard.net). The Vanguard, established in 1935, is a New York legend. All the greats, from Miles to Monk, have played here, and their spirits live on in the new, high-quality talent of frequent performers like Roy Hargrove and Bill Charlap. (See the "Downtown Arts & Nightlife" map.)

It's only rock and roll

In New York, you truly can rock and roll all night (KISS is from Queens, after all).

✔ **Arlene Grocery,** 95 Stanton St., between Ludlow and Orchard streets (☎ 212-358-1633; www.arlene-grocery.com). This funky little Lower East Side club has become a big name in the intimate rock club scene. With covers that rarely peak beyond $7, it's a bargain as well. (See the "Downtown Arts & Nightlife" map.)

✔ **Bowery Ballroom,** 6 Delancey St., at Bowery (☎ 212-533-2111; www.boweryballroom.com). There's plenty of room in this club, but it still has the feel of a more intimate venue. With great sight-lines and sound quality, the Bowery Ballroom attracts excellent alt-rock talent. (See the "Downtown Arts & Nightlife" map.)

✔ **CBGB,** 315 Bowery, at Bleeker Street (☎ 212-982-4052; www.cbgb.com). The launching pad for New York punk and New Wave, this gritty, grungy club is now a living shrine to the Ramones, who made their name here. (The corner of 2nd Street and the Bowery was officially renamed "Joey Ramone Place" in 2003.) It's still a big draw, so come early if you actually want to soak up any of the per-formers' sweat. Two more laid-back performance spaces — CB's Lounge and 313 Gallery — sit next door, where the music offered ranges from acoustic to freeform jazz. (See the "Downtown Arts & Nightlife" map.)

✔ **Irving Plaza,** 17 Irving Place, at 15th Street (☎ 212-777-1224; www.irvingplaza.com). Perhaps the biggest name in New York's rock club scene, this mid-sized music hall is a prime stop for national-name rock bands. The best seats can be found in the upstairs balcony but come early for a spot. (See the "Midtown Arts & Nightlife" map.)

✔ **Mercury Lounge,** 217 E. Houston St., at Essex Street and Avenue A (☎ 212-260-4700; www.mercuryloungenyc.com). Another excel-lent intimate spot for good quality, hard-edged rock and roll, and it doesn't cost a fortune. As a result, the Merc is always packed. (See the "Downtown Arts & Nightlife" map.)

The best of the rest

What follows are clubs that are tough to classify; on one night they may feature jazz or blues, and on another night you could hear cutting-edge rock or world music.

✔ **B.B King Blues Club & Grill,** 237 W. 42nd St., between Seventh and Eighth avenues (☎ 212-997-4144; www.bbkingblues.com). Despite its name, B.B. King's rarely sticks to the blues. Here you can find big-name talent from pop, funk, soul, and rock more from the past than from the present. On Sunday, a gospel lunch is served. (See the "Midtown Arts & Nightlife" map.)

✔ **Fez Under Time Cafe,** 380 Lafayette St., at Great Jones Street. (☎ 212-533-2680; www.feznyc.com). Although the club's most popular attraction is the Mingus Big Band jazz band on Thursday nights, the rest of the week brings an eclectic live music-and-performance art mix. (See the "Downtown Arts & Nightlife" map.)

✔ **The Knitting Factory,** 74 Leonard St., between Broadway and Church Street (☎ 212-219-3055; www.knittingfactory.com). At New York's premier avant-garde music venue, in the four separate spaces within the Knitting Factory, you may hear performances ranging from experimental jazz to acoustic folk to spoken-work to poetry readings. (See the "Downtown Arts & Nightlife" map.)

✔ **Satalla,** 37 W. 26th St., between Sixth Avenue and Broadway (☎ 212-576-1155; www.satalla.com). With performances in Flamenco, Klezmer, Celtic, Middle-Eastern Jazz, and Afro-Cuban to name just a handful, the diversity of music that can be heard on any given night in Satalla is staggering. The room is cozy and most nights you can get in with no admission charge. (See the "Midtown Arts & Nightlife" map.)

✔ **Tonic,** 107 Norfolk St., between Rivington and Delancy streets (☎ 212-358-7501; www.tonicnyc.com). The Tonic, which features alternative jazz and rock, may not be for everyone, but if you like your music challenging and in an intimate setting, this Tonic is for you. (See the "Downtown Arts & Nightlife" map.)

Life is a cabaret

Want the quintessential New York night-on-the-town experience? Take in a cabaret. But be prepared to part with your greenbacks; covers can range from $10 to $60 along with a two-drink or dinner check minimum. Always reserve ahead. New York's top cabarets include:

✔ **Cafe Carlyle,** at the Carlyle Hotel, 781 Madison Ave., at 76th Street (☎ 212-744-1600). This is the room the great Bobby Short made famous. Bobby Short, who has long presided over the room, announced and then rescinded his retirement, but if you want to see him, you'd better head to the Carlyle sooner rather than later. When Short isn't there, you still get the top performers on the cabaret scene. And at prices that range from $65 to $75 per person with a $30 per-person minimum, top quality is what you certainly should get. (See the "Uptown Arts & Nightlife" map.)

✔ **Feinstein's at the Regency,** at the Regency Hotel, 540 Park Ave., at 61st Street (☎ 212-339-4095; www.feinsteinsattheregency.com). If you don't catch song impressario Michael Feinstein playing here at the club he opened, don't despair — high-wattage talent is always on tap. (See the "Uptown Arts & Nightlife" map.)

✔ **The Oak Room,** at the Algonquin Hotel, 59 W. 44th St., between Fifth and Sixth avenues (☎ 212-840-6800). The Oak Room is one of the city's most elegant and sophisticated spots for cabaret and that's saying a lot. You can almost always be sure that top-rated talent is headlining here. (See the "Midtown Arts & Nightlife" map.)

New York Comedy is No Joke

Something about New York makes it a ripe breeding ground for comedians. The names of those who got their start here, from Dangerfield to

Seinfeld, are like a who's who of comedy. And you never know, the neb-
bishy guy or girl up at the mike just may be the next Richard Pryor or
Ellen DeGeneres. New York's top comedy clubs include:

- ✔ **Carolines on Broadway,** 1626 Broadway, between 49th and
  50th streets (☎ 212-757-4100; www.carolines.com). New York's
  biggest and highest-profile comedy club attracts the hottest head-
  liners. (See the "Midtown Arts & Nightlife" map.)

- ✔ **Comedy Cellar,** 117 Macdougal St., between Bleecker and W. 3rd
  streets (☎ 212-254-3480; www.comedycellar.com). This intimate,
  subterranean comedy club is a throwback to the days of the raw,
  hard-edged stand-up comedy that spawned Lenny Bruce and
  Richard Pryor. (See the "Downtown Arts & Nightlife" map.)

- ✔ **Dangerfield's,** 1118 First Ave., between 61st and 62nd streets
  (☎ 212-593-1650; www.dangerfieldscomedyclub.com). If Tony
  Soprano were a comedy fan, this would be his kind of place. Slick,
  mature, and Vegas-like, Dangerfield's gets plenty of respect. (See
  the "Uptown Arts & Nightlife" map.)

- ✔ **Gotham Comedy Club,** 34 W. 22nd St., between Fifth and Sixth
  avenues (☎ 212-367-9000; www.gothamcomedyclub.com). This is
  New York's trendiest comedy club of the moment. Look for theme
  nights like "Comedy Salsa" and "A Very Jewish Christmas." Tuesday
  nights feature new talent. (See the "Midtown Arts & Nightlife" map.)

Hanging Out in New York's Best Bars

You won't have to search far to find a place to sit and have a cocktail in
New York. There are bars on every block, sometimes two or three to a
block. And they come in just about every variety from sleek and hip to
dark and gritty. Check out this small sampling of some of my favorite
New York bars.

For the scene

- ✔ **Pangaea,** 417 Lafayette St., between 4th Avenue and Astor Place
  (☎ 212-353-2992). This African-safari themed restaurant/bar serves
  original cocktails, but the drinks are secondary to the scene. Models,
  model wannabes, and those who can afford the very expensive
  drinks served here prowl the room. (See the "Downtown Arts &
  Nightlife" map.)

- ✔ **Nocturne,** 144 Bleecker St., between La Guardia Place and Thompson
  Street (☎ 212-979-8434). Expect to see lots of posing at this elegant
  beautiful-people hangout where a bottle of Absolut Vodka costs $250.
  (See the "Downtown Arts & Nightlife" map.)

- ✔ **Monkey Bar,** at the Hotel Elysée, 60 E. 54th St., between Madison
  and Park avenues (☎ 212-838-2600). This swanky space is dolled

up like a Hollywood supper club circa the 1930s. The drinks are faultless, and the legendary monkey murals are worth a look alone. Skip the dining room and head directly to the piano bar for the ultimate Monkey Bar experience. (See the "Midtown Arts & Nightlife" map.)

For creative cocktails

✔ **Bemelmans Bar,** in the Carlyle Hotel, 35 E. 76th St., at Madison Avenue (☎ 212-744-1600). The cocktails created by mixologist and self-proclaimed cocktail geek Audrey Sanders are amazing. Also, the bar is a beauty with its whimsical murals painted by children's book illustrator, Ludwig Bemelmans, who created the Madeline books. (See the "Uptown Arts & Nightlife" map.)

✔ **Double Happiness,** 173 Mott St., between Grand and Broome Streets (☎ 212-941-1282). The only indicator to the subterranean entrance of this Chinatown hideaway is a vertical WATCH YOUR STEP sign. Once through the door, you find a beautifully designed speakeasy-ish lounge. You're going to be doubly happy if you try the green tea martini, an inspired house creation. (See the "Downtown Arts & Nightlife" map.)

✔ **Pravda,** 281 Lafayette St., between Houston and Prince streets (☎ 212-334-5015). You can find more than 70 vodkas here from 18 countries. They also offer eight specialty martinis. (See the "Downtown Arts & Nightlife" map.)

✔ **King Cole Bar,** in the St. Regis Hotel, 2 E. 55th St., at Fifth Avenue (☎ 212-744-4300). The supposed birthplace of the Bloody Mary, they continue to make a very mean and tasty one here. If you aren't interested in a Bloody Mary, order something else. You really can't go wrong. Don't forget to admire the very famous Maxfield Parrish mural above the bar. (See the "Midtown Arts & Nightlife" map.)

In 2003, smoke and smoking was made illegal in all restaurants and bars in New York City (except for a few cigar bars). So if you get the urge, join the huddled (and shivering, in the winter) masses outside the bar, in what some not-so-fondly call the "Bloomberg Lounge" (after Mayor Mike, who pushed through the anti-smoking laws).

For old-world charm

✔ **White Horse Tavern,** 567 Hudson St., at 11th Street (☎ 212-243-9260). This circa 1880 pub is where Dylan Thomas supposedly had his very last drink before becoming a bar legend. (See the "Down-town Arts & Nightlife" map.)

✔ **Pete's Tavern,** 129 E. 18th St., at Irving Place (☎ 212-473-7676). This place is so old it is said to have opened when Lincoln was still president. (See the "Midtown Arts & Nightlife" map.)

Downtown Arts & Nightlife

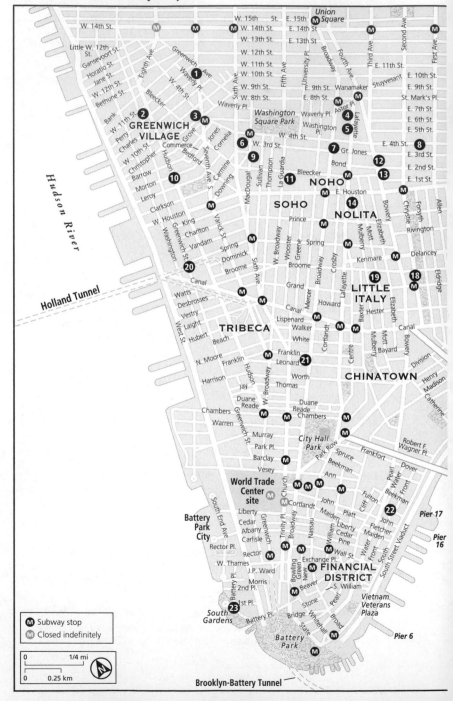

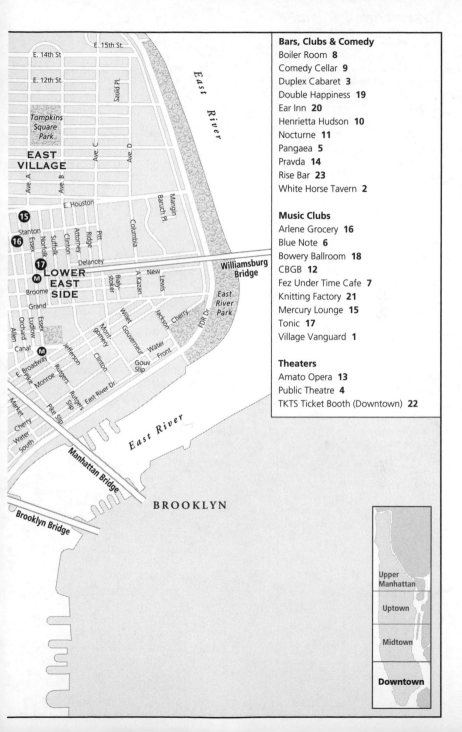

Bars, Clubs & Comedy
Boiler Room **8**
Comedy Cellar **9**
Duplex Cabaret **3**
Double Happiness **19**
Ear Inn **20**
Henrietta Hudson **10**
Nocturne **11**
Pangaea **5**
Pravda **14**
Rise Bar **23**
White Horse Tavern **2**

Music Clubs
Arlene Grocery **16**
Blue Note **6**
Bowery Ballroom **18**
CBGB **12**
Fez Under Time Cafe **7**
Knitting Factory **21**
Mercury Lounge **15**
Tonic **17**
Village Vanguard **1**

Theaters
Amato Opera **13**
Public Theatre **4**
TKTS Ticket Booth (Downtown) **22**

Midtown Arts & Nightlife

Bars, Clubs, and Comedy
Avalon **21**
Barracuda **15**
Carolines on Broadway **3**
Crobar **13**
Gotham Comedy Club **22**
High Bar **23**
Jimmy's Corner **7**
King Cole Bar **30**
Monkey Bar **29**
Oak Room **27**
Old Town Bar & Grill **20**
Pen-Top Bar **30**
Pete's Tavern **19**
Spirit **14**
Subway Inn **31**
Swing 46 **4**

Music Clubs
B.B. King Blues Club & Grill **11**
Birdland **8**
Irving Plaza **18**
Jazz Standard **24**
Satalla **25**

Theaters
Atlantic Theater Workshop **17**
Carnegie Hall **1**
City Center **2**
Joyce Theater **16**
Madison Square Garden **12**
New Victory **10**
New Perspectives **5**
Radio City Music Hall **28**
TADA! Youth Theater **26**
TKTS Ticket Booth **6**
Town Hall **9**

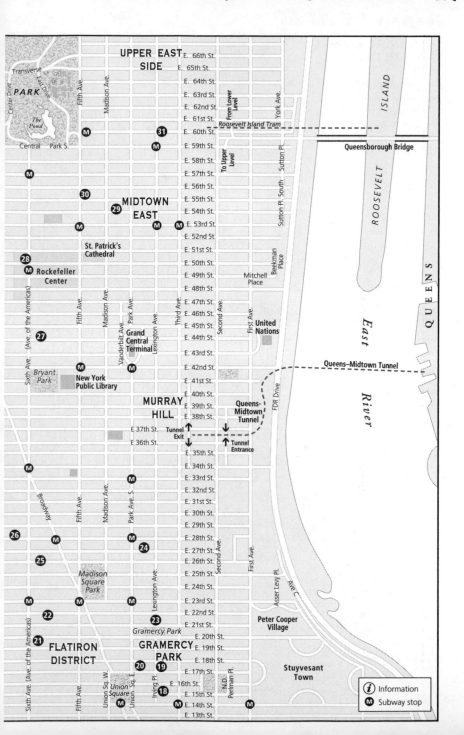

UPPER EAST SIDE

E. 66th St.
E. 65th St.
E. 64th St.
E. 63rd St.
E. 62nd St.
E. 61st St.
Roosevelt Island Tram
E. 60th St.
E. 59th St.
E. 58th St.
E. 57th St.
E. 56th St.
E. 55th St.
E. 54th St.
E. 53rd St.
E. 52nd St.
E. 51st St.
E. 50th St.
E. 49th St.
E. 48th St
E. 47th St.
E. 46th St.
E. 45th St.
E. 44th St.
E. 43rd St.
E. 42nd St.
E. 41st St.
E. 40th St.
E. 39th St.
E. 38th St.
E 37th St.
E. 36th St.
E. 35th St.
E. 34th St.
E. 33rd St.
E. 32nd St.
E. 31st St.
E. 30th St.
E. 29th St.
E. 28th St.
E. 27th St.
E. 26th St.
E. 25th St.
E. 24th St.
E. 23rd St.
E. 22nd St.
E. 21st St.
E. 20th St.
E. 19th St.
E. 18th St.
E. 17th St.
E. 16th St.
E. 15th St.
E. 14th St.
E. 13th St.

MIDTOWN EAST

Transverse
PARK
The Pond
Central Park S.

Fifth Ave.
Madison Ave.
Center Drive
East Drive

St. Patrick's Cathedral

Rockefeller Center

Fifth Ave. (Ave. of the Americas)

Bryant Park

New York Public Library

Madison Ave.

Vanderbilt Ave.

Grand Central Terminal

Park Ave.

Lexington Ave.

Third Ave.

Second Ave.

First Ave.

United Nations

Mitchell Place

Beekman Place

Sutton Pl. South

Sutton Pl.

York Ave.

From Lower Level

To Upper Level

Queensborough Bridge

ISLAND

ROOSEVELT

East River

QUEENS

Queens–Midtown Tunnel

FDR Drive

MURRAY HILL

Tunnel Exit

Queens-Midtown Tunnel

Tunnel Entrance

Broadway

Fifth Ave.

Madison Ave.

Park Ave. S.

Madison Square Park

Lexington Ave.

Second Ave.

First Ave.

Asser Levy Pl.

Ave. C

Peter Cooper Village

Stuyvesant Town

Sixth Ave. (Ave. of the Americas)

FLATIRON DISTRICT

Fifth Ave.

Union Sq. W.

Union Square

Union Sq. E.

Irving Pl.

GRAMERCY PARK

Gramercy Park

N.D. Perlman Pl.

Information

Subway stop

Uptown Arts & Nightlife

Bars, Clubs and Comedy
Bemelmans Bar **8**
Cafe Carlyle **8**
Dangerfield's **7**
Dublin House **2**
Feinstein's at the Regency **5**
79th Street Boat Basin Cafe **3**

Music and Dance Clubs
Decade **6**
Smoke **1**

Theaters
Lincoln Center **4**

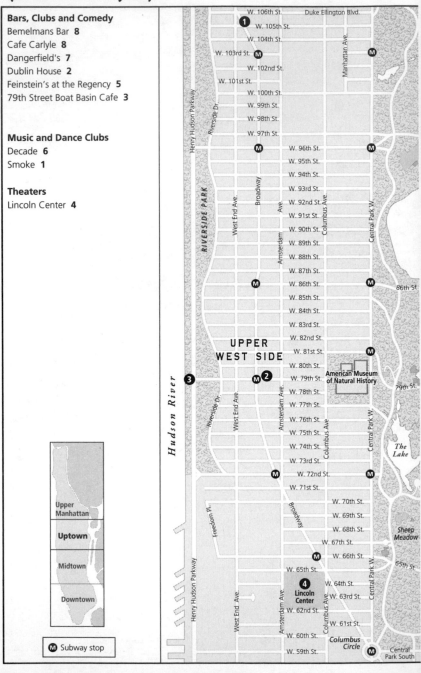

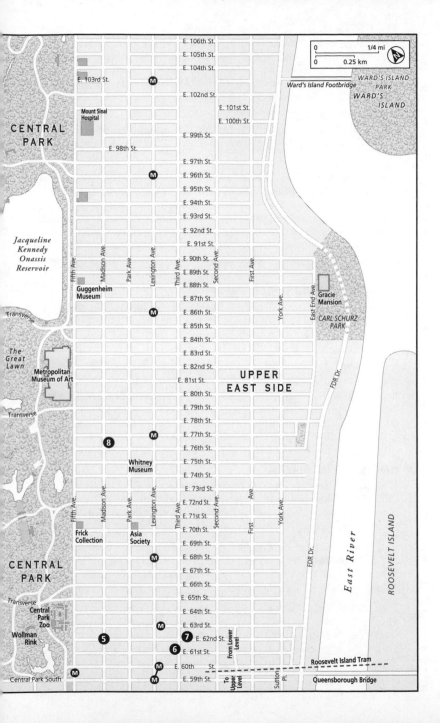

✔ **The Old Town Bar & Grill,** 45 E. 18th St., between Broadway and Park Avenue (☎ 212-529-6732). The bar where food is shuttled to customers via a dumb waiter from the basement kitchen has been featured on film *(The Devil's Own)* and TV (the opening credits of Letterman in his NBC days). (See the "Midtown Arts & Nightlife" map.)

✔ **Ear Inn,** 326 Spring St., between Greenwich and Washington streets (☎ 212-226-9060). This cluttered old, 1870-established pub is a cranky relief in super-chic Soho. (See the "Downtown Arts & Nightlife" map.)

✔ **Dublin House,** 225 W. 79th St., between Broadway and Amsterdam Avenue (☎ 212-874-9528). For years, like a welcoming beacon, the Dublin House's neon harp has blinked invitingly. This very old pub is a no-frills Irish saloon and the perfect spot for a drink after visiting the nearby Museum of Natural History or Central Park. The Guinness is cheap and drawn perfectly by the very able and sometimes crusty bartenders. (See the "Uptown Arts & Nightlife" map.)

For dive bar aficionados

✔ **Jimmy's Corner,** 140 W. 44th St., between Broadway and Sixth Avenue (☎ 212-221-9510). Jimmy's is a tough guy's joint that has happily survived the Disneyfication of Times Square. Beer is cheap and drinks aren't fancy, so skip the theme bars and restaurants in the area and go for an after-theater pop at Jimmy's instead. (See the "Midtown Arts & Nightlife" map.)

✔ **Subway Inn,** 143 E. 60th St., at Lexington Avenue (☎ 212-223-9829). This is my all-time favorite dive and has been around for more than 60 years. No matter what time of day, it's always dark as midnight inside the Subway Inn. (See the "Midtown Arts & Nightlife" map.)

For drinks with a view

✔ **Rise Bar,** at the Ritz-Carlton New York, Battery Park, 2 West St. (☎ 212-344-0800). On the hotel's 14th floor, the bar boasts incomparable views of Lady Liberty and busy New York Harbor. (See the "Downtown Arts & Nightlife" map.)

✔ **Pen-Top Bar,** at the Peninsula Hotel, 700 Fifth Ave., at 55th Street (☎ 212-956-2888). The views of midtown Manhattan are awesome here and make the steep price of the drinks easier to take. (See the "Midtown Arts & Nightlife" map.)

✔ **79th Street Boat Basin Cafe,** 79th St., at the Hudson River (☎ 212-496-5542). As you sip your cocktail, enjoy a beautiful sunset and watch boats bob on the river; you may just forget you're in New York for a moment. Open from May through September. (See the "Uptown Arts & Nightlife" map.)

✔ **High Bar,** 2 Lexington Ave., at 21st Street (☎ 212-475-4320). This bar is located on the rooftop of the legendary Gramercy Park Hotel, just opposite pristine and exclusive Gramercy Park. The scene at the High Bar, where the views of the Met Life Building, Gramercy Park, and the Empire State Building are gorgeous, has gotten so hot that they actually installed outdoor heaters to extend drinking alfresco into the cooler months. (See the "Midtown Arts & Nightlife" map.)

For gay & lesbian nightlife

✔ **Barracuda,** 275 W. 22nd St., between Seventh and Eighth avenues (☎ 212-645-8613). Located in the heart of gay Chelsea, this bar is regularly voted best gay bar in New York by the various local GLBT publications. (See the "Midtown Arts & Nightlife" map.)

✔ **Boiler Room,** 86 E. 4th St., between First and Second avenues (☎ 212-254-7536). This is New York's favorite gay dive bar and a fun East Village hangout. (See the "Downtown Arts & Nightlife" map.)

✔ **Duplex Cabaret,** 61 Christopher St., at Seventh Avenue (☎ 212-255-5438; www.theduplex.com). High camp is the norm at this gay cabaret and piano-bar, still going after 50 years. It once hosted the likes of Woody Allen and Joan Rivers in their early stand-up careers. (See the "Downtown Arts & Nightlife" map.)

✔ **Henrietta Hudson,** 444 Hudson St., at Morton Street (☎ 212-924-3347; www.henriettahudsons.com). This popular lesbian hangout has a great jukebox and a deejay on weekends. (Expect a $5 to $7 cover charge.) (See the "Downtown Arts & Nightlife" map.)

 Some of the hottest "clubs" are actually traveling parties that alight in various spots depending on the day, making them hard for visitors to find. Various publications — *Time Out New York's* Gay & Lesbian section, as well as the GLBT–specific *Homo Xtra, GONYC* magazine, and others I list in Chapter 6 — provide the best up-to-the-minute club information. Another good source is the Web; try the gay NYC site at www.gay center.org.

Hitting the Dance Clubs and Getting Across the Velvet Rope

Dance club fame is transient; one year a club can be white hot, but the next year it's not even hip enough for the Bridge and Tunnel crowd. These dance clubs, as of this writing, are closer to the hot, hot, hot variety.

✔ **Avalon,** 660 Sixth Ave., at 20th Street (☎ 212-807-7780; www.ny avalon.com). The old dance club, the Limelight, once reigned supreme at this location during the decadent 80s; now Avalon has moved into this large, former church with its many "private" rooms. (See the "Midtown Arts & Nightlife" map.)

✔ **Crobar,** 530 W. 28th St., between 10th and 11th avenues (☎ 212-629-9000; www.crobar.com). This 25,000-square-foot club can fit up to 3,000 people, so the odds of you getting in are very good. Once inside, top-name deejays have you sweating in no time. (See the "Midtown Arts & Nightlife" map.)

✔ **Decade,** 1117 First Ave., at 61st Street (☎ **212-835-5979**). Here you find a rare dance club where no matter your age, you won't feel old. The vibe is upscale, and the music is mostly from the 70s, 80s, and 90s. (See the "Uptown Arts & Nightlife" map.)

✔ **Spirit,** 530 W. 27th St., between 10th and 11th avenues (☎ **212-268-9477**; www.spiritnewyork.com). This New Age dance emporium features a healing center and organic vegetarian restaurant, along with a 10,000-square-foot dance floor. (See the "Midtown Arts & Nightlife" map.)

✔ **Swing 46,** 349 W. 46th St., between Eighth and Ninth avenues (☎ **212-262-9554**; www.swing46.com). As its name suggests, the music here, mostly live, is swing. And if swing dancing is new to you, free lessons are offered Wednesday through Saturday. (See the "Midtown Arts & Nightlife" map.)

New York nightlife starts late and finishes *really* late. Things don't start happening until at least 11 p.m. Most places don't take credit cards, so bring cash (or be prepared to fork over a high transaction charge at an in-house ATM). Cover charges can range from $7 to $30 and often increase as the night goes on. The best source for club information is the weekly *Time Out New York* magazine. It lists cover charges for the week's big events and gives sound advice on the type of music *and* the type of crowd each event attracts. (Refer to this chapter's introduction for additional sources of entertainment information.)

If you're somewhat masochistic, enjoy humiliation and ridicule, and are determined to get into that oh-so-trendy club you heard about back home, keep these pointers in mind to help you get beyond the velvet rope.

✔ Be polite.

✔ Dress fashionably.

✔ Don't try to talk your way in.

✔ Arrive early (think 9 p.m.), and then be willing to hang out at a mostly empty club until the action heats up.

Part VI
The Part of Tens

The 5th Wave   By Rich Tennant

"Ooo-look at this—we've got a perfect view of
the Chrysler Building, the Buick Building and
the Chevy Building."

In this part . . .

1 warn you about some New York experiences you should avoid and some that you should definitely seek out, and I give you the lowdown on the top ten movie locations in the city.

Chapter 16

The Top Ten Offbeat New York City Experiences

· ·

In This Chapter

▶ Riding the subway from New York to Korea
▶ Walking the radical way
▶ Heading to the beach, Coney Island style
▶ Biking the Hudson

· ·

*M*ost of this book covers the basics about New York, the top attractions, neighborhoods, restaurants, and hotels. But New York has many layers, and you can find riches within each layer. Check out some of my favorite New York experiences that offer a variety of ways to see the city.

Ride the International Express

The number 7 train is sometimes referred to as the International Express. Take it out of Manhattan and through the borough of Queens, and you pass through one ethnic neighborhood after another, from Indian to Thai, from Peruvian to Columbian, from Chinese to Korean. Get off at any stop along the way and sample the local cuisine and keep repeating to yourself, "I'm still in the United States, I'm still in the United States." Or stay on the train until the 103rd Street stop where, within a few blocks walk, is the **Louis Armstrong House Museum,** 34-56 107th St., Corona (☎ 718-478-8274; www.satchmo.net) where Satchmo lived from 1943 until his death in 1971. After touring the House, have lunch at the nearby Peruvian restaurant, **La Pollada de Laura,** 102-03 Northern Blvd. (☎ 718-426-7818).

Explore the Museum of Sex

Don't be bashful. How many cities can claim their own Museum of Sex? The first exhibit was titled, "NYC Sex: How New York City Transformed Sex in America," and it featured displays of S&M, 19th-century brothels, and videos of Times Square in its sleazy heyday of the 1970s. In 2004, "Sex Among the Lotus: 2,500 Years of Chinese Erotic Obsession" opened displaying explicit imagery dating from the second century B.C. Who knew? Don't miss a trip through the gift shop — definitely not your typical museum shop. This museum is located at 233 Fifth Ave., at 27th Street (☎ **866-MOSEX-NYC** or 866-667-3969; www.museumofsex.com). By subway, take the N, R or 6 trains to 28th Street.

You must be 18 or older to visit the Museum of Sex.

Stroll Riverside Park

Central Park may be the king of New York parks, but if I can't have Central Park, I'll take **Riverside Park** any day. This underrated beauty, designed by Frederick Law Olmstead (the same man who designed Central Park) stretches four miles from 72nd Street to 158th Street. The serpentine route along the Hudson River offers a variety of lovely river vistas, 14 playgrounds, two tennis courts, softball and soccer fields, a skate park, beach volleyball, and the Boat Basin. Strolling folks with the munchies can find two cafes: the **79th Street Boat Basin Cafe** at 79th Street (☎ **212-496-5542**) and **Hurley's Hudson Beach Cafe** at 105th Street (☎ **917-370-3448**). This park also features monuments like the **Eleanor Roosevelt Monument** at 72nd Street, the **Soldiers and Sailors Monument** at 90th Street, and **Grant's Tomb** (Quick: Who's buried there?) at 122nd Street.

Take a Radical Walking Tour

Led by self-proclaimed "radical historian" Bruce Kayton, these are unconventional tours of conventional tourist sights. A tour to Harlem covers the sites pertaining to such groups and historic figures as Black Panthers, Malcolm X, and the Communist Party, and it includes a visit to the Apollo Theater. My favorite is the "Non-Jerry Seinfeld Upper West Side Tour," which visits the home of Fidel Castro when he lived in the neighborhood in the late 1940s, the site of the shootout between Black Panther H. Rap Brown and police, and Lincoln Center (where the tour docent describes how Lincoln Center destroyed what once was a thriving Puerto Rican community). For more information, call ☎ **718-492-0069** or check out the Web site at www.he.net/~radtours. Tours cost $10, and reservations aren't necessary.

Ride the Roosevelt Island Tram

Impress your family and friends with a little-known, but spectacular, view of the New York skyline by taking them for a ride on the Roosevelt Island Tram (☎ 212-832-4543, ext. 1). This is the same tram that King Kong "attacks" in the Universal Studios Theme Park in Florida. (It's also the same tram you have probably seen in countless movies, most recently *Spider-Man.*) The Tram originates at 59th Street and Second Avenue, costs $2 each way ($2 round trip for seniors), and takes four minutes to traverse the East River to Roosevelt Island, where a series of apartment complexes and parks sit. During those four minutes, you're treated to gorgeous views down the East River and of the east side skyline with views of the United Nations and four bridges: the Queensborough, Williamsburg, Manhattan, and the Brooklyn Bridge. On a clear day you may even spot Lady Liberty. The Tram operates daily from 6 a.m. until 2:30 a.m. and until 3:30 a.m. on weekends.

Head to Coney Island

I can't believe I'm calling Coney Island an offbeat experience. This is the same Coney Island that thousands used to flock to on a summer's day. But Coney Island is just a shell of what it once was in its heyday (the early part of the 20th century). That shell and the idea of what it once was make it an intriguing attraction. The almost mythical old amusement ride, the Parachute Jump, which towers over the Boardwalk, is recently refurbished though long inoperable; it stands as a monument to Coney Island.

But don't assume that this is a dead amusement park; Astroland, home of the famed **Cyclone roller coaster,** has some great rides for children and adults. The best amusement of all, however, is the people-watching. Coney Island attracts its fair share of odd, freaky, and funky visitors, and it hosts a handful of events and attractions that many people find a bit offbeat. Each 4th of July at noon, **Nathan's Famous Hot Dogs** holds its hot dog eating contest. And each year (usually on the Saturday closest to the first day of summer) the fabulous and gaudy **Coney Island Mermaid Parade** (www.coneyisland.com/mermaid.shtml), the nation's largest art parade, is presided over by a celebrity "King Neptune" and "Queen Mermaid" and takes place at the end of June. On January 1st, members of the Polar Bear Swim Club show their masochistic gusto by taking a plunge into the icy ocean.

The small **Coney Island Museum,** 1208 Surf Ave., near W. 12th Street (☎ 718-372-5158; www.coneyisland.com/museum.shtml) showcases fun exhibits detailing the history of Coney Island. Open year-round is the **New York Aquarium** at Surf Avenue and West 8th Street (☎ 718-265-FISH, www.nyaquarium.com), a small but interesting branch of the Wildlife Conservation Society that offers underwater exhibits, a touch pool, and performing sea lions. The rides and amusement park are open from Memorial Day until mid-September, which is also the best time to

visit Coney Island. Bring your bathing suit and test the waters. To reach
Coney Island by subway, take trains D, Q, or F to Coney Island-Stillwell
Avenue, Brooklyn.

Catch some real sports

You think the Knicks are New York basketball? You obviously haven't been
to the **West 4th Street** (at Sixth Avenue) courts, where the game is played
at its best. You can spend all afternoon watching the pickup games there,
and you'll be entertained not only by the moves on the court, but by
some of the best trash talking you've ever laid ears on. And although the
Yankees are America's team, if you really want a treat, head to Hecksher
Fields in Central Park during the warm months to watch the co-ed softball
Broadway Show League (☎ **212-944-3849;** www.broadwayshowleague.
com). The co-ed games, which are open for all to watch, can get pretty
intense, and you may be surprised who you see out there shagging flies;
Al Pacino, Matthew Broderick, and Robert Redford have all played in
the league. Cast members from all the major shows (*The Lion King,
The Producers,* and *Hairspray,* to name just a few) compete. The schedule
runs from April through August; check the Web site for more information.

Tour Little Italy in the Bronx

Taking a trip to Little Italy in the Bronx is growing in popularity, thus
making it not so offbeat. Since the near-demise of Little Italy in Manhattan,
the area centered on Arthur Avenue, known as the Little Italy in the Bronx,
is the place to go for old-fashioned Italian charm, food, and ambiance. You
know you've arrived on Arthur Avenue when you smell the fresh-baked
bread, stacks of bacala (dried salt cod), aromatic sausages and cheeses,
and tomato sauce. Spend the day browsing the markets and having lunch
at one of the local restaurants or pizzerias followed by cappucino or
espresso at a cafe. Or even better, combine your visit with a trip to the
nearby Bronx Zoo. To get to Arthur Avenue, take the 4 or D train to
Fordham Road, 12 bus east, 2 or 5 train to Pelham Parkway, 12 bus west,
Metro North Harlem Line to Fordham Road, and shuttle bus to Belmont
and Bronx Zoo.

Bike Along the Hudson River

If walking is just not enough exercise for you, a good alternative is to
rent a bike and ride the length of Manhattan via the work-in-progress
Hudson River Park. As of this writing, you can bike from Battery Park to
Fort Tryon Park near the George Washington Bridge. Although detours
along the way occasionally may take you on and off bike paths, by 2005,
work on the park is supposed to be complete, allowing you to ride unen-
cumbered the whole way. But don't let the detours deter you from a
remarkable bike ride. Along the route you pass the World Trade Center

site, the far West Village, Chelsea Piers, the *USS Intrepid,* Riverside Park, and the George Washington Bridge.

Wander the Streets on Sunday Morning

This may not sound so offbeat, and I've noticed quite a few tourists, usually jet-lagged Europeans, wandering the parks and streets on early Sunday mornings, but try it some time. The city has a special feel on Sunday mornings. The streets are generally deserted, and things are so quiet it's almost eerie. Even though I'm far from alone, I feel as if I have the city to myself early on Sunday mornings, and I find that very exhilarating. Is it worth getting an early wake-up call? That's for you to decide. Or it may be easier not to go to bed at all on Saturday night. . . .

Chapter 17

The Top Ten New York City Movie Locations

- -

In This Chapter

▶ Missing Scorsese's Times Square

▶ Scaling King Kong's Empire State Building

▶ Having what she's having . . . going to the *When Harry Met Sally* deli

- -

*N*ew York has been the backdrop for so many films that it really is a character in itself. Many people who've never been to New York only know the city from the movies — and that's not a bad way to learn about New York. What follows are my favorite New York City movie locations and the movies that best represent them.

Times Square

You can watch the evolution of Times Square in two distinct and very gritty movies. When I say gritty, you should know immediately that neither of these movies was made in and around the Times Square of today. The Times Square of the 1950s is best illustrated in the great film, *The Sweet Smell of Success* (1957) starring Burt Lancaster and Tony Curtis (later made into a Broadway musical starring John Lithgow). The film's setting is a time when Times Square's the place where those who aspired to celebrity come to be discovered. It's tough, but not as tough as the Times Square depicted in the 1976 movie, *Taxi Driver.* Directed by Martin Scorsese, the Times Square of the 1970s is a literal hell where Robert DeNiro's Travis Bickle says: "Someday a real rain will come and wash all this scum off the streets." It's really not at all like that anymore. So maybe we, who lament the bad old days of Times Square, have Scorsese to blame for what it has become now.

Empire State Building

Something about that view from the 86th-story observatory ignites romance. Here, Tom Hanks woos Meg Ryan in *Sleepless in Seattle*

(1993), and Cary Grant waits for his love Deborah Kerr in *An Affair to Remember* (1957). But the greatest love story of all meets its tragic ending at the Empire State Building when King Kong woos Fay Wray in the 1933 masterpiece, *King Kong.* Remember, ". . . it wasn't the airplanes. It was beauty killed the beast."

Little Italy

Not much of Little Italy is left today, especially compared with what is depicted in two movie classics. In the Little Italy of *The Godfather: Part II* (1974), the neighborhood of the early 20th century is a teeming, vibrant place with its own social strata. Who can forget the great scene where young Vito Corleone (played by Robert DeNiro) stalks the local mafia don during the Feast of San Gennaro — when the Feast was truly a feast. We return to the Feast of San Gennaro and Little Italy in the 1970s, this time in Martin Scorsese's *Mean Streets* (1973), when the neighborhood is beginning to disintegrate, as are the proud Vito Corleone–like Mafiosos who are replaced by young small-time thugs.

New York Delis

Woody Allen films all of his movies in New York, not so much because it's such a colorful place, but because he says he likes to sleep at home when he works. His movies have countless memorable New York scenes and one of my favorites, *Broadway Danny Rose* (1984), is no exception. The story of Broadway Danny Rose is told by a group of standup comedians who convene at none other than the **Carnegie Deli** (see Chapter 10) where, it's said, there's a sandwich named after him. New York's best deli is **Katz's** (see Chapter 10) on the Lower East Side. Katz's is famous for their salami and kosher hot dogs. The deli is also famous for Meg Ryan's pretend orgasm in the Rob Reiner-directed film *When Harry Met Sally* (1989). By the way, what is she having anyway? It isn't one of those wieners, is it?

Central Park Reservoir

I'm a regular jogger at the Central Park Reservoir, now known as the Jacqueline Kennedy Onassis Reservoir, where the views of the New York skyline are spectacular. I'm not sure if Dustin Hoffman cares about the skyline views when he runs the track in the thriller, *Marathon Man* (1976). And Keanu Reeves, I think, is more interested in selling his soul than getting a good workout when he hits the track in the movie *The Devil's Advocate* (1997).

Roosevelt Island Tram

What is it about this tram that attracts evildoers? In the Sylvester Stallone movie *Nighthawks* (1981), Stallone plays a New York cop who saves a packed tram from a terrorist. And in *Spider-Man* (2002), Peter Parker (also known as Spiderman) rescues a group of young tram riders from the clutches of the diabolical Green Goblin. Even King Kong gets in the act when he attacks a replica of the tram at the Universal Studios Theme Park in Florida.

New York Subways

People have this morbid fascination with the way the New York subway system used to be. Even though the subways are cleaner, safer, and cooler than they ever were, Hollywood still likes to think of them as dark, dangerous, graffiti-strewn places. One of the best movies about the bad old days on New York subways is *The Taking of Pelham One Two Three* (1974), in which a subway car is hijacked by Robert Shaw, and it's up to transit cop Walter Matthau to crack the crime. The best New York subway movie of all time has very little actual inside-the-subway footage. Most of the action is below the subway, the elevated train to be precise, where Gene Hackman, in a car, is in mad pursuit of a suave heroin dealer on the train above him in *The French Connection* (1971).

Statue of Liberty

Poor Lady Liberty. She carries a heavy burden as the symbol of democratic society. Who can forget the eyes of the immigrants on the boat carrying Vito Corleone to the New World in *The Godfather: Part II* (1974)? But it's because she's such a symbol that Hollywood likes to trash her. It's their unsubtle way of showing how fragile our society is, but it usually takes unusual force to do so, like a tsunami in *The Day After Tomorrow* (2004). Or what happens in my favorite Statue of Liberty scene, in the original *Planet of the Apes* (1968), when Charlton Heston spots her torch coming out of the sand and screams: "You maniacs! You blew it up. Damn you! God damn you all to hell!"

Central Park West

With all the famous streets in New York, you wouldn't think that CPW (as New Yorkers call the street running up the west side of the park) would be one of the most filmed. But think of how many movies feature the Macy's Thanksgiving Day Parade that runs down Central Park West. All five (yes, five!) versions of *Miracle on 34th Street* feature the street, and a scene in *Broadway Danny Rose* (see "New York Delis" earlier in this list) also features the parade and its main thoroughfare. Central

Park West is the street the giant Stay Puft Marshmallow Man lurches up in *Ghost Busters* (1984), on his way to Sigourney Weaver's building at 55 Central Park West (at 66th Street). A few blocks up, at the stately Dakota apartment building at 72nd Street, Mia Farrow discovers some very devilish neighbors in *Rosemary's Baby* (1968). They aren't enough, however, to frighten Farrow from returning years later under better circumstances in Woody Allen's *Hannah and Her Sisters* (1986).

New York City Apartments

Not much irks me more than seeing those palatial digs that television seems to think represent New York City apartments. Most of us live in closets, and some filmmakers actually understand this. Sure, Audrey Hepburn dressed like a rich fashion model in that great New York–based movie, *Breakfast at Tiffany's* (1961), but she lived in a small studio walk-up. That didn't stop her from entertaining, and the party scene in that movie, where the revelers were practically on top of each other, is a classic. Maybe even more realistic is the heatless, cockroach-swarming hovel that Dustin (Ratso Rizzo) Hoffman inhabits and offers to share with country boy Jon Voigt in another tough New York movie, *Midnight Cowboy* (1969).

Chapter 18

Ten New York City Experiences to Avoid

*N*ew York offers plenty of offbeat adventures that you may want to experience (see Chapter 16 for a rundown). Here's the flipside: things, events, and places to avoid. Take note: Some of the experiences I list are often featured prominently in guidebooks as must-do experiences. You may, in fact, have a lifelong dream of ringing in the New Year in Times Square. But my cranky nature leads me to believe otherwise. I'll leave it to you to ultimately decide.

New Year's Eve in Times Square

You see the event on television every year and now you're here. This is your chance to be one of the hundreds of thousands of revelers packed tightly together in the frigid cold to watch the ball drop. *Don't do it!* Find a nice warm restaurant or bar to celebrate in. Or better yet, have room service deliver a delicious meal and some bubbly for you and your loved one, and don't go out at all. Despite the happy faces that you see on television, the whole thing is a miserable experience and not worth the forced elation of blowing on a noisemaker at midnight with half a million others. (You won't find too many New Yorkers here . . . it's very much an out-of-towners' event.)

Chain Restaurants

Oh yes, they're here, probably to stay — and with probably more to come. I'm referring to those restaurants with familiar names like Olive

Garden, Applebee's, Red Lobster, and Domino's. When you begin to feel the pangs of hunger, ask yourself: Did I come to New York to eat exactly what I can eat in every city or town in this country? Or did I come here to experience what makes New York so unique? And that includes the amazing variety of unchained restaurants, from the coffee shops and diners where real New Yorkers eat to the bargain-priced ethnic cuisine and higher-end dining experiences. Bypass the old standards and try something homey, glamorous, or new. You won't regret it.

Three-Card Monte

When you see a crowd gathered around a cardboard box with one man flipping cards, madly enticing innocent rubes into his game while another guy scans the crowd for undercover cops, keep on walking. Don't stop and listen to the dealer's spiel or think you can be the one to beat him at his game. Even if you're *quite* sure which of the facedown cards is the Red Queen, don't put your money down. It won't be the one you pick. Oh, someone who works with the dealer will play and win to make you think you've got a chance. But you don't. Buy a lottery ticket instead. People *do* win that.

Waiting on Lines for Breakfast

(And please note, New Yorkers wait *on* line, not *in* line). Sometimes New Yorkers can be masochistic — and silly. They hear about a restaurant that serves a great breakfast, and they begin lining up on weekend mornings to eat. Sometimes they wait for over an hour, standing outside, winter or summer, to order pancakes, omelets, or whatever else the breakfast menu offers. They do this even though many coffee shops and diners are serving patrons the same foods at much less cost and without more than a minute's wait. Now what would you do?

Brunch

One of the greatest scams in the food biz is the concept of "brunch." Whoever thought of this faux combo of breakfast and lunch was a genius. He or she was aware of the marketing possibilities connected with the concept: Serve a glorified breakfast starting at around 10 or 11 a.m. (so if you're up early and hungry you just have to wait), throw in a watered-down drink or cheap champagne, and inflate the price. Make it a social thing, something for people to "do." Brunch, despite my misgivings, has been a resounding success. But it's not for me. I'm of the "three squares" school: breakfast, lunch, and dinner. On top of everything else, restaurants that serve brunch usually make you wait on line for it. And you know how I feel about lines.

The St. Patrick's Day Parade

On March 17, packs of suburban teenagers (with cases of beer between them) begin arriving early via the Long Island Rail Road, Metro North, or New Jersey Transit. By the time the parade kicks off, they — along with a few off-duty policemen — are sloshed. And even before the parade ends, the fights begin and the vomit flows as freely as the beer did earlier. The pubs are packed, and the already-high price of drinks gets even higher. If you truly yearn for a bit of the Irish on this day, for your own good, stay home and watch *The Quiet Man* or listen to the Irish Tenors sing "Danny Boy."

Electronics Stores

You may notice a wealth of "electronics stores" in and around Times Square and Fifth Avenue or wherever gullible tourists frequent. Many of the stores post banners advertising a GOING OUT OF BUSINESS sale. These guys have been going out of business since the Stone Age. That's the bait and switch; pretty soon you've spent too much money for not enough stereos or cameras or MP3 players. The people who work at these stores are a special breed of shark; they work you hard to take their "deal." Don't even get close enough to let them sink their fangs into you because after they do, you're usually theirs for the taking.

Driving in the City

I warn you about driving in the city in Chapter 7, but it bears repeating. So if you want a world of aggravation, rent a car, tolerate the traffic, maneuver amongst the yellow cabs, and try to find a parking place. And when you do, make sure the parking place is a legal one (read the fine print on the street signs). Or put the car in a garage and watch your vacation budget fritter away. (If you must drive your car to get here, consider staying in a hotel that offers free or discounted parking.) With subways, buses, and your feet, New York has the best and fastest public transportation. A car is a luxury you want no part of.

Getting your car out of the pound

If you come back to the spot on the street where you left your car and it's not there, it *probably* hasn't been stolen, but rather towed. You can call the city information number, ☎ 311, or call the car pound directly at ☎ 212-971-0770, and the personnel there can help you track your car in the system. Or, just head for the Manhattan car pound at Pier 76 on the far West Side (12th Ave. and 38th St.). Take a cab; it's on the other side of the busy West Side Highway. The pound is open from 7 a.m. to 11 p.m. Mondays, until midnight on Tuesdays, 24 hours a day Wednesday through Saturday, and on Sunday from midnight to 6 a.m.

If your car is towed, you should get it out as quickly as possible because the pound charges you $15 a day for storage after the first day. Granted, this may be cheaper than what you're paying at a parking lot, but don't forget that big fine you already have to cover.

When you go to the car pound, bring the car's registration (if it's not in the glove box) or rental agreement and your driver's license. Pound personnel will escort you to the car, if necessary, to identify it if you don't have all the required documentation. Oh, and bring cash (or traveler's checks). It's a minimum of $185 to claim your car, and they don't take credit cards or personal checks. You don't have to pay the (additional) $55 parking ticket when you claim your car.

If you think this information sounds like a first-hand account, believe me, it is!

Horse-Drawn Carriage Rides

Pity those poor beasts of burden. They get dragged out in the heat (though not extreme heat) and cold (though not extreme cold) with a buggy attached to them just to give the passenger the feel of an old world, romantic buggy ride through Central Park. But the horses look so forlorn, as if it's the last thing they want to do. And they don't even get a cut of the generous take: $40 for a 20-minute ride, $60 for 45 minutes, excluding tip. If you want a slow, leisurely ride through Central Park, minus the ripe and frequent smell of horse poop, consider an alternative called Manhattan Rickshaw Company (☎ 212-604-4729). The beast of burden behind the rickshaw has two legs, and the rate is about $1 a minute.

The Feast of San Gennaro

At one time this was a distinct and genuine Italian feast (see the films *Godfather II* and *Mean Streets* for The Feast in the good old days). Its decline pretty much has coincided with the decline of Little Italy, a neighborhood that's a small shell of what it once was. Now, The Feast is just an overblown and overcrowded street fair with bad food, cheap red wine, and games of chance you have no chance of winning. Most of the original Little Italy residents have left, but the ones who are still there make sure to clear out during the Feast and let the Bridge and Tunnel expats take over.

Appendix

Quick Concierge

Fast Facts

American Automobile Association (AAA)

The general number is ☎ 212-757-2000; emergency road service, ☎ 800-222-4357.

Ambulance

Call ☎ 911.

American Express

Several locations, including Macy's in Herald Square (Sixth Avenue at 34th Street, ☎ 212-695-8075); for other New York branches, call ☎ 800-AXP-TRIP.

Area Codes

The area codes for Manhattan are **212** and **646**. The area code for the Bronx, Brooklyn, Queens, and Staten Island is **718**.

ATMs

ATMs are virtually everywhere in New York — even inside small shops, delis, supermarkets, and some restaurants. Banks are on almost every corner in commercial districts; finding one may be harder in less touristed or commerical areas. Most ATMs now accept cards on both the PLUS and Cirrus networks. For information about PLUS ATM locations, call ☎ 800-843-7587 or try www.visa.com. For Cirrus locations, call ☎ 800-424-7787 or try www.mastercard.com.

Baby-sitters

Try the Baby Sitters Guild (☎ 212-682-0227) or the Frances Stewart Agency (☎ 212-439-9222).

Camera Repair

Try Berry Camera Repair, 139 Fourth Ave. between 13th and 14th streets (☎ 212-677-8407); Citi-Photo, 636 Lexington Ave. at 54th Street (☎ 212-980-5878); Professional Camera Repair Service, Inc., 37 W. 47th St. between Fifth and Sixth avenues (☎ 212-382-0550); or Westside Camera Inc., 2400 Broadway at 88th Street (☎ 212-877-8760).

Doctors

For an emergency, go to a hospital emergency room (see the "Hospitals" listing later in this appendix). Walk-in clinics can handle minor ailments; one example is DOCS at New York Healthcare, 55 E. 34th St. between Park and Madison avenues (☎ 800-673-3627), open Mon–Fri 8 a.m.–7 p.m. and Sat–Sun 9 a.m.–2 p.m. The charge is $100 for a visit.

Emergencies

For police, fire, and ambulance, call ☎ 911. For the Poison Control Center, call ☎ 800-222-1222 or 212-340-4494.

Hospitals

From south to north, here are the numbers of specific Manhattan hospitals: New York Downtown Hospital, 170 William St. at Beeckman Street, near City Hall (☎ 212-312-5000); St. Vincent's Hospital, Seventh Avenue at 11th Street (☎ 212-604-7000); Beth Israel Medical Center, First Avenue at 16th Street (☎ 212-420-2000); Bellevue Hospital Center, First Avenue at 27th Street (☎ 212-562-4141); New York University

Medical Center, First Avenue at 33rd Street (☎ 212-263-7300); Roosevelt Hospital Center, Tenth Avenue at 58th Street (☎ 212-523-4000); New York Hospital Emergency Pavilion, York Avenue at 70th Street (☎ 212-746-5050); Lenox Hill Hospital, 77th Street between Park and Lexington avenues (☎ 212-434-2000); St. Luke's Hospital Center, Amsterdam Avenue at 113th Street (☎ 212-523-4000).

Hotlines

The 24-hour Crime Victim Hotline is ☎ 212-577-7777; the Sex Crime Report Line is ☎ 212-267-7273. For local police precinct numbers, call ☎ 212-374-5000; the Department of Consumer Affairs is at ☎ 212-487-4444.

Information

For tourist information, call NYC & Company (formerly the Convention and Visitors Bureau) at ☎ 212-484-1222 or 212-397-8222 (www.nycvisit.com). For telephone directory information, dial ☎ 411 or the area code you're calling plus 555-1212. These calls are free from Verizon public pay phones. Not all public pay phones in New York are affiliated with Verizon, and the ones owned by other companies charge for 411 calls. It's also worth noting that Verizon has dropped the price of a local call from 50¢ to 25¢ at its own pay phones (except in some hotel lobbies and other places out-of-town visitors congregate). For more sources of information, consult "Where to Get More Information," later in this appendix.

Internet Access and Cyber Cafes

Some of the hotels I recommend now offer the option of checking your e-mail even if you didn't bring your laptop along; the alternative is one of the Internet cafes in town. EasyInternetCafé, 234 W. 42nd St. between Seventh and Eighth avenues (☎ 212-398-0724, 212-398-0775; www.easyinternetcafe.com; open 24 hours), has 800 computers and no minimum charge. The price per minute depends on the number of people using the facilities: The more demand, the higher the price, but it's always very reasonable. You get a prepaid card from a machine for the amount of money you want, say $3; the card is valid for 30 days and enables you to log on as many times as you want at the going rate. Other choices are NY Computer Café, 247 E. 57th St. between Second and Third avenues (☎ 212-872-1704; www.nycomputercafe.com; open Mon–Fri 8 a.m.–11 p.m., Sat 10 a.m.–11 p.m., Sun 11 a.m.–11 p.m.), which charges $3 per 15 minutes; and CyberCafe, with two locations: one at 273 Lafayette St. at Prince Street (☎ 212-334-5140, open Mon–Fri 8:30 a.m.–10 p.m., Sat–Sun 10 a.m.–10 p.m.) and the other at 250 W. 49th St. between Broadway and Eighth Avenue (☎ 212-333-4109, open Mon–Fri 8:30 a.m.–11 p.m., Sat–Sun 11 a.m.–11 p.m.). Its Web site is www.cyber-cafe.com, and it charges $6.50 per 30 minutes minimum.

Liquor Laws

The minimum legal age to buy and consume alcoholic beverages in New York is 21. Liquor and wine are sold only at licensed stores, which are open six days a week. Most are closed Sundays, holidays, and election days while the polls are open. You can purchase beer at grocery stores, delis, and supermarkets 24 hours a day, except on Sundays before noon.

Maps

Transit maps for the subways and buses are available free at token booths inside subway stations and at public libraries; bus maps are also available on the buses. Free city maps are available at hotels inside the free city guides. To buy maps of all kinds, go to Hagstrom Map and Travel Center, 57 W. 43rd St. between Fifth and

Sixth avenues (☎ 212-398-1222; open Mon–Fri 9 a.m.–5:30 p.m.). For simple New York City street maps, go to any of the bookstores in town.

Newspapers/Magazines

The three major daily newspapers are the *New York Times,* the *New York Daily News,* and the *New York Post.* Two weekly newspapers distributed free in the city are the *New York Press* and the *Village Voice* (Wednesdays). The *New Yorker* is a weekly magazine that publishes listings of local events, news features, criticism, and short stories. *New York* magazine, also weekly, publishes news and commentaries about the city, along with well-regarded restaurant, film, and theater reviews. *Time Out New York* is an indispensable weekly service-oriented magazine that offers dining, music, and entertainment reviews, shopping news, and insider advice about living in the city, as well as an exhaustive compilation of local events.

Pharmacies

Here are two 24-hour pharmacies, both members of the Duane Reade chain: One is at Broadway and 57th Street (☎ 212-541-9708); the other is at Third Avenue and 74th Street (☎ 212-744-2668). In addition, CVS and Rite Aid have branches throughout the city. For homeopathic cures and other natural medicines, try C.O. Bigelow Pharmacy, 414 Sixth Ave. between 8th and 9th streets (☎ 212-533-2700).

Police

Dial ☎ 911 for emergencies and ☎ 212-374-5000 for the phone number of the nearest police precinct.

Radio Stations

Find National Public Radio on WFUV-FM 90.7, WNYC-AM 820, and WNYC-FM 93.9. WBAI-FM 99.5 and the cluster of college radio stations at the lower end of the radio dial broadcast an interesting mix of music and talk. WBGO-FM 88.3 plays jazz while WQHT-FM 97.1 plays hip-hop and R&B. Find salsa and merengue on the mostly Spanish-language WSKQ-FM 97.9, classical on WNYC-FM 93.9, country on WYNY-FM 107.1, classic rock on WAXQ-FM 104.3, modern rock on WXRK-FM 92.3, light rock at WQCD 101.9, top 40 and contemporary hits at WPLJ-FM 95.5 and WHTZ-FM 100.3, and oldies at WCBS-FM 101.1. Yankees games are broadcast on WCBS-AM 880, and WINS-AM 1010 is an all-news station that provides traffic and weather reports every ten minutes. The Mets, Knicks, Rangers, and Giants are on WFAN-AM 660, an all-sports station.

Restrooms

Public restroom facilities are located in all transportation terminals (Grand Central Terminal, Penn Station, and the Port Authority Bus Terminal), in Central Park and Bryant Park, and in the New York Public Library and some other branch libraries — but in some of these places, cleanliness may leave much to be desired. Department stores, museums, and large hotels have wonderful restrooms (we love the ones in Saks Fifth Avenue and at the Plaza Hotel), as does Trump Tower at 56th Street and Fifth Avenue. Some large coffeeshops, such as Dean & Deluca, Au Bon Pain, and larger Starbucks, as well as some chains such as McDonald's and Houlihan's, also have nice restrooms. If you see a sign that says, "Restrooms for customers only," you may have to buy a token snack or beverage in order to use the facilities.

Safety

New York is reasonably safe, much more so than it was even ten years ago. Still, it's a good idea to keep in mind a few basic tips. The number-one rule is to trust your instincts: If it feels unsafe, it probably is, so go elsewhere. Don't flash money or check your wallet in public; pickpockets sometimes loiter near ATM machines to fleece unsuspecting customers. Modesty pays; keep valuables out of sight. Don't leave a purse or jacket with a wallet inside hanging on your chair in a restaurant; someone could brush by and snag it while you're enjoying your meal. Although most hotel room doors lock automatically these days, it pays to double-check when you're coming and going. Subway stations have off-hours waiting areas, usually near the entrances, with camera surveillance; look for the signs overhead. And whatever you do, don't get sucked into those boisterous three-card monte games being played on the sidewalk. It's a big con game — just think, if these folks had a legitimate operation going on, they wouldn't be playing it on a cardboard box on the street! In the unlikely and unfortunate event that you are mugged, don't be foolish enough to resist. Give the mugger what he or she wants, get to a safe place, and call the police.

Smoking

City regulations forbid smoking in all places of employment and commerce, including offices, bars, restaurants, public transportation, taxis, and indoor arenas. A city tax added to the cost of cigarettes makes them quite expensive. If you're a smoker, bring enough to last your trip, and expect to duck out to the sidewalk if you'd like a smoke when you're at a restaurant, bar or club. You'll have plenty of company in what's sometimes called the "Bloomberg Lounge," after Mayor Bloomberg, who pushed the smoking regulations through.

Taxes

Sales tax is 8.625 percent on meals, most goods, and some services. Hotel tax is 13.25 percent plus $2 per room per night (including sales tax). Parking garage tax is 18.25 percent.

Taxis

Authorized, legal taxis in Manhattan are yellow. Yellow cabs have city medallions posted inside the vehicles that have the driver's name and identification number, in case you need to lodge a complaint (or, heaven forbid, if you leave something in the cab and need to track down the driver). A taxi will cost you $2.50 just for stepping in the door, plus 40¢ per ⅕ mile. The flat rate from JFK Airport is $45 and a surcharge of $1 is applied all rides from 4 to 8 p.m., Monday through Friday.

Time Zone

New York is on eastern standard/eastern daylight time.

Tipping

In restaurants in New York City, you can double the 8.625 percent tax to figure the appropriate tip. Other tipping guidelines: 15 percent to 20 percent of the fare to taxi drivers; 10 percent to 15 percent of the tab to bartenders; $1 to $2 per bag to bellhops; at least $1 per day to hotel maids; $1 per item to checkroom attendants. Tipping theater ushers isn't expected.

Transit Info

For ground transportation to and from all the area airports, call Air-Ride (☎ 800-247-7433). For all transit information, call the MTA (Metropolitan Transit Authority) Transit Information Center (☎ 718-330-1234; operators available daily 6 a.m.–9 p.m.).

Weather

For the current temperature and next day's forecast, look in the upper-right corner of the front page of the *New York Times* or call ☎ 212-976-1212. If you want to know how to pack before you arrive, point your browser to www.cnn.com/weather or www.weather.com.

Toll-Free Numbers and Web Sites

Airlines

Aer Lingus
☎ 800-474-7424 in the U.S.
☎ 01-886-8888 in Ireland
www.aerlingus.com

Air Canada
☎ 888-247-2262
www.aircanada.ca

Air New Zealand
☎ 800-262-1234 or ☎ 800-262-2468 in the U.S.
☎ 800-663-5494 in Canada
☎ 0800-737-767 in New Zealand
www.airnewzealand.com

Airtran Airlines
☎ 800-247-8726
www.airtran.com

Alaska Airlines
☎ 800-426-0333
www.alaskaair.com

American Airlines
☎ **800-433-7300**
www.aa.com

American Trans Air
☎ 800-225-2995
www.ata.com

America West Airlines
☎ 800-235-9292
www.americawest.com

British Airways
☎ 800-247-9297 in the U.S.
☎ 0345-222-111 or 0845-77-333-77 in Britain
www.british-airways.com

Continental Airlines
☎ 800-525-0280
www.continental.com

Delta Air Lines
☎ 800-221-1212
www.delta.com

Frontier Airlines
☎ 800-432-1359
www.frontierairlines.com

Jet Blue Airlines
☎ 800-538-2583
www.jetblue.com

Midwest Express
☎ 800-452-2022
www.midwestexpress.com

Northwest Airlines
☎ 800-225-2525
www.nwa.com

Qantas
☎ 800-227-4500 in the U.S.
☎ 61-2-9691-3636 in Australia
www.qantas.com

Southwest Airlines
☎ 800-435-9792
www.southwest.com

United Airlines
☎ 800-241-6522
www.united.com

US Airways
☎ 800-428-4322
www.usairways.com

Virgin Atlantic Airways
☎ 800-862-8621 in the U.S.
☎ 0293-747-747 in Britain
www.virgin-atlantic.com

Major hotel and motel chains

Best Western International
☎ 800-528-1234
www.bestwestern.com

Clarion Hotels
☎ 800-CLARION
www.hotelchoice.com

Comfort Inns
☎ 800-228-5150
www.hotelchoice.com

Courtyard by Marriott
☎ 800-321-2211
www.courtyard.com or www.
marriott.com

Crowne Plaza Hotels
☎ 800-227-6963
www.crowneplaza.com

Days Inn
☎ 800-325-2525
www.daysinn.com

Doubletree Hotels
☎ 800-222-TREE
www.doubletreehotels.com

Econo Lodges
☎ 800-55-ECONO
www.hotelchoice.com

Fairfield Inn by Marriott
☎ 800-228-2800
www.fairfieldinn.com

Four Seasons
☎ 800-819-5053
www.fourseasons.com

Hilton Hotels
☎ 800-HILTONS
www.hilton.com

Holiday Inn
☎ 800-HOLIDAY
www.holiday-inn.com

Howard Johnson
☎ 800-654-2000
www.hojo.com

Hyatt Hotels & Resorts
☎ 800-228-9000
www.hyatt.com

Inter-Continental Hotels & Resorts
☎ 888-567-8725
www.interconti.com

ITT Sheraton
☎ 800-325-3535
www.sheraton.com

Marriott Hotels
☎ 800-228-9290
www.marriott.com

Quality Inns
☎ 800-228-5151
www.hotelchoice.com

Radisson Hotels International
☎ 800-333-3333
www.radisson.com

Ramada Inns
☎ 800-2-RAMADA
www.ramada.com

Red Roof Inns
☎ 800-843-7663
www.redroof.com

Residence Inn by Marriott
☎ 800-331-3131
www.residenceinn.com

Ritz Carlton
☎ 800-241-3333
www.ritzcarlton.com

Super 8 Motels
☎ 800-800-8000
www.super8.com

Travelodge
☎ 800-255-3050
www.travelodge.com

Westin Hotels & Resorts
☎ 800-937-8461
www.westin.com

Wyndham Hotels & Resorts
☎ 800-996-3426 in the U.S. and
Canada
www.wyndham.com

Where to Get More Information

I packed this book with information, but if you still haven't had enough, you can consult the following resources for additional info.

Tourist information offices

NYC & Company (the former Convention and Visitors Bureau) offers a 24-hour telephone hotline (☎ **800-NYC-VISIT**, 212-397-8222) that you can call to order a kit, which includes a 100-page *Big Apple Visitor Guide* plus a map and other materials; you pay only shipping, and you should receive the kit in seven days. The guide, which you can order separately (and for free), contains tons of information about hotels, restaurants, theaters, events, and so on and is updated quarterly. NYC & Co. also maintains a **Visitor Information Center** at 810 Seventh Ave. between 52nd and 53rd streets (☎ **212-484-1222**; open Monday through Friday 8:30 a.m. to 6 p.m., weekends and holidays 9 a.m. to 5 p.m.; mailing address 810 Seventh Ave., New York, NY 10019).

You can get information about current **theater** productions over the phone through **NYC/On Stage** (☎ **212-768-1818**) and the **Broadway Line** (☎ **888-BROADWAY**, 212-563-2929, 212-302-4111).

For all **transit** information, call the **MTA Transit Information Center** (☎ **718-330-1234**). Call ☎ 718-330-3322 for a copy of *Token Trips Travel Guide*, a brochure that gives you instructions on how to get to New York City's main attractions via mass transit.

Air-Ride (☎ **800-247-7433**) is a service that provides recorded information about ground transportation from all the area airports.

Newspapers and Magazines

New York City has four daily newspapers: *The New York Times*, www.nytimes.com (registration required); *The Daily News*, www.nydailynews.com; *The New York Post*, www.nypost.com; and *Newsday*, www.newsday.com. Each paper offers daily calendars of events and usually runs full sections of weekend listings on Fridays.

The best weekly magazines for information and listings about upcoming events are *Time Out New York*, www.timeoutny.com; and *New York* magazine, www.newyorkmetro.com; and *The New Yorker*, www.newyorker.com. Weekly free newspapers *The Village Voice*, www.villagevoice.com; and *NYPress*, www.nypress.com, also have extensive listings with staff picks and recommendations.

The following are some of the more useful online sources.

✔ **Citysearch** (www.newyork.citysearch.com) is another comprehensive, user-friendly site that lists tons of entertainment and dining prospects. The listings are ample, and the reviews quite useful. Citysearch is now associated with NYC & Company (found later in this list).

✔ The **MTA (Metropolitan Transit Authority)** (www.mta.info) site provides easy access to bus and subway maps and information.

✔ **New York City Reference** (www.panix.com/clay/nyc) is an excellent index of links to other New York–related Web sites — a couple thousand of them — such as the Web sites of all the museums in New York.

✔ **NYC & Company,** New York City's official tourism site (www.nycvisit.com), is the Web site of the former Convention and Visitors Bureau; it provides a wealth of information and links, and you can book hotels online with a few clicks of your mouse.

✔ **NYC.gov** (www.nyc.gov) is the official site of the city of New York. It's very comprehensive and clear and has a bunch of useful links to sightseeing and entertainment information.

✔ www.nyctourist.com offers an excellent selection of very useful information, although it's a little more commercial than the other Web sites I list.

✔ **Frommer's Web site** (www.frommers.com) offers much of the content from Frommer's guidebooks, as well as online updates of changes in the area since the guidebook was published. You can also subscribe to an Internet newsletter that spotlights travel deals and offers articles and service information on destinations worldwide. There are also message boards for travelers to ask for and share traveling tips.

If you're looking for additional guidebooks on New York City, I can recommend (and I wrote!) *Frommer's New York City, Frommer's Portable New York City*, and *Frommer's New York City from $90 a Day* (all published by Wiley). Also check out Suzy Gershman's *Born to Shop New York City*, and *Frommer's Memorable Walks in New York City* (both published by Wiley, too).

Index

See also separate Accommodations and Restaurant indexes at the end of this index

Accommodations Index

Restaurant Index

SPORTS, FITNESS, PARENTING, RELIGION & SPIRITUALITY

0-7645-5146-9   0-7645-5418-2

Also available:
- Adoption For Dummies
  0-7645-5488-3
- Basketball For Dummies
  0-7645-5248-1
- The Bible For Dummies
  0-7645-5296-1
- Buddhism For Dummies
  0-7645-5359-3
- Catholicism For Dummies
  0-7645-5391-7
- Hockey For Dummies
  0-7645-5228-7

- Judaism For Dummies
  0-7645-5299-6
- Martial Arts For Dummies
  0-7645-5358-5
- Pilates For Dummies
  0-7645-5397-6
- Religion For Dummies
  0-7645-5264-3
- Teaching Kids to Read
  For Dummies
  0-7645-4043-2
- Weight Training For Dummies
  0-7645-5168-X
- Yoga For Dummies
  0-7645-5117-5

TRAVEL

0-7645-5438-7   0-7645-5453-0

Also available:
- Alaska For Dummies
  0-7645-1761-9
- Arizona For Dummies
  0-7645-6938-4
- Cancún and the Yucatán
  For Dummies
  0-7645-2437-2
- Cruise Vacations For Dummies
  0-7645-6941-4
- Europe For Dummies
  0-7645-5456-5
- Ireland For Dummies
  0-7645-5455-7

- Las Vegas For Dummies
  0-7645-5448-4
- London For Dummies
  0-7645-4277-X
- New York City For Dummies
  0-7645-6945-7
- Paris For Dummies
  0-7645-5494-8
- RV Vacations For Dummies
  0-7645-5443-3
- Walt Disney World & Orlando
  For Dummies
  0-7645-6943-0

GRAPHICS, DESIGN & WEB DEVELOPMENT

0-7645-4345-8   0-7645-5589-8

Also available:
- Adobe Acrobat 6 PDF
  For Dummies
  0-7645-3760-1
- Building a Web Site For Dummies
  0-7645-7144-3
- Dreamweaver MX 2004
  For Dummies
  0-7645-4342-3
- FrontPage 2003 For Dummies
  0-7645-3882-9
- HTML 4 For Dummies
  0-7645-1995-6
- Illustrator cs For Dummies
  0-7645-4084-X

- Macromedia Flash MX 2004
  For Dummies
  0-7645-4358-X
- Photoshop 7 All-in-One Desk
  Reference For Dummies
  0-7645-1667-1
- Photoshop cs Timesaving
  Techniques For Dummies
  0-7645-6782-9
- PHP 5 For Dummies
  0-7645-4166-8
- PowerPoint 2003 For Dummies
  0-7645-3908-6
- QuarkXPress 6 For Dummies
  0-7645-2593-X

NETWORKING, SECURITY, PROGRAMMING & DATABASES

0-7645-6852-3   0-7645-5784-X

Also available:
- A+ Certification For Dummies
  0-7645-4187-0
- Access 2003 All-in-One Desk
  Reference For Dummies
  0-7645-3988-4
- Beginning Programming
  For Dummies
  0-7645-4997-9
- C For Dummies
  0-7645-7068-4
- Firewalls For Dummies
  0-7645-4048-3
- Home Networking For Dummies
  0-7645-42796

- Network Security For Dummies
  0-7645-1679-5
- Networking For Dummies
  0-7645-1677-9
- TCP/IP For Dummies
  0-7645-1760-0
- VBA For Dummies
  0-7645-3989-2
- Wireless All In-One Desk Reference
  For Dummies
  0-7645-7496-5
- Wireless Home Networking
  For Dummies
  0-7645-3910-8

HEALTH & SELF-HELP

0-7645-6820-5 *†   0-7645-2566-2

Also available:
- Alzheimer's For Dummies
  0-7645-3899-3
- Asthma For Dummies
  0-7645-4233-8
- Controlling Cholesterol For
  Dummies
  0-7645-5440-9
- Depression For Dummies
  0-7645-3900-0
- Dieting For Dummies
  0-7645-4149-8
- Fertility For Dummies
  0-7645-2549-2

- Fibromyalgia For Dummies
  0-7645-5441-7
- Improving Your Memory
  For Dummies
  0-7645-5435-2
- Pregnancy For Dummies †
  0-7645-4483-7
- Quitting Smoking For Dummies
  0-7645-2629-4
- Relationships For Dummies
  0-7645-5384-4
- Thyroid For Dummies
  0-7645-5385-2

EDUCATION, HISTORY, REFERENCE & TEST PREPARATION

 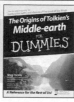

0-7645-5194-9   0-7645-4186-2

Also available:
- Algebra For Dummies
  0-7645-5325-9
- British History For Dummies
  0-7645-7021-8
- Calculus For Dummies
  0-7645-2498-4
- English Grammar For Dummies
  0-7645-5322-4
- Forensics For Dummies
  0-7645-5580-4
- The GMAT for Dummies
  0-7645-5251-1
- Inglés Para Dummies
  0-7645-5427-1

- Italian For Dummies
  0-7645-5196-5
- Latin For Dummies
  0-7645-5431-X
- Lewis & Clark For Dummies
  0-7645-2545-X
- Research Papers For Dummies
  0-7645-5426-3
- The SAT I For Dummies
  0-7645-7193-1
- Science Fair Projects For Dummies
  0-7645-5460-3
- U.S. History For Dummies
  0-7645-5249-X

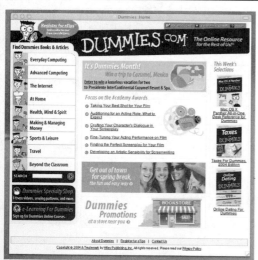

Get smart @ dummies.com®

- **Find a full list of Dummies titles**
- **Look into loads of FREE on-site articles**
- **Sign up for FREE eTips e-mailed to you weekly**
- **See what other products carry the Dummies name**
- **Shop directly from the Dummies bookstore**
- **Enter to win new prizes every month!**

* Separate Canadian edition also available
† Separate U.K. edition also available

Available wherever books are sold. For more information or to order direct: U.S. customers visit www.dummies.com or call 1-877-762-2974.
U.K. customers visit www.wileyeurope.com or call 0800 243407. Canadian customers visit www.wiley.ca or call 1-800-567-4797.